Social Networks and Natural Resource Management
Uncovering the Social Fabric of Environmental Governance

Social network analysis (SNA), a quantitative approach to the study of social relations, has recently emerged as a key tool for understanding the governance of natural resources. Bringing together contributions from a range of researchers in the field, this is the first book to fully explore the potential applications of SNA in the context of natural resource management.

Topics covered include the role of SNA in stakeholder selection; improving fisheries management and conservation; the effect of social network ties on public satisfaction with forest management; and agrarian communication networks. Numerous case studies link SNA concepts to the theories underlying natural resource governance, such as social learning, adaptive co-management, and social movement theory.

Reflecting on the challenges and opportunities associated with this evolving field, this is an ideal resource for students and resear involved in many areas of natural resource management, con biology, sustainability science, and sociology.

ÖRJAN BODIN is an Assistant Professor at the S Centre at Stockholm University, Sweden. He in using network analysis to study various governance.

CHRISTINA PRELL is an Assistant Professor i y at the University of Maryland, College Park. She studies ole social networks play in the ways stakeholders perceive and interact with ecosystems.

Social Networks and Natural Resource Management

Uncovering the Social Fabric of Environmental Governance

Edited by

ÖRJAN BODIN
Stockholm University, Sweden

CHRISTINA PRELL
University of Maryland, USA

CAMBRIDGE UNIVERSITY PRESS
Cambridge, New York, Melbourne, Madrid, Cape Town,
Singapore, São Paulo, Delhi, Tokyo, Mexico City

Cambridge University Press
The Edinburgh Building, Cambridge CB2 8RU, UK

Published in the United States of America by
Cambridge University Press, New York

www.cambridge.org
Information on this title: www.cambridge.org/9780521766296

First published 2011

Printed in the United Kingdom at the University Press, Cambridge

A catalogue record for this publication is available from the British Library

Library of Congress Cataloguing in Publication data
Social networks and natural resource management: uncovering
the social fabric of environmental governance, / edited by Örjan Bodin,
Christina Prell.
    p.   cm.
ISBN 978-0-521-76629-6 (hardback)
1. Natural resources – Management.   2. Social networks.
I. Bodin Örjan, 1969–
II. Prell, Christina.   III. Title.
HC21.S65   2011
333.7–dc22

                                                          2011007347

ISBN 978-0-521-76629-6 Hardback
ISBN 978-0-521-14623-4 Paperback

Contents

Contributors

Örjan Bodin
Stockholm Resilience Centre and
Department of Systems Ecology
Stockholm University
Sweden

Beatrice Crona
Stockholm Resilience Centre
Stockholm University
Sweden

Evans Dawoe
Faculty of Renewable Natural Resources
Department of Agroforestry
Kwame Nkrumah University of Science and Technology
Kumasi, Ghana

Henrik Ernstson
Stockholm Resilience Centre
Stockholm University
Sweden, and African Centre for Cities
University of Cape Town South Africa

Ken A. Frank
Measurement and Quantitative Methods
Counseling, Educational Psychology and Special Education and
Fisheries and Wildlife and Center for Systems Integration and
Sustainability
Michigan State University
USA

Howard Harshaw
Department of Forest Resources Management
University of British Columbia
Canada

Klaus Hubacek
Department of Geography
University of Maryland
USA

Marney Isaac
Department of Physical and Environmental Sciences and
International Development Studies
University of Toronto
Canada

Christina Prell
Department of Sociology
University of Maryland
USA

Saudiel Ramirez-Sanchez
Oceans Directorate
Department of Fisheries and Oceans, Ottawa
Canada

Mark Reed
Aberdeen Centre for Environmental Sustainability and Centre
for Planning and Environmental Management
School of Geosciences
University of Aberdeen
UK

Annica Sandström
Division of Social Sciences at Luleå
University of Technology, and
Stockholm Resilience Centre Stockholm University
Sweden

J. M. Taylor
Department of Forest Resources Management
University of British Columbia
Canada

David B. Tindall
Department of Sociology
Department of Forest Resources Management
Centre for Applied Conservation Research
University of British Columbia
Canada

Foreword

Clearly, successful natural resource management can no longer be constrained to single resources like mineral ore, timber, or food, governed in a sectoral fashion. Humanity is at a stage where we are challenging the biophysical foundation of our own future at the global level. Environmental issues are shifting from a focus on saving the environment as if we were independent of it to finding pathways of sustaining our own development and even existence on a finite planet. How do we adapt to the new situation of global human imprint, in a democratic and respectful manner, sharing ecological, social, and economic burdens and benefits justly among people and nations? The challenge is broader than the climate issue and encompasses an active stewardship of critical processes of people and nature in dynamic landscapes and seascapes in a global context, and in a situation where more than 50% of the human population is living in urban areas.

The social sciences play a central role in the current era of turbulent global dynamics with unprecedented social, ecological, and technological change. The social sciences, although still to some extent suffering from a lack of a common framework in approaching these issues, is rapidly gaining ground in climate and global environmental change research, in resilience thinking and sustainability science. In August 2010, the UN Secretary-General's High-level Panel on Global Sustainability was launched with the objective to reflect on and formulate a new vision for sustainability in the context of planetary boundaries, and research on governance and institutions for collective action to deal with common-pool resource dilemmas characterizing natural resource governance was awarded the 2009 prize in economic sciences in memory of Alfred Nobel.

Clearly, there is tremendous scope for drawing on insights from diverse fields of the social sciences and for generating new understanding of truly integrated systems of people and nature for stewardship of our own future within the biophysical boundaries set by the life-support systems of our planet. The ecosystem approach to natural resource management aims at integrating the social and the ecological but so far mostly in terms of management of dynamic ecosystems. Research that contributes to a deeper understanding of the social dimension that allows for ecosystem stewardship and natural resource governance within the framework of interdependent social-ecological systems is a frontier of great significance. It certainly is important to broaden the social domain from investigating human action in relation to a specific natural resource, like dairy or fruit production, or environmental issue, like climate change, to the challenge of multi-level collaborative societal responses to a broader set of feedbacks and thresholds in social-ecological systems. For example, governance in catchments of the Murray Darling river, Australia has been successful in solving problems, adapting to change and connecting the region to global markets. Dryland cropping, grazing, irrigated dairy and fruit production is widespread and economically lucrative activities are thriving. But, if the analysis is broadened to a social-ecological approach to account for the capacity of the landscape in sustaining the values of the region the picture looks quite different. Widespread clearing of native vegetation and excessive water use for irrigation have created severe salinization problems, so severe that the region seems to be facing serious social-ecological thresholds with possible knock-on effects between them. Crossing such thresholds may result in irreversible changes in the region. Hence, strategies for adaptability that are socially desirable may lead to vulnerable social-ecological systems and persistent undesirable states such as poverty traps or rigidity traps. Similarly, scientists dealing with the environmental domain may conclude that the environment is in a hopelessly degraded state, but if analyzed from a social-ecological perspective, there may be adaptive capacity to turn the situation around, to get out of the trap and start a new pathway of development.

It is in this context that this volume *Social Networks and Natural Resource Management: Uncovering the Social Fabric of Environmental Governance* becomes very relevant. Recent studies have revealed the crucial importance of social, often informal, networks in natural resource governance. Informal networks of resource users and beneficiaries, actor groups, leaders, agencies, knowledge carriers, and institutional entrepreneurs, seem instrumental in trust building and conflict resolution, in mobilizing key resources, in navigating social-ecological transitions when responding to crises, and in transforming unsustainable governance regimes towards adaptive and multi-level stewardship of whole landscapes and seascapes. Social networks are often the glue that ties together the individual with the organizational and the institutional and with key actors operating in networks that span multiple scales and governance levels.

Reading this book will enable more focus, and more precision, in understanding how social networks, and their internal and external characteristics, affect natural resource governance outcomes. Many valuable approaches and tools are presented for how to unravel functions and processes of social networks, what they look like, how they are structured, who participate and their positions, and in what ways all this relates to sustainable ecosystem stewardship. The reader will have the pleasure of further learning and understanding social relations of natural resource governance through applications of methods, tools, and theories that draw on and combine competences and insights from many different research fields within the social sciences with interdisciplinary research on adaptive management, common-pool resource management, and adaptive co-management. The different chapters and studies in the book will take us to a plethora of places and contexts around the world. This journey stretches through contexts such as agro-forestry in Ghana and artisanal fisheries in Kenya and Mexico, through forest management in British Columbia in Canada to the governance of a large urban park in Stockholm, Sweden. The chapters assemble new insights for how interactions and collaborations among different actors in networks contribute to ecosystem stewardship. A true pleasure to read and an important step towards improved understanding of the social dimension of natural resource governance. Read on and enjoy!

Professor Carl Folke
Science Director of the Stockholm Resilience Centre,
Stockholm University
Director of the Beijer Institute of Ecological Economics,
Royal Swedish Academy of Sciences

Part I Introduction

ÖRJAN BODIN, SAUDIEL RAMIREZ-SANCHEZ,
HENRIK ERNSTSON, AND CHRISTINA PRELL

1

A social relational approach to natural resource governance

1.1 THE SOCIAL DIMENSION OF SUSTAINABLE DEVELOPMENT

The magnitude of the impact of human activities on the natural environment is now on a planetary scale (Vitousek *et al.*, 1986; Rockström *et al.*, 2009). The growth of the human population and the growth in amount of natural resources used are altering the Earth in unprecedented ways (Lubchenco, 1998), while humanity at the same time is fundamentally dependent on Earth system processes for a prosperous societal development (Rockström *et al.*, 2009). Hence, natural resource extraction and environmental impact have a deeper meaning than simply correcting for externalities. People are embedded in Earth system processes, dependent on the capacity of ecosystems to generate ecological services for societal development. Therefore, the very notion of "natural resources," as the term is being used in this book, does not only include single extractable resources such as, for example, fish, timber, and minerals; instead natural resource are also perceived in the much broader context of biophysical processes and ecosystem services (see Daily, 1997; Chapin *et al.*, 2010).

Given these insights, it is clearly getting more difficult to justify a dichotomy between social and natural systems. Instead, the intimate connections between our biophysical environments and human health, the economy, social justice, and national security are gaining acceptance across societies (Lubchenco, 1998; Liu *et al.*, 2007). This intimate coupling between the biophysical environment and human

Social Networks and Natural Resource Management: Uncovering the Fabric of Environmental Governance, ed. Ö. Bodin and C. Prell. Published by Cambridge University Press.

societies makes it virtually impossible to perceive the huge, far-reaching, and enormously difficult challenge in accomplishing sustainable management and governance of the world's natural resources only as a consequence of our limited understanding of our biophysical environment and the inherent uncertainties associated with complex systems such as ecosystems (Levin, 1998; Checkland and Scholes, 1999). Although our understanding and knowledge of the complex biophysical environment upon which societal development fundamentally depends is surely increasing, our ability to predict biophysical outcomes of future and ongoing human activities is inevitably and inherently limited (cf. Levin, 1998). To meet the challenge, we need to get a better understanding on how we can change and transform the way we govern our natural environment, and we will need to devise flexible institutions and adaptive governance structure that not only try to sustain and enhance the capacity of ecosystems to generate natural resources and ecosystem services, but also are able to respond to complex dynamics and cope with unpredictabilities (Folke *et al.*, 2005; Duit and Galaz, 2008; Chuenpagdee and Jentoft, 2009; Ernstson *et al.*, 2010).

Accordingly, the quest of accomplishing sustainable management and governance spans over various scientific disciplines, and research engaging both the natural and the social sciences is needed (see Lubchenco, 1998). This clearly poses a tremendous challenge for the research community since that insight cuts across the traditional and well-rooted division between the natural and social sciences. Around the world researchers, practitioners, and policy makers are doing their best to tackle this challenge and significant progress is being made. Research on resource management and governance is increasingly drawing from interdisciplinary/multi-disciplinary teams composed of both social and natural scientists. This development has actually been ongoing since the early 1960s, and has, among other things, led to the establishment of large international research programs focusing on human and social aspects of natural resource-related issues and challenges. The recent global program Millennium Ecosystem Assessment (MEA, see www.millenniumassessment.org), initiated and led by the United Nations during 2001–2005, gathered the largest body of social and natural scientists ever assembled to provide a state-of-the-art scientific appraisal of the condition and trends in the world's ecosystems, the services they provide, and how this links to human wellbeing and societal development. Even more recently, the International Council for Science (ISCU, see www.icsu.

org) has established the Program on Ecosystem Change and Society (PECS) as a follow-up to MEA. A final example of a transdisciplinary research program is the global networked research organization the Resilience Alliance (www.resalliance.org), which engages scientists and practitioners from many disciplines in collaborative research on natural resource governance with a particular emphasis on complexity and the resilience of interdependent social-ecological systems.

In addition to the above-mentioned international initiatives, national research funding agencies are refocusing their funding programs embracing inter- or transdisciplinary approaches as a response to the demand for better understanding of social-ecological systems (see Castán Broto *et al.*, 2009; Stafford *et al.*, 2009). Examples include the Rural Economic and Land Use Program in the UK (www.relu.ac.uk), which is funded by the UK Research Council with the prime aim of supporting research that is interdisciplinary and aimed at knowledge transfer to end-users and policy makers. The newly founded transdisciplinary Stockholm Resilience Centre received one of the largest research grants ever in Sweden, and similar research centers integrating various scientific disciplines are continually being established. For example, two recent initiatives are the Global Institute of Sustainability at Arizona State University in the USA (www.sustainability.asu.edu) and the ARC Centre of Excellence for Coral Reef Studies at James Cook University in Australia (www.coralcoe.org.au).

Conclusively, the sheer presence of humans in all of the world's different ecosystems makes it virtually impossible to find pristine natural environments, and humans are often the dominating factor in shaping the processes and structures of the biophysical environment (Vitousek *et al.*, 1997). Hence, human activities are increasingly harder to disregard in any kind of scientific inquiry about the functioning of the natural environment. Likewise, the fact that societies are inherently embedded in Earth system processes makes it equally unfeasible to perceive and abstract societies as if they were independent of the natural environment. Therefore, we strongly argue that if the inevitable linkages between the social and the natural dimensions are not taken into account in framing scientific inquiries, our ability to gain knowledge and understanding of how we can sustain societal development will be inherently limited. Using this insight as our overarching baseline, our focus in this book is primarily on using a social relational approach to gain a deeper understanding of the social dimension of natural resource governance. This approach is further explained and elaborated below.

1.2   A NEED FOR A SOCIAL RELATIONAL APPROACH IN STUDYING NATURAL RESOURCE GOVERNANCE

Ecological processes typically operate across various spatial and temporal scales, which often make it difficult to conceptually, jurisdictionally, and economically separate different ecological elements from each other in any meaningful way (Cumming *et al.*, 2006; Folke *et al.*, 2007). In other words, ecosystems stretch across human-made jurisdictions and administrative borders such as municipalities, provinces, and states. As a result of this and other factors, natural resources are often characterized by ineffective institutional arrangements and with multiple actors and stakeholders competing for resource use and extraction often leading to overexploitation and the inability to account for dynamic ecosystem processes. As a consequence, scholars nowadays typically refer to *governance* of natural resources instead of *management* or *government*. The very meaning of the term governance implies that the managing process, whatever is being managed, is less formalized, more difficult to control, and involves a multitude of different type of actors (Duit and Galaz, 2008). It is quite recently that the notion of governance made its entrance into the research on natural resources, and the reason it did is to further emphasize the multi-actor and multi-purpose context characterizing use and extraction of resource governance (Folke *et al.*, 2005). Governance should be contrasted with *government* where one designated actor (typically the state in political science) is the one and only actor being in charge, and *management* where focus often is on how to manage the resource from a biophysical perspective only.

Given the multi-actor and multi-purpose context characterizing resource use, effective natural resource management and governance largely rely on the knowledge, expertise, and the willingness/possibilities for negotiation, conflict resolution, collaboration, and coordinated actions among various stakeholders. Social issues of natural resource governance thus range from questions related to designing flexible and adaptable institutions that can handle uncertainties and facilitate stakeholder cooperation to more complex and subtle questions pertaining to issues of class, power, discourse, conflicts, and consensus; and how these aspects shape the way natural resources are governed. Social factors affecting resource governance have, for example, been studied from theoretical perspectives such as social learning (Bandura, 1977; Wenger, 1998), collaborative management (Carlsson and Berkes, 2005; Armitage *et al.*, 2007), and social capital

(Portes, 1998; Pretty and Ward, 2001; Krishna, 2002; Bodin and Crona, 2008), as well as more pragmatic approaches such as stakeholder selection (Maiolo *et al.*, 1992; Prell *et al.*, 2006). Political ecologists, geographers, and anthropologists have also contributed with more critical perspectives and increased the sensitivity by which to approach concepts like "knowledge," "scale," and "resource" to better account for issues of power, equity, and social justice. For instance, what is to be perceived as "proper" knowledge of the natural environment is contested and influenced by power asymmetries (Blaikie, 1985; Nadasdy, 2007) and that resource governance rests upon a "politics of scale," which is not just a reflection of the biophysical scale, but a negotiated product of socially and politically embedded knowledge and moral claims made by scientists, resource managers, and interest groups (Swyngedouw and Heynen, 2003; Ernstson and Sörlin, 2009). Following this, perceptions of what is to be considered as a "natural resource" (or an ecosystem service) can be seen as social constructs, or hybrids (Ernstson, 2008). Furthermore, these fields of research explore how the distribution of environmental benefits are embedded in socio-spatial structures (Harvey, 1996) and world systems (Hornborg, 2009), which influence resource governance in several ways.

In considering social factors that significantly affect the way we succeed or fail in governing the biophysical environment, a fundamental question is: how do we study all these various factors without falling into the traps of either being too narrow in scope, thus risking missing the big picture, or too broad and therefore losing scientific depth and precision? In this book, we propose a social relational approach as both a conceptual and analytical framework for uncovering how social factors affect natural resource governance. In short, this approach seeks to explain and shed light on human and systems behaviors by investigating how patterns of social relations among actors within a system enable and constrain actors and processes. Thus, the approach we advocate here primarily focuses on the social dimensions of natural resource governance in complex social-ecological systems, although it could be extended into a larger modeling framework also involving models of the natural environment (as will be discussed further in the final chapter of this book). Just as understanding of the environment has moved towards a systems' perspective of interacting parts and emergent wholes, so has the notion of understanding human and social behavior moved from an atomist model, where individuals are studied in a case-by-variable format, to one of seeing individuals in the context of their relationships with others (Wellman, 1988). Gaining insight into those relationships, and how the pattern and structure of those relationships influence attitudes, perspectives, and behaviors towards resource governance outcomes is what this book is about.

1.3   A SOCIAL RELATIONAL APPROACH

An old debate in the social sciences has been the part–whole relations, or individual agency and social structure linkages. In the social sciences the study of such connections has more or less adopted one of two philosophical views, individualism or holism. The former puts less emphasis on the social constraints on agency and attempts to analyze and account for social facts in a bottom–up fashion, i.e. from the individual. The latter adopts a top–down approach to the analysis and account of social facts, putting less emphasis on individual interests and initiative (Bunge, 1999). A practical solution to this problem is to use both perspectives. However, such aggregation is always at risk of producing irreconcilable explanations. A more viable approach will seek to merge these perspectives rather than simply aggregating them. A merger requires a referent that is neither isolated individuals (e.g. rational self-interested individuals) nor organic wholes, but related individuals who collectively give rise to emergent properties or qualitative novelty, above all, social structure. Such is one of the main assumptions of a social relational approach (Emirbayer, 1997).

The social relational approach discussed here can be described as using a framework consisting of four elements (Bunge, 1996). This framework consists of the body of background knowledge, problems, aims, and methods advanced by a particular approach. These are briefly described below. Please also note that there are various approaches within the humanities and social sciences that could be labeled under a relational approach. The social relational approach used here is however centered on using quantitative social network analysis.

1.3.1   Body of background knowledge

There are two main philosophical ideas that underpin a social relational approach. First, it conceives cultural, political, and economic facts as relational in nature rather than an aggregate of individual actions. Second, it recognizes that from these relations greater wholes are formed that display emergent or novel properties, above all, social structure (see Blitz, 1992; Schweizer, 1997; Sawyer, 2001 on the issue of emergence). More recently, these two philosophical notions have been articulated in a theoretical movement in sociology called "relational sociology," which stipulates that the structure of relations among actors and their location in this structure have important behavioral, perceptual, and attitudinal consequences for both the actors and the entire social system (Emirbayer and Goodwin, 1994). Relational sociology stipulates that social relations are not completely random, but that they show patterns or particular configurations, which are important features of the lives of the actors who display them. Therefore, how a person lives depends in large part on how s/he is tied into the larger web of social connections. Furthermore, relational sociology notices that categorical affiliations (e.g. race, social status, and social class) alone rarely partition people in a way that confirms with observed action. Thus, social relational analysts argue that human action is organized through categorical affiliations (e.g. race or social classes), but it is motivated by the structure of social relations in which actors are embedded (Emirbayer, 1997).

1.3.2 Problems addressed

All social cognitive problems (economic, cultural, and political) can be addressed through a social relational approach given one condition. The cognitive social problem has to be formulated in relational terms (Emirbayer and Goodwin, 1994; Emirbayer, 1997). For example, social institutions can be conceptualized as the emergent patterns of social activity generated by actors embedded in the structure of social networks (Schweizer, 1997; White, 2008), and power emerges out of the pattern and operation of socio-cultural and socio-psychological relationships among members of a social system (Emirbayer, 1997). A social relational approach can deal with practical problems, but in an indirect way, i.e. by scientifically uncovering the role of political, cultural, and economic relations in social systems and providing this information for designing social policies. In this sense, a social relational approach distinguishes between science and socio-technologies such as policies and management.

1.3.3 Aims

A social relational approach seeks to explain, at least in part, the behavior of human actors and of the system as a whole by appeal to specific features of the connections (structure) among the elements. More specifically, the social relational approach discussed here investigates how patterned relationships among actors within a system enable and constrain human action. Conceiving human actors as part of rather than just as elements of social systems, a social relational approach acknowledges the social embedded condition of human actors and avoids the problems of micro-reduction (which focuses on individuals) and macro-reduction (which focuses on the larger structure) approaches to explain the behavior of systems: it eschews the individualist and holist pitfalls.

1.3.4 Methods

One of the best-developed sociological methods for studying social relations is organized under the rubric of social network analysis (SNA) (Emirbayer and Goodwin, 1994; Wasserman and Faust, 1994; Degenne and Forsé, 1999; Freeman, 2004). Social network analysis focuses on "relationships among entities, and on the patterns and implications of these relations." Social network analysis comprises diverse methods for the study of how resources, goods, and information flow through particular configurations of social ties. From the outset, the network methods of studying human behavior involve two commitments: (1) they are guided by formal theory organized in mathematical terms, and (2) they are grounded in the systematic analysis of empirical data. Thus, fuzzy concepts such as social cohesiveness and social prestige can be formalized and quantified, allowing systematic quantification and comparative studies. Social network data consist of at least one structural variable measured for a set of actors. Structural variables refer to the social relations (measured on pairs of actors) of interest, and are the primary concern of network analysis. However, attributes of individuals such as age, education, work position, place of residence, and so on, can also be used creating a composition-structure framework of explanation. The relations among actors define the structural data, while the attributes of individuals refer to the composition of the social network. The tools for obtaining social network data are similar to the traditional methods used in the social sciences (e.g. interviews, surveys, participant observation, and archival records).

Finally, it is necessary to make some conceptual distinctions between (social) system and (social) network and between network analysis and social network analysis, if only because they are closely related. The similarity and difference between (social) system and (social) network are these: every social network is a social system, but the converse is not true. There are two reasons for this, one conceptual and the other of substance. Conceptually, all (social) networks and all (social) systems can be represented as a graph; i.e. a collection of nodes (e.g. representing individuals, firms, organizations, nations) connected (fully or partially) by lines (social relations). Substantially, however, a social network is held together by pro-social behaviors (e.g. solidarity, friendship, acts of reciprocity), and it is informal and not hierarchical (Bunge, 1996). Thus, a formal organization and a market are social systems but not social networks, yet both can be represented as networks (Podolny and Page, 1998). To be sure, every human is a member of at least one social network, and often we deal and participate through our networks in social systems such as the market (Granovetter, 1985); hence, the relevance of social networks to all social systems, despite the contention that contemporary societies are characteristically structured by impersonal institutions (Polanyi, 1967; Scott, 1976; Coleman, 1993). Another important distinction should also be made between network and social network analysis. While both may use the same mathematical algorithms, network analysis is used to model and analyze practically any kind of system. Again, this is because systems can be represented as graphs. Thus, there are applications of network analysis to a wide range of systems. For example, network analysis has been used to study food webs (Dunne, 2006) and neuro-physiological systems (Smith and Franks, 1999). Clearly, by definition none of them is a social network.

1.4 HOW DOES THE RELATIONAL PERSPECTIVE RELATE TO COMMONLY APPLIED THEORIES IN STUDIES OF RESOURCE GOVERNANCE?

The social relational approach we present in this book allows us to study how patterns of interactions among various actors, stakeholders, agencies, and others can influence and frame activities and outcomes of natural resource management and governance. Although this is clearly not the one and only approach for studying natural resource governance, nor can it provide all the answers, it does provide a unique, yet broad, conceptual and analytical lens. To be sure, the social relational approach is still evolving, and depending on the specific research question, the contextual environment, and practicalities such as data-gathering issues, it will certainly not always be practically and theoretically feasible. With the objective to inform those interested in using this approach, this book explicitly documents some of the key challenges and opportunities in implementing the social relational approach.

Focusing on social relations and the social structures that emerged, the social relational approach discussed above, which we refer to in this book as social network analysis (SNA), provides a conceptual and analytical framework that could be integrated with other research approaches and theoretical frameworks (Dougill *et al.*, 2006; Prell *et al.*, 2007). Sometimes, SNA simply complements other approaches. At other times, SNA helps researchers to more precisely study the relationship between social structures and resource governance outcomes, but again we do not claim that it provides an all-encompassing and stand-alone framework or approach for understanding the human and social aspects of resource governance. The real strength of SNA actually comes when it is applied in combination with other theoretical frameworks. In other words, the relational approach provides for a valuable addition to the various theoretical and methodological toolboxes available in studying resource management and governance. Throughout this book, we try to show how the relational approach gives the researcher the means to uncover and analyze the complex patterns of interactions among actors characterizing most real-world governance settings, and how this can be used to explain various governance outcomes, and also in furthering the development of different theoretical frameworks. To illustrate what we mean, below we exemplify how some key challenges in resources management link to the relational approach. In doing so, we aim to show how a social relational approach can be incorporated in a broader research context.

1.4.1   Common-pool resource management

In the 1960s, Hardin (1968) wrote his seminal paper where he argued that commonly owned resources (or when the ownership is undefined) will inevitable be over-harvested and, in the end, exhausted (termed "the tragedy of the commons"). The solution, he argued, is to either privatize the commons or implement firm state control to avert the tragedy of the commons. Since most natural resources could be characterized as either open access or commonly owned (and assigning ownership and/or exerting effective monitoring schemes is often inherently difficult) resource depletion seems, from this standpoint, as inevitable. Since the publication of Hardin's paper, a large stream of scholarly work has, however, shown that this is not necessarily the case. In the past 30 years, a plethora of studies by a diverse collection of scholars have been published documenting a large number of cases of fisheries, forestry, rangelands, and irrigated farming systems in which various local groups of resource extractors have been able, by themselves, to together devise and implement common rules and practices (or institutions, in short) that regulate their resource extraction and prevent resource depletion (Acheson, 1981; Fenny *et al.*, 1990; Ostrom, 1990; Dyer and McGoodwin, 1994). Elinor Ostrom, who is one of the most well known of these scholars, even received the 2009 Swedish Bank of Treasures annual prize in Economics (commonly referred to as the Nobel prize in Economics) for her immense contributions to the research of common-pool resources.

Furthermore, research has shown that there is a set of specific criteria (or design principles) that characterize long-term success in such locally based approaches of common-pool resources governance (Ostrom, 1990). These principles (e.g. a bounded set of actors, ability for actors to self-organize, actors' commitment in following the commonly devised rules, and their mutual trust in the commitment of others to also comply, etc.) are inherently embedded in social processes and affected by factors such as trust for their long-term operation and effectiveness (e.g. Acheson, 1981; Fenny *et al.*, 1990; Dyer and McGoodwin, 1994; McCay and Jentoft, 1998). In other words, the social arena from where they organize and operate is largely defined by their patterns of social relations.

This, we argue, shows that SNA should be very helpful in unpacking important social factors that define different rates of success (or failure) in governing common-pool resources. For example, what pattern of relations generally defines settings where actors have been able to steer away from the tragedy of the commons and instead have organized themselves around a set of self-imposed institutions regulating their resource extraction? To what extent would such patterns differ depending on the stage of such self-organizing processes (Bodin *et al.*, 2006; Bodin and Crona, 2009)? And is it possible for an external agency to facilitate the development of favorable patterns of relationships (cf. Schneider *et al.*, 2003; Ernstson *et al.*, 2010)?

1.4.2   Developing knowledge of complex ecosystems

The natural environment is characterized by immense diversity and complexity, and, as stated above, our understanding of basic ecological mechanisms is still rather incomplete. Our limited knowledge and capacity to predict how the biophysical environment will respond to different management approaches clearly poses huge management and governance challenges.

Adaptive management was proposed as a response to these challenges in the early 1970s (Holling, 1973). In adaptive management, incomplete knowledge of ecological systems is assumed, and the management should be designed to produce better knowledge through controlled experiments. This explicitly implies that management has to change adaptively as knowledge increases. Since then, this basic idea has been much further developed. Now scholars often refer to adaptive co-management where, among other things, more focus is laid on social aspects of the management processes, and on the involvement of different actors and stakeholders in the governance processes (e.g. Armitage *et al.*, 2007). This is proposed as a way to make better use of different sources of knowledge (among other benefits, as will be further described in Chapter 3).

However, irrespective of whether the interest is specifically on adaptive management or adaptive co-management or in some other related conceptual framework, the generation and distribution of ecological knowledge among actors is clearly important if we are to be able to meet the challenges posed by the complexity of the biophysical environment. Here, we are touching upon fields such as social learning and participatory management (e.g. Bandura, 1977; Johnson *et al.*, 2003). Common threads for these fields are the exchange of information and knowledge among different actors, and the co-production of knowledge (e.g. Stephan *et al.*, 2010). Clearly, the pattern of communication among the various actors will play an important role in determining the outcomes of such processes. Conclusively, SNA can help us to understand how social networks of information and knowledge exchange can help in developing and distributing knowledge of the biophysical environment.

1.4.3 Collaborative management of boundary-spanning natural resources

As stated above, the governance processes, responsibilities, and ownership of natural resources is typically divided among several different actors. The biophysical environment, on the other hand, does not adhere to such man-made borders and division of responsibilities. For example, a municipality may be responsible for the management of all land along a stretch of a coastline, but the management of the marine environment is someone else's responsibility. There are, however, many strong ecological linkages between the terrestrial and the marine environment in the coastal zone. If these biophysical linkages are not accounted for, effective governance of these systems is difficult to achieve since important biophysical linkages are likely to be neglected. Specific for this example, the concept of Integrated Coastal Zone Management (ICZM) has been developed since the 1970s. ICZM proposes, simply speaking, that different management bodies being independently responsible of interdependent natural resources in the coastal zone are to manage these resources collaboratively through integrated planning.

More generally, for management and governance settings where the overall responsibility of a complex system is somewhat diffusively shared among a set of different actors, a likely outcome is that nobody will take responsibility for the whole, but instead focus their efforts on those parts they perceive as being their clearly defined responsibilities. This problem is quite similar to the challenges of common-pool resource management described above, however, here emphasis is on the lack of institutions operating on a higher system level although there might be well-functioning institutions operating on lower sub-system levels (cf. Cumming *et al.*, 2006; Ernstson *et al.*, 2010). One way to come around the dilemma is through exchange and collaboration among various actors (as in ICZM). In particular, collaborations between formal governing bodies such as state agencies and municipalities, and non-governmental organizations and the public at large are conceptualized in the research field of co-management (Pinkerton, 1989; Carlsson and Berkes, 2005). One key success factor for co-management initiatives to succeed is that these actors, which are sometimes in open conflict with each other, develop some level of mutual understanding and trust (e.g. Carlsson and Berkes, 2005). Trust develops over time and is often facilitated by the quality and quantity of social relations among individuals and organizations across organizational and contextual boundaries (Schneider *et al.*, 2003). There are in fact indications that such cross-organizational social networks can be more important for compliance to and enforcement of resource regulations than the development of formal institutions (Scholz and Wang, 2006).

1.4.4   A social relational approach as the common denominator

A common denominator for the briefly described research fields above is the need for various different actors to communicate, collaborate, coordinate activities, and so on. Actors often have different mandates, roles in society, perspectives, interests, backgrounds, objectives, etc.

Making such collaboration work is, accordingly, typically associated with many challenges. Fortunately, research shows that such collaborations are indeed possible and feasible. As mentioned earlier, the research on common-pool resources has shown that there are numerous examples of cases where people have actually managed to come together to collaboratively manage their common resources in a sustainable way over long periods of time (Acheson, 1981; Fenny *et al.*, 1990; Ostrom, 1990; Dyer and McGoodwin, 1994). Much of this research identifies the need for various stakeholders to be able to establish communication channels and to develop trustful relationships (this is often phrased as developing social capital; see e.g. Pretty and Ward, 2001). However, a great deal of this research focuses on institutional analysis and the various social relations that support these often informal institutions are often left unanalyzed.

In all, these examples and discussions have hopefully conveyed the message that SNA can prove very useful in furthering our knowledge on how to take on the challenges associated with sustainable governance of our biophysical environment, and that it can do so due to its ability to significantly contribute to a whole range of different theoretical and conceptual frameworks of importance in researching natural resource governance.

1.5   SOCIAL RELATIONAL APPROACHES IN NATURAL RESOURCE GOVERNANCE RESEARCH UP UNTIL NOW

The relational approach in general, and the explicit consideration of social networks in particular, is increasingly drawing attention in natural resource governance research, particularly with respect to adaptive natural resource governance based on different forms of participation and co-management. Many studies have identified the presence of informal social relationships among various actors and stakeholders in different management and governance settings as instrumental in order to for them to deal with complex tasks and unforeseen situations characterizing natural resource governance (Folke *et al.*, 2005; Hahn *et al.*, 2006). The majority of the research on these issues has not been explicit on the characteristics of such social networks, i.e. what specific structures make them successful or not. There are, however, several studies that have deployed detailed quantitative analyses of these networks, using formal mathematical models, with the objective to link specific structural characteristics of such networks with governance outcomes. In exemplifying this range of approaches we find it useful to divide this literature into three broad (and somewhat overlapping) categories: the binary metaphorical, the descriptive, and the structurally explicit approach. The categories aim to encapsulate how social networks and the relational approach have been commonly used, and should serve to acknowledge increasing levels of analytical precision on what we mean with social networks, and how we can research them. Some of the cited studies could be part of more than one category; especially the first and second categories are sometimes hard to separate from each other, while there is an easily distinguishable jump to the structurally explicit approach.

1.5.1   The binary metaphorical approach

In this category of literature, social networks are often treated as a metaphor for saying that certain actors are closer to each other, or that they exchange information or other resources in an informal way towards attaining a certain goal or objective. Social networks are treated as a quite unspecified binary variable; either there is a network or not, and the internal structural characteristics of these networks (like who is in the network, and how and in what way they are connected) are not explicitly addressed. Typically, the idea is that relevant actors are either socially tied together and that they use these relational ties for various purposes, or they are socially detached from other actors and thus operate more or less on their own. Nonetheless, this approach has been applied in a range of explorative studies, and these studies have established the empirically well-grounded realization that social networks in resource governance are of crucial importance (Olsson et al., 2004a, 2004b, 2007; Hahn et al., 2006; Fabricius et al., 2007). A wide range of effects and outcomes have been attributed to the existence of social networks. Folke et al. (2005), in their highly cited explorative review article, suggest that the existence of social networks is instrumental for building social memory and social capital, mobilizing legal, political, and financial support to ecosystem-based governance initiatives, in identifying knowledge gaps, and in creating "nodes of expertise of significance for ecosystem management that can be drawn upon at critical times." As such, these studies find social networks as instrumental for information sharing and the mobilization of internal and external knowledge across scales, levels, and groups, and as necessary in adaptive co-management. In summary, this category is characterized by studies where social networks in natural resource governance are identified as instrumental, but where little is said about the actual structure or pattern of the social networks themselves. As a consequence, the analytical and explanatory potential of the relational approach is not fully utilized, and at times it is difficult to separate the proposed influence of social networks from other analytical constructs such as social memory, social capital, and collaboration.

1.5.2 The descriptive approach

This category expands beyond the binary metaphorical approach since it starts to address certain key characteristics of the studied social networks. Descriptors of the shape of the social networks, for example them being *horizontal*, *vertical*, *bonding*, *bridging*, and *dense* are commonly used in this category. Often the network descriptors are expressed in relation to aspects of social capital with references to seminal work in the field (Coleman, 1990; Putnam, 1993; Pretty and Ward, 2001). Some illustrative examples where this descriptive approach is used is in the discussions between Tompkins and Adger (2004) and Newman and Dale (2005) regarding the adaptive capacity of community-based coastal management in Trinidad and Tobago; the case study of conflicts and resource use in the Southwestern Highlands of Uganda by Sanginga *et al.* (2007); the book on networks and natural resource management edited by Rydin and Falleth (2006); and the studies by Olsson *et al.* on adaptive co-management (Olsson *et al.*, 2004a, 2004b). As an example, Jones *et al.* (2009), who investigated the influence of social capital on co-management policy instruments, divide social networks into bonding, bridging, and linking ties. This division is, respectively, to be interpreted as collaborative ties within and between homogeneous social groups, and those between social groups with different power and authority (with reference to Putnam, 2000). This division enables more precision in analyzing and discussing how structures of networks might influence various governance outcomes, and thus goes beyond the metaphorical perspective where social networks are treated as either being present or absent. The studies in the descriptive category thus build on the important notion that not all social networks are created equal. However, studies within this category generally lack clear methodological strategies on how to empirically investigate and analytically distinguish between different descriptors of social network structure, which lowers their ability to explain or increase understanding of *how* social network structure matters.

Although we are not arguing that fully fledged and formally and explicitly defined quantitative methods are superior to less stringent studies on the meaning and function of social networks, a well-tried approach to improve understanding on how and why social network structure matters is, however, to measure and quantify aspects of social networks and their structures.

1.5.3   The structurally explicit approach

This third and final category encompasses studies of natural resource governance where the investigated social networks have been measured using systematic data collection methods, and where the relational data have been analyzed using formally defined models and methods. This is the category wherein this book would fit. The ultimate objective of studies within this category is to infer relationships between formally defined and quantified structural characteristics of social networks and various outcomes in natural resource governance. This quantitative approach does not exclude qualitative approaches (on the contrary, as will be shown throughout this book), but the analytical treatment of the networks is to be based upon quantified relational data for any study to fall within this category. In short, for studies to fit in the structurally explicit approach, the analytical treatment of the social network should follow the principles of the social relational approach discussed above (social network analysis).

1.6   WHY DO WE NEED THIS BOOK?

As we have argued earlier, social network analysis (SNA) provides a rigorous, systematic approach to studying how relations and their structuring influence a range of outcome variables and behaviors. For resource management and governance researchers, SNA offers a gateway into testing a range of theories linked to the field (see Chapter 3), and its solid grounding in empirical studies provides a rich array of concepts that can help sharpen the eyes of resource management scholars as they increasingly take a more "relational perspective" to their work.

Although a number of texts do exist that aim to introduce a novice to SNA (e.g. Wasserman and Faust, 1994; Degenne and Forsé, 1999), linking the approach to the field of natural resource management and governance might not be such an easy, straightforward application, and this has to do with the fact that SNA's history lies largely within the fields of social psychology and sociology. In this book, we not only introduce readers to key concepts and methods of SNA, we also show how these link to a range of popular theories within the field of natural resource governance, and we offer a number of case studies to illustrate how this use of SNA has been successfully done in the past. Every case study is also accompanied with a subsection where the authors reflect upon some key issues of importance that typically need to be considered when studying natural resource governance using SNA. In detail, we asked each author to reflect upon the following issues:

- Network boundary issues and how you resolved them? For example, how did you define the social network boundary (if conducting a complete network)?
- If and how were ecological boundaries taken into account in your study (especially in relation to the social network boundaries)?
- How did you decide on the unit of analysis (e.g. individuals, groups, or organizations)?
- Were there any data-gathering problems/issues?
- Any ethical issues, especially in relation to the SNA method?
- Explanatory power of SNA: did you feel that SNA explained the outcome variable of interest or do you think that other issues/ variables held more explanatory value?
- Did you gather any other data alongside your social network data, e.g. qualitative data or additional quantitative data that were not network data? If so, then what sort of benefit or role did these data play, and would you advise a reader to do the same?
- SNA is often accused of portraying networks/relations as static. What is your own experience and/or opinion of this view?

Finally, towards the end of this book, we offer readers not only a summary of where the state of the field now lies, in relation to linking SNA to natural resource management, we reassess where the future potentials lie. We hope this book will serve as a handbook and as a source of inspiration for all researchers and practitioners who are interested in exploring social relational aspects of natural resource governance, but we also hope that it will serve as a starting point from which to develop this emerging field much further.

1.7 WHO SHOULD READ THIS BOOK?

The intended audience for this book is both an audience which is mostly new to social network analysis (SNA), but already familiar with some of the theories and basic issues of natural resource governance, and an audience of scholars and practitioners using SNA and who would be interested in applying such approaches in the field of natural resource governance. The book will meet audience needs of

(1) Wishing to learn about how social networks can enable or constrain resource management and governance.
(2) Understanding some of the stumbling blocks and/or other obstacles one might encounter in applying a social network analytical approach in studying resource governance.
(3) Learning about some useful starting points from empirical research that has put this approach into practice.
(4) Learning about what resources are available for conducting an SNA study and how to get started in a study of this sort.

Typical examples of this audience thus include upper-level undergraduate, graduate, or post-graduate students, and academics fairly new to SNA but already within the multi-disciplinary field of natural resource governance. We hope the book could fit nicely being part of the study course literature for upper-level undergraduate courses on resource governance in more general terms, and more specific graduate/post-graduate courses on various theories and approaches in resource governance research where stakeholder and agency cooperations and interactions are emphasized. Also, more practically oriented individuals and groups (within or external to academia) that are, or work together with, practitioners in resource governance (land-use planners, development agencies, governmental authorities, resource extractors, etc.) would hopefully find this book being of interest and relevance.

1.8 HOW IS THE BOOK ORGANIZED?

This book basically consists of three different parts. Part I introduces the rationale as to why a structurally explicit relational approach in studying natural resource management is beneficial. It comprises this chapter, the following chapter that introduces basic concepts and approaches in SNA, and the third chapter where the social relational approach is contextualized in relation to other theoretical and conceptual frameworks commonly used in contemporary natural resource governance research. The main objectives with this part are twofold. First, we want to provide the reader with enough theoretical, methodological, and conceptual understanding to be able to comprehend and therefore get the most out of the following parts. Second, we use this part (in particular Chapter 3) to gather, synthesize, and elucidate how recent research in this emerging research field have put SNA in contact with other theoretical frameworks. Hence, this part not only introduces the reader to the field, it also provides what we see as a substantial contribution to the research field as such.

Part II constitutes a set of carefully selected studies, each presented as a separate chapter. One of the studies is based solely on theoretical modeling, whereas the remaining studies are based on empirical case studies from different regions of the world. Each study will emphasize different aspects and concepts within the field, and each study will also include some reflective commentary on some of the benefits, limitations, or challenges encountered in using the social network analysis for the particular study in question. Although the studies are quite different, they together provide a coherent presentation of how some key aspects of social network characteristics can affect resource management in various ways. They also give the reader a broad overview of a range of approaches that are applicable in studying natural resource governance utilizing the social relational perspective.

We have arranged the case studies by their primary unit (or level) of analysis. The chapters that are concerned with identifying individual entities (e.g. resource users, organizations) occupying different types of positions in the social network are referred to as node level. The next level is the subgroup. A subgroup is a set of individual entities in the network that are grouped together according to some clearly defined criteria. Chapters focusing on subgroups typically identify subgroups to investigating how these subgroups are related to each other, and who the members of these subgroups are. The third level is the complete network. At this level, focus is on the overall patterns of relations of the complete network.

However, it must be pointed out that irrespective of the chosen level of analysis, the whole network is always taken into consideration. For example, in identifying the individual nodes in the network with the highest betweenness centrality (which is a measure that is defined and quantified at the node level; see Chapter 2), the complete network structure is taken into account. The different studies of Part II are outlined in Table 1.1.

Table 1.1. *The case studies in Part II.*

Chapter	Title	System	Theories and concepts	Authors
Individual (node) level				
4.	Barriers and opportunities in transforming to sustainable governance: the role of key individuals	Artisanal small-scale coastal marine fisheries in Kenya	The role of key individuals in enabling/blocking collective action in natural resource governance	Bodin and Crona
5.	Social network analysis for stakeholder selection and the links to social learning and adaptive co-management	Land management in the Peak District National Park, UK	Stakeholder selection using network analysis, and the links to social learning and adaptive co-management	Prell, Reed, and Hubacek
6.	*Who* and *how*: engaging well-connected fishers in social networks to improve fisheries management and conservation	Artisanal small-scale coastal marine fisheries in Baja California Sur, Mexico	Stakeholder selection using network analysis. How to engage with communities?	Ramirez-Sanchez
7.	The effects of social network ties on the public's satisfaction with forest management in British Columbia, Canada	Forestry in Canada	To what extent are people's perceptions about forestry management influenced by their peers?	Tindall, Harshaw, and Taylor
8.	Social network models for natural resource use and extraction	N/A	Multi-level modeling where both network and other effects can be incorporated	Frank

Table 1.1. (cont.)

Subgroup level

9.	Friends or neighbors? Subgroup heterogeneity and the importance of bonding and bridging ties in natural resource governance	Artisanal small-scale coastal marine fisheries in Kenya	Subgroup composition, subgroup interactions, and effects on local ecological knowledge and collective action	Crona and Bodin
10.	The role of individual attributes in the practice of information sharing among fishers from Loreto, BCS, Mexico	Artisanal small-scale coastal marine fisheries in Baja California Sur, Mexico	Investigation of defining characteristics of subgroup memberships. Links between subgroups and collective action	Ramirez-Sanchez

The network level

11.	Transformative collective action: a network approach to transformative change in ecosystem-based management	Network of civil society organizations in the National Urban Park in Stockholm, Sweden	Pairing SNA with social movement theories to identify network level mechanisms to explain collective action towards transformative change	Ernstson
12.	Social networks, joint image building, and adaptability: the case of local fishery management	Three local fishery management areas in northern Sweden	How network closure and heterogeneity (bridging) support adaptive management processes	Sandström
13.	Agrarian communication networks: consequences for agroforestry	Agroforestry in four rural villages in Ghana	Information and knowledge diffusion. Could social networks be used in scaling up agroforestry management?	Isaac and Dawoe

Finally, in Part III we summarize some key findings from the cases, both from a methodological and a theoretical perspective. We also summarize and synthesize lessons learned by (partly) drawing from the reflections each author provides in his or her chapters in Part II. In doing so, we suggest a set of key areas of importance for future research in this new and rapidly growing research field.

REFERENCES

Acheson, J. M. (1981). Anthropology of fishing. *Annual Review of Anthropology*, **10**, 275–316.

Armitage, D., F. Berkes and N. Doubleday (2007). *Adaptive Co-management: Collaboration, Learning, and Multi-level Governance*. University of British Columbia Press.

Bandura, A. (1977). *Social Learning Theory*. Englewood Cliffs, NJ: Prentice Hall.

Blaikie, P. (1985). *The Political Economy of Soil Erosion in Developing Countries*. Harlow: Longman.

Blitz, D. (1992). *Emergent Evolution, Qualitative Novelty and the Levels of Reality*. Dordrecht: Springer.

Bodin, Ö. and B. Crona (2008). Community-based management of natural resources – exploring the role of social capital and leadership in a rural fishing community. *World Development*, **36**(12), 2763–2779.

Bodin, Ö., B. Crona and H. Ernstson (2006). Social networks in natural resource management – what's there to learn from a structural perspective? *Ecology and Society*, **11**(2), r2.

Bodin, Ö. and B. I. Crona (2009). The role of social networks in natural resource governance: what relational patterns make a difference? *Global Environmental Change*, **19**, 366–374.

Bunge, M. (1996). *Finding Philosophy in Social Science*. New Haven, CT: Yale University Press.

Bunge, M. (1999). Ten modes of individualism – none of which works – and their alternatives. *Philosophy of the Social Sciences*, **30**, 384–406.

Carlsson, L. and F. Berkes (2005). Co-management: concepts and methodological implications. *Journal of Environmental Management*, **75**, 65–76.

Castán Broto, V., M. Gislason and M.-H. Ehlers (2009). Practicing interdisciplinarity in the interplay between disciplines: experiences of established researchers. *Environmental Science and Policy*, **12**(7), 922–933.

Chapin, F. S. I., G. P. Kofinas and C. Folke (2010). *Principles of Ecosystem Stewardship: Resilience-based Natural Resource Management in a Changing World*. New York, NY: Springer Verlag.

Checkland, P. and J. Scholes (1999). *Soft Systems Methodology in Action*. New York, NY: Wiley.

Chuenpagdee, R. and S. Jentoft (2009). Governability assessment for fisheries and coastal systems: a reality check. *Human Ecology*, **37**, 109–120.

Coleman, J. S. (1990). *Foundations of Social Theory*. Cambridge, MA: Belknap Press of Harvard University Press.

Coleman, J. S. (1993). The rational reconstruction of society – 1992 presidential address. *American Sociological Review*, **58**, 1–15.

Cumming, G. S., D. H. M. Cumming and C. L. Redman (2006). Scale mismatches in social-ecological systems: causes, consequences, and solutions. *Ecology and Society*, **11**(1), 14.

Daily, G. C. (1997). Introduction: what are ecosystem services? In *Nature's Services. Societal Dependence on Natural Ecosystems*. Washington, DC: Island Press, pp. 1–10.

Degenne, A. and M. Forsé (1999). *Introducing Social Networks*. London: Sage.

Dougill, A. J., E. D. G. Fraser, J. Holden *et al.* (2006). Learning from doing participatory rural research: lessons from the Peak District National Park. *Journal of Agricultural Economics*, **57**(2), 259–275.

Duit, A. and V. Galaz (2008). Governance and complexity – emerging issues for governance theory. *Governance*, **21**(3), 311–335.

Dunne, J. A. (2006). The network structure of food webs. In *Ecological Networks: Linking Structure to Dynamics in Food Webs*. Oxford: Oxford University Press, pp. 27–86.

Dyer, C. L. and J. R. McGoodwin (1994). *Folk Management in the World's Fisheries: Lessons for Modern Fisheries Management*. Niwot, CO: The University Press of Colorado.

Emirbayer, M. (1997). Manifesto for a relational sociology. *American Journal of Sociology*, **103**, 281–317.

Emirbayer, M. and J. Goodwin (1994). Network analysis, culture, and the problem of agency. *American Journal of Sociology*, **99**, 1411–1454.

Ernstson, H. (2008). In Rhizomia: actors, networks and resilience in urban landscapes. PhD thesis. Stockholm University, Stockholm.

Ernstson, H., S. Barthel, E. Andersson and S. T. Borgström (2010). Scale-crossing brokers and network governance of urban ecosystem services: the case of Stockholm, Sweden. *Ecology and Society*, **15**(4), 28.

Ernstson, H. and S. Sörlin (2009). Weaving protective stories: connective practices to articulate holistic values in Stockholm National Urban Park. *Environment and Planning A*, **41**(6), 1460–1479.

Fabricius, C., C. Folke, G. Cundill and L. Schultz (2007). Powerless spectators, coping actors, and adaptive co-managers: a synthesis of the role of communities in ecosystem management. *Ecology and Society*, **12**(1), 29.

Fenny, D., F. Berkes, B. J. McCay and J. M. Acheson (1990). The tragedy of the commons: twenty-two years later. *Human Ecology*, **18**(1), 1–19.

Folke, C., T. Hahn, P. Olsson and J. Norberg (2005). Adaptive governance of social-ecological systems. *Annual Review of Environment and Resources*, **30**, 441–473.

Folke, C., L. Pritchard, F. Berkes, J. Colding and U. Svedin (2007). The problem of fit between ecosystems and institutions: ten years later. *Ecology and Society*, **12**(1), 30.

Freeman, L. C. (2004). *The Development of Social Network Analysis – A Study in the Sociology of Science*. Vancouver, BC: Empirical Press.

Granovetter, M. (1985). Economic action and social structure: the problem of embeddedness. *American Journal of Sociology*, **91**, 481–510.

Hahn, T., P. Olsson, C. Folke and K. Johansson (2006). Trust-building, knowledge generation and organizational innovations: the role of a bridging organization for adaptive comanagement of a wetland landscape around Kristianstad, Sweden. *Human Ecology*, **34**(4), 573–592.

Hardin, G. (1968). The tragedy of the commons. *Science*, **162**, 1243–1248.

Harvey, D. (1996). *Justice, Nature and the Geography of Difference*. Oxford: Blackwell.

Holling, C. S. (1973). Resilience and stability of ecological systems. *Annual Review of Ecological Systems*, **4**, 1–23.

Hornborg, A. (2009). Zero-sum world: challenges in conceptualizing environmental load displacement and ecologically unequal exchange in the world-system. *International Journal of Comparative Sociology*, **50**(3–4), 237–262.

Johnson, N. L., N. Lilja and J. A. Ashby (2003). Measuring the impact of user participation in agricultural and natural resource management research. *Agricultural Systems*, **78**(2), 287–306.

Jones, N., C. M. Sophoulis, T. Iosifides, I. Botetzagias and K. Evangelinos (2009). The influence of social capital on environmental policy instruments. *Environmental Politics*, **18**(4), 595–611.

Krishna, A. (2002). *Active Social Capital – Tracing the Roots of Development and Democracy*. New York, NY: Columbia University Press.

Levin, S. A. (1998). Ecosystems and the biosphere as complex adaptive systems. *Ecosystems*, **1**(5), 431–436.

Liu, J., T. Dietz, S. R. Carpenter *et al.* (2007). Complexity of coupled human and natural systems. *Science*, **317**(5844), 1513–1516.

Lubchenco, J. (1998). Entering the century of the environment: a new social contract for science. *Science*, **279**(5350), 491–497.

Maiolo, J. R., J. C. Johnson and D. Griffith (1992). Application of social science theory to fisheries management: three examples. *Society and Natural Resources*, **5**, 391–407.

McCay, B. J., and S. Jentoft (1998). Market or community failure? Critical perspectives on common property research. *Human Organizations*, **57**(1), 21–29.

Nadasdy, P. (2007). Adaptive co-management and the gospel of resilience. In *Adaptive Co-Management: Collaboration, Learning and Multi-level Governance*. Toronto: UBC Press, pp. 208–227.

Newman, L. and A. Dale (2005). Network structure, diversity, and proactive resilience building: a response to Tompkins and Adger. *Ecology and Society*, **10**(1), r2.

Olsson, P., C. Folke and F. Berkes (2004a). Adaptive comanagement for building resilience in social-ecological systems. *Environmental Management*, **34**(1), 75–90.

Olsson, P., C. Folke, V. Galaz, T. Hahn and L. Schultz (2007). Enhancing the fit through adaptive co-management: creating and maintaining bridging functions for matching scales in the Kristianstads Vattenrike Biosphere Reserve, Sweden. *Ecology and Society*, **12**(1), 28.

Olsson, P., C. Folke and T. Hahn (2004b). Social-ecological transformation for ecosystem management: the development of adaptive co-management of a wetland landscape in southern Sweden. *Ecology and Society*, **9**(4), 2.

Ostrom, E. (1990). *Governing the Commons: The Evolution of Institutions for Collective Action*. Cambridge: Cambridge University Press.

Pinkerton, E. (1989). *Co-operative Management of Local Fisheries. New Directions for Improved Management and Community Development*. Vancouver, BC: University of British Columbia Press.

Podolny, J. M. and K. L. Page (1998). Network forms of organization. *Annual Review of Sociology*, **24**, 57–76.

Polanyi, K. (1967). *The Great Transformation*. Boston: Beacon Press.

Portes, A. (1998). Social capital: its origins and applications in modern sociology. *Annual Review of Sociology*, **24**, 1–24.

Prell, C., K. Hubacek and M. Reed (2006). Using stakeholder and social network analysis to support participatory processes. *International Journal of Biodiversity Science and Management*, **2**(3), 249–252.

Prell, C., K. Hubacek, M. Reed *et al.* (2007). If you have a hammer everything looks like a nail: traditional versus participatory model building. *Interdisciplinary Science Reviews*, **32**(3), 263–282.

Pretty, J. and H. Ward (2001). Social capital and the environment. *World Development*, **29**(2), 209–227.

Putnam, R. D. (1993). The prosperous community: social capital and public life. *American Prospect*, **13**, 35–42.

Putnam, R. D. (2000). *Bowling Alone: The Collapse and Revival of American Community*. New York, NY: Simon & Schuster.

Rockström, J., W. Steffen, K. Noone *et al.* (2009). A safe operating space for humanity. *Nature*, **461**(7263), 472–475.

Rydin, Y. and E. Falleth (2006). *Networks and Institutions in Natural Resource Management*. Cheltenham: Edward Elgar.

Sanginga, P. C., R. N. Kamugisha and A. M. Martin (2007). The dynamics of social capital and conflict management in multiple resource regimes: a case of the southwestern highlands of Uganda. *Ecology and Society*, **12**(1), 6.

Sawyer, R. K. (2001). Emergence in sociology: contemporary philosophy of mind and social implications for sociological theory. *American Journal of Sociology*, **107**, 551–558.

Schneider, M., J. Scholz, M. Lubell, D. Mindruta and M. Edwardsen (2003). Building consensual institutions: networks and the National Estuary Program. *American Journal of Political Science*, **47**(1), 143–158.

Scholz, J. T. and C.-L. Wang (2006). Cooptation or transformation? Local policy networks and federal regulatory enforcement. *American Journal of Political Science*, **50**(1), 81–97.

Schweizer, T. (1997). Embeddedness of ethnographic cases – a social networks perspective. *Current Anthropology*, **38**, 739–760.

Scott, J. (1976). *The Moral Economy of the Peasant. Rebellion and Subsistence and Southeast Asia*. New Haven, CT: Yale University Press.

Smith, T. S. and D. D. Franks (1999). Introduction: emergence, reduction, and levels of analysis in the neurosociological paradigm. In D. D. Franks and T. S. Smith (Eds.), *Mind, Brain, and Society: Toward a Neurosociology of Emotion*. Stanford: Jai Press, pp. 3–18.

Stafford, S. G., D. M. Bartels, S. Begay-Campbell *et al.* (2009). Now is the time for action: transitions and tipping points in complex environmental systems. *Environment: Science and Policy for Sustainable Development*, **52**(1), 38–45.

Stephan, B., F. Carl and C. Johan (2010). Social-ecological memory in urban gardens – retaining the capacity for management of ecosystem services. *Global Environmental Change*, **20**(2), 255–265.

Swyngedouw, E. and N. C. Heynen (2003). Urban political ecology, justice and the politics of scale. *Antipode*, **35**, 898–998.

Tompkins, E. L. and N. W. Adger (2004). Does adaptive management of natural resources enhance resilience to climate change? *Ecology and Society*, **9**(2), 10.

Wasserman, S. and K. Faust (1994). *Social Network Analysis – Methods and Applications*. Cambridge: Cambridge University Press.

Wellman, B. (1988). Structural analysis: from method and metaphor to theory and substance. In B. Wellman and S. D. Berkowitz (Eds.), *Social Structures: A Network Approach*. Cambridge: Cambridge University Press, pp. 19–61.

Wenger, E. (1998). *Communities of Practice: Learning, Meaning, and Identity*. New York, NY: Cambridge University Press.

White, H. C. (2008). *Identity and Control: How Social Formations Emerge*. Princeton, NJ: Princeton University Press.

Vitousek, P., H. Mooney, J. Lubchenco and J. Melillo (1997). Human domination of earth's ecosystems. *Science*, **277**(5325), 494–499.

Vitousek, P. M., P. R. Ehrlich, A. H. Ehrlich and P. A. Matson (1986). Human appropriation of the products of photosynthesis. *Bioscience*, **36**(6), 368–373.

CHRISTINA PRELL

2

Some basic structural characteristics of networks

In this chapter, I shall try to introduce to you some basic terminology in social network analysis, as well as give you an overview of some of the basic concepts that you will find throughout this book. This chapter will provide the reader with sufficient knowledge and terminology to be able to comprehend the following chapters.

Please note that there are a number of good textbooks and handbooks on the market that offer a thorough introduction to the social network analysis. I recommend the following books for those interested in learning more about social network analysis: de Nooy *et al.* (2005), Prell (2011), Wasserman and Faust (1994), and Scott (2000).

2.1 BASIC VOCABULARY

Social networks are comprised primarily of actors and the social relations linking these actors together. All of us are involved in different social networks, and thus, it is perhaps easiest to start understanding social networks through thinking about one's own. For example, who are your close friends? Who are your immediate family members? With whom do you work closely within your profession? The answers you offer to each of these questions represent a unique social network: friendship, family, and work colleagues.

Below is a hypothetical list of answers to just one of the questions, i.e. "who are your close friends?" The person answering this question is David, and you will see his answers in Table 2.1.

Social Networks and Natural Resource Management: Uncovering the Fabric of Environmental Governance, ed. Ö. Bodin and C. Prell. Published by Cambridge University Press.
© Cambridge University Press 2011.

Table 2.1. *David's close friends.*

Name	Gender	Age
Jan	Female	38
Alice	Female	46
Ken	Male	48

Table 2.1 thus offers you a list of responses from David regarding who David considers to be his close friends. We can call this list of people David's "friendship network." Each individual person in David's network is considered an actor, and David holds a unique kind of social relation with each of these actors, i.e. a relation of friendship. Actors in network analysis are also referred to as nodes and vertices.

In addition, the friendship network for David, shown above, reflects a special kind of social network, i.e. an ego network. An ego network consists of a focal actor (called *ego*) and the actors to whom ego is directly connected are referred to as *alters*. So here, David is ego and his alters are Jan, Alice, and Ken. I have also included in Table 2.1 some additional information about these alters, i.e. their gender and age. Thus, in looking at social networks, we not only consider the people within the network, but also additional characteristics about those people. In this book, you will see many instances where data are gathered not just on the social network, but on the actors themselves.

Ego networks, such as the one described above, are generally contrasted against the idea of a complete network. For example, suppose David, Jan, Alice, and Ken were all members of the same local ski club. As an analyst, I am interested in the friendship dynamics of the people in this club. As such, I am not just interested in David's network, I am interested in all the actors within this ski club, and further, how all these actors within this particular club are related to one another through friendship ties. In specifying a particular set of actors and describing the friendships linking them together, I am studying a *complete friendship network*. A complete network is one where a set of actors and the entire set of ties linking these actors together are studied. Figure 2.1 offers a visual comparison between an ego network and a complete network: the first graph is an ego network, and the middle and third ones are complete networks:

Please note that in Figure 2.1, David appears in all graphs. That is, a complete network can be composed of many ego networks. When I

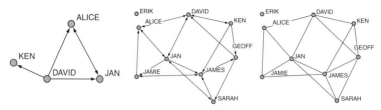

Figure 2.1 Ego network and Ski Club network (ego network, digraph of ski club, graph of ski club).

approached David and asked him who his close friends were, if my intention was to study a complete network, as opposed to an ego network, I could have structured my question to David differently, to focus my data-gathering efforts towards the complete network. Thus, my question could have been altered by saying, "Who are your close friends *within this particular ski club*?" In focusing David's attention to the ski club, I created a *boundary* around the friendship network I wish to study. In other words, I defined (to myself and to David) the scope of possible actors to be considered as part of this network, and simultaneously, implied which ones are outside my realm of interest. Thus, although David most likely has close friendships outside the ski club, as a researcher, I am not interested in those. I am only interested in tracing the friendship ties within the bounded network of the ski club. Further, by specifying the boundary to be the members of the ski club, I have, in essence, specified my population of interest for this particular network study. As you will see, the authors in this book pay considerable attention to the ways in which network boundaries are drawn for their research.

From just this simple example, I can now offer you a more complex definition of a social network: a social network consists of a set of relations that apply to a set of social actors, as well as any additional information on those actors and relations.

I will now move more quickly through some additional vocabulary: Figure 2.1 displays the friendship network of the ski club as a *digraph*, which is a visual depiction of a network showing a set of directed lines among a set of nodes. Sometimes networks are displayed without directional arrowheads on their lines, and such depictions are referred to as *graphs*. Digraphs thus show "who nominates whom" in a network; the directed lines making up the digraph are referred to as *arcs*, and these arcs have *senders* and *receivers*. Senders are actors who nominate, and receivers are the nominees. When two actors both nominate one another, we say that the directional tie they share with one another is a *reciprocal*, or *mutual* tie. In the present example, Jamie and James share a reciprocal tie as they have both nominated one another as friends. In contrast, graphs do not have arcs, but rather *edges* (lines with no directional arrowheads); graphs do not distinguish between senders and receivers, but merely show the presence of a tie between two actors/nodes as an edge. Figure 2.1C also shows the ski club network as a simple graph.

You will notice in Figure 2.1 that Erik sits apart from the rest of the network. This particular kind of actor receives a special name in network analysis, i.e. an *isolate*. An isolate is an actor (or node) that shares no ties with any other actors in the network.

The next figure (Figure 2.2) displays the same digraph of the ski club friendship network, but here, you will notice the thickness of the lines vary. Some lines appear thicker than others, and line thickness reflects the intensity or strength of the friendship tie between two actors.

Thus Jan and James have a stronger friendship tie than David and Ken. Intensity of a friendship relation, or strength of tie, can be measured in a variety of ways; one can look at things such as the frequency of interaction between two actors, as well as the intensity of feelings and perceptions of intimacy and mutual trust. For example, we could ask a respondent, "with whom are you friends in this ski club?" and in addition, ask that respondent to rate their perception of the closeness or intensity of that friendship on a scale from 1–5. In addition, we could

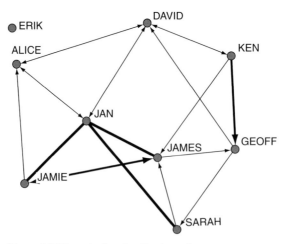

Figure 2.2 Digraph showing tie strength.

ask about the frequency of their interaction, and so forth. Such additional information provides valued social network data, which can be used as an indicator for tie strength.

The above section attempted to lay out some basic vocabulary regarding social networks. This section gives an overview of many of the concepts you will find in subsequent chapters in this book. I have chosen to organize these concepts according to levels of analysis, e.g. the actor, tie, subgroup, and network levels.

2.2.1 Actor level concepts: ego networks and centrality in complete networks

Key social network concepts that pertain to the individual actor first involve a distinction between ego networks and complete networks. Ego networks, by their very nature, focus on the individual actor level, and here, one is primarily concerned with seeing how egos compare across certain features of their individual, personal networks. For example, do some egos have larger networks than others? In addition to comparative sizes of ego networks, an ego network analysis would also consider the following structural features: (i) extent to which the alters in an ego network share ties with each other (referred to as ego network density); (ii) the attributes of egos and alters (e.g. are females more likely to be friends with other females); and (iii) comparing the tie strength across ego networks.

Thus, for example, a male 35-year-old ego may have three close friends who are female and similar in age, and who are likewise friends with each other. In contrast, a female 22-year-old ego may have only one close friend who is male and older than herself.

These differences and/or similarities across ego networks are then generally studied in relation to certain outcome variables; for example, would our 35-year-old male ego generally feel more "supported" by his circle of female friends than the female ego by her one male friend? Such comparison of structural features of an ego network and outcome variables is not only common for ego network studies, but across network analysis in general.

When considering complete networks, the most common actor-level concept used in network analysis is that of centrality. In general, centrality reflects ideas of relative importance, prestige, power, or popularity. When you look at a network and see that certain actors have a disproportionate number of ties compared with other actors, one generally concludes that these actors are more "central" to the network. In Figure 2.1, James and Jan are the most central actors as they hold more ties than any other actor in the network.

Centrality typically gets broken down into different measures, which are as follows: degree (as above, which can be further distinguished according to indegree and outdegree); eigenvector; betweenness; closeness; and beta-centrality. Each of these are briefly described below (readers are strongly encouraged to read Freeman, 1979).

Degree centrality: is simply the number of immediate contacts an actor has in a network. To measure degree centrality, you simply count how many actors are directly tied to your focal actor, ignoring both the direction and value of the tie. If you wish to pay attention to the direction of a tie, then you can focus on how many incoming ties a focal actor receives (referred to as indegree) or how many outgoing ties a focal actor gives (referred to as outdegree). Distinguishing between indegree and outdegree usually suggests slightly different social dynamics in a network; an actor with high levels of indegree centrality is generally seen as a "popular" person, if the relation in question is a positive one such as friendship or advice. In contrast, outdegree centrality can be seen more as an indicator for involvement or dependence; here the focal actor turns to many others either for help, friendship, or advice.

Eigenvector centrality: is a measure that builds upon degree centrality. Here, a central actor is one who is connected to others who themselves have high-degree centralities. Thus, eigenvector centrality is the sum of an actor's connections to other actors, weighted by those other actors' degree centrality. With eigenvector centrality, your attention encompasses a wider view of the network, and as such, it can be seen as a more refined version of degree centrality (Borgatti, 1995).

Betweenness centrality: captures a different dimension of the notion of centrality. Here, one's centrality score increases the number of times that actor rests on the geodesic (shortest path) *between* two actors. In communication networks, betweenness centrality measures how much potential control an actor has over the flow of information. If an actor rests between many other actors in the network, then this actor can choose to withhold or distort information she or he receives, thereby influencing the network as a whole.

Closeness centrality: Like betweenness and eigenvector, closeness centrality is considered a more global measure of centrality, in that it takes into consideration the entire network of ties when calculating the centrality of an individual actor. Closeness is measured by looking at the *distance* between actors, e.g. if an actor needs to pass through many intermediaries to reach another actor, then that actor is quite distant from the other. Thus, actors who have the *shortest distance* to other actors are seen as having the most closeness centrality. Closeness centrality emphasizes an actor's *independence* in that an actor who is close to others in a network tends to not rely on many intermediaries in the network (Bavelas, 1950, Freeman, 1979).

Beta centrality: Phillip Bonacich (1987) developed "beta-centrality" as both critique and alternative to other centrality measures. Bonacich realized that previous research into the different centrality measures offered up conflicting evidence: in some cases, the centrality scores would reveal the most important, or powerful, actor in a network, but in other situations, the most powerful actors would be the semi-peripheral ones, not the central ones (Cook *et al.*, 1983). Keep in mind that "power" in these instances was conceptualized differently, according to the research context. In addition, there were differences across studies according to whether the social networks were composed of "positive" relations such as communication or liking, or "negative" relations, such as exchange networks or networks based on feelings of dislike. With positive relations, previous centrality measures would reliably predict the most powerful person, e.g. the person most responsible for mobilizing a network or diffusing information. For negative relations, the centrality measures would give mixed results or sometimes fail altogether.

To address these issues regarding the relationship between centrality and power, Bonacich developed what he called "beta centrality," which makes use of a parameter (called "beta" or β) that can be controlled by the analyst. The parameter beta reflects the extent to which power is linked to the centrality of others. Thus, if an analyst assigns small values of beta to the equation, the analysis is weighted towards the local structure surrounding ego. Larger values weight the equation towards the wider network structure, and thus, the metric becomes similar to the measure of eigenvector centrality. In addition, beta is assigned a positive or negative value depending on whether it is good for the focal actor to be connected to highly central people (a positive value would indicate that it was, and a negative value would indicate it was more advantageous to stay away from central others).

These measures present some trade-offs and comparisons. Briefly, to summarize some of the main differences/similarities across the measures, I have compiled for you the list below. Again, I also suggest readers take a look at the following literature for further information on centrality (Freeman, 1979; Mizruchi and Potts, 1998; Borgatti, 2005).

- Eigenvector and beta centrality consider the degree centrality of other actors in the network. Degree, betweenness, and closeness do not.
- Degree centrality does not consider the direction of ties. Indegree and outdegree centrality do take into consideration the direction of a tie. Closeness and betweenness centrality can also be calculated on directional data.
- Betweenness centrality draws attention to who is critical for a network's information flow, i.e. who connects different segments of the network together and is an important intermediary or broker. The distribution of betweenness centrality scores in a network is also considered better at capturing the variation in actors' centralities (Wasserman and Faust, 1994). Thus, the contrast between central and non-central actors are more highly contrasted when one makes use of betweenness.
- In contrast to betweenness, degree-based measures are considered less capable for unveiling stark differences/variations in centrality scores among actors.
- Degree centrality measures an individual's *involvement* in the network. Indegree centrality reveals "*popular*" actors and outdegree centrality focuses on the *expansion* of a focal actor's network.
- Eigenvector is sensitive to instances where an actor with low-degree centrality can be connected to someone with high-degree centrality, and gain an advantage from that connection.

2.2.2 Tie level

Earlier I have discussed some of the different ways to describe the ties linking actors together. This includes considering the direction of ties (arcs) or not (edges), looking to see if ties are reciprocal or not, and also considering tie strength. I shall address these in a bit more detail here, as well as one or two additional topics, in the context of how such considerations of ties can be included in analyses of networks.

With regards to the distinction between arcs and edges, there are a number of measures that can only be used on graphs, i.e. networks composed of edges. These include many of the centrality measures described above, such as degree, closeness, eigenvector, and beta. In addition, network density (described below) is typically run on edge data. Thus, in making use of certain measures, network analysts often-times must manipulate their data to make sure they conform to the requirements of the analyses.

Yet aside from these more technical requirements, analysts often-times might gather valued, directional network data only to manipulate those data in particular ways to focus attention on certain relational aspects of the data. For example, if a researcher has gathered data on the frequency of communication ties amongst a set of actors, she or he may decide to dichotomize the data to focus attention only on the most frequent ties in the data set. Similarly, one can extract only the reciprocal ties from a network and run analyses on those (i.e. only the reciprocal ties in a digraph are kept when converting the network to the simpler graph representation).

Another consideration regarding ties is whether a researcher wishes to gather data on more than one kind of relation, i.e. the distinction between multi-relational networks and single relation networks. For example, in a closed, complete network, an analyst might ask a respondent to comment on the number of friends she has, to whom she goes for advice, and with whom she communicates with regularly. Those individuals whom the respondent nominates for two or more of these relations (friendship, advice, and communi-cation) would be considered individuals with whom the respondent shares a *multi-relational tie*. As will be seen shortly, such multi-relational data are very useful when one wishes to conduct a role analysis (see below).

Multi-relational data can also be combined into a single net-work to form a multiplex network. Multiplex relations are typically represented as valued data, e.g. a 1 would represent that two actors only share one sort of relation (friendship), whereas a 2 would indicate two types of ties (friendship and advice) shared between two actors, and so forth. Multiplex relations are seen by some as proxies for strong ties, especially if all the relations under consid-eration can be considered dimensions of a strong relation between two actors, e.g. friendship, high frequency of communication, and presence of trust all combine together to indicate a strong relation between two actors.

2.2.3   Subgroups: cohesive subgroups (modularity); roles and positions (blocks, equivalence, core–periphery)

Beyond looking at individual actors, one can consider how a whole network breaks down into different subgroups. In this book, you will come across two different ways of conceptualizing and approaching subgroups. One approach looks at subgroups as "cohesive sub-sections" of a network, while the other approach conceives of subgroups as subsets of actors who share a similar "position" or "role" in a network.

Cohesive subgroups: A cohesive subgroup in network analysis generally refers to a subset of actors in a network where a high proportion of these actors are connected to one another via some kind of positive tie, e.g. friendship or communication (Wasserman and Faust, 1994). Classic approaches for uncovering subgroups according to this conceptualization include a clique analysis or n-clique analysis; here, the analyst is looking for the extent to which actors are bound together into a cohesive subgroup. A clique is the more strict definition; here, all members of the clique must hold mutual ties with one another. An n-clique relaxes this criterion by stating that members can be indirectly tied to one another by n length (e.g. a two path or three path).

Positions and roles: Looking for areas in the network where a high proportion of the actors are interconnected is not the only way to think about subgroups. One can also locate subsets of actors by studying how similar actors are according to their position in a network. This alternative way of thinking about subgroups involves positional and role analysis. Here, actors are grouped together into subgroups based on their similarity of positions within the networks. For example, in an organizational setting, certain actors "manage" other actors. The relation of "who manages whom" places certain actors in one position, i.e. the managerial position, and other actors in a different position, i.e. the managed position. Further, the nature of the relationship between the two positional blocks implies inherent roles in the network. Thus, one subset of actors play the role of "managers" and the others play the role of "being managed." Not all managers interact with all the same "managed" personnel, but the similarity in patterning is enough to distinguish two different "subgroups" of actors in this network, and to assign them different roles.

What I have described above essentially offers the basic logic behind positional analysis; subsets of actors are grouped together into "blocks" or "classes," and these subsets are derived from how actors within the same block share similar ties to others in a different block. More complicated analyses involving multi-relational data, and also the reduction of data into more simplified forms such as image matrices or reduced graphs, can lead an analysis into uncovering the different "roles" within a network; here the emphasis shifts from looking at individual actor positions (e.g. five actors all appear to locate a "core" position in the network), to understanding how the "classes" or "blocks" derived from the network data stand in relation to one another (e.g. how the "manager" block of positions stands in relation to the "managed" block). Looking for subgroups of actors according to a positional/role analysis is a rather involved process. However, there are some texts available that can lead you through this process in greater detail, explaining the different options along the way. See for example de Nooy *et al.* (2005), Prell (2011), and Wasserman and Faust (1994).

2.3   NETWORK LEVEL

We have proceeded from looking at individual actors, to subsections or subgroups of the network, and now we are considering the network as a whole. When thinking about concepts and measures on the network level, a typical question asked by an analyst is "how cohesive is this network?" Cohesion is an important concept in the social sciences, especially in sociology, and stems from early thinkers such as Tönnies (1887), whose discussion of "Gemeinschaft" emphasized the relational belonging of community members; as well as Kurt Lewin (1951), a social psychologist who discussed cohesion as a field of forces that keep people in a group (or network) together. Thus, when discussing cohesion, feelings of belonging are seen as going hand-in-hand with relational belonging (Friedkin, 1984; Moody and White, 2003), and groups that are tied together relationally are also seen as composed of individuals who share similar beliefs and values (Friedkin, 1984; Collins, 1988; McPherson *et al.*, 2001).

In the previous section on subgroups, I offered one view of subgroups that emphasized a cohesion in the form of relational belonging. On the network level, cohesion is again typically understood as the extent to which actors are interconnected via some kind of social tie. Two measures are typically used conjointly to get at this notion of cohesion, and these are density and centralization.

2.3.1 Density and centralization

Density looks at the extent to which actors in a network are directly tied to one another. More specifically, density refers to the proportion of potential ties in a network that are actually present. If a high proportion of the potential ties are realized, then the network is considered a dense network, and some would say, a cohesive one.

Yet density is known to be riddled with problems: for example, large networks tend to have lower density levels simply because the potential number of ties is so large, thus making it difficult, if not impossible, for actors to create and maintain a large number of ties. In addition, it is not so clear that a high proportion of ties automatically implies a cohesive network. What if a network has a high density score, but the majority of these ties flow via a single actor? Would such a network, where the degree centrality of one actor is so much higher than the others, reflect our intuitive understanding of cohesion?

A good way to see the extent to which your graph's density score depends on the ties of one individual node is to make use of the degree centralization score. *Degree centralization* looks at the extent to which one actor in a network is holding all of the ties in that network. Like density, centralization is measured as a proportion, where a network with a centralization score of 1 indicates all ties centering around one actor, and a score of 0 reflects a network where all actors have the same number of ties. Using density and centralization together can help one better ascertain the extent to which a network is cohesive; thus, a network with high density and high centralization would be less cohesive than one with the same density score, but a lower centralization score. Figure 2.3 illustrates this comparison.

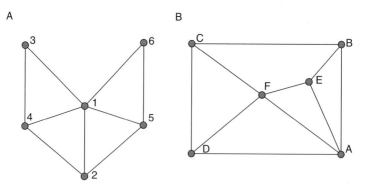

Figure 2.3 Two graphs: Graph A with density 0.53; centralization 0.60, Graph B with density 0.56; centralization 0.20.

In Figure 2.3, both graphs have the same number of nodes and have similar density levels, yet the first graph has a much higher centralization score, given the prominent central position of node 1. One could argue, therefore, that the second graph is the more cohesive one, as the centralities of the nodes are more evenly dispersed (Prell, 2011). See Sandström (Chapter 12) for a more in-depth discussion on density and centralization and how these, in combination, can be used to estimate levels of cohesion.

2.4   SUMMARY AND CONCLUSIONS: MIXING LEVELS OF ANALYSIS

Wellman (1988) notes how actors and network ties rarely, if ever, exist independently, but rather, come part of a "network package." Thus, to study any sort of local feature of a network, for example centrality, implies the need to think about or at least acknowledge the wider network structure. Indeed, this chapter has shown instances whereby the wider network structure plays a role in computing different measures of structure, e.g. centrality, subgroups, roles, and positions. Even though one can think about networks as being broken down into "levels" ranging from the actor to the network level, in many cases, these levels intermix and affect one another. In fact, this interrelationship between "lower levels" such as reciprocal ties and "higher levels" of analysis, such as cliques, lies at the heart of current statisticians' concerns in modeling and explaining network structure (Robins et al., 2007a, 2007b; Snijders, 2005; Snijders et al., 2010). This will be considered further in the final chapter.

In this book, you will find examples whereby authors not only use measures that draw upon the the complete network structure, but also instances of using measures at different levels, e.g. comparing centrality with network density and/or centralization. Thus, in Chapter 5, Prell et al. make use of positional analysis and centrality measures to locate individuals within subgroups; in Chapter 9, Crona and Bodin make use of an approach that in a integrated fashion uses the concepts of subgroups and centrality in order to identify different types of potentially influential actors. Sandström (Chapter 12) makes use of network-level concepts in combination with other measures.

The case studies provided in this book will not only illustrate in greater detail the concepts and terms presented in this chapter, but also show interesting ways of how these concepts and measures can be intermixed. Finally, you will also discover how authors have mixed the social network data with attribute data or with qualitative data. Taken together, the rest of this book will provide you with a range of examples and illustrations for making use of SNA, and in doing so, will provide you with some critical reflection on the strengths and limitations of SNA within the context of resource management and governance.

REFERENCES

Bavelas, A. (1950). Communication patterns in task-oriented groups. *Journal of Acoustical Society of America*, **57**, 271–282.
Bonacich, P. (1987). Power and centrality: a family of measures. *American Journal of Sociology*, **92**, 1170–1182.
Borgatti, S. P. (1995). Centrality and AIDS. *Connections*, **18**, 112–115.
Borgatti, S. P. (2005). Centrality and network flow. *Social Networks*, **27**, 55–71.
Collins, R. (1988). *Theoretical Sociology*. San Diego, CA: Harcourt Brace Jovanovich.
Cook, K., R. Emerson, R. Gilmore and T. Yamaguchi (1983). The distribution of power in exchange networks. *American Journal of Sociology*, **89**, 275–305.
de Nooy, W., A. Mrvar and V. Batagelj (2005). *Exploratory Social Network Analysis with Pajek*. Cambridge: Cambridge University Press.
Freeman, L. C. (1979). Centrality in social networks. *Social Networks*, **1**, 215–239.
Friedkin, N. E. (1984). Structural cohesion and equivalence explanations of social homogeneity. *Sociological Methods and Research*, **12**, 235–261.
Lewin, K. (1951). *Field Theory in Social Science; Selected Theoretical Papers*. New York, NY: Harper.
McPherson, M., L. Smith-Lovin and J. M. Cook (2001). Birds of a feather: homophily in social networks. *Annual Review of Sociology*, **27**, 415–444.
Mizruchi, M. S. and B. B. Potts (1998). Centrality and power revisited: actor success in group decision making. *Social Networks*, **20**, 353–387.
Moody, J. and D. R. White (2003). Structural cohesion and embeddedness: a hierarchical concept of social groups. *American Sociological Review*, **68**, 103–127.
Prell, C. (2011). *Social Network Analysis: History, Theory, and Methodology*. London: Sage.
Robins, G., P. Pattison, Y. Kalish and D. Lusher (2007a). An introduction to exponential random graph (p*) models for social networks. *Social Networks*, **29**, 173–191.
Robins, G., T. Snijders, P. Wang, M. Handcock and P. Pattison (2007b). Recent developments in exponential random graph models for social networks. *Social Networks*, **29**, 192–215.
Scott, J. (2000). *Social Network Analysis: A Handbook*. Newbury Park, CA: Sage.
Snijders, T. A. B. (2005). Models for longitudinal network data. In P. Carrington, J. Scott and S. Wasserman (Eds.), *Models and Methods in Social Network Analysis*, New York, NY: Cambridge University Press, pp. 215–247.
Snijders, T. A. B., C. E. G. Steglich and G. G. van de Bunt (2010). Introduction to actor-based models for network dynamics. *Social Networks*, **32**, 44–60.
Tönnies, F. (1887). *Gemeinschaft und Gesellschaft; Abhandlung des Communismus und des Socialismus als empirischer Culturformen*. Leipzig: Fues.

Wasserman, S. and K. Faust (1994). *Social Network Analysis: Methods and Applications*. Cambridge: Cambridge University Press.

Wellman, B. (1988). Structural analysis: from method and metaphor to theory and substance. In B. Wellman and S. D. Berkowitz (Eds.), *Social Structures: A Network Approach*, Cambridge: Cambridge University Press, pp. 19–61.

BEATRICE CRONA, HENRIK ERNSTSON, CHRISTINA PRELL,
MARK REED, AND KLAUS HUBACEK

3

Combining social network approaches with social theories to improve understanding of natural resource governance

3.1 INTRODUCTION

For much of the twentieth century natural resource management centered on efforts to control nature in order to harvest products from it, while reducing risks to society. The central tenet was to achieve predictable outcomes, a strategy that almost invariably led to reduced biological diversity and a reduction of the range of variation in natural systems. However, reduced diversity, in turn, tends to create more sensitive systems, both ecological and social (Levin, 1999), and examples of this today are the highly controlled systems of conventional agriculture and forestry that are experiencing increasing problems, fighting pest outbreaks and declining populations of natural pollinators (Chapin et al., 2000; Lundberg and Moberg, 2003). From the 1970s onwards (Holling, 1973, 1978), it has been suggested that such attempts to control highly complex and non-linear systems inevitably lead to surprises and/or societal and environmental crises (Holling and Meffe, 1995). On the basis of these arguments, conventional resource management, or command-and-control management as it is often referred to, has been heavily criticized (Holling, 1973; Holling et al., 1995; Wondolleck and Yaffee, 2000; Folke et al., 2005, among many others) and several approaches have been proposed to overcome some of its limitations. These include, among others, adaptive management (Holling, 1978), cooperative management (Pinkerton, 1989; Jentoft,

Social Networks and Natural Resource Management: Uncovering the Fabric of Environmental Governance, ed. Ö. Bodin and C. Prell. Published by Cambridge University Press.
© Cambridge University Press 2011.

2000), collaborative management (Borrini-Feyerabend and Borrini, 1996; Wondolleck and Yaffee, 2000), and adaptive co-management (Ruitenbeek and Cartier, 2001; Olsson *et al.*, 2004a). These concepts share many similarities and readers are referred to Folke *et al.* (2005) and Armitage *et al.* (2008a, 2008b) for more in-depth reviews.

The goal of this book is to outline how social network analysis can be used as a conceptual tool and an analytical method for uncovering a variety of social factors affecting resource governance, particularly as it is conceptualized by these more recent perspectives. We will therefore confine our discussion to adaptive co-management (hereafter ACM), in an attempt to show how this theory, and related concepts, are linked to other theories of importance for natural resource governance, and how social network analysis can help further our understanding in this domain. In doing this we do not suggest that ACM is necessarily better than other concepts or theoretical frameworks available. We have sim-ply chosen to use ACM as a platform upon which to base our discussion of how a variety of social theories and concepts can be integrated with the help of a social network perspective. Throughout the remainder of this chapter we will touch on a number of concepts and theories which all contribute to our understanding of the process of natural resource governance. We will briefly describe each of these, how they are linked to resource governance, and discuss how social network analysis can contribute to a fuller understanding of this link. For the remainder of this chapter we will use both the terms governance and management when we discuss natural resources. To avoid confusion it is important to clarify how we differentiate the two. By management we mean the specific actions that are carried out to accomplish the goals of any resource management scheme, such as carrying out agricultural experi-ments or trial fishing to assess stocks. By governance, however, we refer to the broader system of formal or informal institutions in which the management actions are embedded and which provide the essential direction, resources, and structure needed to meet the overarching resource governance goals.

3.2   A NEW APPROACH TO NATURAL RESOURCE GOVERNANCE

As mentioned in the Introduction there are a number of related concepts all describing approaches and theoretical perspectives that challenge conventional resource governance. We focus here on ACM as it is a participatory and iterative approach to environmental governance, where those responsible for managing social-ecological systems systematically adapt their practices as they "learn by doing" (whether through experimentation or modeling) (Armitage *et al.*, 2008b). Thus this approach links learning (through experimentation) and cooperation, and it represents a wider theme within much of the resource governance literature that emphasizes the need for collaboration and learning between researchers, stakeholders, and resource managers (Dougill *et al.*, 2006; Stringer *et al.*, 2006; Reed *et al.*, 2009). Adaptive management first stemmed from Holling's studies of ecosystem functioning (Holling, 1973), initiating a trend away from theories of equilibrium within the ecological sciences, towards an understanding of nature as a dynamic, self-organizing, complex system (Levin, 1992). Growing recognition that our knowledge of social-ecological systems is uncertain (Levin, 1999) therefore revealed the limitations of predictive approaches, and with this grew the awareness that understanding of these systems requires inclusion of multiple knowledge bases (Carpenter and Gunderson, 2001).

This intellectual move to include a variety of knowledge bases in the governance process necessitates a broadening of what has until recently been considered the realm primarily of scientists and managers. Groups with stakes in the resource to be managed often have significant amounts of local knowledge about the resource (Johannes, 1981; Becker and Ghimire, 2003; Ghimire *et al.*, 2004). Understanding who the stakeholders of any governance context are, especially those that are knowledgeable of the resource is therefore of primary concern.[1] Proponents of co-management describe numerous potential benefits compared with management by a central agency. These include increased effectiveness of management, greater legitimacy of management actions, enhanced understanding of natural and human systems, increased trust between government agencies and stakeholders, reduced enforcement expenditures and transaction costs, and increased public awareness of conservation issues (Pinkerton, 1989; Ostrom, 1990; Borrini-Feyerabend and Borrini, 1996). The process of mobilizing or selecting stakeholders can, in itself, be seen as an integral process of ACM, which we will discuss further below.

This paradigm shift in research and practice has sparked an enormous interest in exploring the social side of resource governance where a row of studies have focused on the difficulties in achieving

---

[1] Other stakeholders, such as certain owners or businesses, may have limited knowledge of the resource or affected ecosystems, but must often still be included on the premise of securing the legitimacy of the ACM process.

ACM or other forms of collective action in a way that produces sustainable, as well as legitimate and salient, resource outcomes (see Pinkerton, 1989; Ostrom, 1990, 2005; Baland and Platteau, 1996; Wondolleck and Yaffee, 2000; Armitage *et al.*, 2007). As alluded to in the Introduction, Elinor Ostrom (Ostrom, 1990, 1998, 2005; Ostrom *et al.*, 1994, 1999) has been instrumental in putting focus on the role of rules and norms in influencing governance of common pool resources, such as fisheries, forests, or water for irrigation. Her work has contributed to an increased awareness that the complexity of most ecosystems is matched by equally complex social settings, and that these social complexities must be considered in order to understand how natural resources can be sustainably managed in ways that are just for all members of society. Ostrom has studied these important aspects of natural resource governance primarily from the perspective of institutional economics. Her extensive work with multiple case studies has led to the development of a number of design principles seemingly essential for the development of well-functioning common-pool resource governance at the local level (Ostrom, 1990, 2005). Many of these design principles, such as formation of rules, conflict resolution, graduated sanctioning and monitoring, are fundamentally linked to and dependent on social interactions.

As should thus be evident, concepts and theories have been developed in a diverse set of disciplines, which are all relevant for understanding different social aspects of ACM including the collaborative and learning component itself, as well as how norms, rules, and institutions grow out of such interactions and feed into the ACM process and natural resource governance over time. In this chapter we have selected what we consider to be some of the most interesting theories and concepts. These include (but are not limited to) theories of (i) *social learning* (Diduck, 2004; Diduck *et al.*, 2005), (ii) *social capital* (Bordieu, 1986; Coleman, 1990; Putnam, 1993; Fukuyama, 1995; Lin, 1999; Putnam, 2000), and (iii) *social movements* (Touraine, 1981; Melucci, 1995; Diani and McAdam, 2003; della Porta and Diani, 2006), complemented with theories linked to (iv) *social influence* and *institutional entrepreneurs* (Maguire *et al.*, 2004; Westley *et al.*, 2006), and network-related ideas surrounding (v) *stakeholder selection*. Somewhat simplified, the first three theories can be seen as largely focusing on the dynamics of groups of individuals and the mechanisms and processes that generate, sustain, and change collective action in some form. This collective action perspective is complemented by (iv) which focuses more on capturing how individual actors have been shown to play important roles in nurturing and steering ACM processes. Together these concepts and theories allow us to address the interplay between (individual) agency and structural position. We have chosen to also include stakeholder selection as a fifth topic because it exemplifies a more applied way of thinking about social networks in a resource governance context, and it draws upon the literature developed around the more practical problem of who to include in collaborative processes.

All these theories and concepts strive to capture processes that in different ways relate to social interaction. A social network perspective therefore has much to offer each of them. In some cases the network perspective and SNA can be used as a tool to identify actors for participatory processes, while in other cases it can serve as an analytical tool to understand an ongoing collaborative resource governance process or why an ACM initiative has stalled. Figure 3.1 is a conceptual diagram showing how the five main concepts and theories discussed in this chapter relate to more recent approaches to natural resource governance, encompassed by, for example, ACM. As noted above, the literature identifies two principal elements to overcome the limitations of command-and-control approaches: (i) continuous learning, achieved through (ii) the inclusion of multiple sectors of society and their diverse knowledge. But achieving this new form of natural resource management is dependent on a fundamental understanding of important social processes at play. Each of the five theories in focus here contributes in different ways to our understanding of natural resource governance, and SNA can play several different roles in this context. This is outlined in Figure 3.1 and in the subsequent sections we will elaborate in more detail how the theories relate to natural resource governance and how SNA can contribute to a fuller understanding of this link. We will begin by examining the process of collaboration. We then move on to discuss how the theories in focus here relate to learning.

The structure of this chapter will follow an imaginary ACM process – starting with the identification of stakeholders and resource mobilization, and moving on to address different aspects of collaboration and learning. Linking to Figure 3.1, Section 3.3 thus aims to provide an integrated account of how the different theories outlined relate to collaboration, while in Section 3.4 we turn our attention to the learning component of ACM and explore how the different social theories addressed here relate to learning, as well as how SNA can contribute to our understanding of this process.

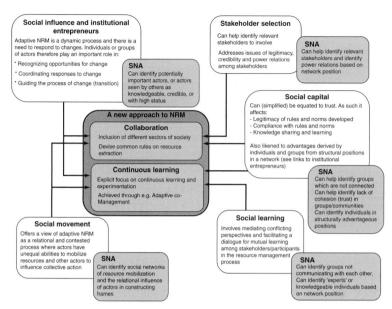

Figure 3.1 Conceptual diagram showing how the five main concepts and theories discussed in this chapter relate to more recent approaches to natural resource governance, encompassed by, for example, adaptive co-management. NRM, natural resource management; SNA, social network analysis.

3.3 COLLABORATIVE PROCESSES AND RESOURCE GOVERNANCE – EXPLORING THE LINK THROUGH SOCIAL NETWORK ANALYSIS

3.3.1 Stakeholders and resource mobilization

Any collaborative process hinges on a good understanding of who the actors involved in the process are, or ought to be – in cases where marginalization of actors occurs. We therefore begin by examining some of the literature that relates to *stakeholder selection*. This literature cannot be classified as an example of social theory as such, but rather as a set of methodological tools used by authorities, land holders, consultants, or researchers aimed at making informed choices on whom to invite to dialogues regarding resource governance (Clarkson, 1995; Grimble and Chan, 1995; Grimble and Wellard, 1997; Brugha and Varvasovszky, 2000; Hare and Pahl-Wostl, 2002; Friedman and Miles, 2006; Prell *et al.*, 2009; Reed *et al.*, 2009). As such, theories regarding participatory governance and democracy feed into this literature, yet the aim remains primarily practical. Several issues are of prime importance for understanding social dynamics which can inform whom to invite to more focused dialogues. These include (i) which stakeholders comprise the stakeholder social network; (ii) how these stakeholders are linked together; (iii) the nature of the ties that link them; and (iv) how the ties are structured into certain patterns. Theories from the social movement literature offer a more theoretical perspective on these issues, especially in how we can theorize voluntary action processes.

Diani and Bison (Diani, 2002; Diani and Bison, 2004) distinguish between different types of voluntary-based collective action – from conflictual social movement processes to consensus- or coalition-based collective action – that are all based on collaboration between individuals and/or organizations who, through informal social networks, exchange resources and construct interpretation frames that guide or steer collective action. Building on this, Ernstson and colleagues (Ernstson *et al.*, 2008; Ernstson and Sörlin, 2009, see also Chapter 11 in this book) argue that this perspective allows us to also view ACM as a relational, networked but often contested process where actors strive to influence how the management process should be performed and framed. To understand this process better we can utilize theories from the social movement literature and combine them with SNA (Diani, 1992, 2003; Diani and McAdam, 2003). Two of these theories are resource mobilization theory (McCarthy and Zald, 1977; Zald and McCarthy, 1980) and framing theory (Benford and Snow, 2000; della Porta and Diani, 2006). The former discusses the fact that any individual or organization necessarily needs to locate and aggregate a variety of resources in order to carry out action. Resources can be economic (money through membership fees, funds, etc.), labor (activists or voluntary members), material (copy machines, a place to meet, etc.), or symbolic (information, or "reputation"), which can be shared between movement organizations, or competed for while they strive to attract resources from the wider society. The theory hypothesizes that certain actors within a whole field of mobilizing actors ("social movement industries") will be more successful in aggregating resources than others, in part by developing certain organizational structures (career paths, tactics, etc.). These ideas can be merged with a social network perspective by measuring the relations of resource exchange, along with organizational attributes, so that attributes and/or patterns of interactions can be used to explain why some actors are more central than others, with greater potential to influence unfolding collective action, and why some are seen as "leaders" (Diani, 2003; Ernstson *et al.*, 2008). Framing theory is partly a critique of resource mobilization theory, which was seen as treating actors as too rational, and without analyzing how movements turn preferences or grievances into action (Melucci, 1995). Framing theory states that collective action is guided by socially constructed interpretation frames aimed at explaining the world and what needs to be done, while mobilizing yet other actors to join collective action (Benford and Snow, 2000). These frames are based on concrete social practices, and should be analyzed as emergent from negotiations between a larger set of actors (Boström, 2004). As such, frame construction can also be analyzed from a social network perspective, where the patterns of interaction can guide interpretation on who is most influential in the construction of dominant frames for action (Ernstson and Sörlin, 2009). We will return to framing theory below.

Social network analysis thus provides a number of possibilities to link theories of social movements and voluntary-based collective action to natural resource governance. For example, Ernstson *et al.* (2008) applied SNA to understand collaboration and power asymmetries surrounding the protection of highly contested urban green spaces in Sweden, and how these patterns also influenced the framing of the park's values (Ernstson and Sörlin, 2009; Chapter 11). In a similar vein, Isaac *et al.* (2007; Chapter 13) used core–periphery analysis of information exchange networks among farmers to study the link between innovation of agricultural practices and community involvement.

The success of collaborative processes depends to some degree on the involvement of "the right" actors. Who the "right" actors are depends largely on the goal of the governance process and, if looked at through the lens of social movement theory, it can also be seen as a highly contested issue. In fact, viewed in this way, identification of stakeholders is a form of "mobilization" of stakeholders. Nonetheless, identification of stakeholders can be greatly facilitated by SNA. As outlined above, it can identify central and peripheral actors, as well as actors linking the various parts of the network together. This sort of information, combined with information on stakeholder categories (e.g. a conservationist versus a government official) can help managers or other practitioners locate areas of a network that may need more "work" in the form of building bridging ties, and identify which areas of the network that are sufficiently represented (Prell *et al.*, 2010).

For example, if all conservationists in a network appear as the most central actors in the network, it is clear that these conservationists have a larger potential of high influence in the network – they tend to regularly communicate with more members of the network than any others, and thus both have a good sense of others' views, as well as ample opportunities for getting their own views heard (as discussed earlier on regarding framing).

3.3.2   Agency and entrepreneurship in natural resource governance

Once an ACM process is underway the maintenance of continuous collaboration becomes a key feature. In the next two subsections we explore how focusing on the interplay between network structure and both individual and collective agency (and how it relates to SNA) can help us understand the process of collaboration, and how some of the social theories in focus here can add to this endeavor. Adaptive natural resource governance is a dynamic process which implies a continuous need to respond to changes over time. Individuals or groups of actors therefore play an important role in recognizing opportunities for change (or "windows of opportunities"), coordinating responses to change, initiating new initiatives, and guiding the process of change (transition) (Olsson *et al.*, 2004b, 2006; Hahn *et al.*, 2008). As outlined above, SNA can be a valuable tool for analysts in mapping patterns of relations between actors in any natural resource governance context. It can be particularly useful for locating individuals who occupy advantageous positions in the network by, for example, linking isolated components of the network and therefore acting as potential bridges between components. The value of such positions to an actor wanting to affect change is considerable and has been explored in great detail (Burt, 2003, 2004, 2005). Such key players have also been shown to play important roles as change agents in natural resource governance, facilitating a move from unsustainable practices to more sustainable regimes (Olsson *et al.*, 2006; Schultz, 2009).

   The notion that individuals can significantly shape the development of a broader system is certainly not a new one. Within the social sciences there is a long-standing debate on agency versus structure and how to best explain social system changes. In other words, whether system changes are predominantly an effect of individual agency or if they emerge out of unintentional, iterative interactions between actors, and to what degree resistance is embedded in social structures

(Emirbayer and Mische, 1998; in a resource management setting see Ernstson *et al.*, 2010). There is a rich literature focusing on the individuals who "make things happen," drawing from several disciplines. Some have called them champions (Gilmour *et al.*, 1999; Napier *et al.*, 2005; Stankey *et al.*, 2005), policy entrepreneurs (Shannon, 1991), change agents (Crawford *et al.*, 2006), or brokers (Bebbington, 1997), while others have chosen to call them organizational entrepreneurs (Hahn *et al.*, 2006), key stewards (Olsson *et al.*, 2007), transformative/ visionary leaders (Leach and Pelkey, 2001; Westley, 2001; Olsson *et al.*, 2007), or social innovators (Westley *et al.*, 2006) and institutional entrepreneurs (Maguire *et al.*, 2004; Garud *et al.*, 2007). In the same way that many of the new approaches to natural resource governance discussed earlier share similarities, many concepts of key individuals resemble each other. In this chapter we choose to use the term institutional entrepreneurs, but our discussion could apply equally to many of the other, similar concepts.

The term institutional entrepreneurship refers to the "activities of actors who have an interest in particular institutional arrangements [*such as new natural resource governance institutions*] and who leverage resources to create new institutions or to transform existing ones" (Maguire *et al.*, 2004: 657). We choose to adhere to the concept of entrepreneurs because the use of the term entrepreneur, as opposed to leader, moves the focus away from the relationship between leaders and followers to the process of transformation itself. This includes the mobilization of resources and the social construction of frames that can support the acceptance of innovation and collective action as discussed previously in relation to social movement theory. Literature has shown that individuals who play key roles in shaping change within a system often do not do so through explicit leadership (Westley and Mintzberg, 1989; Olsson *et al.*, 2004b, 2007). Work on transformative leadership, concerned with leadership involved in moving an organization from one state to another (Bennis, 1982), and institutional entrepreneurship (Maguire *et al.*, 2004; Garud *et al.*, 2007), which focuses on the agency required to produce transformation at broad institutional levels, both nicely illustrate this point. This body of work emphasizes how much of the work of institutional entrepreneurs occurs "behind the scenes." They often influence the construction of visions or framings that help people organize around certain tasks or towards a certain direction, while also building broad alignment with multiple constituencies, giving them the opportunity to focus on building and strengthening the desired direction and maintaining the momentum. To achieve the desired goal and move in the direction of the new vision, the entrepreneurs continuously harness the energy and talents of the people around them (Bennis, 1982; Westley *et al.*, forthcoming) in line with the resource mobilization theories outlined above.

Much of the literature on agency and institutional change is concerned with the skills of institutional entrepreneurs. Cultural skills, such as visioning, marketing, and framing have been suggested as important (Rao, 1998: 917; see also Perkmann and Spicer, 2007). Others have emphasized political skills such as creating incentives, forming coalitions, bargaining, and mobilizing and leveraging resources (DiMaggio, 1998), or setting agendas (Fligstein, 1997). Many of these skills are clearly linked to personal attributes, such as personality, or human capital such as for example education, experience, and perhaps even financial resources. However, much of the work carried out by institutional entrepreneurs is directly reliant on the social networks in which these individuals are themselves embedded. If we agree with the notion that system change is an effect of agency, and not the result of unintentional, iterative change, then it is easy to see that no significant system change is likely to happen without the ability of entrepreneurs to draw on the resources of the network that surrounds them, or spread their ideas through their relations.

The network perspective allows us to conceptualize the relation between agency and structure. Since social network patterns are an outcome of localized interactions between pairs of actors, then no actor can fully control the emergent structure (Degenne and Forsé, 1999). Relations beyond the control of the single actor will influence information and resource flows in the network, and thus to a certain extent control the type and amount of resources that the individual actor can harness. This captures how the structure "acts back" on the individual actor, demonstrating that most actors in a network are constrained to some degree by the social structures around them (Emirbayer and Goodwin, 1994; Ernstson *et al.*, 2010). Utilizing the network perspective we can also distinguish between two forms of agency. If one part lies in harnessing and utilizing resources and spreading information, another part lies in the ability of single actors to change at least part of the network structure through strategically interacting with new actors (Ernstson *et al.*, 2010, with reference to Burt, 2005). In relation to both types of agency, it has been widely shown that the network position that an actor has attained is important for their ability to access resources (Bebbington and Perreault,

1999; Lin, 2002; Burt, 2003, 2004, 2005); and in natural resource governance (see for example Schneider *et al.*, 2003; Ernston *et al.*, 2008; Bodin and Crona, 2009). The structural network position is therefore a key entry point for analysts to understand how individuals in any natural resource governance setting succeed in shaping the development of the system in which they operate.

The role of SNA in this respect is clear. Network analysis provides a number of different ways in which actors can be categorized based on features of the network, ranging from relatively simple measures of degree, betweenness, and eigenvector centrality (Bonacich, 1972; Freeman, 1979; Wasserman and Faust, 1994), to more elaborate measures of structural equivalence or other positional approaches (Burt, 1976; Everett and Borgatti, 1990). Part II of this book will offer a range of case study examples illustrating these various features and measures of social networks and how they can be applied in an empirical context.

3.3.3 Social influence and social capital – oiling the machinery of natural resource governance

Why would someone who is central in a network be better placed to shape the process of change towards new resource governance institutions? And why should we pay attention to individuals with high betweenness? Answering these two questions requires an understanding of the role social networks and their structures play in influencing individuals and groups as a whole. In this section we will discuss how social influence and social capital can contribute to our understanding of how individuals initiate and guide natural resource governance systems through change.

In the social network literature, social influence theory has received a lot of empirical support as a means of understanding how social relations and their structure influence actors' attitudes and behaviors. Simply put, social influence states that two actors who share a tie with one another will influence one another over time, leading to increased similarity between the two actors involved (Friedkin, 1998). In addition to sharing a tie, sharing a tie that is either strong (e.g. close friend) or multiplex (e.g. both a friend and a colleague) increases the likelihood for similarity amongst the individuals involved (McPherson *et al.*, 2001; Ruef *et al.*, 2003). Finally, similarity seems to increase more when the individuals socially tied to one another are likewise embedded in a circle of friends or other kind of cohesive subgroup structure (Krackhardt, 1992; Krackhardt and Kilduff, 2002).

In the context of natural resource governance, some research shows a tendency for similar stakeholders to think and behave similarly with regards to resource governance (Prell *et al.*, 2010). But social influence can be hypothesized to result in different outcomes depending on initial conditions and context. For example, if stakeholders in a network all have similar, sustainable practices in relation to particular common-pool resources, then the network structure could ensure that stakeholders monitor one another's behavior; thus ensuring that potential conflicts or misuses of the resources get dealt with in a relatively efficient manner, without the need for outside institutions (Ostrom, 1990). However, if the situation calls for diverse views and knowledge regarding ecosystem dynamics and current resource governance practice, high social cohesion could obstruct external attempts to encourage stakeholders to question and re-think their current practices (Newman and Dale, 2005; Crona, 2006; Prell *et al.*, 2010). Nonetheless, if such an impasse can be broken, e.g. if a member of the community with high status can be persuaded to adopt a new view or practice, strong social ties can help diffuse new ideas as well as the adoption process. Such scenarios are commonly discussed in the literature examining the role of social networks for diffusion (Katz and Lazarsfeld, 1955; Rogers, 1995; Valente, 1996; Valente and Davis, 1999).

In the sections above we have shown how social influence is relevant to studies of natural resource governance because it can help us understand the effect of network structure on outcomes such as conflict resolution, or adoption of new practices. Let us now turn to a hypothetical example for a moment to explore the role of network structure and individual agency in triggering change. Let us suppose that a fisher who is first to adopt a new view of gear effects and consequently changes his practices does not do so simply on a whim. In fact, upon hearing about the new regulations he first discussed it with an old friend, and former fishing colleague, who now works for the Fisheries Department and through such repeated discussions the adopting fisher eventually came around to the idea and even saw the potential for competitive benefits. He decided to switch gears during a trial period and as he was well respected in the community of local fishers, and the cohesion among them was high, others soon adopted the new practices as well. He effectively became an opinion leader (for an empirical analysis of potential opinion leaders and use of SNA see Crona and Bodin, 2010). The change at the system level (i.e. the whole network) would not have happened if it was not for the interactions between the first adopting fisher and his former colleague, i.e. because of the adopting fisher's ties to contacts outside his closed community of fellow fishers. The reason for this is that social innovation can be thought of as "a compound of two very different network mechanisms; contagion by cohesion through opinion leaders gets information into a group, while contagion by equivalence triggers adoptions within the group" (Burt, 1999). For further discussion on contagion and structural equivalence readers are referred to Burt (1976, 2003, 2004). What Burt terms opinion leaders are effectively what we have chosen to call institutional entrepreneurs in this chapter. They are often not people at the top of an institutional or social hierarchy, but more often operate at the edge of social groups, working across these and thus spanning social boundaries. Through their brokering position they are able to pick up information and trends from a number of different groups, and can introduce these into new social settings using their boundary-spanning contacts. This advantage, derived through their structural position in the social network, has often been referred to as social capital (Lin, 1999; Burt, 2003).

Social capital as a concept is multi-faceted (for review see Coleman, 1988; Portes, 1998; Lin, 1999; Woolcock and Narayan, 2000; Krishna, 2002) and the unit of analysis can vary from the individual to the group (Borgatti *et al.*, 1998; Portes, 1998). As shown above, some argue that social capital is something that accrues to individual actors (Lin, 2002; Burt, 2003), while others discuss social capital at the scale of whole communities, even nations (Putnam, 1993). There is a lack of agreement of what actually constitutes social capital. Putnam (1993) defines social capital as features of social organization such as networks, norms and social trust that facilitate coordination and coop-eration for mutual benefit. Others suggest social capital can be defined as resources embedded in a social structure which are accessed and/or mobilized in purposive actions (Lin, 1999), thus leaving out collective assets such as trust and norms. The latter of these interpretations of social capital and its relevance for natural resource management was described above in our discussion of institutional entrepreneurs. Before we end this section we will now briefly turn our attention to the former definition and its role for understanding resource gover-nance outcomes.

Social capital has been invoked as an important contributing factor to natural resource governance and conservation (Adger, 2001; Pretty and Ward, 2001; Pretty, 2003; Pretty and Smith, 2004). In this context social capital has been regarded as the social ties that foster and promote trust and reciprocity among members of a community. Trust is regarded as the key ingredient that enables or facilitates, for example, monitoring, sanctioning, and resolution of conflicts; all argued to be instrumental for governance of natural resources, particularly those considered to be common property (see Ostrom, 1990, 2005 for a more in-depth discussion of factors affecting management of common property resources). Trust lubricates interaction between people and lowers transaction costs. As such it facilitates the development of rules, the compliance with agreed-upon rules and norms increases as actors deem them legitimate, and in many cases trust also promotes knowledge sharing and learning. It also underpins the processes of resource mobilization and collective action discussed above. When conceptualized in this way, social capital is less related to structural positions of individuals and more concerned with the cohesiveness based on the existence of reciprocal ties among actors in a network (Coleman, 1990; Putnam, 2000). It is important to note that social capital, viewed this way, rests on the important assumption of reciprocity, and therefore should not be equated with mere density of unreciprocated social ties in a network. Social capital can thus be measured through SNA by, for example, density and transitivity (Granovetter, 1973; Weimann, 1982). As an example, Bodin and Crona (2008) used density and level of network fragmentation (number of network components) to examine how the ratio between bonding and bridging ties among groups of resource users could be linked to resource governance issues in small-scale fisheries.

This concludes our attempt at bringing together multiple social theories with SNA to better understand collaboration in natural resource governance settings. Next we turn to the second component of ACM, namely learning.

3.4   LEARNING – TOWARDS MORE ADAPTIVE RESOURCE GOVERNANCE

As noted above, one of the central tenets in the emerging new approaches to natural resource management, such as adaptive co-management, is learning. Continuous learning and adjustment of management and extraction practices becomes important once we recognize that ecosystems are dynamic, and surprise is a rule rather than an exception. Like other concepts discussed in this chapter (e.g. social capital), learning is multi-faceted and can be defined and studied in many different ways. It has been studied within psychology, organizational development, and business management, although aspects of social learning theory (Argyris and Schon, 1978), transformative learning theory (Mezirow and Associates, 2000), and experiential learning theory (Kolb, 1984) provide the base for much of the work around natural resource management (see for example Jovchelovitch, 2006 for more in-depth treatment; Armitage *et al.*, 2008b). Learning can occur in different ways; through experience or through interaction with other people. The purpose of this chapter is not to review the different theories surrounding learning but to point out the ways in which analysis of social networks can help us understand learning in the context of natural resource governance.

Experiential learning is when knowledge is acquired through experience and observation. Any knowledge which is not acquired through experience therefore has to be communicated. The general hypothesis behind learning in networks is that networks provide access to novel information and influence the way information is being processed. Access to novel information is provided by regular communication with other network members. These also exert influence on information processing, for example by copying from others (Bandura, 1977) or through deliberative processes in which arguments are exchanged and perceptions change through persuasion. But learning is not always a straightforward task. While transfer of explicit knowledge can occur freely across most social ties, conveying a complex phenomenon to someone who has not experienced it can be difficult. Transfer of such tacit knowledge (i.e. knowledge which is difficult to transfer to another person by means of writing it down or verbalizing it), for example, how to use complex equipment, requires strong ties and more frequent interaction (Reagans and McEvily, 2003). As such, the same mechanisms of social influence and trust discussed above become important when striving to understand how resource users and other actors in a natural resource management setting share information with each other.

Social network structure is thus important for how and what people in a network learn, and it has implications for the ability of groups to solve problems and hence for collective action in a natural resource governance context (Crona and Bodin, 2006). A network structure that enhances one feature may simultaneously inhibit another. Take as an example centrality. A high degree of centrality may facilitate the process of solving simple tasks because relevant information can be relayed and synthesized to a few actors who can make a decision and take action (Leavitt, 1951). For the same reason, high centrality can be beneficial in times of change when effective coordination of actors and resources may be needed. On the other hand, social networks in which a few individuals have a high degree of centrality may lead to increasingly centralized decision making, which in turn can have long-term negative effects on learning because it reduces the access of individual actors to multiple sources of information (Weimann, 1982; Abrahamson and Rosenkopf, 1997) and does not allow for diversity of knowledge to be fed into the decision-making procecss. Another example is density. As discussed earlier, high density and cohesion can promote trust (also equated with social capital) and increase the possibility for social control (Granovetter, 1985; Coleman, 1990; Pretty and Ward, 2001). This can reduce the risks and costs associated with collaboration and can promote the development of, and compliance with, norms (Ostrom, 1990; Cohen *et al.*, 2001; Burt, 2003). It can also benefit the spread of information through increased accessibility to information (Weimann, 1982; Abrahamson and Rosenkopf, 1997). However, high density of relations among actors can result in homogenization of experiences and knowledge (Oh *et al.*, 2004; Bodin and Norberg, 2005; Crona and Bodin, 2006). This occurs, for example, through a high density of interaction among individuals that leads to a situation in which all individuals tend to adopt similar perceptions of issues at hand. From a natural resource governance perspective such homogenization can have disastrous effects, as exemplified by Bodin and Norberg (2005) in their models of farmers learning and adapting to change.

In most natural resource governance settings the actors who are in some way linked to the natural resource all possess some knowledge of it. These knowledges and perceptions may sometimes be conflicting but they can nonetheless be important for mutual and holistic understanding of the resource dynamics. Homogenization of perceptions and knowledge is likely to occur within dense groups of similar actors. For example, farmers may have dense networks and more similar knowledge about land management practices, while conservationists resemble other conservationists more than other actor categories (Prell *et al.*, 2010). For multiple, and sometimes conflicting views to be able to contribute to resource management, deliberation is essential. Stemming from the ideas of Habermas (1981), deliberation refers to a genuine exchange of ideas and arguments regardless of societal power asymmetries. Networks are expected to provide opportunities for deliberation, for example through group interactions (Newig *et al.*, 2010). Seen in this way, networks of groups of dissimilar actors are expected to produce more creative ideas and solutions as compared to the homogeneous groups discussed above.

Social learning is a line of inquiry which has received increasing attention in recent years. It has been defined as "learning that occurs when people engage one another, sharing diverse perspectives and experiences to develop a common framework of understanding and basis for joint action" (Schusler et al., 2003: 311). In addition, it recognizes the need to also learn "about the mental frames that shape decision making" (Pahl-Wostl, 2002: 401), and it is cited as an essential process for addressing the complexity and uncertainty inherent in natural resource governance (Lee, 1993; Dryzek, 1997).

In contrast to individual learning, social learning refers not only to cognitive and behavioral changes in individuals within a network, but also to the process in which individual changes in cognition and action lead to modifications in collective rules or institutions, either by consensus or by some other mode of decision making. These may, in turn, feed back to learning processes at the individual level (Newig et al., 2010). Social learning thus contributes to collaboration by creating new relationships, building upon cooperative relationships, and transforming adversarial ones. These changes occur as people learn about the character and trustworthiness of others and develop new networks and norms of interaction that can enhance their capacity for joint action (Greenwood and Levin, 1998; Forrester, 1999). When deliberation enables social learning, actors in a network evolve in their understanding of the relevant facts, problems, opportunities, and areas of agreement and disagreement in relation to specific issues (Schusler et al., 2003). But perhaps most importantly, they gain an insight into their own beliefs and values and those of others (Yankelovich, 1991).

However, not all deliberative processes are successful in this respect. When they succeed, they can empower action and enhance learning and democratic processes (Forrester, 1999). But although the definition of deliberation notes that power asymmetries should not be allowed to impinge on communication, deliberative processes often become arenas where politics of power are played out. Social movement theory, introduced in the sections above, places strong emphasis on the struggle among actors to establish their socially constructed "frames" of what is at stake and what to do about it (i.e. what learning should be done and about what). In resource management, such as ACM, framing can be compared to "vision building," where visions in

ACM need to fulfill the dual task of mobilizing stakeholders and re-framing natural resources as outcomes of complex ecological processes that demand collaboration (Olsson *et al.*, 2004a, 2006, 2008; Folke *et al.*, 2005). However, frames should not be seen as given or taken, but as socially constructed and contested. Furthermore, different actors have different abilities to participate in the framing activities establishing what the problem is, what should be done, and why actors should join in collective action (diagnostic, prognostic, and motivational frames; see Benford and Snow, 2000). Thus, social movement theory can add to our understanding of learning as well by analyzing the "vision building" and social learning of ACM as an (unequal) struggle to establish hegemonic meta frames, where certain actors would be more influential while the framings of others would be suppressed or deemed less important (Boström, 2004).

A social network perspective has much to offer someone interested in exploring the issues of power, influence, and framing which surrounds learning in natural resource governance settings. By influence we refer not merely to the ability of actors to impose sanctions but rather the way by which they can promote certain learning efforts, and how the same individuals often become seen as good representatives and dialogue partners to authorities, media, and other outsiders (Diani, 2003). A simple measure of influence is the number of collaboration or alliance ties an actor receives from others in the network (indegree; Freeman, 1979), providing an estimate of the extent that others choose them as partners in collaborative efforts and how "visible" they are to others (Diani, 2003). A more refined version of this measure would take into account not only direct ties, but also indirect ties; an actor with ties to other actors that in turn have many ties, would have greater influence over the flow of resources in the network, than an actor with an equal amount of direct ties, but to actors with very few other ties. One could think of it in terms of local versus more regional or global influence in a network. Here the measures of "prominence" and eigenvector centrality in network analysis can be used (see Wasserman and Faust, 1994; Degenne and Forsé, 1999 and references therein). A third version would be to measure the amount of social brokerage capacity an actor has, i.e. the tendency of an actor to link actor groups that would otherwise not be linked. This provides an indication of the general capacity to steer information and resource flows in the network, but also a greater sensitivity to construct overarching frames that could make a larger set of actors collaborate and possibly to reach longer-lasting consensus agreements (Wasserman and Faust, 1994;

Degenne and Forsé, 1999). Here the measurement of betweenness centrality, based solely on network data, is useful. Gould and Fernandez (1989) have also developed a brokerage algorithm that takes into account the direction of ties and categorized several different types of brokerage positions. A more refined version would take into account the ability to link actors separated by vested interests or social, cultural, or political barriers (Diani, 2003). In network terms this would entail measuring not only betweenness centrality (or type of brokerage), but also the attributes of actors, and the diversity of attributes that are linked through the broker. In ACM processes aimed at supporting social learning across scales, this approach has been used to explore the existence of "scale-crossing brokers," i.e. actors that link groups interacting with ecosystem processes at different scales (Ernstson et al., 2010).

To summarize this section, a network perspective helps us interpret how influential actors play a role in ACM learning processes, by using their position to create overarching frames (or visions) to which a diversity of actors, across various scales, can subscribe. This in turn can facilitate consensus agreements, while also blocking certain other actors that could jeopardize this consensus. The opposite is also true. Influential actors can generate frames that incorporate authorities and thus appear to link well across scales, but where frames exclude actors that interact with ecosystems on a daily basis. This would effectively exclude the capacity of the collaborative process to draw on local ecological knowledge consequently undermining social learning about ecosystem dynamics (Ernstson et al., 2008; Ernstson and Sörlin, 2009; Chapter 11).

3.5   CONCLUDING REMARKS

As outlined in the initial sections of this chapter, the emerging new view on resource governance departs significantly from prior approaches by explicitly acknowledging the role of a range of different actors as well as non-academic knowledge in natural resource governance (Pinkerton, 1989; Borrini-Feyerabend and Borrini, 1996; Berkes et al., 1998; Carpenter and Gunderson, 2001; Becker and Ghimire, 2003; Ghimire et al., 2004). In this initial phase of the changing natural resource governance discourse social interaction was acknowledged as crucial to sustainable governance but social networks were largely treated as a binary variable; they were either present or not. But social networks are ubiquitous. More recent work has therefore sought to explore the role of social networks in resource governance in more depth, and complement the emerging new view of natural resource governance with a wider range of analytical perspectives incorporated from social network analysis (Crona and Bodin, 2006; Prell *et al.*, 2006; Bodin and Crona, 2008, 2009; Ernstson *et al.*, 2008; Ramirez-Sanchez and Pinkerton, 2009). This chapter has taken the next step, and shown how a network perspective can serve as a tool to integrate theories of social interaction to enhance natural resource governance understanding.

We have outlined the paradigm shift in research and practice surrounding natural resource governance, and we have discussed the two central tenets in this emerging paradigm; collaboration and learning. Letting adaptive co-management represent one form of this new governance approach we have used it as a platform to link and integrate four theories addressing social processes which we deem important for improved understanding of natural resource governance: social influence and institutional entrepreneurs, social movements, social capital, and social learning (Figure 3.1). At the core of each of these concepts lie processes which in different ways relate to social interaction. A social network perspective in general, and social network analysis in particular, therefore offer an ideal means of weaving them together and integrating theories with the goal of enhancing our understanding of the factors that affect natural resource governance. The remainder of this book will illustrate this further as a number of different authors show how they use various network approaches to analyze and understand natural resource governance processes in a diverse range of cultural settings.

REFERENCES

Abrahamson, E. and L. Rosenkopf (1997). Social network effects on the extent of innovation diffusion: a computer simulation. *Organization Science*, **8**(3), 289–309.

Adger, W. N. (2001). *Social Capital and Climate Change*. Tyndall Centre for Climate Change Working Paper No. 8. Norwich: Tyndall Centre for Climate Change.

Argyris, C. and D. Schon (1978). *Learning Organizations: A Theory of Action Perspective*. Reading, MA: Addison-Westley.

Armitage, D., F. Berkes and N. C. Doubleday (2007). *Adaptive Co-Management: Collaboration, Learning, and Multi-Level Governance*. Vancouver, BC: UBC Press.

Armitage, D., M. Marschke and R. Plummer (2008a). Adaptive co-management and the paradox of learning. *Global Environmental Change*, **18**(1), 86–98.

Armitage, D., R. Plummer, F. Berkes *et al.* (2008b). Adaptive co-management for social-ecological complexity. *Frontiers in Ecology and the Environment*, **7**(2), 95–102.

Baland, J.-M. and J.-P. Platteau (1996). *Halting Degradation of Natural Resources. Is There a Role for Rural Communities?* Oxford: Clarendon Press.

Bandura, A. (1977). *Social Learning Theory.* Englewood Cliffs, NJ: Prentice-Hall.

Bebbington, A. (1997). Social capital and rural intensification: local organizations and islands of sustainability in the rural Andes. *The Geographical Journal*, **163**, 189–197.

Bebbington, A. and T. Perreault (1999). Social capital, development, and access to resources in highland Ecuador. *Economic Geography*, **75**(4), 395–418.

Becker, C.D. and K. Ghimire (2003). Synergy between traditional ecological knowledge and conservation science supports forest preservation in Ecuador. *Conservation Ecology*, **8**(1), 1.

Benford, R.D. and D.A. Snow (2000). Framing processes and social movements: an overview and assessment. *Annual Review of Anthropology*, **26**, 611–639.

Bennis, W. (1982). Leadership transforms vision into action. *Industry Week*, **54**.

Berkes, F., I. Davidson-Hunt and K. Davidson-Hunt (1998). Diversity of common property resource use and diversity of social interests in the western Indian Himalaya. *Mountain Research and Development*, **18**, 19–33.

Bodin, Ö. and B.I. Crona (2008). Management of natural resources at the community level: exploring the role of social capital and leadership in a rural fishing community. *World Development*, **36**(12), 2763–2779.

Bodin, Ö. and B.I. Crona (2009). The role of social networks in natural resource governance: what relational patterns make a difference? *Global Environmental Change*, **19**, 366–374.

Bodin, Ö. and J. Norberg (2005). Information network topologies for enhanced local adaptive management. *Environmental Management*, **35**(2), 175–193.

Bonacich, P. (1972). Factoring and weighting approaches to status scores and clique identification. *Journal of Mathematical Sociology*, **2**(1), 113–120.

Bordieu, P. (1986). The forms of capital. In J.G. Richardson (Ed.), *Handbook of Theory and Research for the Sociology of Education.* New York, NY: Greenwood Press.

Borgatti, S.P., C. Jones and M. Everett (1998). Network measures of social capital. *Connections (INSNA)*, **21**(2), 27–36.

Borrini-Feyerabend, G. and G. Borrini (1996). *Collaborative Management of Protected Areas: Tailoring the Approach to the Context.* Gland: IUCN.

Boström, M. (2004). Cognitive practices and collective identities within a heterogenous social movement: the Swedish environmental movement. *Social Movement Studies*, **3**, 73–88.

Brugha, R. and Z. Varvasovszky (2000). Stakeholder analysis: a review. *Health and Policy Planning*, **15**, 239–246.

Burt, R. (1976). Positions in social networks. *Social Forces*, **55**, 93–122.

Burt, R. (1999). The social capital of opinion leaders. *Annals of the American Academy of Political and Social Science*, **566**, 37–54.

Burt, R. (2003). The social capital of structural holes. In M.E. Guillen, R. Collins, P. England and M. Meyer (Eds.), *The New Economic Sociology: Developments in an Emerging Field.* New York, NY: Russell Sage Foundation, pp. 148–189.

Burt, R. (2004). Structural holes and good ideas. *American Journal of Sociology*, **110**(2), 349–399.

Burt, R. (2005). *Brokerage and Closure: An Introduction to Social Capital.* Oxford: Oxford University Press.

Carpenter, S.R. and L.H. Gunderson (2001). Coping with collapse: ecological and social dynamics in ecosystem management. *Bioscience*, **51**(6), 451–457.

Chapin, F.S. III, E.S. Zavaleta, V.T. Eviner *et al.* (2000). Consequences of changing biodiversity. *Nature*, **405**(6783), 234–242.

Clarkson, M. B. E. (1995). A stakeholder framework for analyzing and evaluating corporate social performance. *Academy of Management Review*, **20**, 65–91.

Cohen, M. D., R. L. Riolo and R. Axelrod (2001). The role of social structure in the maintenance of cooperative regimes. *Rationality and Society*, **13**(1), 5–32.

Coleman, J. S. (1988). Social capital in the creation of human capital. *American Journal of Sociology*, **94**, 95–120.

Coleman, J. S. (1990). *Foundations of Social Theory*. Cambridge, MA: Harvard University Press.

Crawford, B., M. Kasmidi, F. Korompis and R. B. Pollnac (2006). Factors influencing progress in establishing community-based marine protected areas in Indonesia. *Coastal Management*, **34**, 39–64.

Crona, B. I. (2006). Supporting and enhancing development of heterogeneous ecological knowledge among resource users in a Kenyan seascape. *Ecology and Society*, **11**(1), art 32, http://www.ecologyandsociety.org/vol11/iss1/art32/.

Crona, B. I. and Ö. Bodin (2006). What you know is who you know? Patterns of communication as prerequisites for co-management. *Ecology and Society*, **11**(2), art 7.

Crona, B. I. and Ö. Bodin (2010). Power asymmetries in small-scale fisheries – a barrier to governance transformability? *Ecology and Society*, **15**(4): art 32.

Degenne, A. and M. Forsé (1999). *Introducing Social Networks*. London: Sage.

della Porta, D. and M. Diani (2006). *Social Movements: An Introduction*. Oxford: Blackwell Publishing.

Diani, M. (1992). The concept of social movement. *Sociological Review*, **40**, 1–25.

Diani, M. (2002). Britain re-creates the social movement: contentious (and not-so-contentious) networks. In *Contentious Politics and the Economic Opportunity Structure*, University of Crete, Rhetimno, 17–18 October.

Diani, M. (2003). 'Leaders' or brokers? Positions and influence in social movement networks. In M. Diani and D. McAdam (Eds.), *Social Movements and Networks: Relational Approaches to Collective Action*. Oxford: Oxford University Press, pp. 105–122.

Diani, M. and I. Bison (2004). Organizations, coalitions and movements. *Theory and Society*, **33**, 281–309.

Diani, M. and D. McAdam (Eds.) (2003). *Social Movements and Networks: Relational Approaches to Collective Action*. Oxford: Oxford University Press.

Diduck, A. (2004). Incorporating participatory approaches and social learning. In B. Mitchell (Ed.), *Resource and Environmental Management in Canada: Addressing Conflict and Uncertainty*. Toronto, ON: Oxford University Press, pp. 497–527.

Diduck, A., N. Bankes, D. Clark and D. Armitage (2005). Unpacking social learning in social-ecological systems: case studies of polar bear and narwhal management in northern Canada. In *Breaking Ice: Renewable Resource and Ocean Management in the Canadian North*. Calgary, AB: Arctic Institute of North America and University of Calgary Press, pp. 269–290.

DiMaggio, P. (1998). The new institutionalism: avenues of collaboration. *Journal of Institutional and Theoretical Economics*, **154**(4), 696–705.

Dougill, A. J., E. D. G. Fraser, J. Holden *et al.* (2006). Learning from doing participatory rural research: lessons from the Peak District National Park. *Journal of Agricultural Economics*, **57**(2), 259–275.

Dryzek, J. (1997). *The Politics of Earth*. Oxford: Oxford University Press.

Emirbayer, M. and J. Goodwin (1994). Network analysis, culture and the problem of agency. *American Journal of Sociology*, **99**, 1411–1454.

Emirbayer, M. and A. Mische (1998). What is agency? *American Journal of Sociology*, **103**(4), 962–1023.

Ernstson, H., S. Barthel, E. Andersson and S. Borgström (2010). Scale-crossing brokers and network governance of urban ecosystem services: the case of Stockholm, Sweden. *Ecology and Society*, **15**(4), art 28.

Ernstson, H. and S. Sörlin (2009). Weaving protective stories: connective practices to articulate holistic values in Stockholm National Urban Park. *Environment and Planning A*, **41**, 1460–1479.

Ernstson, H., S. Sörlin and T. Elmqvist (2008). Social movements and ecosystem services – the role of social network structure in protecting and managing urban green areas in Stockholm. *Ecology and Society*, **13**(2), art 39.

Everett, M. and S.P. Borgatti (1990). A testing example for positional analysis techniques. *Social Networks*, **12**, 253–260.

Fligstein, N. (1997). Social skills and institutional theory. *American Behavioral Scientist*, **40**, 397–405.

Folke, C., T. Hahn, P. Olsson and J. Norberg (2005). Adaptive governance of social-ecological systems. *Annual Review of Environment and Resources*, **30**, 441–473.

Forrester, J. (1999). The logistics of public participation in environmental assessment. *International Journal of Environment and Pollution*, **11**(3), 316–330.

Freeman, L. (1979). Centrality in social networks. Conceptual clarifications. *Social Networks*, **1**, 215–239.

Friedkin, N.E. (1998). *A Structural Theory of Social Influence*. Cambridge: Cambridge University Press.

Friedman, A. and S. Miles (2006). *Stakeholders: Theory and Practice*. Oxford: Oxford University Press.

Fukuyama, F. (1995). *Trust: The Social Virtues and the Creation of Prosperity*. London: Hamish Hamilton.

Garud, R., C. Hardy and S. Maguire (2007). Institutional entrepreneurship as embedded agency: an introduction to the special issue. *Organization Studies*, **28**, 957–969.

Ghimire, S.K., D. McKey and Y. Aumeeruddy-Thomas (2004). Heterogeneity in ethnoecological knowledge and management of medicinal plants in the Himalayas of Nepal: implications for conservation. *Ecology and Society*, **9**(3), online.

Gilmour, A., G. Walkerden and J. Scandol (1999). Adaptive management of the water cycle on the urban fringe: three Australian case studies. *Conservation Ecology*, **3**(1), art 11.

Gould, R.V. and R.M. Fernandez (1989). Structure of mediation: a formal approach to brokerage in transactions networks. *Sociological Methodology*, **19**, 89–126.

Granovetter, M. (1973). The strength of weak ties. *American Journal of Sociology*, **76**(6), 1360–1380.

Granovetter, M. (1985). Economic action, social structure, and embeddedness. *American Journal of Sociology*, **91**, 481–510.

Greenwood, D. and M. Levin (1998). *Introduction to Action Research*. Thousand Oaks, CA: Sage.

Grimble, R. and M.K. Chan (1995). Stakeholder analysis for natural resource management in developing countries: some practical guidelines for making management more participatory and effective. *Natural Resources Forum*, **19**, 113–124.

Grimble, R. and K. Wellard (1997). Stakeholder methodologies in natural resource management: a review of concepts, contexts, experiences and opportunities. *Agricultural Systems*, **55**, 173–193.

Habermas, J. (1981). *The Theory of Communicative Action: Reason and the Reationalization of Society*. Boston, MA: Beacon Press.

Hahn, T., P. Olsson, C. Folke and K. Johansson (2006). Trust-building, knowledge generation and organizational innovations: the role of a bridging organization for adaptive co-management of a wetland landscape around Kristianstad, Sweden. *Human Ecology*, **34**(4), 573–592.

Hahn, T., L. Schultz, C. Folke and P. Olsson (2008). Social networks as sources of resilience in social-ecological systems. In J. Norberg and G. Cumming (Eds.), *Complexity Theory for a Sustainable Future*. New York, NY: Columbia University Press, pp. 119–148.

Hare, M. and C. Pahl-Wostl (2002). Stakeholder categorization in participatory integrated assessment. *Integrated Assessment*, **3**, 50–62.

Holling, C. S. (1973). Resilience and stability of ecological systems. *Annual Review of Ecological Systems*, **4**, 1–23.

Holling, C. S. (1978). *Adaptive Environmental Assessment and Management*. New York, NY: John Wiley & Sons.

Holling, C. S. and G. K. Meffe (1995). Command and control and the pathology of natural resource management. *Conservation Biology*, **10**(2), 328–337.

Holling, C. S. D. W. Schindler, B. Walker and J. Roughgarden (1995). Biodiversity in the functioning of ecosystems: an ecological synthesis. In C. Perrings, K.-G. Maler, C. Folke and C. S. Holling (Eds.), *Biodiversity Loss: Economic and Ecological Issues*. Cambridge: Cambridge University Press, pp. 44–83.

Isaac, M., B. H. Erickson, S. J. Quashie-Sam and V. R. Timmer (2007). Transfer of knowledge on agroforestry management practices: the structure of farmer advice networks. *Ecology and Society*, **12**(2), art 32.

Jentoft, S. (2000). Co-managing the coastal zone: is the task too complex? *Ocean and Coastal Management*, **43**(6), 527–535.

Johannes, R. E. (1981). *Word of the Lagoon: Fishing and Marine Lore in the Palau District of Micronesia*. Berkley, CA: University of California Press.

Jovchelovitch, S. (2006). *Knowledge in Context. Representations, Community and Culture*. London: Routledge.

Katz, E. and P. F. Lazarsfeld (1955). *Personal Influence; The Part Played by People in the Flow of Mass Communications*. Glencoe, IL: Free Press.

Kolb, D. A. (1984). *Experiential Learning: Experience as the Source of Learning and Development*. Englewood Cliffs, NJ: Prentice Hall.

Krackhardt, D. (1992). The strength of strong ties: the importance of philosophy in organizations. In R. G. Eccles and N. Nohria (Eds.), *Networks and Organizations: Structure, Form, and Action*. Boston, MA: Harvard Business School Press, pp. 216–239.

Krackhardt, D. and M. Kilduff (2002). Structure, culture and Simmelian ties in entrepreneurial firms. *Social Networks*, **24**, 279–290.

Krishna, A. (2002). *Active Social Capital. Tracing the Roots of Development and Democracy*. New York, NY: Columbia University Press.

Leach, W. D. and N. W. Pelkey (2001). Making watershed partnerships work: a review of the empirical literature. *Journal of Water Resources Planning and Management*, **127**, 378–385.

Leavitt, H. (1951). Some effects of certain communication patterns on group performance. *Journal of Abnormal and Social Psychology*, **46**, 38–50.

Lee, K. N. (1993). *Compass and Gyroscope: Integrating Science and Politics for the Environment*. Washington, DC: Island Press.

Levin, S. A. (1992). The problem of pattern and scale in ecology. *Ecology*, **73**, 1943–1967.

Levin, S. A. (1999). *Fragile Dominion*. Reading, MA: Perseus Books.

Lin, N. (1999). Building a network theory of social capital. *Connections*, **22**, 28–51.

Lin, N. (2002). *Social Capital: A Theory of Social Structure and Action*. Cambridge: Cambridge University Press.

Lundberg, J. and F. Moberg (2003). Mobile link organisms and ecosystem functioning: implications for ecosystem resilience and management. *Ecosystems*, **6**(1), 87–98.

Maguire, S., C. Hardy and T. B. Lawrence (2004). Institutional entrepreneurship in emerging fields: HIV/AIDS treatment advocacy in Canada. *Academy of Management Journal*, **47**, 657–679.

McCarthy, J. D. and M. N. Zald (1977). Resource mobilization and social movements: a partial theory. *American Journal of Sociology*, **82**, 1212–1241.

McPherson, M., L. Smith-Lovin and J. M. Cook (2001). Birds of a feather: homophily in social networks. *Annual Review of Sociology*, **27**, 415–444.

Melucci, A. (1995). *Challenging Codes. Collective Action in the Information Age*. Cambridge: Cambridge University Press.

Mezirow, J. and Associates (2000). *Learning as Transformation: Critical Perspectives on a Theory in Progress*. San Francisco, CA: Jossey-Bass.

Napier, V., G. Branch and J. Harris (2005). Evaluating conditions for successful co-management of subsistence fisheries in KwaZulu-Natal, South Africa. *Environmental Conservation*, **32**, 165–177.

Newig, J., D. Gunther and C. Pahl-Wostl (2010). Neurons in the network. Learning in governance networks in the context of environmental management. *Ecology and Society*, **15**(4), art 24.

Newman, L. L. and A. Dale (2005). Network structure, diversity, and proactive resilience building: a response to Tompkins and Adger. *Ecology and Society*, **10**(1), art 2.

Oh, H., M.-H. Chung and G. Labianca (2004). Group social capital and group effectiveness: the role of informal socializing ties. *Academy of Management Journal*, **47**(6), 860–875.

Olsson, P., C. Folke and F. Berkes (2004a). Adaptive comanagement for building resilience in social-ecological systems. *Environmental Management*, **34**(1), 75–90.

Olsson, P., C. Folke, V. Galaz, T. Hahn and L. Schultz (2007). Enhancing the fit through adaptive co-management: creating and maintaining bridging functions for matching scales in the Kristianstads Vattenrike Biosphere Reserve, Sweden. *Ecology and Society*, **12**(1), art 28.

Olsson, P., C. Folke and T. Hahn (2004b). Social-ecological transformation for ecosystem management: the development of adaptive co-management of a wetland landscape in southern Sweden. *Ecology and Society*, **9**(4), 2.

Olsson, P., C. Folke and T. P. Hughes (2008). Navigating the transition to ecosystem-based management of the Great Barrier Reef, Australia. *Proceedings of the National Academy of Sciences USA*, **105**, 9489–9494.

Olsson, P., L. Gunderson, S. Carpenter *et al.* (2006). Shooting the rapids: navigating transitions to adaptive governance of social-ecological systems. *Ecology and Society*, **11**(1), art 18.

Ostrom, E. (1990). *Governing the Commons: The Evolution of Institutions for Collective Action*. Cambridge: Cambridge University Press.

Ostrom, E. (1998). Scales, polycentricity, and incentives: designing complexity to govern complexity. In L. D. Guruswamy and J. A. McNeely (Eds.), *Protection of Global Diversity: Converging Strategies*. Durham, NC: Duke University Press, pp. 149–167.

Ostrom, E. (2005). *Understanding Institutional Diversity*. Princeton, NJ: Princeton University Press.

Ostrom, E., J. Burger, C.B. Field, R.B. Norgaard and D. Policansky (1999). Revisiting the commons: local lessons, global challenges. *Science*, **284**(5412), 278–282.

Ostrom, E., R. Gardner and J. Walker (1994). *Rules, Games and Common-pool Resources*. Ann Arbor, MI: University of Michigan Press.

Pahl-Wostl, C. (2002). Towards sustainability in the water sector – the importance of human actors and processes of social learning. *Aquatic Sciences*, **64**, 394–411.

Perkmann, M. and A. Spicer (2007). Healing the scars of history: projects, skills and field strategies in institutional entrepreneurship. *Organizational Studies*, **28**(7), 1101–1122.

Pinkerton, E. (1989). *Co-operative Management of Local Fisheries: New Directions for Improved Management and Community Development*. Vancouver, BC: University of British Columbia Press.

Portes, A. (1998). Social capital: its origins and applications in modern sociology. *Annual Review of Sociology*, **22**(1), 1–24.

Prell, C., M. Reed, L. Racin and K. Hubacek (2010). Competing structures, competing views: the role of formal and informal social structures in shaping stakeholder perceptions. *Ecology and Society*, **15**(4), art 34.

Prell, C., K. Hubacek and M. Reed (2006). Using stakeholder and social network analysis to support participatory processes. *International Journal of Biodiversity Science and Management*, **2**, 249–252.

Prell, C., K. Hubacek and M. Reed (2009). Stakeholder analysis and social network analysis in natural resource management. *Society and Natural Resources*, **22**, 501–518.

Pretty, J. (2003). Social capital and the collective management of resources. *Science*, **302**, 1912–1914.

Pretty, J. and D. Smith (2004). Social capital in biodiversity conservation and management. *Conservation Biology*, **18**(3), 631–638.

Pretty, J. and H. Ward (2001). Social capital and the environment. *World Development*, **29**(2), 209–227.

Putnam, R.D. (1993). *Making Democracy Work. Civic Traditions in Modern Italy*. Princeton, NJ: Princeton University Press.

Putnam, R.D. (2000). *Bowling Alone: The Collapse and Revival of American Community*. New York, NY: Simon & Schuster.

Ramirez-Sanchez, S. and E. Pinkerton (2009). The impact of resource scarcity on bonding and bridging social capital: the case of fishers' information-sharing networks in Loreto, BCS, Mexico. *Ecology and Society*, **14**(1), art 22.

Rao, H. (1998). Caveat emptor: the construction of nonprofit consumer watchdog organizations. *American Journal of Sociology*, **103**, 912–961.

Reagans, R. and B. McEvily (2003). Network structure and knowledge transfer: the effects of cohesion and range. *Administrative Science Quarterly*, **48**(2), 240–267.

Reed, M., A. Graves, N. Dandy *et al.* (2009). Who's in and why? Stakeholder analysis as a prerequisite for sustainable natural resource management. *Journal of Environmental Management*, **90**, 1933–1949.

Rogers, E. (1995). *Diffusion of Innovations*. New York, NY: Simon & Schuster.

Ruef, M., H. Aldrich and N.M. Carter (2003). The structure of founding teams: homophily, strong ties, and isolation among U.S. entrepreneurs. *American Sociological Review*, **68**, 195–222.

Ruitenbeek, H.J. and C. Cartier (2001). The invisible wand: adaptive co-management as an emergent strategy. *Complex Bio-Economic Systems*,

Occasional Paper No. 34, Center for International Forestry Research, Indonesia.

Schneider, M., J. Scholz, M. Lubell, D. Mindruta and M. Edwardsen (2003). Building consensual institutions: networks and the National Estuary Program. *American Journal of Political Science*, **47**(1), 143–158.

Schultz, L. (2009). Nurturing resilience in social-ecological systems. PhD thesis, Systems Ecology. Stockholm University, Stockholm.

Schusler, T. M., D. J. Decker and M. J. Pfeffer (2003). Social learning for collaborative natural resource management. *Society and Natural Resources*, **16**(4), 309–326.

Shannon, M. A. (1991). Resource managers as policy entrepreneurs. *Journal of Forestry*, **89**, 27–30.

Stankey, G. H., R. N. Clark and B. T. Bormann (2005). Adaptive management of natural resources: theory, concepts, and management institutions. Portland, OR: US Department of Agriculture.

Stringer, L., A. J. Dougill, E. D. G. Fraser *et al.* (2006). Unpacking 'participation' in the adaptive management of social-ecological systems: a critical review. *Ecology and Society*, **11**(2), art 39.

Touraine, A. (1981). *The Voice and the Eye. An Analysis of Social Movements.* Cambridge: Cambridge University Press.

Valente, T. W. (1996). Social network thresholds in the diffusion of innovations. *Social Networks*, **18**(1), 69–89.

Valente, T. W. and R. Davis (1999). Accelerating the diffusion of innovations using opinion leaders. *Annals of the American Academy of Political and Social Science*, **566**, 55–67.

Wasserman, S. and K. Faust (1994). *Social Network Analysis – Methods and Applications.* Cambridge: Cambridge University Press.

Weimann, G. (1982). On the importance of marginality: one more step into the two-step flow of communication. *American Sociological Review*, **47**(6), 764–773.

Westley, F. (2001). Devil in the dynamics. In L. S. Gunderson and C. S. Holling (Eds.), *Panarchy: Understanding Transformations in Human and Natural Systems.* Washington, DC: Island Press, pp. 333–360.

Westley, F. and H. Mintzberg (1989). Visionary leadership and strategic management. *Strategic Management Journal*, **10**, 17–32.

Westley, F., O. Tjörnbo, P. Olsson *et al.* (forthcoming). Agency and leadership strategies for innovation and transformation of social-ecological systems.

Westley, F., B. Zimmerman and M. Patton (2006). *Getting to Maybe: How the World is Changed.* Toronto, ON: Random House Canada.

Wondolleck, J. M. and S. L. Yaffee (2000). *Making Collaboration Work. Lessons from Innovation in Natural Resource Management.* Washington, DC: Island Press.

Woolcock, M. and D. Narayan (2000). Social capital: implications for development theory, research and policy. *The World Bank Research Observer*, **15**(2), 225–249.

Yankelovich, D. (1991). *Coming to Public Judgment. Making Democracy Work in a Complex World.* Syracuse, NY: Syracuse University Press.

Zald, M. N. and J. D. McCarthy (1980). Social movement industries: competition and cooperation among movement industries. In *Research in Social Movements, Conflict, and Change.* Greenwich, CT: Jai Publisher.

Part II Case studies

4

Barriers and opportunities in transforming to sustainable governance: the role of key individuals

4.1 INTRODUCTION

There are numerous examples of successful natural resource management. Some of the more notable and well documented include mountain agriculture in the Swiss alps (Ostrom, 1990), irrigation systems in different parts of the world (Ostrom, 1990), Kristianstad Water Kingdom in Sweden (Olsson et al., 2004b; Schultz, 2009), and the Maine lobster fishery (Acheson, 1988). However, in many settings, governance for sustainable resource management remains an elusive goal and the current state of affairs is characterized by rigidity and inertia. This is sometimes a result of power struggles and elite capture (Barratt, 2009), but also because of lack of incentives and poor problem perception (Crona and Bodin, 2006; Bodin and Crona, 2008) or failure of top-down regulatory mechanisms (Ostrom, 1990). Transforming a system experiencing such inertia can be difficult and, among other things, requires appropriate leadership. The process of change has been likened to navigating turbulent rapids (Olsson et al., 2006) and the role of leadership has been hailed as one of the key factors in enabling transformation.

Leadership can take many forms, from working behind the scenes to connecting people in "shadow networks" (sensu Olsson et al., 2006) in preparation of change (see also Burt, 2005), to providing a vision (Olsson et al., 2004a), or being able to use social capital within a community to foster development (Krishna, 2002). Individuals who

Social Networks and Natural Resource Management: Uncovering the Fabric of Environmental Governance, ed. Ö. Bodin and C. Prell. Published by Cambridge University Press.
© Cambridge University Press 2011.

have successfully undertaken the challenge of initiating larger scale changes (i.e. transformations) have also been referred to as institutional entrepreneurs (Maguire *et al.*, 2004; Garud *et al.*, 2007; see also Chapter 3).

Implicit in this way of looking at leaders and leadership is both the importance of social networks and personal characteristics, and the interplay between the two. This interplay can be thought of as the activities and strategies employed by the individuals initiating change. Social networks largely provide the vehicle through which successful leaders spread their ideas, garner support, and ultimately move the system through a transformation. Hence, how the leaders are positioned within such networks becomes important since occupying favorable positions gives these individuals some means to exert influence. Reversely, in occupying a favorable position, a person becomes a potential leader. So, what constitutes a favorable position? To be able to effectively spread a vision, produce a common understanding (sensemaking), and prepare the system for change, you need to be socially well connected (Burt, 2005; Olsson *et al.*, 2006). Being well connected, in this sense, can be seen as the sheer number of social ties. But who you are linked to is equally important. Put differently, being well connected or highly central within your own group of peers can be a good way to influence those close to you, but without links to other groups your ideas are unlikely to spread very far, and it is unlikely that any greater system transformation will be achieved.

But social position is not everything. What you do, who you are, and how you choose to use your social position in reaching your objectives have been shown to play a significant role in successful entrepreneurship, in social ventures, business as well as natural resource management settings (Aldrich, 1999; Burt, 2005 and references therein; Olsson *et al.*, 2006). Accordingly, the interplay between structural position in networks and the personal characteristics contributes to individual agency of potential leaders (e.g. Bodin and Crona, 2009), which could then be used for successful navigation of transformations as outlined above. This is the focus of this chapter.

Because who you are connected to, and how well connected you are, both appear to play a central role in enabling agency, social network analysis (SNA) emerges as a method well suited for furthering our understanding of these issues. Social network analysis can help to identify key individuals (i.e. potential leaders) based on their centrality in social networks and, in combination with both quantitative and qualitative approaches in measuring the key individuals' personal characteristics, it can provide valuable insights on the factors that enable agency for change in natural resource governance. In this way, we are given a powerful analytical framework that could help us to start exploring these issues. In this chapter we will show, using a case study of a rural fishing village, how SNA can be used to identify key individuals based on a categorization of centrality in a social network of fishers sharing local ecological knowledge. There are a number of different ways in which network centrality can be conceptualized, as outlined in Chapter 2. Here we focus on degree centrality (an actor's number of social ties), but we differentiate an actor's degree centrality depending on the extent to which he or she is linked to others beyond the immediate social neighborhood. In other words, to what extent an actor is linked to others within his or her own social subgroup versus to others outside that subgroup. To accomplish that we use a method that stems from the generalized field of network analysis of complex systems and is not targeted for analyzing social networks in particular. However, the method suits our objective because it does not only measure degree centrality but also takes into account to what degree an individual is connected to others within or outside their own subgroup, and the scale at which this subgroup crossing interaction takes place. Hence, the method per necessity also identifies subgroups, which is further elaborated in Chapter 9. The method divides all actors of a network into several categories of centrality based on (1) the number of ties an actor possesses, and (2) whether these are within versus between subgroup. Again, this differentiation is important since it captures whether an actor is mostly oriented towards his or her own peers, or if his or her social contacts span across various subgroups.

As discussed above, agency at least partly appears to emerge from the interplay between structural position in a social network and the personal characteristics of these key individuals occupying these positions. We therefore go on to examine how the characteristics of the identified key individuals in the social network may explain why the studied community has *not* been able to change the way they extract natural resources, thus failing to address declining fish stocks and environmental degradation. This chapter complements the analysis in Chapter 9 where we focus on the interactions within and between subgroups and how such patterns could contribute to our understanding of possible causes for the studied community's inability to collectively respond to the ongoing environmental degradation.

4.2   THE CASE SETTING

This chapter analyzes data from the same community explored in Chapter 9. The system in focus is a rural fishing village on the south coast of Kenya. Of the approximately 1000 inhabitants (206 households) a large portion (44% of households) rely on fishing as a main occupation while many others depend indirectly on fisheries resources for their livelihood. Farming and small-scale businesses represent some alternative livelihoods. For more details on fishing practices and institutional arrangements please refer to Chapter 9 and/or Crona and Bodin (2006).

The population of coastal Kenya comprises two main ethnic groups; the Mijikenda of Bantu origin and the Swahili who are of mixed Bantu, Asian, and Arabic descent (King, 2000). The Mijikenda comprise nine tribes, of which Digo is the predominant ethnicity of inhabitants in the study area. However, other coastal tribes such as Bajuni, historically associated with the Lamu region of the north coast, have migrated south and are present in the studied community. Many Bajuni families have traditionally been involved in mangrove cutting and trading, as well as fishing, accumulating substantial wealth, while the Mijikenda were primarily farmers who, in the last century, diversified their livelihoods to include fisheries. This now constitutes a substantial portion of incomes (King, 2000). It is worth noting that although a minority, Bajuni families constitute a disproportionate number of the households in the upper income bracket in this community, while households of Digo and other Mijikenda descent constitute the large majority of the poorest families. More recently, a third ethnic group has emerged in the community, accounting for approximately 26% of households and consisting of semi-migrant fishers from the Tanzanian island of Pemba, where they return on a regular basis. This migration is linked to both economic factors and kinship ties. During the high season, migrating fishers return to the study area to fish and are often assisted with travel expenses and permits by local middlemen (fishmongers) operating out of the village. At the same time, kinship ties play a significant role in who is recruited to come along as crew for the duration of the season. The most dramatic influx of Tanzanian fishers occurred after the 1964 overthrow of the Zanzibar-Pemba government, resulting in large seine crews establishing more or less semi-permanent operations along the Kenyan coast (Glaesel, 1997). The majority of Pembas currently residing in the village primarily use ring nets (a variant of purse seines). They operate from larger vessels, employing crews of up to 30 men or more, and are often referred to as deep-sea fishers by themselves as well as others in the community.

For a fuller description of the studied community, how we defined the study population, and how the social networks data were collected, please see Chapter 9. In this section, we present only the methodological issues that are specific for this chapter.

4.3.1   Which social network is most relevant?

In this study we focus on the social network used by villagers to communicate local ecological knowledge. This means essentially any information shared among people in the village concerning the status of the natural resource, any changes in the environment, or information on the abundance of fish and other resources. The rationale for focusing on this network is that it may be a suitable vehicle for initiating change of current resource management and governance practices. Individuals who appear as highly central in this network are likely to be influential in transmitting their knowledge but are also well placed to receive diverse information. Hence, these key individuals thus appear as having a significant potential in providing leadership for change.

4.3.2   Personal characteristics of relevance

We are concerned with identifying key individuals in a network and then linking their position to personal characteristics, such as who they are and what they do. We do this to investigate, in an explorative way, how their individual agency is, or is not, put in use in the social-ecological system in which they operate. However, measuring personal characteristics is certainly not a trivial task. First you need to define, given your underlying theories, hypotheses, and research questions, what kinds of characteristics are relevant and which ones you determine are feasible to obtain. Ideally, as many of these relevant characteristics as possible should be measured but there is always a trade-off in terms of the time and resources available and the amount of data which can be collected. The issue of respondent fatigue, i.e. tiring your respondents should also not be neglected. Once data on personal characteristics are collected, you can proceed to statistically infer which types of characteristics best explain the outcome you are concerned with (see Krishna, 2002 for an example of a similar inquiry where he identified some key characteristics of village leaders that seemingly defined their ability to lead their villages to better economic development). Krishna's work is exemplary in its thoroughness, use of multiple and somewhat competing theories, and large sample size. However, this is not always attainable when working on one or a few cases.

For the sake of this study we instead relied on a range of characteristics which were fairly easy to measure, but still based on what we believe to be well-founded assumptions about how they affect and possibly also constrain an individual's capacity (and willingness) to act in favor of changing the way resources are being utilized as a response to ongoing resource degradation. As briefly described earlier, tribal affiliation is an important characteristic in the studied community since it to a large extent defines who you are, what you do, and with whom you are likely to be most loyal. Furthermore, in our previous studies of the community (Crona and Bodin, 2006; Bodin and Crona, 2008), occupational affiliation was shown to, in a similar way, define a person's social circle related to resource extraction and communication. For fishers in particular, the type of gear used is of key importance in defining a person's occupational identity. In addition, occupational affiliation to some extent frames the setting within which a person's local ecological knowledge is obtained. Finally, we included ownership of gear. This can be important in determining how reliant a fisher is on others in order to access and extract marine resources. We argue that gear ownership is important for agency since, given the low average income levels in this community, both ring nets and seine nets are highly capital intensive gear. This means that a significant amount of capital has been invested in this fishing gear and such sunken costs are likely to prevent individuals from changing their fishing practices, even when deemed unsustainable. Also, owning gear typically puts a person in a more powerful position compared to the ones relying on him or her to gain access to this gear.

4.3.3   Identifying the key individuals

A primary task in this study is to identify centrally located individuals in the network used to communicate local ecological knowledge. There are several different ways of approaching this task in social network analysis, all conceptually focused on defining the level of centrality of individual actors (nodes). Degree centrality is the most basic way to measure centrality and tells you the number of others an actor is directly linked to. High degree centrality could indicate that an individual is influential in shaping others' perception in a communication network such as the one studied here (e.g. Degenne and Forsé, 1999). Another way of approaching the concept of centrality is to look at betweenness centrality, i.e. to identify individuals located in-between others and therefore potentially able to control the flow of resources (see e.g. Burt, 2005). If the key objective is to capture those individuals most likely to be important in terms of both influence and control of resource flow, using a combination of degree centrality and betweenness centrality measures is advised. An example of this can be found in a previous study where we used a combination of centrality measures in different networks to assess the most influential individuals (Bodin and Crona, 2008). However, in this chapter our focus is on unpacking degree centrality further by clearly distinguishing between different aspects of degree centrality and using this differentiation to identify key individuals that are occupying influential positions *of different kinds.*

We make use of a method that is devised for analyzing not only social networks but essentially networks of any kind. It is used to categorize nodes into seven universal roles/types, independent of system type. For instance, this method has been successfully applied in such diverse networks as metabolic pathways, airport networks, and networks of collaborations among researchers in chemical engineering (Guimerà and Amaral, 2005a). It is an interesting method because it teases apart an actor's degree centrality based on the number of links within his or her subgroup and other subgroups, as well as the extent to which these group-crossing relations exist.

The method consists of the following steps. First, the network is divided into subgroups (see further description in Chapter 9 and in Guimerà and Amaral, 2005a, 2005b). Nodes are then categorized as being a hub or not. To be a hub, a node should possess significantly more links than its fellow subgroup member. This is captured by the within-subgroup degree z_i (Equation 4.1):

$$z_i = \frac{k_i - k_s}{\sigma_{k_s}} \qquad (4.1)$$

Where k_i is the degree centrality of node i, k_s is the average degree centrality of the nodes in i's subgroup s, and σ_{k_s} is the standard deviation of the degree centrality in subgroup s. To be categorized as a hub, the value of z_i must exceed the threshold z_t that was originally set to 2.5.

As explained in Guimerà and Amaral (2005b), this threshold was defined by investigating structural characteristics of several different networks of different types. In this study, we relaxed the threshold value in several steps as explained below.

Next, each node is further categorized depending on how many of its links fall outside its own subgroup as defined by the participant coefficient P_i in Equation (4.2):

$$P_i = 1 - \sum_{s=1}^{N_M} \left(\frac{k_{is}}{k_i}\right)^2 \tag{4.2}$$

where k_{is} is the number of links of node i to nodes in subgroup s, and k_i is the total degree of node i. N_M is the number of subgroups. Following the same approach as when defining the threshold on the within-subgroup degree above, Guimerà and Amaral (2005b) analyzed the same set of networks to define a set of five different threshold values of the participant coefficient (see Figure 4.1). Using three of these thresholds of the participant coefficient, the non-hub nodes are categorized into four different universal roles. These consist of: (R1) ultra-peripheral nodes which are nodes with all their links within their subgroup; (R2) peripheral nodes which are nodes with most but not entirely all of their links within their subgroup; (R3) non-hub connector nodes which are nodes with quite a few of their links to other subgroups; or (R4) non-hub kinless nodes which are nodes with all their links fairly equally distributed among all subgroups (Guimerà and Amaral, 2005b) (Figure 4.1).

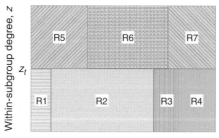

Figure 4.1 Categorization of nodes into seven different roles (adapted from Guimerà and Amaral, 2005b). The threshold z_t defines whether a node is a hub or not, and this threshold value was set to 2.5, 2.0, and 1.5 in three different consecutive rounds of categorization.

If, on the other hand, a node is identified as a hub, it is categorized into one of the following three categories based on the remaining
two threshold values of the participation coefficient: (R5) provincial
hubs which are hub nodes with the vast majority of links directed at
nodes within their subgroup; (R6) connector hubs which are hubs with
a fair number of links to other subgroups; or (R7) kinless hubs which
are hubs with links equally distributed among all subgroups (Guimerà
and Amaral, 2005b).

In our data the spread around the mean (i.e. the standard deviation) of reported relations concerning the exchange of ecological information among respondents was fairly low (average of 2.51 reported
relations with a standard deviation of 1.48 among the 121 respondents
who reported any such relations). We believe that our use of the recall
method to elicit the social ties of the respondents could be one reason
for the low variability in reported ties among individuals. This stems
from the fact that respondents have a limited ability to remember all of
their relations and memory bias skews reported ties to those most
frequently or most recently used (see also Marsden, 1990; Freeman,
1997 for a review of this issue). Since the overall spread in our data set is
rather low, the within-subgroup degree z_i values were also relatively
low overall and therefore only very few individuals got a value that
exceeded the predefined threshold defining a node as a hub (as
described above). Because the recall method may have affected the
spread of reported relations we decided to relax the threshold z_t in
three separate rounds to compare how the stringency of the hub/non-
hub criteria affects the identification of key individuals. In the first
round the threshold z_t was set to 2.5 as in the original outline of the
methods (Guimerà and Amaral, 2005a, 2005b); the second time the
criteria was relaxed to $z_t = 2$; and in the third round it was further
relaxed to $z_t = 1.5$.

4.3.4   A note on the direction of causality

Before we continue with the analysis it is important to discuss the
issue of causality in network analysis. Given our interest in potential
agents of change, also referred to as institutional entrepreneurs
(sensu Maguire *et al.*, 2004), a legitimate question would be: Are
these individuals who they are because of where they are placed in
their network of relations, or have they acquired their position in the
network as a result of their personal characteristics? This question
illustrates well one of the main differences distinguishing different

social network studies. So far, the bulk of network research has been concerned with the consequences of networks (Borgatti and Foster, 2003) and not so much with the causes of the structures themselves. The latter type of research is, however, increasing rapidly although those types of studies are conducted within various fields not directly related to SNA and are thus perhaps less visible (Borgatti and Foster, 2003). In this study we adhere to the former perspective and regard the present network structure as given while investigating its potential consequences. Having said that, we would like to acknowledge that a key personal characteristic of individuals who are able to provide leadership for transformations appears to be their ability to create and maintain relations of trust to various groups and individuals (Westley and Mintzberg, 1989; Olsson et al., 2004a; Schultz, 2009). Further investigation of this important issue is, however, beyond the scope of this chapter.

4.4   IDENTIFYING POTENTIAL AGENTS OF CHANGE

In applying the most stringent criterion ($z_t = 2.5$) in our first round we find only two individuals who can be considered hubs and both are of the type termed connector hubs (type R6) (Figure 4.2A and Table 4.1). Six individuals are classified as type R3, i.e. non-hub connector nodes or nodes with many links to other subgroups but not enough links relative to others within their subgroups to be considered as hubs. Using this criterion, we thus find that the majority of the population are classified as ultra-peripheral (R1) or peripheral nodes (R2) (94 and 57, respectively).

If we relax the criterion ($z_t = 2.0$) a different pattern starts to emerge. Seven more individuals now get classified as connector hubs (Figure 4.2B and Table 4.1) and we also see the emergence of a new category, namely the so-called provincial hubs or hub nodes with the vast majority of their links within their subgroup. One individual is classified as a provincial hub in the second round while the majority of the population remain non-hubs. Relaxing the criterion even further ($z_t = 1.5$) results in an additional three provincial hubs and three connector hubs (Figure 4.2C and Table 4.1). In both rounds 2 and 3, the individuals classified as type R3 (i.e. non-hub connector nodes) in the first round remain with this classification.

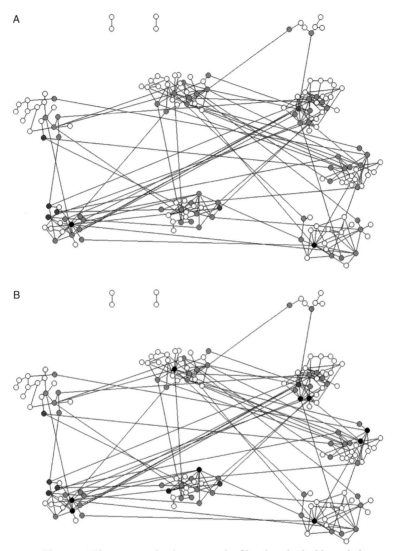

Figure 4.2 The communication network of local ecological knowledge. The spatial clustering of the nodes is in accordance with their subgroup membership, and the subgroups themselves are arranged using the spring embedding technique (using NetDraw which is part of the software program UCINET; Borgatti *et al.*, 2002). Each node is colored according to its categorization (black = R6, dark gray = R5, gray = R3, R2 = light gray, R1 = white). A is based on $z_t = 2.5$, B is based on $z_t = 2.0$, and C is based on $z_t = 1.5$. The software program Pajek was used to produce the figure.

C

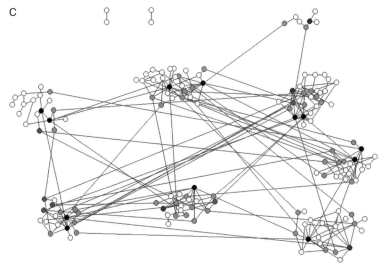

Figure 4.2 (cont.)

We can thus see that by successively relaxing the criterion related to the spread of reported ties around a subgroup average we can start to get a fuller picture of who the key individuals are, based on different characteristics of centrality in the communication network of local ecological knowledge. It is important here to tie back to the discussion on methodological choices in this chapter and throughout the different chapters in this book. In using SNA to address relevant research questions for natural resource management we need to constantly be cognizant of methodological issues, as in this case where the relaxation of a criterion had to be considered in light of issues related to the chosen data-gathering method. This adaptive approach provides for more relevant results. The key is to explicitly disclose any adaptations done to a particular method.

Looking at our combined results from using three different values of z_t (Figure 4.2A–C), do individuals occupying potentially influential positions in the network exist, and if so, who are they? The first and most obvious conclusion is that there are very few provincial hubs. Instead it appears that if respondents have many relations compared to others within their subgroup (high z_i), they also tend to have many links to other subgroups. This gives rise to the higher number of connector hubs (type R6) than provincial hubs (type R5), showing that in the studied community those who are well

Table 4.1. *Identified connector and provincial hubs in the communication network of local ecological knowledge*

	Hub type	Tribal affiliation	Occupation	Owner
Round 1 ($z_t = 2.5$)	Connector hub (R6)	Pemba	Fisher ring net	X
		Pemba	Fisher ring net	X
Round 2 ($z_t = 2.0$)	Connector hub (R6)	Digo	Fisher ring net	X
		Digo	Fish trader	–
		Bajuni	Businessman	X
		Digo	Fisher ring net	–
		Bajuni	Fisher ring net	X
		Pemba	Fisher seine net	X
		Bondoi	Fisher seine net	X
	Provincial hub (R5)	Digo	Other occupation	–
Round 3 ($z_t = 1.5$)	Connector hub (R6)	Bajuni	Fish trader	X
		Digo	Fisher seine net	–
		Digo	Fisher gillnet	–
	Provincial hub (R5)	Digo	Other occupation	–
		Pemba	Fisher seine net	X
		Pemba	Fisher ring net	–

connected tend to be well connected both within their own subgroup as well as connected to many other subgroups in the network. In terms of our research question relating to existence of potential agents for transformation this appears promising. As the literature suggests, these types of bridging or brokering individuals can play important roles in enabling collective action around resource-related problems, or spark new ideas for entrepreneurial ventures (Westley and Mintzberg, 1989; Olsson *et al.*, 2004a; Burt, 2005; Newman and Dale, 2005; Bodin and Crona, 2009). But before we can venture any further into an analysis of such potential change agents we need to look at the characteristics of the key individuals we have identified as having these structurally advantageous positions (i.e. categorized as hubs of type R5 or R6).

4.5   INDIVIDUAL CHARACTERISTICS AND POTENTIAL AGENCY FOR CHANGE

Looking more closely at the individuals occupying the hub positions (R5 and R6) we find that the two connector hubs (R6) revealed in the first round are both ring net fishers from Pemba (Table 4.1). No provincial hub (R5) was identified in the first round. In the second round, another seven connector hubs were found. Of these, three were also fishers using ring nets, two were fishers using seine nets, one is a fish trader, and another runs a local business. The one and only provincial hub revealed in the second round was occupied by a person with an unspecified non-fishery related occupation. In the third round three more provincial hubs emerged: one more person with unspecified occupation and two fishers using seine net and ring net, respectively. Finally, in the third round three more connector hubs emerged. Of these, one was a fisher using seine nets, one was a fisher using gill nets, and the third was a fish trader.

How can this information help us understand the social fabric surrounding local ecological knowledge exchange in the village and how it may affect the ability of the community to transform from a situation of virtual impasse, towards the direction of sustainable fisheries management? To begin, it is interesting to note that as we relax the criterion, ring net fishers keep on occupying the role of connector hubs. Furthermore, seine net fishers increase in importance and both types of fishers are highly over-represented in our list of hubs, particularly connector hubs (of 12 connector hubs only four had a different occupation although these two kinds of fishers only constitute approximately a third of the community at large; see Bodin and Crona, 2008). This could, although only partially, be attributed to the fact that the communication network of ecological knowledge was used in identifying key persons; thus non-resource related occupations such as local businessmen may have been discriminated against. This does not, however, explain why there are no other types of fishers, farmers, or fish traders (except two) among these individuals. In this context it is also worth noting that beach seine net fishing has been illegal in Kenya for several years. It seems highly unlikely that someone engaged in an illegal fishing practice would coordinate or garner support for new or better fishing regulations and enforcement. These results concur with previous findings regarding the skewed representation of identified key individuals versus the community at large, and how this might contribute to the lack of collective initiatives to deal with resource degradation (Bodin and Crona, 2008; Crona and Bodin, 2010).

Second, we see that all seine net fishers, and all but two ring net fishers, are owners of the gear which could make these individuals more inclined to preserve the status quo (Table 4.1). Third, ring net fishers have been shown in a previous study to focus their fishing efforts mostly outside the lagoon and reef where most of the current degradation has occurred (Crona, 2006). These fishers target reef-associated but semi-pelagic stocks which migrate outside the range of the community seascape. This has been suggested as one reason why ring net fishers do not appear to be concerned with declining fish stocks (Crona and Bodin, 2006; Bodin and Crona, 2008). Finally, from a broader perspective, homogeneity among the identified key individuals is likely to reduce their collective ability to perceive and synthesize new information and knowledge of different kinds (see e.g. Reagans and McEvily, 2003; Oh et al., 2004). As such it reduces their ability to adapt to new circumstances (e.g. the decline of fish stocks), potentially contributing to lowering the community's adaptive capacity (e.g. Berkes et al., 2003) and the ability to respond to change and disturbances by initiating transformation towards more sustainable practices.

Approximately a third of identified connector and provincial hubs (i.e. the key individuals) originate from Pemba. This may seem like an insignificant number but it should be kept in mind that these are semi-migrant fishers, usually with homes and families in their place of origin as well. This is likely to have a negative impact on their sense of place and responsibility for the local resource, as has been demonstrated in previous work (Crona and Bodin, 2006).

As stated, so far all this largely concurs with our previous findings (Crona and Bodin, 2006; Bodin and Crona, 2008, Crona and Bodin, 2010). However, there are some findings that deserve further attention. One is the fact that connector hubs are much more common than provincial hubs. As said above, connector hubs are likely very important in bringing different subgroups together and allowing for new information and knowledge to be shared among actors otherwise not well connected (assuming that they, in their potential role as gate keepers, actually allow for such exchange). In this community, there appears to be no immediate shortage of such subgroup-spanning brokers. The characteristics of the persons occupying this role are however a skewed representation of the village as a whole which, as discussed above, could be problematic. Nonetheless, given the existence of many potential brokers among subgroups who could help in, for example, instigating the development of common resource regulations, why has the inertia in resource management, alluded to above, not been overcome? In order to extend our suggested explanations even further, we will now direct our attention to the subgroups.

As said previously, there are very few provincial hubs (R5). The original threshold z_t had to be relaxed from 2.5 to 1.5 in order to identify more than just one individual of this type. This relative abundance of connector hubs but lack of provincial hubs tells us that when it comes to communication of local ecological knowledge strictly *within* subgroups, there are few individuals who, at this level, possess a central position. Remember that a provincial hub mainly has links within his or her own subgroup whereas a connector hub has relatively more links to other subgroups. In other words, at the subgroup level there are few subgroup members who possess significantly more within-subgroup links than any other member (as revealed by the very low number of provincial hubs). In network terminology, all this implies that the level of *centralization* within subgroups is quite low (Freeman, 1979).

Hence, of the fairly limited number of hubs, most of them have a relatively large proportion of their links to members of other subgroups (i.e. them being connector and not provincial hubs). The abundance of links crossing subgroup borders might make these hubs less focused on what is going on strictly within their own group (i.e. they might be less "loyal" to their subgroup). This could present a barrier to change since initiating change and collective action requires the ability of a group of actors to prioritize and coordinate activities (Olsson *et al.*, 2004a; Ostrom, 2005), and these abilities have been shown to be constrained by low degrees of network centralization (Leavitt, 1951; Sandström, 2008). As such, the coordinating and prioritizing ability at the *subgroup* level may be quite limited. It should be noted that there are other structural characteristics of networks that have been found to be positively associated with collective action which we have not investigated here (e.g. level of cohesiveness). Nonetheless, since the literature suggests that the possibility for large change in a system (such as transformations) is enhanced if there are opportunities for change to take place incrementally in smaller steps and/or at smaller scales (Ostrom, 1990), the lack of centralization at the subgroup level, along with the suggested negative impacts this may have on subgroups' abilities for collective action, presents a challenge and perhaps a barrier to transforming to sustainable governance. Observed inertia in a system such as the one studied here could therefore be caused by the fact that the ability to coordinate activities and achieve "small wins" at the subgroup level seems quite limited due to the lack of provincial hubs. If this is true, any initiative to successfully change the current situation would have to take place at the community level since there are so few provincial hubs to facilitate change at the smaller subgroup level. In other words, there appears to be less possibility for small wins and incremental change at scales below that of the entire village. Furthermore, of the few identified provincial hubs, only two of four are involved in fishing (for the most relaxed criteria where $z_t = 1.5$), and these two fishers are semi-migrant fishers likely to be least inclined to change the current state of affairs. This appears to further limit the possibility for subgroups to initiate a transformation to more sustainable resource management practices.

In summarizing our findings we can see that although our network analysis identified a number of hubs (which we suggest puts them in potential key positions for enabling collective action for change), most of them were found to be connector hubs, as opposed to provincial hubs. When we combine this analysis with a more in-depth look at the characteristics of the individuals occupying each hub position we can discern patterns that may explain the lack of collective action surrounding the fishery in the community studied here. We also suggest that lack of provincial hubs to initiate change and collective action at the subgroup level may have hampered the process of change. However, the difficulty in inferring causality from one case study naturally remains and we note that without longitudinal data much of our argumentation must remain speculative at this point. Furthermore, it is essential to note that for change to happen in a system such as this one, where inhabitants are reliant on largely common-pool resources, hoping for and promoting small wins may not necessarily be a viable way towards change in fishing practices and governance. The reason for this is that changes in harvesting behaviors of a subset of fishers using the same resources as other fishers not willing to change resembles a prisoner's dilemma (Ostrom *et al.*, 1994). As such, changing behavior at the subgroup level might be highly irrational even though the current situation is characterized by over-harvesting (c.f. Hardin, 1968). Network analysis cannot solve this dilemma but can help researchers understand some of the social aspects contributing to governance outcomes which are difficult to investigate using other approaches.

Reflections

Since this study relies on the same data set as in Chapter 9, our reflections on social network and ecological system boundaries, units of analysis, data-gathering issues, and ethical concerns are presented in Chapter 9 and are not duplicated here.

Explanatory power of SNA

Due to the nature of the study (a single case study), we were not able to infer whether the identified characteristics of either the network or the individuals actually had something to do with the outcome variable (i.e. the lack of common initiative to deal with the declining fisheries). However, we feel that the SNA approach allowed us to come up with a set of elaborated and hopefully well-grounded hypotheses that could be taken as inputs to more elaborated studies preferably adopting a multi-case study approach.

Non-network data

Data were gathered on the personal characteristics of all respondents. However, a more elaborate study of which personal characteristics can account for an actor's ability to make the most use of an influential position in a network would require a more developed and theoretically grounded approach and would typically involve a combination of quantitative and qualitative methods.

Social network analysis is static?

As briefly discussed, in this chapter we treat the structure of the network as fixed. However, we acknowledge that the structure itself is an outcome of social processes and deliberate action. Fortunately, the number of studies that addresses networks as outcome variables is increasing. Thus, we believe that the dichotomy of whether network structures should be seen as causes or consequence is going to be less relevant since we foresee a development where both perspectives will become more integrated and the mutual feedback mechanism between structure and processes is made more explicit.

REFERENCES

Acheson, J. (1988). *The Lobster Gangs of Maine*. Hanover, NH: University Press of New England.

Aldrich, H. (1999). *Organizations Evolving*. London: Sage.

Barratt, C. (2009). Netting the benefits now or later? Exploring the relationship between risk and sustainability in Lake Victoria fisheries, Uganda. PhD thesis. School of International Development, University of East Anglia, Norwich.

Berkes, F., C. Folke and J. Colding (2003). *Navigating Social-Ecological Systems: Building Resilience for Complexity and Change*. Cambridge: Cambridge University Press.

Bodin, Ö. and B. I. Crona (2008). Management of natural resources at the community level: exploring the role of social capital and leadership in a rural fishing community. *World Development*, **36**(12), 2763–2779.

Bodin, Ö. and B. I. Crona (2009). The role of social networks in natural resource governance: what relational patterns make a difference? *Global Environmental Change*, **19**, 366–374.

Borgatti, S. P., M. G. Everett and L. C. Freeman (2002). *UCINET for Windows: Software for Social Network Analysis*. Harvard, Cambridge, MA: Analytic Technologies.

Borgatti, S. P. and P. C. Foster (2003). The network paradigm in organizational research: a review and typology. *Journal of Management*, **29**(6), 991–1013.

Burt, R. (2005). *Brokerage and Closure: An Introduction to Social Capital*. Oxford: Oxford University Press.

Crona, B. I. (2006). Supporting and enhancing development of heterogeneous ecological knowledge among resource users in a Kenyan seascape. *Ecology and Society*, **11**(1), art 32, http://www.ecologyandsociety.org/vol11/iss1/art32/.

Crona, B. I. and Ö. Bodin (2006). What you know is who you know? Patterns of communication as prerequisites for co-management. *Ecology and Society*, **11**(2), art 7.

Crona, B. I. and Ö. Bodin (2010). Power asymmetries in small-scale fisheries: a barrier to governance transformability? *Ecology and Society*, **15**(4), art 32.

Degenne, A. and M. Forsé (1999). *Introducing Social Networks*. London: Sage.

Freeman, L. (1979). Centrality in social networks. Conceptual clarifications. *Social Networks*, **1**, 215–239.

Freeman, L. C. (1997). Uncovering organizational hierarchies. *Computational and Mathematical Organization Theory*, **3**(1), 5–18.

Garud, R., C. Hardy and S. Maguire (2007). Institutional entrepreneurship as embedded agency: an introduction to the special issue. *Organization Studies*, **28**, 957–969.

Glaesel, H. (1997). Fisher, parks and power: the socio-environmental dimentions of marine resource decline and protection on the Kenya coast. PhD thesis. University of Wisconsin-Madison.

Guimerà, R. and L. A. N. Amaral (2005a). Cartography of complex networks: modules and universal roles. *Journal of Statistical Mechanics: Theory and Experiments*, art P02001.

Guimerà, R. and L. A. N. Amaral (2005b). Functional cartography of complex metabolic networks. *Nature*, **433**, 895–900.

Hardin, G. (1968). The tragedy of the commons. *Science*, **162**, 1243–1248.

King, A. (2000). Managing without institutions: the role of communication networks in governing resource access and control, PhD thesis. University of Warwick.

Krishna, A. (2002). *Active Social Capital. Tracing the Roots of Development and Democracy*. New York, NY: Columbia University Press.

Leavitt, H. (1951). Some effects of certain communication patterns on group performance. *Journal of Abnormal and Social Psychology*, **46**, 38–50.

Maguire, S., C. Hardy and T. B. Lawrence (2004). Institutional entrepreneurship in emerging fields: HIV/AIDS treatment advocacy in Canada. *Academy of Management Journal*, **47**, 657–679.

Marsden, P. V. (1990). Network data and measurement. *Annual Review of Sociology*, **16**, 435–463.

Newman, L. L. and A. Dale (2005). Network structure, diversity, and proactive resilience building: a response to Tompkins and Adger. *Ecology and Society*, **10**(1), art 2.

Oh, H., M.-H. Chung and G. Labianca (2004). Group social capital and group effectiveness: the role of informal socializing ties. *Academy of Management Journal*, **47**(6), 860–875.

Olsson, P., C. Folke and F. Berkes (2004a). Adaptive comanagement for building resilience in social-ecological systems. *Environmental Management*, **34**(1), 75–90.

Olsson, P., C. Folke and T. Hahn (2004b). Social-ecological transformation for ecosystem management: the development of adaptive co-management of a wetland landscape in southern Sweden. *Ecology and Society*, **9**(4), 2.

Olsson, P., L. Gunderson, S. Carpenter *et al.* (2006). Shooting the rapids: navigating transitions to adaptive governance of social-ecological systems. *Ecology and Society*, **11**(1), art 18.

Ostrom, E. (1990). *Governing the Commons: The Evolution of Institutions for Collective Action*. Cambridge: Cambridge University Press.

Ostrom, E. (2005). *Understanding Institutional Diversity*. Princeton, NJ: Princeton University Press.

Ostrom, E., R. Gardner and J. Walker (1994). *Rules, Games and Common-pool Resources*. Ann Arbor, MI: University of Michigan Press.

Reagans, R. and B. McEvily (2003). Network structure and knowledge transfer: the effects of cohesion and range. *Administrative Science Quarterly*, **48**(2), 240–267.

Sandström, A. (2008). Policy networks: the relation between structure and performance. PhD thesis. Business Adninistration and Social Sciences. Luleå, Luleå Technical University.

Schultz, L. (2009). Nurturing resilience in social-ecological systems. PhD thesis, Systems Ecology. Stockholm, Stockholm University.

Westley, F. and H. Mintzberg (1989). Visionary leadership and strategic management. *Strategic Management Journal*, **10**, 17–32.

5

Social network analysis for stakeholder selection and the links to social learning and adaptive co-management

5.1 INTRODUCTION

There is now widespread recognition in the academic and wider community that those who are affected by, or who have the power to affect environmental decision-making processes, have a right to be consulted (e.g. the EU's Aarhus Convention[1] enshrines this right in law). There is also growing evidence that their involvement may enhance the quality of decisions made (Prell *et al.*, 2008). However, these benefits depend upon appropriate representation of stakeholders, and this poses significant challenges. In many cases, the population of stakeholders is unknown, and thus, locating a representative sample is difficult. In addition, different stakeholders are likely to have different views about what are the relevant issues, and who are the most relevant parties to invite to the table. In this chapter, we put forward social network analysis as a complementary tool to help unravel who is a relevant stakeholder. In doing so, we argue that including a network analysis of stakeholders demonstrates another dimension to the idea of "diversity" in considering "wide representation" of stakeholders. In addition to trying to capture a diversity of perspectives from diverse stakeholder categories, we argue for considerations of diversity based on social networks, i.e. diverse positions within a wider network structure, and demonstrate how social network analysis can be used for uncovering such positions.

[1] http://www.unece.org/env/pp/

Social Networks and Natural Resource Management: Uncovering the Fabric of Environmental Governance, ed. Ö. Bodin and C. Prell. Published by Cambridge University Press.
© Cambridge University Press 2011.

This chapter thus details the process of stakeholder selection from our own experiences in the Peak District National Park, located in England. In particular, we discuss how social network analysis was combined with data from interviews, focus groups, and questionnaires, as well as knowledge of the local geography, to uncover and situate the range of relevant stakeholders. We learned as we went along, tacking back and forth between different kinds of data and emerging concerns of stakeholders. Uncovering the social network of stakeholders involved rounds of interviews and analyses to reveal different communication patterns and network structural features. In addition, our network findings provided powerful heuristics for stakeholders to see some of the communication patterns found within the Peak District community. Thus, in what follows, we offer readers not only a detailed description of the processes by which we came to use social network analysis within the context of stakeholder selection, but also offer some guidelines and insights into how we see this tool best being used for other resource management initiatives that aim to involve a small, yet representative group of participants.

Our study in the Peak District (Prell *et al.*, 2007, 2008) is not the first one to make use of SNA for stakeholder selection (see e.g. Maiolo *et al.*, 1992), and we have also continued to refine our understanding and use of this tool for stakeholder selection purposes (Prell *et al.*, 2009; Reed *et al.*, 2010). Guiding our approach have been the theoretical and methodological frameworks regarding learning (Kolb, 1984), social learning (Reed *et al.*, in press), and adaptive co-management (Armitage *et al.*, 2008). These frameworks, all important to discussions regarding natural resource management and governance, have been introduced in Chapter 3 of this book, and at the end of the current chapter, they will be discussed in relation to the case study described in the following sections.

5.2 UNCERTAINTIES AND LEARNING: OUR PROJECT AIMS

Land managers in UK uplands are faced with a number of challenges. Such challenges include regulations introduced by the EU, declining subsidies, unstable market prices, increasing input costs, and a changing population in rural areas (CRC, 2010; Reed *et al.*, 2010). Sensitive to this context in which stakeholders were embedded, our research team's wider aims were to bring stakeholders together through a learning process, aimed at combining knowledge from local stakeholders, policy makers, and social and natural scientists to help land managers better anticipate, monitor, and sustainably manage rural change in UK uplands (Dougill *et al.*, 2006).

The study our team developed involved a three-phase cycle, where social network analysis was situated in the first phase of that cycle, and consequently, affected all other aspects of the research. The first phase emphasized "understanding the context" as well as developing an understanding of the boundaries of the social-ecological system implied in the term "UK uplands." This first phase was done collaboratively, i.e. through meetings with our research team and through engaging with stakeholders. The second phase involved identifying sustainability goals, strategies that could be used to reach these goals, and indicators to measure progress towards these goals. The third phase (which we are still implementing) uses integrated modeling tools to evaluate the management options that emerge from this process in a multi-stakeholder, participatory framework. Taken together, our learning process has sought to integrate knowledge from different sources, and then transfer that knowledge back out into the social-ecological system to help land managers make more informed decisions about their day-to-day practices. Social network analysis has been critical for the first phase of this process, where we were challenged to define the context and boundaries of both the ecological and social system(s). As will be seen in the following discussion, social network analysis was part of an overall iterative stakeholder selection process, and it was closely intertwined with stakeholders' opinions and views regarding land management, ecological scales, and ecosystem services.

5.3   STUDY SITE: THE PEAK DISTRICT NATIONAL PARK[2]

The Peak District National Park (PDNP) was established in 1951 as the UK's first national park. Its location between the major cities of Manchester to the west, Sheffield to the east, and Leeds to north, and the fact that almost 50% of England's population lives within reasonable traveling distance, makes the PDNP one of the world's most visited national parks (Peak District National Park, 2004). UK national parks do

---

[2] We had three sites, two of which involved social network analysis. For detailed information on SNA in research site two, visit Prell *et al.* (forthcoming).

not exclude people from living and working within them, and in the case of the PDNP, approximately 38 000 people are resident within the park boundaries (AONB Office, 2009). In addition, most of the land is in private ownership rather than owned by national government (with a share of less than 2%).

The PDNP is typical of the UK uplands and many marginal mountain areas of Europe that are facing pressures from demographic change, policy reform, and environmental problems. As people retire to or buy holiday homes in rural areas, key workers are forced out, thus creating labor shortages; farming is economically marginal and reliant on subsidies, which are currently undergoing major changes due to reform of the EU's Common Agricultural Policy; and much of the PDNP falls within environmentally sensitive areas containing internationally important habitats and Sites of Special Scientific Interest (SSSIs), which are threatened by soil erosion, biodiversity loss, and climate change (see Dougill *et al.*, 2006 for more information on the study site).

In addition, the PDNP provides a range of ecosystem services which encourage and support uses such as sheep grazing, recreation, drinking water provision, grouse shooting, and agriculture (Hubacek *et al.*, 2009). Taken together, this complex context of challenges and ecosystem services with different spatial extensions and boundaries made the process of identifying stakeholders and stakes difficult for our research team; uncovering who and what was relevant involved a tacking back and forth between different dimensions of the overall social-ecological system. Thus, geographical boundaries, scales, and ecosystem services were balanced against knowledge of the stakeholders' social network and stakeholder categories.

5.3.1   The first phase: scoping study

5.3.1.1   *Establishing study region boundaries*

Our project began with a scoping study, with the aim of uncovering important contextual information regarding the PDNP uplands areas. The first step for our team involved reaching agreement on what defined an upland area, and then agreeing upon a geographical boundary for our research site. Although stakeholders and members of our research team could often point to areas of a map and identify regions as being uplands, there was no clear definition of what uplands were. For example, uplands could be defined via their soil characteristics (i.e. peat lands) or vegetation (i.e. moorlands and blanket bogs). They could also be identified as land above the upper limit of enclosed farmland, or land classed by the EU as "Less Favored Areas" because of their low agricultural productivity (Averis *et al.*, 2004; Reed *et al.*, in press). For the purposes of this research, we chose altitude (specifically land above 300 m elevation) as the main criterion for defining uplands. Such a criterion, we realized, automatically identified land that matched the other identifying characteristics listed above. Later prioritization of *which* particular uplands areas would be our study's focus would come at a slightly later stage in the project, through consultation with stakeholders.

5.3.1.2   *Identifying ecosystem services and associated stakeholders*

In the next step, members of our team approached an initial group of stakeholders through use of a gatekeeper organization, i.e. the Moors for the Future (MFF). The MFF was deemed by our team as a good, initial contact as this organization itself comprised various groups and individuals in the Peak District dealing with issues of conservation and land management (Hubacek and Reed, 2009). As such, the MFF had wide knowledge of many of the relevant groups and stakeholders, and they offered that knowledge to us to help in organizing an initial focus group. This focus group comprised members of the MFF team, as well as representatives from the Peak District National Park Authority and the National Trust. Representatives from these organizations were selected due to their cross-cutting interests that included conservation, farming, game management, carbon management, and recreation.

The purpose of this focus group was twofold: first, to develop a list of stakes, issues, and services relevant to uplands management in the Peak District; and second, to identify which kinds of organizations and individuals were deemed relevant for the issues and services found on the list. The list of ecosystem services and associated land uses included sheep farming, biodiversity, provision of drinking water, recreation, carbon storage, field sports and game management, and forestry.[3] The list of issues, which were tightly intertwined with these

---

[3] At the beginning of the project in 2005 many of the stakeholders were not yet familiar with the notion of ecosystem services (ES) and we used the concept fairly loosely. Interestingly, the knowledge and use of the terminology has improved since then given the considerable focus on government agencies on ES (see Millennium Ecosystem Assessment, 2005).

uses, included CAP reform, heather- and grass-burning regulations, carbon offsetting opportunities, and climate change. After this list of stakes, issues, and ecosystem services and land uses was developed, the focus group then brainstormed relevant individuals and organizations that could represent these different interests. This brainstorm resulted in a list of over 200 names. All who were nominated were seen as involved in or affected by upland management in some capacity in the Peak District.

5.3.1.3   Categorization based on ecosystem services or land uses

In an attempt to gain a handle on this large list of names, our focus group participants helped us develop a categorization scheme that was largely based upon the services participants had identified in these areas. After the focus group, our team checked and refined these categories through interviews with eight other stakeholder respondents who had not been present in the original focus group. As a result of this categorization process, six categories emerged: water companies; recreation and tourism; agriculture; conservationists; hunting grouse (consisting of owners/managers and game keepers); and statutory bodies.

We were keenly sensitive to the fact that this categorization scheme was imperfect; certain stakeholders fell under more than one category, and it was perceived that certain groups and individuals found in the original list of 200+ names were now potentially being excluded. These included residents and schools, which were not categories we ended up with, and we justified their exclusion by noting that these individuals were represented in other respects by categories such as "land owners," "tourists and recreationists," and "land managers." Although imperfect, we nonetheless opted to maintain the list we had finalized through interacting with our stakeholders.

5.3.1.4   Issue selection, geographic boundary, and ecological scale

Although the categorization of stakeholders we adopted did help to organize our list of stakeholder names, we were constrained by time and budget to a few months of data collection and analysis. This was a scoping study project, and as such, there was no opportunity to explore in depth the many issues relevant to the PDNP uplands (Reed *et al.*, 2005). Consequently, one question we asked participants in our focus group was which issue was deemed the most pressing for upland managers at the time. The issue participants offered was that of heather burning, which was receiving a lot of attention due to an ongoing and highly contentious government review of the Heather and Grass Burning Code. This review was seen by many as potentially leading to greater regulation of burning practices, and as such, burning was seen as an issue that had the potential to affect all the ecosystem services in the region. Thus, in focusing on heather burning, we were focusing our attention, directly or indirectly, on a fairly wide range of stakeholders and interrelated issues.

This decision to focus on heather burning immediately impacted our research site's geographic boundary; in the Peak District, heather burning only took place in the Dark Peak area, dominated by deep peat soils and heather moorland. In turn, these areas primarily existed in the northern parts of the park. This decision to focus on the Dark Peak in turn informed the next stages in our research study, as we were now focusing our attention on a more specific area of land with a more focused topic. Consequently, we needed to revisit our initial identification of stakeholders from earlier phases in our study.

5.3.1.5   *Social network analysis and larger ecological context*

Despite the focus on a relatively nicely bounded area we were confronted with the problem that different ecosystem services have different spatial boundaries or are even of national interest. This fact was implicitly considered by the earlier focus groups as we had a number of regional or national stakeholders in our list representing stakeholder groups or interests beyond the Dark Peak.

The initial list of 200+ names generated in our focus group applied, broadly, to the entire PDNP uplands areas. Through re-adjusting our focus to a smaller-scaled area in the Peak District, i.e. the Dark Peak, we were now no longer certain of the extent to which this 200+ boundary might need to be adjusted. Our team was also aware that the time frame for the scoping study was drawing to an end, and we wanted to explore deeply one pressing issue (heather burning), before the study's completion. Such an exploration would draw from natural scientists' previous UK upland research (Worrall *et al.*, 2003; Holden, 2005a, 2005b) as well as our own analysis of the social context in which these stakeholders were embedded.

Understanding of social context emerged partially from our focus group and interviews; this is how we had learned about

many of the economic and historical challenges currently facing
land managers of PDNP Dark Peak areas. However, we also wanted
to conduct a social network analysis to identify some additional
features of this social context. In particular, we wanted to see how
stakeholders within the Dark Peak boundary were socially tied to
one another; who communicated with whom on land management
issues, who agreed with whom on land management practices, and
where conflict relations (or difficult relations) lay between stakeholders. Answering questions of this sort would give us more
precise knowledge of the social context our team was studying,
which in turn would help inform the learning cycle we were
attempting to develop for later stages in the project.

Given our tight time schedule, we decided to sample within the
stakeholder categories we had derived, and further, to target stakeholders we knew worked or lived within the Dark Peak areas. A total of
22 interviews were conducted with respondents who were representative of the six categories and the Dark Peak area.

Social network data were gathered through a fixed-recall name
generator technique. More specifically, for each interview, we asked
the respondent the following question, "Do you communicate with
anyone from (stakeholder category named here) on upland management issues in the Peak District National Park? Please list up to five
names." We asked our respondents this question for each of the six
stakeholder categories. Although this name-generator question took
the form of a fixed-recall question, i.e. we were constraining our
respondents to only nominating five names, this limitation was
deemed necessary, given our time frame. Further, the five names
were multiplied across the six stakeholder categories, and so respondents could potentially nominate up to 30 names. In spite of this con-
straint in name-generator technique, we found that most respondents
only nominated two to three names for each category. Only two
respondents told us they wished to nominate more than five for a
particular category. The name-generator question resulted in a total
of 147 nominations. Although these nominations largely reflected the
200+ names originally derived from our initial focus group, we had
only gathered network data as such from the 22 respondents. Thus,
only 22 of the 147 actors of the resulting social network had informed
the network's structure. This was a real limitation to the network
analysis, and yet in spite of this limitation, we now had some indicators
of the network structure, and as will be seen shortly, the network data
we gathered provided a powerful heuristic for launching a discussion

with stakeholders on the communication and other social dynamics existing amongst certain stakeholder categories. Our name-generator question was followed by more detailed questions on the nature of the relational tie. In particular, we asked respondents how frequently they communicated with each nominee; the extent to which respondents perceived the tie they shared with others as being positive or "difficult," and the extent to which respondents felt their views regarding land management were in agreement with the views of their socially tied partners.

The findings from these data offered us a multi-dimensional view of the network. Respondents felt, for the most part, that they and their socially tied alters shared similar views regarding land management. Very few respondents described their relations to others as being difficult, and in those cases, the same stakeholders were repeatedly nominated, indicating that a few difficult characters existed in the group. By and large, respondents felt they got along reasonably well with those to whom they were socially tied. Finally, patterns of communication emerged between different stakeholder categories: recreationists tended to not communicate much with other categories of stakeholders, although a high number of agriculture and grouse-hunting stakeholders communicated with one another frequently. In addition, conservationist and water companies communicated frequently with one another.

5.3.1.6   *Presenting initial findings to stakeholders: building bridges with stakeholders*

These findings were presented back to our stakeholders at a conference organized by MFF, which included a mixture of academics and stakeholders (all of whom came from the 200+ list of names). In our presentation, we displayed digraphs showing the results we uncovered regarding communication patterns, levels of perceived agreement, and perceived "difficult" relations in the network. Our digraphs also indicated which actors were the most central actors, and we discussed how such central actors played bridging roles across different segments of the network.[4] We noted that our network data were incomplete, and as such, our findings and calculations for centrality could

---

[4] The actual centrality measure we used was betweenness centrality, which looks at the number of instances an individual rests on the geodesic (shortest path) between two others (see Chapter 2).

only be seen as heuristics and rough indicators of some of the communication patterns in the network. In spite of these limitations, the digraphs generated a lot of discussion; some audience members chuckled out loud at the portrayal of communication patterns within the network, audibly validating that such a portrayal was pretty accurate of the communication (or lack thereof) between certain stakeholder categories. Some audience members attempted to label the central nodes (some of the guesses were accurate), and others attempted to locate themselves in the network (again, some of the guesses were accurate). Although we kept silent during this guessing game, given our confidentiality agreement with respondents, we were nonetheless secretly pleased that these data, although incomplete, nonetheless managed to capture some important dynamics of communication amongst stakeholders.

A final positive outcome of the conference was that our network analysis was used to inform a new selection of partners for the MFF Partnership. We held a discussion with MFF about how they were selecting partners, and offered some suggestions on whom to include, based largely on our network analysis (see Prell *et al.*, 2009). Some of our suggestions were heard (not all), and the list of partners in the partnership was adjusted.

5.3.2   Second phase: more funds, stakeholder involvement, and new social network analysis

Shortly after the MFF conference, our team received news that we would receive another three years' worth of funding.[5] The first of these three years was to continue work within the Peak District, involving stakeholders in an iterative learning cycle that would focus primarily on the issue of heather burning, but also address additional concerns and issues of stakeholders. The subsequent two years would focus on other uplands areas elsewhere in the UK, including the Nidderdale Area of Outstanding Natural Beauty in the Yorkshire Dales, and a series of catchments in Galloway, Scotland.

One issue that was brought forward during the previous year's scoping study was that some stakeholders, in particular those that worked and managed the land directly, felt uncomfortable and not

---

[5] Funded by ESRC and the Rural Economy & Land Use Programme (co-sponsored by DEFRA and SEERAD with funding in-kind from Moors for the Future).

well adept at discussing land management issues in structured environments like focus groups, conferences, or workshops. Further, many felt that policy makers and others could learn more about what land managers faced, in a day-to-day manner, if they were to visit land manager's farms and other managed regions (for a detailed description of these site visits, see Reed *et al.*, in press). As a consequence of these concerns, our research team made the decision that we would devise a small number of site visits that would involve a small group of stakeholders. These site visits would take place at different estates owned or managed by a select few stakeholders. Now that we had additional funds to expand upon our goals for learning and adaptive management in the Peaks, we felt responding to this particular stakeholder request would be suitable for meeting our research aims of creating opportunities for mutual learning amongst stakeholders and researchers (for a reflection on these processes see Hubacek *et al.*, 2009).

5.3.2.1   *Social network analysis for social learning interventions and diffusion*

This decision to design site visits for stakeholders was an exciting opportunity to develop learning interventions, and from our earlier network analysis, we had a strong sense for some of the gaps in communication between certain stakeholder groups. Thus, designing site visits would provide one opportunity for some meaningful communication between different stakeholders.

Selecting stakeholders for these site visits was a delicate matter. We wanted the group to be small to allow for deliberation and a certain level of intimacy among participants. Such a desire stemmed from our larger research aims to support (social) learning among stakeholders and researchers (see discussion in Section 5.4 below). Yet we also wanted these site visits to have as wide an impact as possible. In particular, we wanted the information exchanged and the knowledge gained in these small groups to be communicated back to the larger stakeholder network in the Dark Peaks and the wider PDNP. This second desire reflected our understanding of the role social networks play in diffusing information through a larger social system (Valente, 1995); that is, if we could identify which actors might help diffuse information through the network, given these individuals' structural position within the network, we could make efforts to include these individuals in the site visits. Past research on diffusion and networks suggested we focus on uncovering who were the central actors in the network (Valente, 1995; Valente and Davis, 1999), as such central actors could act as "hubs" linking different segments of the network together, thus helping to both mobilize and diffuse information out quickly to network areas.

Taken together, we realized a more detailed network analysis on stakeholders would best aid us in selecting a subset of stakeholders for our site visits. In particular, a more precise understanding of the social network, combined with information on stakeholder categories, would help us make strategic decisions regarding stakeholder selection; different categories of stakeholder were interested in sustaining the provision of different ecosystem services from uplands, and hence tended to develop more specialist knowledge about different parts of the upland system. Thus, including a range of diverse categories could reflect these differences in use, interest, and potential knowledge. In contrast, a more rigorous network analysis could reveal which actors were central, along with a detailed view of the different subsections of the network. We were looking for central individuals who could diffuse information to the wider network structure, and thus we wanted these individuals to also represent different stakeholder categories, as well as different peripheral areas of the network.

During this time, MFF had re-designed their MFF Partnership, and this new partnership had been constructed partly on the basis of some of the insights provided by our team's earlier scoping study (see Section 3.1). Thus, we focused our attentions on this new partnership, and conducted our new social network analysis on this group. Towards this end, we administered a questionnaire to all partners present ($n = 51$) at one of the partnership meetings. The questionnaire contained a roster of 60 names, where all members listed on the roster were members of the MFF Partnership. Each respondent was asked to circle names on the roster of those whom they knew, and then to answer the same set of questions about each circled name found on the roster. The questions asked included the frequency of communication stakeholders held with one another; perceptions of understanding regarding others' views on land management; and levels of perceived agreement on issues of land management. In addition, respondents were asked to categorize themselves as falling under one of the following stakeholder categories: (i) water; (ii) agriculture; (iii) grouse; (iv) conservation; (v) statutory bodies; and (vi) recreation and tourism. These data were then organized into a set of matrices, and a number of analyses performed. These analyses are discussed below.

As with the scoping study, our first analyses looked at measures of centrality. As different centrality measures capture slightly different conceptualizations of the term, we applied two measures of centrality to identify two slightly different communication roles in the network; *degree centrality*, which is calculated from counting the number of direct ties to others an actor holds, was used as an indicator to measure which stakeholders were the most "active communicators" in the network; *betweenness centrality*, which reflects the number of times an individual falls on the shortest path between two (otherwise) disconnected others, was used in our study to alert us to individuals who seemed to hold different segments of the network together.

Our findings showed a small portion of stakeholders with relatively high centrality scores across both measures, and these central individuals tended to be conservationists and grouse-hunters. As such, we felt reliance only on centrality measures biased our selection too much in the direction of only two stakeholder categories. At the same time, randomly selecting from the larger portion of "less central" stakeholders was not an appealing solution, i.e. we wanted selections to ultimately stem from a more rigorous analysis of the network structure. Towards this end, we re-analyzed our network data to look at structural features beyond those of centrality. In particular, we made use of a *positional analysis procedure*, which clusters individuals together according to their similarity in social ties to others, and as such, identifies unique areas or subgroupings within the network. Essentially, a positional analysis looks at the extent to which any given pair of actors holds the same or similar pattern in their ties to others, and if two actors are linked to *exactly* the same others, they are considered "*structurally equivalent*," and as such, they occupy the same "position" in the network (see Chapter 2 for more details).

In locating which stakeholders occupied which positions in the network, we were able to gain a more refined sense of the structure of the network, and this provided a means for selecting stakeholders that represented different areas within the overall network structure. Thus, we combined our positional analysis results with the results of our centrality analyses, and these two pieces of information gained from the network were combined with information on stakeholders' categories. Our resulting list included individuals from the network who (i) represented unique network positions; (ii) were the most central stakeholders within these positional groupings; and (iii) represented the range of six stakeholder categories. More specifically, our selection process took the following steps:

(i)   We first took the most central stakeholder from each network position. This first step ended in a list that was still dominated by stakeholders from the conservation category.

(ii) To include other categories, we over-sampled from the network positions that held the most diverse composition of stakeholder categories (these were positions 7–9 in Table 5.1). Again, our final choices from these two positions were guided by stakeholder category and centrality scores.

Our final list is shown in Table 5.1.

These new findings were presented to six key stakeholders during a focus group, who believed the new proposed combination of participants were more likely to be able to learn from each other, and to bring that knowledge back to their peers in the wider community. The only major change that was suggested during this focus group was to supplement this participant list with more high-level (Peak District National Park) decision-makers, so that the site visits could have greater influence over national policy. This last major change in including national decision-makers is an issue we shall address in more detail in the last section of the chapter.

Figure 5.1 summarizes the different steps leading to our final stakeholder selection found in Table 5.1.

Table 5.1. *Final selection based on new social network analysis, stakeholder category, and centrality scores.*

Stakeholder [1]	Category	Position ID	Betweenness score	Degree score
Alison	Conservation	1	29	21
Fred	Conservation	4	168	46
Jeremy	Agriculture	6	19	26
Dave	Agriculture	7	128	46
Eric	Grouse	7	33	35
Judy	Recreation & tourism	8	5	10
Julian	Statutory body	8	208	51
Katy	Water	9	1	17

[1] All names have been changed for confidentiality purposes.

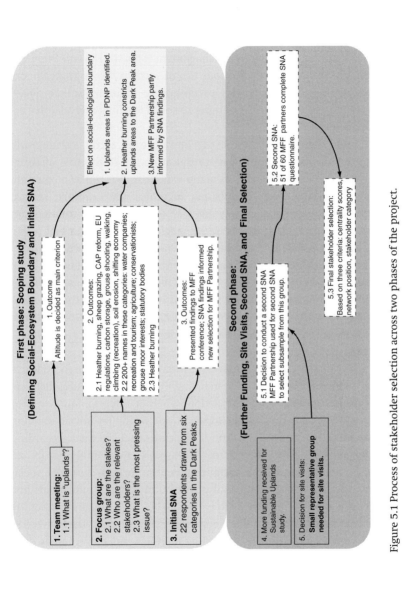

Figure 5.1 Process of stakeholder selection across two phases of the project.

5.4   CONNECTING TO THE WIDER LITERATURE

The above discussion offers a detailed description of our team's use of social network analysis, alongside other methods and tools, for stakeholder selection. Selecting stakeholders was key to meeting larger aims of the project pertaining to participatory, stakeholder involvement, social learning, and adaptive management. This section will therefore highlight in more detail how our use of social network analysis connects with wider discussions pertaining to natural resource governance, i.e. the literature pertaining to social learning and adaptive co-management.

As noted in Chapter 3, the literature on social learning and adaptive co-management pays special attention to the role of social networks. Social networks, in many ways, can be seen as a common thread binding these discussions together: for example, several authors note that the management of social-ecological systems can benefit from relevant individuals engaging with one another, learning from one another, and hence enhancing their adaptive capacity to manage these complex environments (Fazey and Marton, 2002; Fazey *et al.*, 2005; Folke *et al.*, 2005). Thus, adaptive co-management is linked to ideas of learning via social interaction and the practices of a community (Lave and Wenger, 1991; Wenger, 1998), and it is through social networks that such interaction occurs (Wellman, 1988).

Given this emphasis on social interaction to enhance social learning, and hence, adaptive co-management, it is not surprising that support exists on how such interaction, whether intentionally designed (e.g. via participatory workshops) or not facilitates social learning (Cundill, 2010) and the quality of decisions that are made regarding management options (Bandura, 1977; Pea, 1993; Pahl-Wostl, *et al.*, 2007). As noted above, social interaction occurs through social networks; the social relationships that build between individuals in a network allow for diverse perspectives to be shared, leading hopefully to common frameworks of understanding (Schusler and Decker, 2003), and joint problem-solving regarding complex, uncertain issues (Lee, 1993; Dryzek, 1997).

Research on social networks has long shown how networks can influence people's opinions, behaviors, and views (Hunter *et al.*, 1991; Friedkin, 1998; Katz and Lazarsfeld, 2006; Winter *et al.*, 2007; Schwenk and Reimer, 2008; Mercken *et al.*, 2009). Such influence can occur on a one-to-one basis (Erickson, 1988); but more often, the larger network structure in which individual actors are embedded play an important role in influencing what people know, whom they interact with, and who emerges as powerful (Cook *et al.*, 1983; Coleman, 1990; Krackhardt, 1998; Yamaguchi, 2000; Prell *et al.*, forthcoming). Finally, if deliberation (as opposed to simple knowledge transmission) occurs via networks, this can allow for further opportunities to influence network members, and hence, encourage learning (Rist *et al.*, 2007; Newig *et al.*, 2009).

Thus, one contribution of our team to this literature on social learning, adaptive co-management, and networks was to move an *appreciation* for the role of social networks to a more *formal*, analytical approach. In doing so, our team attempted to harness this knowledge of networks and the structure of these networks, alongside other information on the research context, for the practical purpose of stakeholder selection. Such a shift is rather significant; much of the literature on social learning focuses on the interactions themselves, e.g. the importance of deliberation, trust, and exchanges of information that flow through social relations (Cole and Engestrom, 1993; Pea, 1993; Leeuwis and Pyburn, 2002; Davidson-Hunt, 2006). Yet in the absence of systematic tools and knowledge regarding social networks, such attention to social interaction remains partial. That is, it is not enough to look at how social interaction can lead to meaningful deliberation and learning, but rather, one needs to take a look at the *wider network* in which such interactions take place, as well as the *structure* of that wider network to fully understand the potential for individual network members, and the network as a whole, to change and/or learn. Uncovering which actors are central, which are peripheral, the different positions within a network and the overall network structure can help analysts and practitioners to understand, and even possibly predict, the extent to which deliberative dialogues, and hence learning, might be feasible. For example, one might ask, "is the network fragmented into disconnected subnets, or are there only a few central actors holding a network together?" If the latter, then one might not find much cohesion in the network as a whole (Prell, 2011), and hence not much deliberation over resource management matters (Newig *et al.*, 2009). Thus, understanding, and harnessing, the knowledge of a network's structure can help in designing participatory processes geared towards social learning and adaptive management.

5.5 CONCLUSIONS

This chapter described an iterative, mixed method approach to stakeholder analysis and selection, where social network analysis proved key in not only identifying the range of stakeholders via their communication paths, but also in helping make well-informed choices about how to select a subsample of stakeholders for participatory dialogues. Guided by literature and past research on stakeholder participation, social learning, and adaptive co-management, we devised an approach that included a mixture of individuals from different categories and from different areas of the network to create a more balanced configuration of individuals for participatory dialogue. Time constraints have not allowed us to evaluate the extent to which individuals and the network, as a whole, "changed" as a result of our carefully designed subgroup of stakeholders and our site visits. Our intention and hope, however, has been that diverse stakeholders could challenge stereotypes and break down traditional barriers between categories and groups as they build relations with each other and/or strengthen those already in existence. In this way, it may be possible to build trust and forge multi-stakeholder partnerships that can over time accommodate multiple views, and work constructively towards negotiated goals regarding management of the uplands.

Reflections

Deciding the unit of analysis

We attempted to use the individual as the unit of measurement and analysis for both research sites, yet we experienced some problems along the way. When we asked individual respondents, "with whom do you discuss land management issues pertaining to [Nidderdale or the Peak District]?" the responses given to us were not always other individuals. Some respondents opted to simply name an organization, e.g. "Natural England," whilst others simply stated a category of users such as "other farmers in the area." Our field workers tried to probe for actual individual names, e.g. "Is there anyone within this organization, in particular, you speak with on a regular basis?" Yet sometimes this strategy failed as well. Some respondents simply felt uncomfortable nominating other individuals, and we had to respect these respondents' wishes to refrain from offering actual names.

When it came time for analysis, we did toy with the idea of doing an analysis on the organizational or categorical level as opposed to the individual level, yet ultimately opted to remain at the individual level of analysis. This had to do with the fact that we, ultimately, were trying to select a small subsample of individual stakeholder participants for our project. Thus, in instances where respondents did not offer concrete names, we had to treat these data as omissions for purposes of analysis.

Defining network boundaries

We started with a focus group, where approximately 200 names of individuals and organizations were listed by participants. We then approached eight other stakeholders, who had not participated in the focus group, to get their nominations. This list was large, and we conducted an initial "scoping" social network analysis, by interviewing 22 individuals, each representing a different stakeholder category. These respondents largely replicated the list of 200 names, and we were able to run some initial analyses to get a "feel" for the network and network structure. These data helped to inform the final list of partners to be included in the MFF Partnership. The MFF Partnership that emerged during the course of our study included 60 partners, and it was this list of 60 partners that we used for our second social network analysis in the Peak District. Thus, the 60 partners upon which we conducted our second network analysis were not reflective of the "full" network of 200+ names, yet for purposes of studying how a defined group of individuals might be related to one another, we made the decision to treat the partnership of 60 individuals as the complete network.

Data-gathering issues

Gathering SNA data is very time consuming; one name-generator question, followed by some name-interpreter questions, can generate a lot of data and take a lot of time from a respondent. We also felt that the data needed to be gathered through interviews, as this would better ensure that respondents were understanding the nature of the data we were trying to gather (SNA questionnaires are still relatively unfamiliar to many people).

In situations where we needed to rely on snowball sampling to outline the network boundary, we used more name-generator questions; for example, we asked "with whom do you communicate" but we also asked other questions, such as "are there places or meetings where land management issues tend to get discussed? [and then who was present at the meeting]" and "Think back on your last decision regarding land management. With whom (if anyone) did you discuss this issue/decision?" In some instances, respondents offered the same list of names for each name-generator question, but in the majority of cases, different name-generator questions elicited different nominations.

Ethical issues

These have already been touched upon: respondents felt uneasy offering names of individuals. In addition, there was great interest in the digraphs that could be drawn from the data gathered, yet we were not able to portray the names of nodes in the digraph for confidentiality reasons. Thus, many respondents, upon seeing the digraphs, felt slightly frustrated; they saw the potential power of such an analysis and digraph, yet not being able to see the names associated with the nodes offered little real value when looking at the digraph.

Explanatory power of SNA

We were amazed at how much SNA data seemed to explain (or predict) similarity in stakeholder views regarding land management. Typically, the literature suggests that user groups or stakeholder categories are better predictors for how people think and behave in relation to land; in our case, these sorts of variables did not predict respondents' views very well, and individuals seemed to agree more with those to whom they were socially tied, regardless of the other person's stakeholder category.

Non-network data

Our entire stakeholder analysis relied on a mixture of methods; we used focus groups and interviews to explore the range of relevant issues and stakeholders. SNA provided more precision when it came to understanding how stakeholders communicated with one another, and the data also helped us categorize stakeholders according to their position within the communication network.

Is social network analysis static?

All cross-sectional research can be criticized for only offering a snapshot of the social phenomenon of interest. The same is true of social network data that have been gathered in the context of cross-sectional studies. Longitudinal research, however, can be done with networks, and there are now applications and statistical models to handle such "dynamics." Further, the use of agent-based modeling is often used as a tool for exploring network formation and change.

REFERENCES

AONB Office (2009). *Nidderdale Area of Outstanding Natural Beauty Management Plan 2009–2014.* Pateley Bridge: AONB Office, pp. 1–40.

Armitage, D., M. Marschke and R. Plummer (2008). Adaptive co-management and the paradox of learning. *Global Environmental Change,* **18**, 86–98.

Averis, A. M., A. B. G. Averis, H. J. B. Birks *et al.* (2004). *An Illustrated Guide to British Upland Vegetation.* Peterborough: Joint Nature Conservation Committee.

Bandura, A. (1977). *Social Learning Theory.* Englewood Cliffs, NJ: Prentice Hall.

Bodin, Ö. and B. I. Crona (2009). The role of social networks in natural resource governance: what relational patterns make a difference? *Global Environmental Change,* **19**, 366–374.

Cole, M. and Y. Engestrom (1993). A cultural historical approach to distributed cognition. In G. Salomon (Ed.), *Distributed Cognitions: Psychological and Educational Considerations.* New York, NY: Cambridge University Press, pp. 1–46.

Coleman, J. S. (1990). *Foundations of Social Theory.* Cambridge, MA: Belknap Press of Harvard University Press.

Cook, K. S., R. M. Emerson, M. R. Gilmore and T. Yamagishi (1983). The distribution of power in exchange networks: theory and experimental results. *American Journal of Sociology,* **89**, 275–305.

CRC (2010). High ground, high potential: a future for England's upland communities, Summary Report. In *Rural Communities.* Cheltenham: Commission for Rural Communities, pp. 1–24.

Cundill, G. (2010). Monitoring social learning processes in adaptive co-management: three case studies from South Africa. *Ecology and Society,* **15**(3), 28.

Davidson-Hunt, I. (2006). Adaptive learning networks: developing resource management knowledge through social learning forums. *Human Ecology,* **34**, 593–614.

Dougill, A.J., E.D.G. Fraser, K. Hubacek *et al.* (2006). Learning from doing participatory rural research: lessons from the Peak District National Park. *Journal of Agricultural Economics*, **57**, 259–275.

Dryzek, J. (1997). *The Politics of Earth*. Oxford: Oxford University Press.

Erickson, B. (1988). The relational basis of attitudes. In B. Wellman and S.D. Berkowitz (Eds.), *Social Structures: A Network Approach*. Cambridge: Cambridge University Press, pp. 99–121.

Fazey, I., J.A. Fazey and D.M.A. Fazey (2005). Learning more effectively from experience. *Ecology and Society*, **10**, 4 (online), http://www.ecologyandsociety.org/vol10/iss2/art4/.

Fazey, J.A. and F. Marton (2002). Understanding the space of experiential variation. *Active Learning in Higher Education*, **3**, 234–250.

Folke, C., T. Hahn, P. Olsson and J. Norberg (2005). Adaptive governance of social–ecological systems. *Annual Review of Environment and Resources*, **30**, 441–473.

Friedkin, N.E. (1998). *A Structural Theory of Social Influence*. Cambridge: Cambridge University Press.

Holden, J. (2005a). Controls of soil pipe frequency in upland blanket peat. *Journal of Geophysical Research*, **110**, doi: 10.1029/2004JF000143.

Holden, J. (2005b). Piping and woody plants in peatlands; cause or effect? *Water Resources Research*, **41**, doi: 10.1029/2004WR003909.

Hubacek, K., N. Beharry, A. Bonn *et al.* (2009). Ecosystem services in dynamic and contested landscapes: the case of UK uplands. In M. Winter and M. Lobley (Eds.), *What is Land For? The Food, Fuel and Climate Change Debate*. London: Earthscan, pp. 167–188.

Hubacek, K. and M. Reed (2009). Lessons learned from participatory planning and management in the Peak District National Park, England. In C. Allan and G. Stankey (Eds.), *Adaptive Environmental Management: A Practical Guide*. New York, NY: Springer, pp. 189–202.

Hunter, S.M., I.A. Vizelberg and G.S. Berenson (1991). Identifying mechanisms of adoption of tobacco and alcohol use among youth: the Bogalusa heart study. *Social Networks*, **13**, 91–104.

Katz, E. and P.F. Lazarsfeld (2006). *Personal Influence: The Part Played by People in the Flow of Mass Communications*, 2nd Edition. New Brunswick, NJ: Transaction Publishers.

Kolb, D.A. (1984). *Experiential Learning: Experience as the Source of Learning and Development*. Princeton, NJ: Prentice-Hall.

Krackhardt, D. (1998). Simmelian ties: super, strong and sticky. In R. Kramer and M. Neale (Eds.), *Power and Influence in Organizations*. Thousand Oaks, CA: Sage, pp. 21–38.

Lave, J. and E. Wenger (1991). *Situated Learning: Legitimate Peripheral Participation*. Cambridge: Cambridge University Press.

Lee, K.N. (1993). *Compass and Gyroscope: Integrating Science and Politics for the Environment*. Washington, DC: Island Press.

Leeuwis, C. and R. Pyburn (2002). *Wheelbarrows Full of Frogs: Social Learning in Rural Resource Management*. Assen, the Netherlands: Koninklijke van Gorcum.

Maiolo, J.R., J.C. Johnson and D. Griffith (1992). Application of social science theory to fisheries management: three examples. *Society and Natural Resources*, **5**, 391–407.

Mercken, L., T.A.B. Snijders, C. Steglich and H.D. Vriesa (2009). Dynamics of adolescent friendship networks and smoking behavior: social network analyses in six European countries. *Social Science and Medicine*, **69**, 1506–1514.

Millennium Ecosystem Assessment (2005). *Ecosystems and Human Well-being: Synthesis*. Washington, DC: Island Press.

Newig, J., D. Günther and C. Pahl-Wostl (2009). Learning in governance networks in the context of environmental management. Paper presented at the 7th IHDP Open Meeting. Bonn, Germany. April 26.

Pahl-Wostl, C., M. Craps, E. Dewulf, D. Tabara and T. Taillieu (2007). Social learning and water resources management. *Ecology and Society*, **12**(2), art 5.

Pea, R. (1993). Practices of distributed intelligence and designs for education. In G. Salomon (Ed.), *Distributed Cognitions: Psychological and Educational Considerations*. Cambridge: Cambridge University Press, pp. 47–87.

Peak District National Park (2004). *State of the Park Report (update)*. Bakewell: Peak District National Park Authority.

Prell, C. (2011). *Social Network Analysis: History, Theory, and Methodology*. London: Sage.

Prell, C., K. Hubacek, C. Quinn and M. Reed (2008). 'Who's in the network?' When stakeholders influence data analysis. *Systemic Practice and Action Research*, **21**, 443–458.

Prell, C., K. Hubacek and M. Reed (2009). Stakeholder analysis and social network analysis in natural resource management. *Society and Natural Resources*, **22**(6), 501–518.

Prell, C., K. Hubacek, M. Reed *et al.* (2007). If you have a hammer everything looks like a nail: 'traditional' versus participatory model building. *Interdisciplinary Science Review*, **32**, 263–282.

Prell, C., K., Hubacek, M. Reed and L. Racin (forthcoming). Competing views, competing structures: the role of formal and informal structures in shaping stakeholder perceptions. *Ecology and Society*.

Reed, M., A. Bonn, W. Slee *et al.* (2010). The future of the uplands. *Land Use Policy*, **26S**, S204–S216.

Reed, M., A. Evely, G. Cundill *et al.* (in press). What is social learning? *Ecology and Society*,

Reed, M.S., K. Hubacek and C. Prell (2005). Sustainable upland management for multiple benefits: a multi-stakeholder response to the Heather & Grass Burning Code Consultation. In *Review of the Heather and Grass Etc. (Burning) Regulations 1986 and the Heather and Grass Burning Code 1994*. Food Department for Environment, and Rural Affairs Department for Environment, Food, and Rural Affairs

Rist, S., M. Chidambaranathan, C. Escobar, U. Wiesmann and A. Zimmermann (2007). Moving from sustainable management to sustainable governance of natural resources: the role of social learning process in rural India, Bolivia and Mali. *Journal of Rural Studies*, **23**, 23–37.

Schusler, T.M. and D.J. Decker (2003). Social learning for collaborative natural resource management. *Society and Natural Resources*, **15**, 309–326.

Schwenk, G. and T. Reimer (2008). Simple heuristics in complex networks: models of social influence. *Journal of Artificial Societies and Social Simulation*, **11**(3), 4.

Valente, T.W. (1995). *Network Models of the Diffusion of Innovations*. Cresskill, NJ: Hampton Press.

Valente, T.W. and R. Davis (1999). Accelerating the diffusion of innovations using opinion leaders. *Annals of the American Academy of Political and Social Science*, **566**, 55–67.

Wellman, B. (1988). Structural analysis: from method and metaphor to theory and substance. In B. Wellman and S. D. Berkowitz (Eds.), *Social Structures: A Network Approach*. Cambridge: Cambridge University Press, pp. 19–61.

Wenger, E. (1998). *Communities of Practice: Learning, Meaning, and Identity*. New York, NY: Cambridge University Press.

Winter, S., H. Prozesky and K. Esler (2007). A case study of landholder attitudes and behaviour toward the conservation of Renosterveld, a critically endangered vegetation type in Cape Floral Kingdom, South Africa. *Environmental Management*, **40**, 46–61.

Worrall, F., M. Reed, J. Warburton and T. Burt (2003). Carbon budget for a British upland peat catchment. *Science of the Total Environment*, **312**, 133–146.

Yamaguchi, K. (2000). Power in mixed exchange networks: a rational choice model. *Social Networks*, **22**, 93–121.

6

Who and *how*: engaging well-connected fishers in social networks to improve fisheries management and conservation

6.1 INTRODUCTION

The Loreto Bay National Marine Park was conceived as a people-oriented park where protection and sustainable use of marine resources were to be achieved. There have been advances towards these goals since the park was created, but the involvement of resource users in natural resource management and conservation still remains a challenge as in many other people-oriented parks worldwide (Brechin *et al.*, 2002; Wilshusen *et al.*, 2002; Adams *et al.*, 2004). Many factors determine in *what* aspects, *when*, and *how* resource users could be involved in resource management and conservation. However, in all cases natural resource managers face the issue of identifying and involving resource users who could spread ideas and practices to improve natural resource management and conservation. This issue becomes increasingly relevant in large-scale initiatives (e.g. ecosystem-based management initiatives) where it is more effective and efficient to find representatives who can participate in planning processes and then communicate with, and engage, their peers (Layzer, 2008; Kubo and Supriyanto, 2010). Thus, the issue of identifying and involving resource users is also affected by the scale at which a management and conservation initiative is intended.

Deciding on *who* to involve in a management or conservation initiative can follow two approaches. We can rely on individual attributes or relational attributes. In both cases, it is assumed that the

Social Networks and Natural Resource Management: Uncovering the Fabric of Environmental Governance, ed. Ö. Bodin and C. Prell. Published by Cambridge University Press.
© Cambridge University Press 2011.

individual or relational attribute is a reliable indicator of importance within a social system. For instance, in a fisheries management strategy, one could potentially involve those fishers who are captains of all existing boats fishing in a particular area or the most senior fishers. Alternatively, we could select those who have extensive social relations in a particular fishery and/or an area (Maiolo and Johnson, 1988). Moreover, social network analysis can be used to make sure different groups (some of them marginalized) are being represented in participatory processes for natural resource management (Prell *et al.*, 2008; see also Chapter 5). By focusing on social relations, social network theorists have developed methods to identify central or well-connected actors in social networks (Wasserman and Faust, 1999).

6.1.1   Centrality in social networks

Social network researchers have conceptualized centrality in different ways (Borgatti and Everett, 2006). The most basic conceptualization of social network centrality is degree centrality, which refers to the direct ties in which an actor is involved (Freeman, 1979). Thus, degree centrality indicates how important each actor is in a network by the "volume" or number of direct ties in which she or he is involved. In this measure, important actors have a large number of direct ties. For instance, in communication networks, an actor with a high-degree centrality can be said to be in the "thick of things" and likely to be a major channel of information – actors with high-degree centrality values are "focal points of communication, at least with respect to the others with whom he [the actor] is in contact" (Freeman, 1979: 219–220). Indeed, the importance of highly connected individuals in social networks resides in their capacity to spread ideas, practice, or resources as the result of their interpersonal transmission along friendship or other durable or trustworthy channels (Borgatti and Foster, 2003). Another conceptualization of centrality is provided by Bonacich's power-based centrality measure (Bonacich, 1987). Bonacich proposes that an individual's centrality is a function of both the individual's connections to others and the connections of those she or he is connected to (see also Chapter 2 in this book). Bonacich proposes a parameter β to weigh the extent to which an individual's centrality depends on the centrality of those to whom he or she is connected. This β parameter can be positive or negative. For instance, in a communication network, a positive value of β is appropriate because the extent to which an individual can, for instance, spread ideas and practice is positively related to the number of contacts of those with whom the person is directly connected (Bonacich, 1987).

In a bargaining situation, however, it is advantageous to be connected to those who have few options: "power [in exchange networks] comes from being connected to those who are powerless" (Bonacich, 1987: 1171). A negative value of β is appropriate because the power of an individual over others is reduced by the higher centrality of those to which the individual is connected. It is in this second application that Bonacich (1987) studied dependency or power in exchange networks (see Cook and Whitmeyer (1992) and Molm (2003) for reviews on network exchange theory). This chapter is not concerned with power. However, I discuss the practical implications that natural resource managers may face when involving highly connected individuals in social networks. I use degree centrality and Bonacich's power-based centrality (β = +) to identify individuals with the capacity *to* spread ideas and practice that can improve fisheries management and conservation.

The idea of identifying central individuals in social networks to improve natural resource management is not new. For instance, Maiolo and Johnson (1988) used a social network approach to identify well-connected fishers in various fisheries. Moreover, they tested factors (i.e. individual attributes like a fisher's subscription to fisheries publications) that may forecast fishers' centrality in social networks to assess the possibility of using these factors to simplify the identification of central figures in social networks. Finding factors that forecast the centrality of individuals in social networks is important in light of the high costs typically involved in gathering social network data.

6.1.2 Forecasting centrality using individual attributes

Finding individual attributes that could forecast the centrality of individuals in social networks may simplify the process of identifying central actors (Maiolo and Johnson, 1988). In the context of information sharing on their fishing activity, fishers display different tendencies towards participation depending on their socio-demographic characteristics and social roles (Stiles, 1972; Maiolo and Johnson, 1988; Gatewood and McCay, 1990; Crona and Bodin, 2006). There is no consensus, however, among scholars on what attributes may forecast the centrality of individuals in exchanges of information in the context of the fishing activity. Moreover, different attributes may forecast the importance of resource users in information exchanges even within the same economic sector (Maiolo and Johnson, 1988). Thus, the extent to which actors' attributes can forecast their centrality is, by and large, an empirical question.

6.1.3   Network centrality and scale

Once the boundaries of the population of interest have been defined (e.g. a community) in a social network study, the system is assumed closed for analytical purposes in the formal methods of social network analysis. Social network analysts are well aware of this assumption and recognize that systems are not closed but nested. Clearly, an actor who is centrally positioned in a social network at the community level may not be necessarily central in a regional network (e.g. among multiple communities). This is an important consideration for managers when deciding *who* to involve in management and conservation issues whose scope may range from the local to the regional level as is typically the case in ecosystem-based management initiatives (Layzer, 2008). Indeed, Kubo and Supriyanto (2010) report evidence that local communities engaged in forest conservation were able to control the over-exploitation of forest at the local level. However, local communities made little to no contribution to forest ecosystem conservation of a scale beyond the community.

6.1.4   Engaging actors in conservation and natural resource governance

Regarding the issue of *how* to promote the efficient and effective involvement of resource users in natural resource management and conservation – understood here as a sustained commitment of resource users to achieve management and conservation goals – one could draw from at least two views. The first view focuses on the individual and seeks to provide the *right* incentives either through market (Christy, 1996) or community-based institutions (Ostrom, 1990). This view assumes complete or bounded rationality in individuals who assess and act upon a situation based on the structure of incentives and social/economic costs associated with not following common agreements provided by institutions. Alternatively, one can focus on social relations and their emergent structures as a means to mobilize groups towards the achievement of supra-individual goals (Bodin and Crona, 2009). This view does not make any particular claims regarding individual rationality. However, its main thesis is that human action unfolds as part of social relations among actors and not by independent self-contained interacting individuals. In this sense, identifying and engaging well-connected actors in social networks can facilitate the spreading of ideas and practices by virtue of their social relations.

In this chapter, I focus on the issues of *who* and *how* to involve fishers to improve fisheries management and conservation using network centrality measures and social network mechanisms. I use degree centrality (Freeman, 1979) and Bonacich's power-based centrality (Bonacich, 1987) to identify fishers within and among communities with the capacity to spread ideas and practices by virtue of the social relationships. In addition, I test the hypothesis that years living in the community and years of fishing experience are reliable indicators of fishers' centrality in their social networks. I draw on social network data of information exchanges on the state and location of fish resources among fishers from seven coastal fishing communities adjacent to the Loreto Bay National Marine Park, Baja California Sur, Mexico. I will draw from some unpublished work on an event initiated by a large NGO where the objective was to engage fishermen from different localities in the Northwest of Mexico and Chile when I discuss my results. Finally, based on social network mechanisms, I argue that building trusting social relations between resource users and managers is the best strategy to implement a participatory policy for conservation and natural resource governance.

6.2 METHODS

6.2.1 Study area

The Loreto municipality is located on the eastern side of Baja California Sur, Mexico, and contains several rural small coastal communities (Figure 6.1). The social network data I use in this chapter are from fishers who reside in the communities of Ramadita, San Nicolás, Colonia Zaragoza, Juncalito, Ligüí, Ensenada Blanca, and Agua Verde, which were selected because of their strong dependence on small-scale fisheries. Tourism and the service sector have been growing rapidly in the municipality of Loreto; however, commercial small-scale fishing of clam, conch, octopus, squid, crustaceans, shark, and finfish has been and continues to be the main, and often only, economic activity available in most of the rural coastal communities (Gutiérrez-Barreras, 2001).

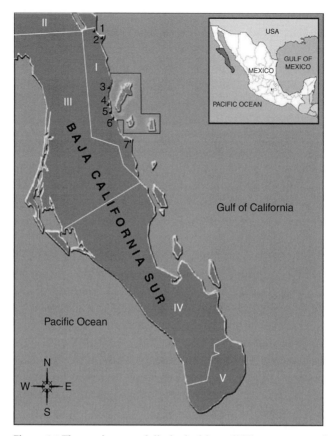

Figure 6.1 The marine area delimited with a solid line represents the limits of Loreto Bay National Marine Park. Communities studied: 1. Ramadita (RM); 2. San Nicolás (SN); 3. Colonia Zaragoza (CZ); 4. Juncalito (JC); 5. Ligüí (LG); 6. Ensenada Blanca (EB); 7. Agua Verde (AV); municipalities in the state of Baja California Sur: I. Loreto; II. Mulegé; III. Comondú; IV. La Paz; V. Los Cabos.

In 1996, the Loreto Bay National Marine Park was created after an influential group of local entrepreneurs directly requested the Mexican President to help them protect their marine resources from poachers and non-resident shrimp trawling fleets. The creation of the park strengthened the right of local groups to participate in the management of local marine resources. Indeed, the overarching goal set out by the management plan of the park is to protect and restore the natural resources of the park and, at the same time, promote the social development of the communities adjacent to the park (CONANP, 2002).

Park managers are committed to involving resource users in the management of the park, and so far, community involvement has been formally attempted through the formation of a Technical Advisory Committee.

6.2.2 Fieldwork and analysis

To collect the network data, a survey questionnaire was given to fishers to assess the personal contacts they rely on to obtain trustworthy information within their community and with other fishing communities in the area on the state and location of fish. Trustworthy information refers to information provided "in good faith according to the best of competence" where opportunism is limited or absent (Noteboom, 2007: 35). Two questions were asked: who do you consult to obtain trustworthy information regarding abundant fishing areas in (1) your community, and (2) six other rural fishing communities in the Loreto municipality? Each fisher was presented with a list of fishers from his community to answer the first question, and, for the second, the fisher was asked to name his personal contacts from the other communities.

To further refine the analysis of fishers' centrality and factors affecting it, I look at these aspects at two geographical levels: local (community) and regional (among communities). I do this by analyzing the social ties that exist among fishers from the same community (local level) and by considering all ties among fishers from the seven fishing study communities (regional level). I use degree centrality and Bonacich's power-based centrality to assess each fisher's centrality as proxy of their capacity to communicate ideas and practice. I determine degree centrality and Bonacich's power centrality using UCINET (Borgatti *et al.*, 2002), which can also estimate the value of β as the absolute value of the reciprocal of the largest eigenvalue of the network. It is recommended to use a value of β smaller than the value estimated by UCINET (Borgatti *et al.*, 2002). There is no guidance as to how smaller the value of β from the ones calculated in the UCINET program should be. The key point, however, is that the magnitude of β affects the extent to which distant ties are taken into account (Bonacich, 1987). Thus, a β value of zero when using Bonancich's power-based centrality produces the same results as degree centrality (Bonacich, 1987). I use network visualizations created using Netdraw (a program distributed by UCINET) to display the different types of centrality at the local and regional level.

Finally, I use regression analysis to test the extent to which years living in the community and years of fishing experience forecast the fishers' network centralities. In the case of the social networks on information sharing in the Loreto area, it is likely that the more experienced a fisher is, the more likely he will be consulted by others, thus making him more central than others in the social network. To evaluate this hypothetical relationship, I use years of fishing experience to determine the extent to which this variable forecasts fishers' centrality values. Time of residence may also be a good predictor of actors' centrality values. All personal contacts reported by fishers from Loreto were perceived as trustworthy, which is a characteristic most likely developed over time. Thus, it is possible that a fisher who has lived longer in a community may be perceived as more trustworthy than one who has just recently arrived. To explore this hypothetical relationship, I use years of residence to determine the extent to which this variable forecasts fishers' centrality values.

6.3   RESULTS

A total of 123 fishers who were members (all males) of households agreed to participate in the research from the seven coastal fishing communities. These 123 fishers represent 75% of all households involved in fishing. I analyze the networks among 121 fishers because the other two did not report consulting with anybody regarding the state and location of fish. The 121 fishers reported a total number of 638 ties.

6.3.1   Degree and power-based centrality

Figure 6.2 shows the overall pattern of ties among the 121 fishers, who are clustered by their community affiliation and are represented with nodes (circles) that have sizes proportional to their degree centrality values at the local (Figure 6.2A) and regional (Figures 6.2B) levels. To highlight differences between the two levels of aggregation, fishers with the highest centrality values in each community network in Figure 6.2A are located at the top and fishers with lower centrality values follow in a counter-clockwise direction. This order was repeated in Figure 6.2B to highlight how fishers' centrality may vary with the level of aggregation (local and regional levels). For instance, fishers CZ27 and CZ46 represent the fishers with the highest and lowest degree centrality values, respectively, in the Colonia Zaragoza community (Figure 6.2A). When degree centrality values of fishers are compared between the local and regional levels, we notice that a fisher may not be necessarily a central actor at these two levels of aggregation. For example, fisher CZ67 from Colonia Zaragoza community, roughly located in the middle of the distribution of degree centrality values at the local level (Figure 6.2A), becomes one of the central actors at the regional level (Figure 6.2B). Another case is fisher RM08 from Ramadita community, who appears to have very similar degree centrality as other fishers within his community at the local level (Figure 6.2A) but becomes very prominent at the regional level (Figure 6.2B). The opposite can also occur. Fishers who are central at the local level can become less prominent at the regional level. Such is the case, for example, of fisher LG08 from the Ligüí community (Figure 6.2A), who becomes less central when calculating his centrality at the regional level (Figure 6.2B). Another example is fisher AV06 from Agua Verde community, who is one of the central figures at the local level but becomes less prominent at the regional level. In sum, a visual

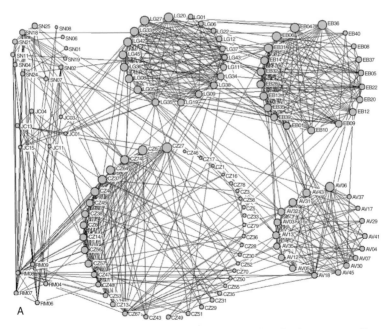

Figure 6.2 Social network of information showing the degree centrality values for each fisher with different node sizes at the local (A) and regional (B) levels. Agua Verde (AV), Colonia Zaragoza (CZ), Ramadita (RM), San Nicolás (SN), Juncalito (JC), Ligüí (LG), and Ensenada Blanca (EB).

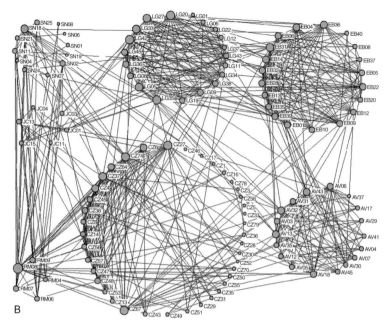

B

Figure 6.2 (cont.)

exploration helps us to quickly identify who is a central figure at the local and regional levels, and to grasp the fact that a fisher may not be equally central at both levels of aggregation.

Similarly, Figure 6.3 displays the overall pattern of ties among the 121 fishers, who are clustered by their community affiliation and are represented with nodes (circles) that have sizes proportional to their power-based centrality values at the local (Figure 6.3A) and regional (Figure 6.3B) levels. The community networks depicted in Figure 6.3A and 6.3B follow the same arrangement as described for Figure 6.2A and 6.2B. That is to say, fishers with the highest power-based centrality values in each community network in Figure 6.3A are located at the top and fishers with lower centrality values follow in a counter-clockwise direction. This order was repeated in Figure 6.3B to highlight how fishers' centrality may vary with the level of aggregation (local and regional levels). At the regional level (i.e. considering ties within and between communities), a $\beta = 0.066$ was used to calculate the power-based centralities of all fishers (Figure 6.3B). This value was smaller than the one calculated by UNICET (0.667) as recommended in this program (Borgatti *et al.*, 2002). At the local level, the power-based

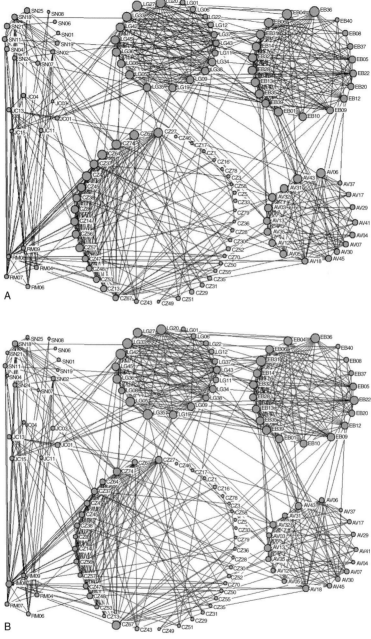

Figure 6.3 Social network of information showing the Bonacich's power-based centrality values for each fisher with different node sizes at the local (A) and regional (B) levels. Agua Verde (AV), Colonia Zaragoza (CZ), Ramadita (RM), San Nicolás (SN), Juncalito (JC), Ligüí (LG), and Ensenada Blanca (EB).

centralities of each fisher were calculated using a β for each community as follows: AV (0.105); CZ (0.095); EB (0.084); JC (0.368); LG (0.086); SN (0.273); and RM (0.214). In all cases, the same magnitude (0.001) was subtracted from the values calculated by UCINET to conform to the rule of using smaller values of β than the ones calculated. In Figure 6.3A and 6.3B, differences in a fisher's power-based centralities can be found at the local and regional levels. For instance, many of the fishers from Colonia Zaragoza who are prominent at the local level (CZ4 to CZ48 in a counter-clockwise direction) become less prominent at the regional level. Moreover, fisher CZ67 who was originally in the middle of the distribution of power-based centrality values at the local level becomes one of the most prominent actors at the regional level.

Visually, a comparison between the two centrality measures at the local level (Figures 6.2A and 6.3A) indicates a more subtle difference than between levels of aggregation for the same centrality measure. Indeed, the relative size of each node (fisher) appears very similar in Figures 6.2A and 6.3A. The main difference is in terms of the order of importance of each fisher that can be observed within each community. For instance, many fishers appear to maintain their order of importance in Agua Verde, Juncalito, San Nicolás, and Ramadita networks whether we use degree centrality (Figure 6.2A) or power-based centrality (Figure 6.3A). However, this is less the case in the Colonia Zaragoza and Ensenada Blanca community networks, where most fishers change their order of importance.

In sum, the level of aggregation (local and regional) affects the centrality of fishers. That is to say, a fisher may not necessarily be both a central actor at the local and regional levels. It was possible to see these changes through a visual exploration of Figures 6.2 and 6.3. A more subtle effect exists between the two centrality measures at each level of aggregation where the relative order of fishers within each community may change more or less. The visual exploration method used to identify central fishers served to illustrate the effects of levels of aggregation and type of centrality measure. The numerical centrality values can also be used to do a quantitative analysis, for instance when testing for factors that may forecast the centrality of actors.

6.3.2   Factors forecasting centrality

When all fishers are considered (without distinction by community), only number of years living in the community and degree centrality are significantly correlated ($F = 4.63866$; $\alpha < 0.05$). Years of fishing experience is not significantly correlated with degree centrality ($F = 3.55$;

$\alpha > 0.05$) or power-based centrality ($F = 0.32$; $\alpha > 0.05$). However, various significant correlations emerge when analyzing centrality at the community level (Table 6.1). The variable of years living in the community has more cases of significant correlation with fishers' centrality than years of fishing experience at the community level. Identifying other factors that may account for this variability is beyond the scope of this chapter. However, and for the purpose of this chapter, the evidence indicates that neither years living in the community nor years of fishing experience may serve as reliable proxies to simplify the identification of central figures from each community.

Table 6.1. F *values of regression analyses for the independent variables of Years Living in the Community and Years of Fishing Experience with each of the two power measures (degree centrality and Bonacich's power-based centrality, β positive) at regional and local levels by community. Statistically significant values are marked with an asterisk ($\alpha \leq 0.05$).*

| | Years living in the community | | | |
| | Regional | | Local | |
Community	Degree	Power-based	Degree	Power-based
Agua Verde	3.65	6.43*	1.00	0.99
Colonia Zaragoza	3.61	3.76	4.67*	6.23*
Ensenada Blanca	1.08	2.44	0.52	0.84
Juncalito	1.10	0.00	3.61	5.23
Ligüí	9.25*	9.39*	11.92*	16.62*
San Nicolás	27.77*	0.07	2.00	3.14
Ramadita	0.08	2.53	2.38	2.38

| | Years of fishing experience | | | |
| | Regional | | Local | |
Community	Degree	Power-based	Degree	Power-based
Agua Verde	10.42*	10.74*	6.82*	7.01*
Colonia Zaragoza	0.02	0.03	0.00	0.64
Ensenada Blanca	1.28	1.10	0.84	0.66
Juncalito	0.00	0.13	1.15	1.93
Ligüí	1.63	1.56	0.45	0.94
San Nicolás	1.87	0.63	0.21	0.28
Ramadita	2.78	0.72	0.74	0.74

6.4 DISCUSSION

In people-oriented parks where conservation and sustainable resource use are to be achieved through a participatory approach (Brechin *et al.*, 2002; Wilshusen *et al.*, 2002; Adams *et al.*, 2004) engaging well-connected individuals in social networks could facilitate their effectiveness. By virtue of their social relations, these individuals could diffuse ideas and practice to improve natural resource governance. Therefore, natural resource managers could benefit from first identifying the actors who are well connected in social networks through the use of methods and centrality measures demonstrated in this chapter. However, identifying *who* to involve is a necessary but insufficient condition to tap on the capacity of well-connected individuals to diffuse ideas and practice. In the context of participatory governance of natural resource management and conservation, *how* to involve/ engage these well-connected individuals is also critical (Kubo and Supriyanto, 2010).

My discussion covers two aspects. First, I discuss the importance and differences between the two centrality measures (degree and power-based centrality) and the role of individual attributes in identifying well-connected individuals by using an unpublished example from a conservation initiative that was aimed at bringing together small-scale fishers from various communities in Mexico and Chile to exchange ideas and experiences on conservation and sustainable use of fisheries. Second, I reflect on the issue of *how* to involve well-connected resource users in conservation and natural resource management initiatives that are framed within a participatory policy contrasting a social relational with the institutional view proposed by neo-institutional economists. I conclude by suggesting that both views have an important contribution to natural resource governance.

6.4.1 Degree and power-based centrality

There are different ways to index individuals' importance from a social network perspective. All of them depend on the extent to which local and global structures are weighted and whether that weight should be positive or negative (Bonacich, 1987). Thus, a fisher with many direct ties has multiple alternative ways to satisfy his needs and may also be able to spread ideas and influence others to change or adopt new practices. This is the basic idea underpinning the use of degree centrality to index an actor's importance, which focuses on the local structure (direct ties). Bonacich's power-based centrality places positive or negative weight on the centralities of a fisher's contacts. In other words, it focuses more on the larger structure to assess centrality and in the case of a negative weighting, power as dependency (see Bonacich, 1987 for his treatment of power in exchange networks). As visually demonstrated in this chapter, a fisher may be a central actor at the local but not at the regional level for the same centrality measure. The effect of the two centrality measures at the same level of aggregation was much less apparent and mostly observed in terms of changes in the relative order of importance of fishers' centralities. What, then, is the appropriate centrality measure to identify actors with a high capacity to spread ideas and practices? An example can help to grasp the importance of one measure over the other.

In 2003, *Comunidad y Biodiversidad*, a Mexican NGO, sponsored an event called *De Pescador a Pescador* (from fisher to fisher), for small-scale fishers from various communities in Mexico and one from Chile to exchange ideas and experiences on the role of marine reserves to improve fisheries. In 2006, a sequel of this event (*De Pescador a Pescador II*) was co-sponsored by *Comunidad y Biodiversidad* and *Sociedad de Historia Natural Niparajá*. Using the same approach of exchanging ideas and experiences among small-scale fishers, the event focused on the responsibilities, rights, and opportunities of small-scale fishers to enable sustainable fisheries in Mexico. Valuable information was exchanged and documented, and overall participants were pleased with the structure and output of the event. In 2004, I was able to interview one of the fishers who participated in the first event. The fisher was very pleased with the event, and the approach of the event based on exchange of ideas among peers seemed to have had a positive effect on him regarding the possibility of improving the health of fish stocks in the Loreto area. The Loreto park managers invited him to attend the event in the first place because of his years of experience as a fisher and his predisposition and openness to innovations in fisheries management and conservation. After he participated in the event, he shared his knowledge and experience with his son-in-law and *compadre* (god-father of one of his sons), who were also the contacts he reported to share information on the abundance of fish in the area (Ramirez-Sanchez, 2007). In turn, his son-in-law and *compadre* were also poorly connected to the rest of their community network.

From the example above, it is evident that a study on social networks could have better informed managers *who* to engage to participate in the conservation initiative, and influence their direct contacts (degree centrality) and/or spread ideas beyond their immediate circle of contacts (Bonacich's power-based centrality). Park managers, however, relied on an attribute-based approach. In particular, they used the years of experience and predisposition to new ideas to decide who to invite to the *De Pescador a Pescador* event. Although these individual attributes may be important, they were not reliable indicators of the capacity of a fisher to spread ideas and influence the adoption of new practices to many fishers in a community. In addition, when dealing with issues beyond the scope of the community and its adjacent waters (e.g. ecosystem-based management initiatives), a better strategy would have been to target fishers with both intra- and inter-community social ties (in this chapter referred to as regional level of aggregation).

The work and resources necessary to carrying a social network study has led some researchers to test the possibility of identifying individual attributes that can serve the same role of network centrality measures, i.e. identifying central actors. In their study, Maiolo and Johnson (1988: 274) identified the problem of communication between managers and their constituency in the context of what they refer to as "upward aggregation of responsibility and authority" in fisheries management in the USA. To address this problem in the king mackerel fishery in the southeast USA, the authors assume that the effectiveness of this communication could be improved by identifying key leaders or central members in the communication networks who could then be appointed as representatives of the industry in key advisory committees. In particular, these authors sought to produce a series of protocols for identifying central figures. While they found variations in the socio-economic characteristics that forecast actors' degree centrality values by state (Florida, North and South Carolina in the USA) and type of fishery (mackerel and shrimp), they tentatively concluded that in their case studies, organizational affiliation and subscriptions to information outlets are good proxies for selecting advisors. Yet, they acknowledged that it is advisable to carry out a full-scale network study rather than simplifying the identification of central figures by assuming socio-economic characteristics identified in one study will hold everywhere. Similar to the overall conclusion of Maiolo and Johnson (1988), I found that the individual attributes, time of residence and years of fishing experience, may not always be reliable indicators of fishers' centrality. The discussion of other factors (individual attributes) that may be contributing to the specific patterns of the study networks is out of the scope of this chapter. However, Ramirez-Sanchez (2007) and Ramirez-Sanchez and Pinkerton (2009) provide a discussion on community factors that may be influencing the network structure of these communities.

It is important to recognize that while well-connected individuals in social networks may have a high capacity to spread ideas and practice, they simply may not have the motivation to participate in a conservation initiative. Thus, while social network centrality measures can provide us with good insights as to *who* has the capacity to diffuse information and practice, some individual attributes need to be considered to make a choice as to *who* to involve in a conservation or resource management initiative. In this case, the purpose is not to find individual attributes that substitute for the relational variable as tested in this chapter and by Miolo and Johnson (1988). Instead, the purpose is to find individuals that have both suitable individual and relational attributes given some particular tasks and objectives. Indeed, although it was found in this chapter that years of fishing experience and years living in the community may not be reliable indicators of centrality, combining these attributes with centrality measures can be more effective than just using centrality or individual attributes on their own. It is beyond the scope of this chapter to discuss some methods to integrate relational and individual attributes. However, a multi-criteria analysis is a relatively simple method that can consider both relational and individual attributes to rank fishers (see Triantaphyllou, 2002 for a detailed description on multi-criteria analysis).

Assuming that using a combination of individual and relational attributes leads to the identification of resource users most suitable to promote conservation and natural resource initiatives, resource managers still face the problem of *how* to engage these resource users. *How* or more precisely what mechanisms can natural resource managers use for effective involvement of resource users is still under debate. In the Introduction of this chapter, an individualistic and a relational view were mentioned as two contrasting perspectives that can be used to engage natural resource users in conservation and natural resource governance. I will argue that building social relations is a necessary condition for natural resource governance institutions to be viable and more generally to implement a participatory policy for conservation and natural resource governance.

6.4.2   Participatory policies for conservation and natural resource governance

Modern natural resource management and biological conservation were initially conceived as the application of biophysical scientific knowledge to the rational use and protection of biodiversity (Mascia et al., 2003; Ewert et al., 2004). While scientific knowledge of the biophysical world identifies the possibilities for managing and conserving biological diversity, environmental policies target social systems (Brechin et al., 2002; Mascia et al., 2003). Yet, providing policy recommendations is especially challenging in protected areas that have been established with the dual purpose of protecting biological diversity and promoting development of local communities through sustainable natural resource use (Songorwa et al., 2000; Brechin et al., 2002; Wilshusen et al., 2002; Adams et al., 2004; Berkes, 2004; Locke and Dearden, 2005). However, it is widely accepted that one of the guiding principles for managing people-oriented protected areas is the effective involvement of local groups in the decision-making process. Indeed, participatory approaches to conservation and natural resource management are becoming increasingly prominent (Ashby, 2003; Pahl-Wostl and Hare, 2004).

6.4.3   New institutionalism in conservation and natural resource management

Participatory policies emerged from academic views that advocate sustainable use, participation of rural populations in research and development, and inclusion of local perspectives and knowledge in environmental management (Ashby, 2003; Berkes, 2004). Conceived under diverse circumstances, multiple programs have been guided and implemented in alternative ways, for instance, under the people-oriented parks policy (e.g. community-based natural resource management and integrated conservation development projects (Brechin et al., 2002); and community-based wildlife management (Songorwa et al., 2000)). It has been difficult to establish why such programs sometimes work and at other times fail, but most of the advocates of people-oriented conservation and natural resource management agree that failure or success lies in the design of institutions and social organizations created to implement such programs (Brechin et al., 2002; Berkes, 2004; Mansuri and Rao, 2004; Pretty and Smith, 2004).

Institutional design is the major concern of the "the choice-within-constraints" new institutionalism (in short: new institutionalism) that asserts that actors pursue their interests by making choices within institutional constraints (Ingram and Clay, 2000). This view has become influential in participatory approaches to conservation and natural resource management (Ostrom, 1990; Agrawal and Gibson, 1999; Berkes, 2004; Pretty and Smith, 2004). These researchers assumed bounded rationality and argue that in the absence of institutions transaction costs can frustrate collective ends. Ingram and Clay (2000) provide an insightful critique about the new institutional school of thought and the reader is encouraged to consult it. What is relevant to the discussion in this chapter is the neglect of social relations and emergent structures and properties such as social trust by the new institutionalism practice in natural resource management and conservation. Indeed, the extreme focus on individuals' choices leads scholars using the new institutionalism to argue that "promising programs may falter if individuals start to burn out, believing that investments in social capital are no longer paying off" in conservation initiatives (Pretty and Smith, 2004: 637). These same authors add that "rules and sanctions give individuals the confidence to invest in the collective good, knowing that others will also do so, and sanctions ensure that those who break the rules know they will be punished" (Pretty and Smith, 2004: 633). Others have argued that organizations, institutions, and political processes built on a pluralistic view and rationality tend to be ephemeral and evanescent (Earle and Cvetkovich, 1995; Vandergeest, 2006), and that rules and sanctions are a functional substitute and not a producer of social trust (Granovetter, 1985; Molm, 2003). To be sure, new institutional scholars acknowledge the need for trust and social relations to facilitate cooperation in natural resource governance, but these critical factors are rarely analyzed (Ostrom *et al.*, 1994).

6.4.4   The social relational view

Social relational theorists argue that it is by building trusting relations that social networks are created and that key properties of social systems like solidarity, trust, and reciprocity emerge (Molm, 2003). For instance, initial conceptions of social exchange (Blau, 1964; Lévi-Strauss, 1969) have led a group of social relational theorists to distinguish between negotiated (e.g. Cook and Whitmeyer, 1992) and reciprocal exchanges (Blau, 1964; Lévi-Strauss, 1969; Molm *et al.*, 2000;

Molm, 2003). When actors in negotiated exchanges engage in a joint decision process in which they seek agreement on the terms of exchange (i.e. contract), such agreement is strictly binding. This is exactly the same conception adopted by new institutionalists who have studied cooperation through game theory (e.g. Ostrom, 1999). In contrast, actors in reciprocal exchanges start the exchanges individually by "performing a beneficial act for another (such as giving assistance or advice), without knowing whether, when, or to what extent the other will reciprocate" (Molm, 2003). The key findings of experiments in exchange networks are that reciprocal exchanges induce lower power use and inequality, higher levels of trust and feelings of affective commitment, and stronger perception of fairness than negotiated exchanges (Molm *et al.*, 2000).

Interestingly, the need for trust and social relations to facilitate cooperation in natural resource governance is acknowledged by scholars who endorse new institutionalism. Thus, new institutionalists remind us that those who have developed trust and social capital "can utilize these assets to craft institutions that avert the CPR [common-pool resource] dilemma and arrive at reasonable outcomes" (Ostrom *et al.*, 1994: 329). This implies that participatory policies for conservation and natural resource management should not be only concerned with the creation of institutions "as rules of the game," but the often taken-for-granted social relations and pro-social behaviors and cultural understandings that are necessary to make such institutions-as-rules viable.

The networks of information exchanges studied in this chapter qualified as reciprocated exchange networks and not as negotiated exchange networks. The main reason is that the exchange is not negotiated but occurs on an opportunistic basis and among actors who over time have developed trust through reciprocated exchanges. *How*, then, can natural resource managers engage resource users effectively?

6.4.5   Social and emotional engaging strategy

Managers could become leaders or central figures in social networks of the resource users they are trying to engage in conservation and management. Indeed, formal arrangements in hierarchical organizations often become secondary in practice, and individuals engage in information exchanges and collaborations that do not correspond to formal channels (Brass, 1984; Granovetter, 1985; Brown and Duguid, 2000).

Institutionalized rules cannot capture this social phenomenon, but in a figure of speech, they piggyback on such informal practices to achieve its goals.

Interestingly, the relevance of informal channels and practical understanding to achieve participation has been recognized by the managers of the Loreto Bay National Marine Park (LBNMP). In 2001, the director at the time of the LBNMP commented that the progress they were making in involving fishermen in the management process was the result of one staff member's efforts to establish social relations with resource users: "you always see him having coffee or interacting with fishers in informal settings." If resource managers could carry out a systematic study of the social networks of resource users, a park manager should be in a good position to tap into these social networks. An example of such systematic study of social networks was demonstrated in this chapter by identifying well-connected fishers using two centrality measures, and as I argued, deciding on *who* to involve could be more effective by combining relational and individual attributes. There is a caveat, however. For an individual to mobilize a social network, she or he must be a central and legitimate figure in a network. In my study of the social networks of fishers, a condition of trustworthiness characterizes all the personal contacts used by fishers. Thus, a resource manager, external to the network of resource users, who wishes to efficiently tap into the potential capacity of the social network, needs to become a legitimate figure in social networks and connect with centrally connected actors (e.g. leaders). This requires long-term commitments to a conservation area (Kubo and Supriyanto, 2010) and, perhaps more importantly, an understanding of what it means to be socially embedded in social networks for a resource manager to accomplish that. The experts (social scientists, neuroscientists, social psychologists, and social network analysts) tell us that this implies becoming socially and emotionally engaged (Krackhardt and Hanson, 1993; Goleman, 1998; Bechara and Bar-On, 2006).

Evidence is already being produced as to how a new attitude of front-line staff towards community engagement is having positive effects towards conservation and sustainable development in the context of people-oriented parks. Kubo and Supriyanto (2010) have found evidence that building trusting social relations between resource users and front-line staff has provided a key condition for them to transform the governance of local forests in a national park in Indonesia. They argue that trusting social relations enable the transformation of the local governing system of forests by creating common understanding (mutual learning) and changes in perceptions and behaviors of both front-line staff and local villagers. Recognizing the limited capacity of front-line staff in building direct relationships with many people in villages, front-line staff identified local leaders who were respected and built interpersonal relationships with them with the idea of having these leaders taking the role of delivering conservation messages and practices. Kubo and Supriyanto (2010) indicate that resource degradation was effectively halted at the village level but this did not necessarily lead to the rehabilitation of forest ecosystems. Extending the approach of engaging well-connected individuals in multiple communities as illustrated in this chapter seems a logical and feasible strategy to address conservation and resource management issues at the broader ecosystem level.

Emphasizing the involvement of front-line managers in local and regional social networks of resource users as a primary strategy for participatory conservation and management of natural resources does not imply that building institutions-as-rules does not play an important role. It does imply, however, that institutions-as-rules are necessary but insufficient for understanding the dynamics of social systems and enabling the transformation of governing systems. Thus, rules cannot be the only or primary policy concern to ensure conservation and effective natural resource governance.

6.5 CONCLUDING REMARKS

Different ways on how to measure centrality, and how such approaches could be used in participatory processes were elaborated and discussed in this chapter. I demonstrated that the centrality of an actor depends on the type of centrality used and whether centrality is assessed within or among communities. I argued that a social relational strategy to improve fisheries management and conservation through the engagement of well-connected individuals could be more effective if managers become socially and emotionally engaged in social networks rather than being simply concerned about building institutions-as-rules.

Reflections

Network boundary issues

I used a snowball network sampling technique to define the boundary of my network. This technique focuses on an initial small set of actors who are asked to report on who they consider to be a fisher in their community. The identified contacts are then consulted, and so on, until all fishers from a community are identified. The implicit assumption in defining my population of interest using this technique is that fishers had to be regarded as such by their peers rather than being selected using a researcher's theoretical categories such as occupation (e.g. sport and commercial fisher), years living in the community, alternative sources of income, etc. The approach of identifying boundaries as perceived by the actors themselves is referred to in the literature as the realist approach, while a nominal approach is based on the theoretical concerns of the researcher (Wasserman and Faust, 1999). To be sure, in this chapter, I used the communities as parameters to set the boundaries.

Ecological boundaries

My study was regional from a municipal rather than an ecological perspective. However, the municipal perspective allowed me to cover a set of small communities operating within and outside a marine park created on some ecological considerations.

Decide on the unit of analysis

I focused on fishers as actors because during my first visit to the area, theories based on individuals as (bounded) rational individuals were inconsistent with my field observations of fishers sharing information on location and abundance of fish stocks that were already over-harvested. I wanted to forecast this; an inconsistent fact to mainstream theories in natural resource management and conservation.

Data-gathering issues

One of the main assumptions in a social network analysis and, in general, of survey questionnaires is that respondents will recall all information accurately, for instance, the individuals with whom they have a social tie of a certain kind. To deal with the issue of forgetting, I disaggregated my network-related questions on the personal contacts used by fishermen into several questions, and added the qualifier "trustworthy" (*de confianza*) to each question. Disaggregating the question on the personal contacts prompts respondents to concentrate their attention on specific situations and reduces the demand on respondents' cognitive effort to recall names. Furthermore, the subjective qualifier "trustworthy" may have had the additional effect of focusing attention on associated emotional events or important personal experiences (e.g. whose information has proven to be trustworthy) that seem to enhance an individual's facility for recalling past information. In cases where the number of network members is not too large, a recognition method to collect network data may be appropriate. Using this method, a list with all the names of the study network is presented to each interviewee to determine with whom the interviewee has a social connection.

Ethical issues

My main ethical issue emerged when I considered how park managers could use the information without revealing the identity of my informants. My dissertation, reports, and subsequent publications did not include any names of my participants.

Explanatory power of social network analysis

In my study, I did not measure management/governance outcomes directly (e.g. outcomes in terms of improved participatory approaches). However, while social network analysis cannot provide all the answers, it may be a powerful tool. In this chapter, I argued that rather than using individual or relational attributes, a combination or integration of both is likely to produce better results. The reason is that social networks/systems have composition, relationships, and structure.

Non-network data

It is critical to obtain data on individual attributes and contextual factors. Individual attributes tell us about the composition of the network and contextual factors (e.g. community dynamics and social programs) help us to have a better sense if social networks have been operating as a dependent or independent variable. Indeed, where do social networks come from in the first place, and once formed, what is their effect in social life? Both are legitimate questions even though most emphasis has been given to the latter. Whether one or the other, the goal is to find the mechanisms that produce social networks (see for example Ramirez-Sanchez and Pinkerton, 2009) and the social network mechanisms that affect social life.

Is social network analysis static?

There are studies that have followed networks over time to understand how networks change. A perhaps more critical question is whether or not a "static" study of social networks can suffice to understand the conditions and mechanisms that allow networks to discharge certain functions (e.g. better coordination) critical to, for instance, natural resource governance. I do not think there is a priori reason to believe static studies cannot identify such conditions and mechanisms.

ACKNOWLEDGMENT

Saudiel Ramirez-Sanchez currently works as policy analyst in the Oceans Directorate of the Department of Fisheries and Oceans, Canada. The International Development Research Centre (IDRC) and the Canon National Parks Science Scholar Program supported this research.

REFERENCES

Adams, W. M., R. Aveling, D. Brockington *et al.* (2004). Biodiversity conservation and the eradication of poverty. *Science*, **306**(5699), 1146–1149.

Agrawal, A. and C. C. Gibson (1999). Enchantment and disenchantment: the role of community in natural resource conservation. *World Development*, **27**(4), 629–649.

Ashby, J. (2003). Introduction: uniting science and participation in the process of innovation – research for development. In B. Pound, S. Snapp, C. McDougall and A. Braun (Eds.), *Managing Natural Resources for Sustainable Livelihoods. Uniting Science and Participation.* London: IDRC and Earthscan Books, pp. 1–15.

Bechara, A. and R. Bar-On (2006). Neurological substrates of emotional and social intelligence: evidence from patients with focal brain lesions. In J. T. Cacioppo, P. S. Visser and C. L. Pickett (Eds.), *Social Neuroscience. People Thinking about Thinking People*. Cambridge, MA: MIT Press, pp. 13–40.

Berkes, F. (2004). Rethinking community-based conservation. *Conservation Biology*, **18**(3), 621–630.

Blau, P. M. (1964). *Exchange and Power in Social Life*. New York, NY: Wiley.

Bodin, O. and B. Crona (2009). The role of social networks in natural resource governance: what relational patterns make a difference? *Global Environmental Change*, **19**(3), 366–374.

Bonacich, P. (1987). Power and centrality: a family of measures. *American Journal of Sociology*, **92**(5), 1170–1182.

Borgatti, S. P. and M. G. Everett (2006). A graph-theoretic perspective on centrality. *Social Networks*, **28**, 466–484.

Borgatti, S. P., M. G. Everett and L. C. Freeman (2002). *UCINET for Windows: Software for Social Network Analysis*. Harvard, MA: Analytic Technologies.

Borgatti, S. P. and P. C. Foster (2003). The network paradigm in organizational research: a review and typology. *Journal of Management*, **29**(6), 991–1013.

Brass, D. J. (1984). Being in the right place: a structural analysis of individual influence in an organization. *Administrative Science Quarterly*, **29**, 518–539.

Brechin, S. R., P. R. Wilshusen, C. L. Fortwangler and P. C. West (2002). Beyond the square wheel: toward a more comprehensive understanding of biodiversity conservation as social and political process. *Society and Natural Resources*, **15**(1), 41–64.

Brown, J. S. and P. Duguid (2000). *The Social Life of Information*. Boston, MA: Harvard Business School Press.

Christy, F. T. (1996). The death of open access and the advent of property right regimes in fisheries. *Marine Resource Economics*, **11**, 287–304.

CONANP (2002). *Programa de Manejo Parque Nacional Bahía de Loreto, México*. México, D.F.: Comision Nacional de Areas Naturales Protegidas y Secretaria del Ambiente y Recursos Naturales.

Cook, K. S. and J. M. Whitmeyer (1992). Two approaches to social structure: exchange theory and network analysis. *Annual Review of Sociology*, **18**, 109–127.

Crona, B. and O. Bodin (2006). What you know is who you know? Communication patterns among resource users as a prerequisite for co-management. *Ecology and Society*, **11**(2), 7.

Earle, T. C. and G. T. Cvetkovich (1995). *Social Trust. Toward a Cosmopolitan Society*. Westport, CT: Praeger.

Ewert, A. W., D. C. Baker and G. C. Bissix (2004). *Integrated Resource and Environmental Management. The Human Dimension*. New York, NY: CABI Publishing.

Freeman, L. C. (1979). Centrality in networks: I. Conceptual clarification. *Social Networks*, **1**, 215–239.

Gatewood, J. B. and B. J. McCay (1990). Comparison of job-satisfaction in 6 New-Jersey fisheries – implications for management. *Human Organization*, **49**(1), 14–25.

Goleman, D. (1998). What makes a leader? *Harvard Business Review*, November–December, 9–102.

Granovetter, M. (1985). Economic action and social structure: the problem of embeddedness. *American Journal of Sociology*, **91**(3), 481–510.

Gutiérrez-Barreras, J. A. (2001). *Reporte marino y costero del Municipio de Loreto, BCS, México*. Loreto, Baja California Sur: GEA y PNBL.

Ingram, P. and K. Clay (2000). The choice-within-constraints new institutionalism and implications for sociology. *Annual Review of Sociology*, **26**, 525–546.

Krackhardt, D. and J. R. Hanson (1993). Informal networks: the company behind the charts. *Harvard Business Review*, **71**(4), 104–111.

Kubo, H. and B. Supriyanto (2010). From fence-and-fine to participatory conservation: mechanisms of transformation in conservation governance at the Gunung Halimun-Salak National Park, Indonesia. *Biodiversity Conservation*, **19**, 1785–1803.

Layzer, J. A. (2008). *Natural Experiments: Ecosystem-based Management and the Environment*. Cambridge, MA: MIT Press.

Lévi-Strauss, C. (1969). *The Elementary Structure of Kinship*. Boston, MA: Beacon.

Locke, H. and P. Dearden (2005). Rethinking protected area categories and the new paradigm. *Environmental Conservation*, **32**(1), 1–10.

Maiolo, J. R. and J. Johnson (1988). Determining and utilizing communication networks in marine fisheries: a management tool. Gulf and Caribbean Fisheries, St. Thomas, USVI.

Mansuri, G. and V. Rao (2004). Community-based and -driven development: a critical review. *The World Bank Research Observer*, **19**(1), 1–39.

Mascia, M. B., J. P. Brosius, T. A. Dobson *et al.* (2003). Conservation and the social sciences. *Conservation Biology*, **17**(3), 649–650.

Molm, L. D. (2003). Theoretical comparisons of forms of exchange. *Sociological Theory*, **21**, 1–17.

Molm, L. D., N. Takahashi and G. Peterson (2000). Risk and trust in social exchange: an experimental test of a classical proposition. *American Journal of Sociology*, **105**(5), 1396–1427.

Noteboom, B. (2007). Social capital, institutions and trust. *Review of Social Economy*, **LXV**(1), 29–53.

Ostrom, E. (1990). *Governing the Commons: The Evolution of Institutions for Collective Action*. New York, NY: Cambridge University Press.

Ostrom, E. (1999). Coping with tragedies of the commons. *Annual Review of Political Science*, **2**, 493–535.

Ostrom, E., R. Gardner and J. Walker (1994). *Rules, Games, and Common-pool Resources*. Ann Arbor, MI: University of Michigan Press.

Pahl-Wostl, C. and M. Hare (2004). Processes of social learning in integrated resource management. *Journal of Community and Applied Social Psychology*, **14**, 193–206.

Prell, C., K. Hubacek, C. Quinn and M. S. Reed (2008). 'Who's in the network?' When stakeholders influence data analysis. *Systemic Practice and Action Research*, **21**, 443–458.

Pretty, J. and D. Smith (2004). Social capital in biodiversity conservation and management. *Conservation Biology*, **18**(3), 631–638.

Ramirez-Sanchez, S. (2007). A social relational approach to the conservation and management of fisheries: the rural communities of the Loreto Bay National Marine Park, BCS, Mexico. PhD thesis. School of Resource and Environmental Management, Simon Fraser University, Burnaby, BC.

Ramirez-Sanchez, S. and E. Pinkerton (2009). The impact of resource scarcity on bonding and bridging social capital: the case of fishers' information-sharing networks in Loreto, BCS, Mexico. *Ecology and Society*, **14**(1), 22.

Songorwa, A., T. Buhrs and K. F. D. Hughey (2000). Community-based wildlife management in Africa: a critical review of the literature. *Natural Resource Journal*, **40**, 604–643.

Stiles, R. G. (1972). Fishermen, wives and radios: aspects of communication in a Newfoundland fishing community. In R. Andersen and C. Wadel (Eds.), *North Atlantic Fishermen. Anthropological Essays on Modern Fishing*. St. Johns,

Newfoundland and Labrador: Institute for Social and Economic Research (ISER), pp. 35–60.

Triantaphyllou, E. (2000). *Multi-criteria Decision Making Methods: A Comparative Study. Applied Optimization Series*, 44. Dordrecht: Kluwer Academic.

Vandergeest, P. (2006). CBNRM communities in action. In S.R. Tyler (Ed.), *Communities, Livelihoods and Natural Resources. Action Research and Policy Change in Asia*. Intermediate Technologies Development Group Publishing/ International Development Research Centre, pp. 321–346.

Wasserman, S. and K. Faust (1999). *Social Network Analysis. Methods and Applications*. Cambridge: Cambridge University Press.

Wilshusen, P.R., S.R. Brechin, C.L. Fortwangler and P.C. West (2002). Reinventing a square wheel: critique of a resurgent protection paradigm in international biodiversity conservation. *Society and Natural Resources*, **15**(1), 17–40.

DAVID B. TINDALL, HOWARD HARSHAW, AND J. M. TAYLOR

7

The effects of social network ties on the public's satisfaction with forest management in British Columbia, Canada

7.1 INTRODUCTION

In the past several decades there has been a growing interest in the human/social dimensions of forestry and other natural resource industries.[1] In the past several years a specific interest in the role of social networks in these domains has arisen (Hubacek *et al.*, 2006, Prell *et al.*, 2009). There are many possible ways in which social networks might be important to societies/communities and natural resources. Communities themselves can be thought of as social networks (Wellman, 1979). Networks play an important role in diffusing information (Coleman *et al.*, 1966). Beliefs, values, and attitudes are formed partly in the context of network structures (Erickson, 1988; Harshaw and Tindall, 2005). Individuals are connected to one another through organizations (Breiger, 1974) in what are sometimes called two-mode networks. Political economists sometimes look at interorganizational ties, and the ways in which business leaders are linked through interlocking directorships (Carroll, 2004). Collective actions and social movements usually have a network basis (Diani and McAdam, 2003).

---

[1] The survey study described in this chapter was part of a larger research project that sought to understand social sustainability in the context of forestry. The larger project was led by Thomas Beckley. We would like to acknowledge the support of a Sustainable Forest Management Network research grant for this research project.

Social Networks and Natural Resource Management: Uncovering the Fabric of Environmental Governance, ed. Ö. Bodin and C. Prell. Published by Cambridge University Press.
© Cambridge University Press 2011.

Network analysts have examined the role of social networks in environmental movements that have arisen vis-à-vis various environmental and natural resource issues (Diani, 1995; Tindall, 2002, 2004).

7.1.1 Objectives/contents of this chapter

The objective of this chapter is to examine the effects of personal network ties on people's satisfaction with forest management.[2] More specifically, it will examine whether having ties to environmentalists, and to forestry professionals, is associated with one's level of satisfaction with forest management.

In this chapter we draw upon, and make connections across several quite distinct literatures. While this book focuses on social networks and natural resources – a theme shared by our chapter – our research has also been motivated by theory and literature in the broader social networks field, social movements research, and social psychology. Thus we will review some key ideas and studies from several of these areas. More specifically, we briefly touch upon the social networks and social capital literature, and then discuss work on social movements and social networks. Following this we provide a short overview of work on social networks and natural resources. Next we introduce our research questions, and then provide a justification for examining satisfaction with forest management (our main dependent variable). In order to provide some context for this chapter we briefly describe environmentalist campaigns over forestry. Next we provide our hypotheses, and provide justification for them in the literatures of diffusion of information, and social influence. We then turn to methods, and findings. We analyze survey data on the general public in three communities in British Columbia (BC) in order to investigate the relationship between network ties (to

[2] While we use the phrase "satisfaction with forest management" (and similar designations) we mean this in a relatively broad sense. We are referring to how the forests of British Columbia are managed, and relatedly their condition, and the effects of their management. There are a number of actors involved in the management of the "forests," including people working for the Ministry of Forests in British Columbia, loggers, professional foresters, engineers, and others. "Satisfaction" should not be implied as restricted solely to the performance of "professional forest managers" "or "professional foresters" but rather to the broader state of the forests, and the array of actors involved in managing them – most of whom work either in private sector forestry, or in the public sector managing forests, but of whom only a portion are "professional foresters."

environmentalists, and to forestry professionals) and satisfaction with forest management. Finally, we discuss the theoretical and practical implications of our findings and limitations of our study.

7.2   LITERATURE/BACKGROUND

7.2.1   Social networks and social capital

Putnam defines social capital as "features of social organization such as networks, norms, and trust that facilitate coordination and cooperation for mutual benefit" (1993: 36). A useful distinction is made in the social capital literature between "bonding social capital" which refers to linkages which are mainly or exclusively among members of the same group, and "bridging social capital" in which linkages exist amongst members of different groups. Social capital is:

> defined by its function. It is not a single entity, but a variety of entities having two characteristics in common: They all consist of some aspect of social structure, and they facilitate certain actions of individuals who are within the structure. (Coleman, 1990: 302)

Conceived as such, social capital includes social goods such as information, values, and social influence, which are produced and dissipated through social relations. The present study focuses on the effects of environmental organization members' ties on the general public. We partly conceptualize this effect as an instance of social capital. While there is some theoretical overlap between the social capital and social movement literatures, these are generally treated as distinct phenomena. Thus we will now turn to specifically consider some key ideas from the social movement literature.

7.2.2   Social movement and social networks

In recent years social movement scholars have given considerable attention to social networks in social movements (Knoke, 1990; Diani, 1995; Diani and McAdam, 2003; Mische, 2008). Four types of network processes have been explored, though these are not entirely separate phenomena. The basic types are: (1) personal networks that are implicated in the initial recruitment and ongoing mobilization of social movement members; (2) interorganizational networks that link members of distinct social movement groups; (3) network structures that help transmit ideas and other aspects of culture; (4) networks that produce social capital for group members.

A number of these studies have examined environmental movements (e.g. Diani, 1995; Tindall, 2002). The environmental movement has been an important force in shaping various natural resource industries, such as forestry in British Columbia (Wilson, 1998; Tindall, 2002).

The central thread of the argument linking social movement activities, networks, and social capital is as follows: environmental organizations mobilize individuals to engage in a variety of environmental movement activities. In the context of these activities, and their everyday lives, environmental organization members develop ties with people both inside and outside the environmental movement (Diani, 1997, Tindall *et al.*, 2010). The ties that are formed through mobilization can be thought of as a type of network social capital that has potential implications for other aspects of social capital. Through these bridging ties to people outside the movement, environmental organization members influence people's values, attitudes, and more generally, environmental concern (which can be thought of as a form of social capital). This "environmental concern" ultimately benefits the wider society by playing a part in influencing government policy, and motivating action on the part of various actors. The social influence that occurs through "bridging ties" is only one of a variety of ways in which the environmental movement potentially has an effect on society. Indeed this is probably a relatively minor aspect of the total influence of the environmental movement, and interpersonal social influence is generally an informal and unplanned process. In the present study, however, we argue that "environmental concern" is a measurable outcome that can be translated as "level of satisfaction with forest management." To the extent that this "environmental concern effect" (as indicated by decreased satisfaction in forest management) leads to policy and legislative responses that help to protect the environment, then we can see this as a collective benefit or a form of social capital. In terms of broader effects of environmental movement mobilization, the movement has arguably influenced the creation of new forest practices legislation (the Forest Practices Code), a Commission on land use (Commission on Resources and the Environment; CORE), various land-use planning processes that incorporated the participation of stakeholders (such as Land and Resource Management Plans; LRMPs), and the rise of forest certification in the province. In the present study we only set out to empirically document the "social influence" effect of these bridging ties, not the formation of the ties themselves, the consequences of diminished satisfaction with forest management, or these other processes. We have examined some other aspects of this argument elsewhere (Cormier *et al.*, 2007, Tindall *et al.*, 2010).

7.2.3   Social networks and natural resources

The application of social network analysis to public issues in natural resource management is helpful as it can permit examinations of social structure beyond typical groups, and can encompass broader, non-geographically bounded communities of interest (Stokowski, 1990; Stokowski and Lee, 1991; Blackshaw and Long, 1998). For example, one popular public use of forest lands is for outdoor recreation; as outdoor recreation activities are dependent on physical settings and managerial settings, people often look beyond their immediate communities for desired recreation opportunities, and people can become familiar with (and develop affinities for) forested landscapes in a broader sense. Further, by providing opportunities for outdoor recreation (a socially significant pursuit), forest management may support the creation of associational memberships, or weak ties (Stokowski, 1990; Putnam, 1995; Hemingway, 1999). Although, actual applications of social network analysis to forest management issues have been few, Prell *et al.* (2009) suggest that "the resource management community is beginning to realize that social networks matter" (p. 504).

Social network analysis may help to address traditional limitations in identifying, categorizing, and understanding the relationships of forest stakeholders. Harshaw and Tindall (2005) employed a social network approach to examine the role that social capital plays in the relationships that people have with forested landscapes, and identified the implications of these relationships to forest land-use planning. These authors drew two conclusions: (1) network diversity is directly related to identity diversity, which can mediate the relationship between network diversity and forest value diversity; and (2) strong ties are relatively more important than weak ties in explaining the formation of identity and diversity in forest values.

Social network analysis has also been used to investigate the roles and influence of different land-use stakeholders in the Peak District of the UK by examining people's positions within stakeholder networks (Hubacek *et al.*, 2006; Prell *et al.*, 2009). Prell *et al.* (2009) concluded that weak ties can make natural resource networks more resilient and adaptive to environmental change, as weak ties help to keep the network connected; this study also concluded that stakeholder selection can benefit from an investigation of the centrality of stakeholders in the context of tie strength and type of stakeholder as communicative and brokering individuals can be identified.[3]

A further study by Klenk *et al.* (2009) employed social network analysis to identify the network of interacting stakeholders (e.g. academic researchers, landowners, workers, First Nations, communities, industry, government) in Canadian forestry research. These authors concluded that such analyses can be useful in determining whether power and the control in information is concentrated or diffuse, and who may have influence on network dynamics. These studies provide some context in the natural resources literature for our research question, which we will now introduce.

7.2.4   Research questions

The general research question that guides the analysis in this chapter is,

RQ1.   *How are social network ties related to satisfaction with forest management?*

We ask two more specific subquestions:

RQ 1.1.   *How are ties to people in environmental organizations related to satisfaction with forest management?*
RQ 1.2.   *How are ties to forestry professionals related to satisfaction with forest management?*

Immediately below we will explicate the relevance of the dependent variable: satisfaction with forest management.

7.2.5   Why is understanding satisfaction with forest management important in British Columbia?

Perhaps the earliest use of satisfaction as an indicator of acceptability in natural resource management can be found in the field of outdoor recreation management, which has considered satisfaction to evaluate communication between forest managers and the public. Expectancy theory has framed the use of satisfaction in outdoor recreation management, as people engage in recreation activities with an expectation

---

[3] In the present study we consider whether weak ties or strong ties are more or less important in affecting satisfaction. We also argue that different types of processes might be associated with weak versus strong ties.

that they will be able to fulfill specific needs or motivations (Manning, 1999; Needham and Rollins, 2009). This is consistent with Inglehart (1977), who suggested that satisfaction "reflects the gap between one's aspiration level and one's perceived situation" (p. 118). In this sense then, satisfaction becomes the means of measuring the congruency between expectations and outcomes.

Manning's (1999) framing of visitor satisfaction for outdoor recreation management as a measure of quality seems appropriate for examining expectations of forest management. Quality can be considered an underlying goal of forest management: managers want to provide high-quality forestry outcomes (e.g. revenue for companies, employment for communities, maintenance/enhancement of biodiversity, public access) and the public desire high-quality benefits (e.g. local economic contributions, jobs, ecological health, opportunities for outdoor recreation). In this sense, satisfaction, as a measure of quality, is consistent with a sustainable forest management approach. Manning's (1999) conceptual model of recreation satisfaction (Figure 7.1) posits that overall satisfaction is a function of situational variables mediated by subjective evaluations.

The influence of people's socioeconomic and cultural characteristics, experience, and values introduces degrees of subjectivity in assessments of satisfaction. Several important patterns can be detected in the relationship between satisfaction and socioeconomic characteristics: education level is a better predictor of

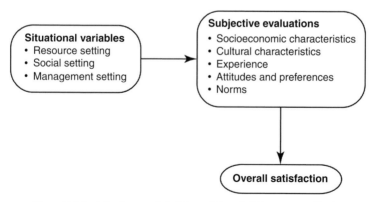

Figure 7.1 Satisfaction model. Adapted from Whisman & Hollenhorst, (1998) with kind permission of Springer Science and Business Media; and Manning (1999) with kind permission of Oregon State University Press.

satisfaction with one's life situation than income, as education is a relatively stable attribute; political and social life are also important components in understanding satisfaction (Inglehart, 1977). Within the context of natural resource management, satisfaction is a multi-dimensional concept, as biophysical, social, and management factors can each (and in combination) exert an influence on people's assessments of satisfaction. For example, high levels of satisfaction are linked to active solicitation of public opinion (Sargent-Michaud and Boyle, 2002).

Understanding people's satisfaction with forest management outcomes is important for helping managers to assess their success in meeting land-use objectives (Harshaw, 2008a). Such assessments of satisfaction can be useful for forest managers to be able to identify and quantify the impact of management and planning decisions – satisfaction can provide a measure of this (Horne *et al.*, 2005). The use of satisfaction as an indicator of "successful" forestry management in BC is apt, as past land-use management planning exercises (e.g. the Commission on Resources and the Environment, regional Land and Resource Management Plans) and sustainable forest management initiatives (e.g. forest certification, public advisory groups) have served to raise the public's awareness and expectations of forest management (Harshaw *et al.*, 2009). This begs the question, have people's expectations of forest management been met?

Understanding of people's satisfaction with land-use planning outcomes is important information for managers to utilize in assessing their success in meeting land-use objectives. In a survey of the West Kootenay region of BC, respondents reported moderate levels of satisfaction with the management of forest resources; the levels of reported satisfaction were generally lower than both respondents' knowledge of these forest resources and the importance that respondents had placed on these forest resources (Sheppard *et al.*, 2006). Harshaw (2008b) asked individuals from nine timber-dependent communities in BC to indicate their satisfaction with ten forest management outcomes often at issue in BC forest management; satisfaction was assessed for each outcome at local and provincial scales. Respondents' satisfaction was higher for local forest management outcomes than for provincial forest management outcomes, although there was a relatively high degree of uncertainty surrounding respondents' satisfaction with some forest management outcomes (especially at the provincial scale). Although satisfaction can provide a measure of the degree to which the public's expectations have been met, it is what is done with these assessments that matters: "If decision-makers do not satisfy the public that they are listening and considering what members of the public say, then the political process begins to break down" (Vining and Tyler, 1999: 23).

7.2.6   Environmentalist campaigns over forestry

It is our contention that the campaigns of environmentalists about the protection of old-growth forests, and about better forest management more generally have influenced satisfaction with forest management. Thus we will briefly describe some aspects of this campaign.

Williams *et al.* (1998) claim that "BC has been the site of some of the most contentious land use conflicts in Canada's history" (p. 861). During this contentious period, environmental interests gained prominence over the forest industry's hold over the framing of forest land-use through media and marketing campaigns that resulted in what has been characterized as the "war in the woods." Evidence of this conflict included protracted court actions, public demonstrations, acts of sabotage to logging equipment, economic boycotts of forest products, public conflicts between conservationists and industrial interests, and legal battles over native land claims and wilderness protection such as Clayoquot Sound, the Stein Valley, and Gwaii Haanas (Wilson, 1998).

One of the prominent policy initiatives in BC that responded to the forest management crisis and focused environmental campaigns in the 1990s was the Forest Practices Code, a consolidation and stream-lining of forestry legislation and regulations into enforceable guidelines for recommended operational practices and desired forest management results that were generally seen by environmentalists as a stronger regulatory approach (Wilson, 1998). The other important policy initiative that was a consequence of this crisis period was the development of land-use policies through consensus-based processes. A result of the increased influence in forest policy that environmentalists gained through these media battles, as well as the desire of the provincial government to achieve peace in the woods, was the initiation of processes that incorporated high degrees of stakeholder participation through shared decision making in land-use and resource planning, such as CORE and LRMPs (Cashore *et al.*, 2001; Halseth and Booth, 2003; Frame *et al.*, 2004). One outcome of these processes was a doubling of the area of parks and protected areas in the province

(Cashore *et al.*, 2001), evidence that the dominant position of the resource sector was being successfully challenged by environmental constituencies.

Driven by market forces that have been influenced by the environmental lobby, forest certification has also become a significant influence on forestry practices in BC. These standards have been adopted by forestry companies that seek certification that their management and operational practices are both ecologically and socially sustainable so that they can be competitive in the global timber market (Cashore *et al.*, 2001). The forest industry's adoption of certification frameworks like the Canadian Standards Association (CSA) and the Forest Stewardship Council (FSC) is changing the ways that land-use planning is practiced on tree farm licenses. Management plans developed under these frameworks recognize the role of non-timber products and amenity values, and go beyond existing regulatory requirements to incorporate public participation into the development of measures of criteria and indicators of sustainable forest management as well as in the monitoring of management practices to ensure that sustainability requirements are met (Canadian Standards Association, 2002; Forest Stewardship Council Canada Working Group, 2004).

7.2.7   Hypotheses and theoretical rationale

Above we introduced our research questions, talked about the relevance of satisfaction with forest management, and talked about some of the general ways in which the environmental movement has influenced views about forestry. Linked to these research questions, we offer two hypotheses. Our main hypothesis is:

H1.   *Ties to members of environmental organizations will be negatively associated with satisfaction with forest management.*

A secondary hypothesis is:

H2.   *Ties to forestry professionals will be positively associated with satisfaction with forest management.*

The rationale for these hypotheses is rooted in the processes of information diffusion, social comparison, and social influence.

7.2.8   Diffusion of information

Regarding information diffusion, there is a substantial literature on the diffusion of information through social networks (see Coleman *et al.*, 1966; Valente, 1995; Rogers, 2003). This argument posits that people learn, in part, about novel information through their social network contacts. Further, processes of social comparison (Gartrell, 1987) also occur in the context of social network structures. People compare their attitudes, opinions, experiences, and abilities with significant others in their personal networks.

With regard to forestry, an important source of information for the general public is the news media (Cormier and Tindall, 2005). However, people generally obtain information through multiple modalities, and personal contacts – or social network ties – are another important source. Indeed, some scholars have argued that people often utilize their interactions with social network ties to help them evaluate information from the media and other sources (Knoke, 1990).

7.2.9   Social comparison and social influence

The diffusion and development of values, attitudes, and opinions are also influenced by social network structures (Erickson, 1988). Explanations for social influence (Friedkin, 1998) are rooted in balance theory (Heider, 1958), and social comparison theory (Suls and Miller, 1977). For example, attitude formation is partly based on making comparisons with others in one's personal network. If ego compares with an alter about a particular attitude regarding object X, and the alter has a positive attitude towards X, then ego will be motivated to also develop a positive attitude towards X.

Different types of specific models have been developed, including those rooted in social cohesion, and structural equivalence (Burt, 1987; Erickson, 1988). Consistent with the broader "networks and social influence" theoretical argument, it is asserted here that bridging ties from environmental organization members to non-environmental organization members serve as a conduit for social influence concerning forestry issues. Parallel arguments apply to ties between forestry professionals and the general public.

This study is part of a series of interrelated projects on environmentalism and forestry in British Columbia where we have conducted survey research, interviews, field research, and analysis of available documents. Questioning the public about their views about forest management is not an esoteric thing in British Columbia. Forestry has historically been one of the most important industries in the province, and conflicts over forestry have dominated the local and regional news periodically over the past several decades. Field research, interviews, and other sources have shown how environmentalists have been very dramatic and persuasive in their critiques of forestry – especially criticism of, and opposition to, clearcut logging of old-growth rain forests. People working in forestry have been equally engaged in dismissing environmentalist criticisms of forestry often by ridiculing environmentalist claims, and by engaging in ad hominem critiques of environmentalists (e.g. "hippies on welfare," "cappuccino sucking condo dwellers"). Almost everyone in BC has an opinion about the management of forests. They are shaped to a large extent by the media, partly by direct experience, and it is our claim that opinions are also partly shaped through interpersonal interactions in social networks.

To reiterate, in the context of the present study we argue that some members of the general public will learn about forestry through their contact with environmental organization members, some people will learn about forestry through their contact with forestry professionals, and some people will obtain information from both of these sectors of their social networks. As the environmental movement has for a considerable period of time been highly critical of various aspects of the forest industry, we would expect having ties to environmental organization members to be negatively correlated with satisfaction with forest management. Conversely, as forestry professionals make their livelihood from forestry, and have been socialized in forestry schools, companies, and communities, they are generally much more positive about forest management. Thus we would expect having ties to forestry professionals to be positively correlated with satisfaction with forest management. While we have described expected correlations between network ties and satisfaction with forest management, it is our contention that several overlapping and possibly reinforcing processes are at work: information diffusion, social influence, and social comparison processes (amongst others).

7.3 METHODS

This section documents the survey and sample design, the questions posed to respondents, and the analytical methods.

7.3.1 Sample design

The questionnaire utilized in this study was mailed to residents of three communities in British Columbia, Canada, with varying levels of direct and/or indirect dependence on forests and forestry: Greater Vancouver, Kelowna, and Armstrong. (See Figure 7.2 for a map depicting the locations of these three communities.) These communities also provide useful variation in terms of size and location. Greater Vancouver is on the coast of BC, is a large metropolitan center, and has relatively less direct dependence on the forest industry. Kelowna is located in the southern interior of BC, it is a middle-sized urban center, and is quickly transforming from a resource-based community to a community that is an important retirement and tourism destination. Armstrong is also located in the southern interior of BC. It is much smaller in size, and compared to the other two communities it is much more directly connected to the forestry sector.

The specific sampling procedure was systematic sampling with a random start. A total of 572 responses from all communities were received between November 20, 2005 and May 23, 2006, which represents an overall response rate of 31.5% after correcting for undeliverable addresses. Response rates were highest from Armstrong and lowest from Vancouver. Descriptive analysis suggests that men are somewhat over-represented in the sample, and younger people are

Figure 7.2 Community locations in British Columbia.

somewhat under-represented. The former bias may be due to a greater interest in forestry issues on the part of men, and perhaps also to a greater likelihood of phone lines being listed in men's names. The latter (age) bias may be due to the fact that we were using a mailing list based on traditional landline telephone numbers. It may be that younger people with cell phones were less likely to be on the list; it is also possible that younger people are more mobile, and thus less likely to be on the list; lastly, it is also possible that younger people may see forestry as being less relevant to their lives.

To remedy unit response bias the sample has been weighted by age and gender for each community to match the parameters for the census. Thus the sample is demographically representative in terms of age and gender by community. Of course it is possible that there are still some sampling biases related to other variables.[4]

Earlier analysis revealed no significant differences between the three communities for key variables such as satisfaction with forest management. This provides justification for pooling the three samples, to increase the N for multi-variate statistical analysis. Nevertheless, in the multiple regression analyses that follow we do include dummy variables for the different communities in order to rule out "community effects." (Kelowna is the reference category that is omitted from the regression models; see Table 7.1.)

7.3.2   Survey design

The survey design followed the principles of the Tailored Design Method, which identifies procedures to maximize survey return rates and minimize survey error (Salant and Dillman, 1994; Dillman, 2000). The questionnaire was 26 pages in length.[5] Although the questionnaire sought opinions and beliefs about a wide range of forestry-related

---

[4] These sampling biases may have some effect on descriptive univariate results, but should have little influence on the multi-variate results where we test theoretical arguments. More specifically, if two variables are thought to be correlated based on theory then they should be correlated even if there is some sampling bias for the two variables (as long as there is reasonable variation for the two variables). In other words, while specific parameter estimates may not be precise, pairs of variables should still be significantly correlated (for more on these arguments see Opp, 1986).

[5] While the questionnaire is somewhat lengthy by ideal standards, ten pages were primarily composed of photographs, and three additional pages did not include substantive questions, so there were only 13 pages of questions.

topics the results reported here focus on items related to residents' satisfaction with forest management. Data were also collected about demographic information (e.g. gender, age, personal income, years of education), and on social network ties to people from different occupations/organizations.

7.3.3   Measures

We describe the key independent and dependent variables below.

7.3.3.1   Satisfaction with forest management (dependent variable)

Single item appraisals of satisfaction may be too broad and not specific enough to elicit useful information for management activities (Manning, 1999). We employed facet appraisal (Needham and Rollins, 2009) as people's degree of satisfaction may differ for the various aspects of sustainable forest management, and to capture the multi-dimensional aspects of sustainable forest management (e.g. resource, social, and management settings). As noted above, we may expect differences between local and provincial assessments of satisfaction as people's familiarity with sustainable forest management at different scales can vary; additionally, forest planning and management occurs at different scales (Harshaw et al., 2009). Thus it seems appropriate to gauge people's satisfaction with sustainable forest management at different scales. Seven facets of sustainable forest management were identified (i.e. quality of life: social, ecological, community cohesion, participation in decision making, outdoor recreation, ecological processes, and aesthetics and landscape) and were measured with 20 items.

Respondents indicated their level of satisfaction with each aspect of forest management at both local and provincial scales for each question. Respondents indicated their degree of satisfaction with each statement on a five-point scale from "not at all satisfied" (1) to "extremely satisfied" (5); respondents were also given the option of indicating that they did not know enough, or did not have an opinion, about a particular statement.

Issues regarding reliability and validity were statistically assessed through the use of Cronbach's alpha, and factor analysis. Cronbach's alpha for the satisfaction items at the local level was quite high: $\alpha = 0.93$. This indicates a high degree of inter-item reliability across the 20 questionnaire items. Cronbach's alpha for the items at the provincial level was identical: $\alpha = 0.93$.

Factor analysis of the items for local satisfaction suggested a single factor solution. There was a large drop off in the scree plot between factor 1 and factor 2. Factor 1 accounts for 44.8% of the total variation in the items, a moderate amount. The factor loading for each of the items was ≥ 0.46.

The results of the factor analysis for the items for provincial satisfaction were virtually identical to those reported above for local satisfaction. For the provincial satisfaction items factor 1 accounts for 45.1% of the total variation in the items. The factor loading for each of the items was ≥ 0.48. Again this is reasonable evidence for a single factor solution.

In sum, the results show a very good level of inter-item reliability for the indicators for the two satisfaction scales, and the factor analysis provides moderately strong evidence that the items load on a single dimension (in each case), which we interpret theoretically as satisfaction with forest management activities. Thus each of these two sets of variables were summed together (and divided by 20, the number of indicators) to form an index for satisfaction at the local level, and satisfaction at the provincial level.[6]

7.3.3.2 *Social network ties (independent variables)*

To measure social network ties, a social position generator, similar to those developed by Lin *et al.* (2001) and Erickson (1996), was employed in the questionnaire. In this analysis, we focused on the range of weak and strong ties that respondents had to particular structural positions. The position generator was modified to ensure coverage of occupations and organizational affiliations related to forestry, natural resources more generally, and the outdoors (as well as other occupations and positions). Respondents were presented with a list of 45 positions and asked to indicate what relationship (if any) they had associated with each position: acquaintances, close friends, relatives, and/or whether they themselves were a member of the position. For the purposes of the analyses in this chapter we focus on ties to people who belong to environmental organizations, and ties to people who belong to a set of traditional forestry occupations.

[6] Where respondents indicated "don't know" for an item, we recoded this item as "3" (the neutral or midpoint of the scale) in order to limit loss of cases due to missing data. Otherwise if anyone said "don't know" to any of the 20 items – then the case would have been deleted in the multiple regression analyses.

With regard to environmental organizations, if the respondent knew an acquaintance who was a member of a local environmental organization they received a score of 1; otherwise 0. Similarly if the respondent knew an acquaintance who belonged to a regional, provincial, or national environmental organization they received a score of 1; otherwise 0. These questions were repeated for close friends, and for relatives. Also the respondents were asked about their own membership status in these organizations. Then, within each type of tie (e.g. acquaintances) the scores for environmental organization members were summed. The values for weak ties (acquaintances) to environmental organizations thus ranged from 0 to 2. Similarly, the values for ties to close friends who belonged to environmental groups, and for relatives who belonged to environmental groups, ranged from 0 to 2.

The same format was used to ask respondents about their ties to people involved in forestry. Respondents were asked whether or not they knew an acquaintance/close friend/relative who was: (1) a BC Ministry of Forests manager or employee, (2) a private sector forestry consultant, (3) a forestry sector manager or worker involved in harvesting (e.g. a logger), (4) a saw mill manager or worker, (5) a pulpmill or fine paper mill manager or worker, (6) a reforestation/silviculture manager or worker. The responses for each of these categories (for each type of tie: acquaintance, close friend, or relative) were coded as 1 (if they knew an acquaintance) or 0 (if they did not know anyone). The set of responses for the six categories were then summed together. Thus weak ties (or acquaintances) is a sum of ties to these six categories for the acquaintance category. Parallel measures were also constructed for ties to close friends in forestry, and relatives in forestry. The potential scores for the forestry network measures ranged from 0 to 6.

To operationalize respondent's employment status, we utilized the same six categories above, with reference to whether or not the respondent was a member of these categories. The responses were again summed together to create a measure for employment (employed in forestry). The potential scores for this measure ranged from 0 to 6.

7.4   RESULTS

For our analysis we utilize OLS multiple regression. The multiple regression models are displayed in Table 7.1. Standardized regression coefficients are shown. Two different dependent variables are utilized: level of satisfaction with forest management at the local level, and level of satisfaction with forest management at the provincial level.

Table 7.1. *Models predicting satisfaction with forest management (standardized regression coefficients are shown).*

	Model with ENGO WTs		Model with ENGO STs		Model with both ENGO WTs and STs	
Independent variables	Model 1: Satisfaction with FM local	Model 2: Satisfaction with FM provincial	Model 3: Satisfaction with FM local	Model 4: Satisfaction with FM provincial	Model 5: Satisfaction with FM local	Model 6: Satisfaction with FM provincial
Socio-demographic-economic						
Gender (female = 1)	0.03	−0.09	0.04	−0.08	0.05	−0.08
Education	−0.04	−0.08	−0.05	−0.07	−0.04	−0.06
Income	0.04	−0.05	0.06	0.03	0.05	−0.03
Age	−0.15***	−0.16***	−0.14***	−0.16***	−0.15***	−0.15***
Community: Armstrong	−0.05	−0.04	−0.05	−0.03	−0.06	−0.05
Community: Vancouver	0.12*	0.07	0.10	0.05	0.13*	0.07
Network variables (social ties)						
Weak ties to ENGO members	−0.13*	−0.12*	-----	-----	−0.13*	−0.11*
Strong ties to ENGO members (close friends)	-----	-----	−0.10	−0.18***	−0.08	−0.16***
Ties to relatives who are ENGO members	-----	-----	-----	-----	0.02	0.02

Membership in ENGOs	0.02	0.03	0.05	0.08	0.03	0.06
Employment in forestry	0.08	0.06	0.08	0.07	0.08	0.07
Close friend to someone in forestry	0.04	−0.09	0.04	−0.09	0.06	−0.06
Weak ties to someone in forestry	0.06	0.03	0.00	−0.01	0.06	0.04
Relative in forestry	−0.02	0.01	−0.04	−0.02	−0.02	0.01
R^2	0.06**	0.06**	0.06*	0.08***	0.07**	0.08***
N	436	414	437	414	436	414

$^*P \leq 0.05$, $^{**}P \leq 0.01$, $^{***}P \leq 0.005$.

To test H1, as an independent variable we alternatively utilize weak ties to environmental organization members, and ties with close friends (as an indicator of strong ties) who belong to environmental organizations as indicators of "ties to environmental organization members." To test H2, as an independent variable we alternatively utilize weak ties to forestry professionals, and ties with close friends who are forestry professionals.

As we are framing this analysis – in part – as an example of exploring a potential social movement outcome, our main focus is on the effects of ties to environmental organization members and H1. However, in the process of examining the effects of ties to environmental organization members, we control for ties to forestry professionals, and thus this allows us to simultaneously test H2.

In the regression models we also control for several standard socio-demographic-economic variables (gender, education, income, and age) and for the community of the respondents (as the survey was conducted in three different communities).

Models 1 and 2 examine the effects of weak ties (acquaintances) to ENGO members on satisfaction with forest management (at the local and provincial level) but omit the effects of ties to close friends who are members of ENGOs. Models 3 and 4 examine the effects of ties to close friends who belong to ENGOs on satisfaction with forest management (at the local and provincial level) but omit the effects of weak ties (acquaintances) who are members of ENGOs. Models 5 and 6 examine the effects of both weak ties, and ties to close friends who belong to ENGOs on satisfaction with forest management (at the local and provincial level) and in addition control for ties to relatives who are ENGO members.

In addition to the above, we also control for membership in environmental organizations (to ensure any association between ENGO ties and satisfaction with forest management is not simply a function of the respondent's ENGO membership), and for employment in forestry (to make sure that any association between ties to forestry professionals and satisfaction with forest management is not simply a function of the respondent's employment in forestry). Finally, in all of the tables we also control for whether or not the respondent has a tie to a relative employed in forestry.[7]

---

[7] Sometimes in the social network literature ties to close friends and ties to relatives are combined as indicators of strong ties. We chose to keep these analytically separate here because the ties to relatives measure did not distinguish immediate family living in the household (which is often used as an indicator of strong ties) and more distant relatives (which are not necessarily indicative of strong ties).

7.4.1   Using weak ties to ENGO members to predict satisfaction with forest management

Column 1 of Table 7.1 provides a multiple regression model that statistically explains level of satisfaction with forest management at the local level. In terms of the socio-demographic-economic variables, age and community (Vancouver) have effects. Older respondents are less satisfied with forest management at the local level. This is a somewhat surprising effect, and it is contrary to some of the literature in environmental sociology on age cohorts and attitudes about environmental issues. Residents of Vancouver are more satisfied with forest management at the local level. This is perhaps not too surprising as there is no ongoing industrial logging in the Greater Vancouver area. (Although it should be noted that there is ongoing management of urban forests, and Greater Vancouver has more forested land in its city limits than most comparable cities.)

In terms of the network variables, the only variable with a significant effect is weak ties (acquaintances) to ENGO members. Having weak ties to ENGO members is negatively associated with satisfaction with forest management at the local level. This provides support for our main hypothesis (H1). It should be noted that this effect persists even when controlling for ENGO membership. Thus it is not simply the case that ENGO members have a greater number of weak ties to ENGO members, and also have lower satisfaction with forest management. Rather, it is the case that regardless of whether or not someone belongs to an ENGO, if they have weak ties to ENGO members they tend to be less satisfied with forest management at the local level.

Regarding H2, none of the variables for ties to forestry professionals are significantly associated with satisfaction with forest management at the local level.

Overall the model explains only a modest amount of satisfaction with forest management ($R^2 = 0.06$). However, this is not too surprising as we have not included "objective" measures of the quality of forest management. It is nevertheless interesting that patterns of social network ties play a statistically significant role in explaining subjective satisfaction with forest management.

Column 2 (Model 2) of Table 7.1 provides the identical model as column 1 except now the dependent variable is level of satisfaction with forest management at the provincial level. Substantively the results here are similar to those for the first model with the exception that the community effect (Vancouver) is no longer significant. There are significant effects only for age, and for weak ties to ENGO members. Thus again H1 is supported, but H2 is not supported.

7.4.2   Using ties to close friend ENGO members to predict satisfaction with forest management

Model 3 of Table 7.1 provides a multiple regression model that statistically explains level of satisfaction with forest management at the local level. In term of the socio-demographic-economic variables, only age has an effect. Older respondents are less satisfied with forest management at the local level. None of the network ties variables are significant; thus these results fail to support either H1 or H2. Again, the model explains a relatively small amount of variation in the dependent variable.

Column 4 of Table 7.1 provides the identical model as Model 3 except now the dependent variable is level of satisfaction with forest management at the provincial level. Substantively the results of this model are similar to Model 4 with the important exception that now there is a significant network effect. Again, the only "control variable" that is significant is age; older respondents are less satisfied. In terms of networks, there is a significant effect for ties to close friends who belong to ENGOs. Respondents who have close friends who belong to environmental organizations tend to be less satisfied with forest management at the provincial level. Thus this effect seems to exist for satisfaction with forest management at the provincial level, but not at the local level. None of the other network ties variables are significant. Thus H1 is supported, but H2 is not supported. Again, a modest amount of variation in the dependent variable is explained by the independent variables in the model.

7.4.3   Full model comparing weak ties to strong ties with ENGO members to predict satisfaction with forest management

Model 5 of Table 7.1 provides a multiple regression model predicting satisfaction with forest management at the local level, and this time includes both weak ties to ENGO members, ties to close friends who belong to ENGOs, and also controls for ties with relatives who belong to ENGOs. The objective here is to test for the earlier observed effect while including a full set of controls. In terms of the control variables we observe an effect for age; older respondents are less satisfied. In terms of the network ties variables, the only significant effect is for weak ties to ENGO members. People with weak ties to ENGO members were less satisfied. Thus this provides partial support for H1, but again H2 is not supported.

Finally, Model 6 of Table 7.1 provides a multiple regression model predicting satisfaction with forest management at the provincial level, and includes both weak ties to ENGO members, ties to close friends who belong to ENGOs, and also controls for ties with relatives who belong to ENGOs. In terms of the control variables only age has an effect. Again older respondents are less satisfied. In terms of the network ties variables the results here contrast with those provided in Model 5. There are significant effects for *both* ties to close friends who belong to ENGOs, and for weak ties. None of the other network ties variables had a significant effect. Again, these results provide partial support for H1, but again H2 is not supported. Also, again the model explains a modest amount of variation.

Thus Models 5 and 6 reveal some subtle differences between satisfaction with forest management at the local level and the provincial level. Based in part on these findings, and in part on theory, we speculate that strong ties are slightly more important for explaining satisfaction at the provincial level, while weak ties are slightly more important for explaining satisfaction at the local level. In terms of network theory, strong ties are more likely to be implicated in social influence processes, while for weak ties the process of information diffusion is generally more important than social influence. Thus it seems plausible that a social influence effect is occurring at the provincial level, while an information diffusion effect is happening at the local level. These findings should only be considered to be suggestive and generalizing from these findings should be cautioned as the effects, and the overall R^2, are quite modest.

7.5 DISCUSSION

There are several premises that underlie this research. First, we argue that satisfaction with forest management is of some consequence. In extreme situations, dissatisfaction can lead to conflict and social strife in communities (such as the road blockades in Clayoquot Sound in the summer of 1993; see Shaw, 2002). But it can also affect perceived quality of life, and tangible things such as housing prices (Beckley *et al.*, 2002). As such we argue that satisfaction with various facets of forest management can be seen as an indicator of the subjective aspect of social sustainability.

Second, we argue that satisfaction with forest management will partly be affected by "objective phenomena" – such as the actual job that forest managers are doing – and the objective characteristics of opportunities for public participation, but will also be influenced by characteristics of citizens, including their socio-demographic-economic factors and social networks. Hence the same objective condition could be evaluated differently by different populations or sub-populations, and this could have consequences for forest managers and land-planning processes. In the present analysis we have focused on the social characteristics of the general public in three British Columbian communities.

Third, social networks have consequences for natural resource management. In this instance, we have shown how social network ties are associated with the level of satisfaction that members of the general public have with forest management. We argue that satisfaction is relevant for the relationship that community members have to forest managers, can affect wellbeing, and is one of the factors that precipitate conflict over forests.

The main focus of this book is on the linkage between social networks and natural resource governance and management. However, we have also tried to link our analysis to several other literatures. One of these is the literature on social movement outcomes. The environmental movement in British Columbia has done a variety of things to influence forest management in British Columbia. They have engaged in publicity campaigns that have seemingly influenced public opinion. They have promoted forest certification, which in turn has influenced some management practices. They have met with governments and pressured them (both directly and indirectly) to change policies and legislation regarding forestry. They have developed working relationships with First Nations, forestry workers, and other stakeholders. These are all ways in which they have arguably influenced forest management. And while the above processes have not been the focus of this specific study, some of these processes involve social networks. Beyond the ways in which leaders and formal organizations have tried to influence governments and society through formal strategies and tactics, informal interpersonal relations also have an effect. Indeed it is our argument that an "informal outcome" of social movement mobilization is the social influence of environmentalists on members of the general public. We have demonstrated that consistent with the critical perspective that environmentalists have taken regarding forestry in BC, if a member of the general public has social ties to environmentalists then they tend to be less satisfied with forest management.

Returning to the theme of social networks and natural resources, social network analysis can include both formal organizations and informal relationships. Indeed, social network analysis can make a very important contribution to understanding social processes by documenting informal social structures, and their consequences.

We have shown several statistically significant effects of weak ties and strong ties to environmentalists on the public's satisfaction with forest management. However, there were no corresponding statistically significant effects for ties to forestry professionals. This suggests that regarding the subject of satisfaction with forestry, environmentalists are more influential than foresters are. It should be cautioned that the effect sizes presented here are relatively small. However, this is an interesting pattern of findings, and should be of concern to forestry professionals.

To understand our results some attention should be paid to the context of this case. The results reported here are in part a legacy of the environmental movement's campaign to protect old-growth forests in British Columbia, which occurred over the preceding 20 years or so. Environmentalists engaged in demonstrations and logging-road blockages. They documented alleged bad forestry practices in video documentaries, posters, coffee-table books, and slide shows (Tindall and Begoray, 1993; Wilson, 1998; Shaw, 2002; Tindall, 2002; Cormier and Tindall, 2005). While forestry professionals are generally seen as having a vested interest in their claims that they have managed the forests well, environmentalists have no direct financial stake in the forests, and this – in part – makes them (on the whole) more credible spokespeople on the topic.

It is possible that the social ties to ENGO members versus social ties to forestry professionals effect is due in part to environmentalists having different patterns of ego-centric network ties. We have not investigated this possibility in the current study.[8] But elsewhere we have documented a statistically significant difference in the diversity

---

[8] For several reasons we cannot fully test the idea suggested here. Most importantly, the position generator we used focused on a set of occupations and positions that we speculated might be related in various ways to forestry. The sample is representative of the general public, but the list of occupations in the

of occupationally related social network ties between forestry professionals and non-foresters (Harshaw and Tindall, 2005). Thus, it may also be the case that ENGO members are more influential because of the characteristics of their networks. This is a topic for future research.

There are several limitations to this analysis, and as such the findings reported here should be considered "suggestive." First, as noted earlier, the effects and the R^2s reported here are relatively modest. It is possible that they are due to sampling error. Second, and not previously discussed, in the network literature a distinction is sometimes made between networks as the cause (sometimes called social influence effects) and networks as the effect (sometimes called selection effects). We have been arguing that network ties (namely to people in environmental organizations) have an impact on satisfaction with forest management – thus network ties partially cause satisfaction with forest management. However, it is also plausible that people who are more concerned about forest management (and have lower levels of satisfaction) go out of their way to make ties to people in environmental organizations. Because of the cross-sectional survey design of this study we are limited in distinguishing between these two different effects. However, one piece of evidence in support of the argument proffered here is that the network ties effect holds even when membership in ENGOs is controlled for. To elaborate, we would expect people who are more concerned about forest management to be more likely to join an environmental organization. Further, we would expect those who belong to environmental organizations to be more likely to have ties to ENGO members. Now if the association between network ties to ENGO members and satisfaction with forest management were entirely due to "selection effects" then we might

position generator questionnaire item is not representative of the occupations in the general population. Thus we cannot easily test the relative patterns of ties that environmentalists and forestry professionals have to occupations in the general public. Further, the respective Ns for both environmental organization members and forestry professionals in the sample were relatively small (both < 30). Nevertheless, exploratory analysis showed that with regard to the number of ties that environmental organization members had to the occupations in the position generator, environmental organization members tended to have a statistically greater number of ties to different occupations than non-environmental organization members (for weak ties, close friends, and relatives). Similarly, forestry professionals had a statistically greater number of ties to different occupations than non-forestry professionals (for weak ties, close friends, and relatives). However, for these two small subsamples, there were no statistically significant differences between them in total ties to the 45 different occupations.

expect the association to disappear when ENGO membership is controlled. But it does not. So this constitutes some support in favor of the social network argument made here, i.e. that social ties influence levels of satisfaction.

The main argument of this study is that network ties affect "satisfaction with forest management." Our theoretical claim is that this is a result of social influence and/or information diffusion through social networks. We have tried to couch this analysis in the broader framework of the social capital literature, though our central argument about network effects still holds independent of this framework. An often overlooked observation about social capital is that it exists to some extent in the eyes of the beholder. Social capital is very often "useful" for some actors, and not for others. In the context of the present study, claims about forest management in the BC case are contentious. And whether or not the negative effects of ties to ENGO members on satisfaction with forest management among the general public are a "public good" or a "public bad" is to some extent a matter of perspective. To the extent that forest management could be improved, and that concern about forest management motivates improvement, then we could see this to be a "public good." To the extent that forest management has been of relatively high quality in BC, then the negative influence of ENGO ties on the public's views about forest management constitute an unnecessary and somewhat harmful influence, and thus could be viewed as a "public bad." It is not our objective in this chapter to resolve this debate, but rather to point out that interpreting these results is somewhat relative to one's perspective.[9]

What are the implications of this research for practitioners? As suggested above, the implications of this research depend upon one's point of view. Environmental organization leaders might be heartened to learn that informal interpersonal interactions between ENGO members and the general public can influence the views of the latter. Thus ENGO leaders might want to use this as motivation to encourage more "grassroots activism" where grassroots environmental organization members engage average citizens on forestry and other environmental

---

[9] While this sounds like a "social constructionist" argument, the authors work within the "realist" tradition in that they believe there are "real environmental problems." However, the current analysis focuses on social processes, and thus resolving the status of quality forest management in British Columbia is not our task here.

topics. Forest managers might use the findings of this research to motivate them to try to work collaboratively with environmentalists. In fact, this has already started to happen in some cases in British Columbia. Some examples include particular First Nations–forestry company joint ventures that have been supported by environmental organizations (such as Iisaak in Clayoquot Sound), and the Great Bear Rainforest agreement that involved collaboration amongst the forestry industry, environmentalists, First Nations, the provincial government, and others. These are only two amongst a variety of possible implications. More generally, these findings suggest that incorporating an analysis of social ties in research on people's views about natural resources can help to shed light on trends regarding environmental concern. It should be stressed that in this analysis we have only examined social ties to two types of potential influential actors. Future studies might consider analyzing ties to a wider array of stakeholders and other actors. Also, from the perspective of "monitoring" indicators of social sustainability, it would be useful to track key statistical predictors of satisfaction with forest management (like social network ties) as these will be useful for understanding and predicting trends over time. Without tracking these types of indicators it becomes impossible to understand whether changes in satisfaction are due to forest management practices, or to changes in the characteristics and organization of the population. Knowledge of these trends might also be useful in providing context for engaging relevant civil society organizations in public participation processes.

Reflections

Social network boundaries

These are not applicable since this was not a whole network study.

Ecological boundaries

Our study focused on samples of three communities in British Columbia. Forests are managed at the provincial level in Canada, thus it was appropriate to have British Columbia serve as a "political boundary." The province itself is made up of many ecosystems. These three communities were selected because they varied in size (large, medium, small), and in terms of their level of direct reliance on the forest industry.

Decide on unit of analysis

Our study focuses (indirectly) on interpersonal influence, thus the individual unit of analysis is most appropriate.

Data-gathering issues

For the analysis presented in our chapter we just focused on ties to environmental organization members, and to people working in forestry. We also collected data on respondents' ties to people with other types of occupations and relations to the forest, but we did not include these in the present analysis – for strategic reasons of focusing our analysis. These data could also be analyzed.

We used the position generator methodology to collect our data. We might have used a different approach, such as a name generator. If we had done this, it would have been interesting to collect data on the ties amongst the alters. But this was not possible with the approach we adopted.

Ethical issues

The approach we adopted allowed us to avoid the ethical problems of techniques such as the name roster approach.

Explanatory power of social network analysis

It was not really our intention to compare the explanatory power of the SNA approach to other approaches for explaining the outcome variable. We were simply focused on the theoretical issue of examining whether or not there was an effect for network ties to particular types of contacts, controlling for some other key variables. In the case of our study, networks are theoretically relevant at a number of different levels, in a number of different ways. We only measured one of about half a dozen network processes that were likely ultimately implicated in affecting people's perceptions about forest management. Thus we cannot make claims about the relative explanatory power of the SNA approach compared to others because we are probably underestimating the explanatory power of the SNA approach.

Non-network data

We gather a great deal of additional quantitative data, most of which we did not include in the present study as the present analysis is just one of a number of planned analyses. Certainly it is at least useful to collect data that will allow one to rule out alternative explanations, and the effects of third variables.

Is social network analysis static?

Most social science research is static in the sense that it is usually based on cross-sectional designs. Social network analysis is no more susceptible to this criticism than other forms of explanation. To address this criticism one needs to collect longitudinal data.

REFERENCES

Beckley, T., J. Parkins and R. Stedman (2002). Indicators of forest-dependent community sustainability: the evolution of research. *Forestry Chronicle*, **78**(5), 626–636.

Blackshaw, T. and J. Long (1998). A critical examination of the advantages of investigating community and leisure from a social network perspective. *Leisure Studies*, **17**(4), 233–248.

Breiger, R. L. (1974). The duality of persons and groups. *Social Forces*, **53**, 181–190.

Burt, R. S. (1987). Social contagion and innovation: cohesion versus structural equivalence. *American Journal of Sociology*, **92**, 1287–1335.

Canadian Standards Association (2002). CAN/CSA-Z809-02. *Sustainable Forest Management: Requirements and Guidance. A National Standard of Canada* (approved May 2003), 2nd Edition. Mississauga, ON: Canadian Standards Association.

Carroll, W. K. (2004). *Corporate Power in a Globalizing World: A Study in Elite Social Organization*. Don Mills, ON: Oxford University Press.

Cashore, B., G. Hoberg, M. Howlett, J. Rayner and J. Wilson. (2001). *In Search of Sustainability: British Columbia Forest Policy in the 1990s*. Vancouver, BC: UBC Press.

Coleman, J. S., E. Katz and H. Menzel (1966). *Medical Innovation*. New York, NY: Bobbs-Merrill.

Cormier, J. J. and D. B. Tindall (2005). Wood frames: framing the forests in British Columbia. *Sociological Focus*, **38**(1), 1–24.

Cormier, J., D. B. Tindall and M. Diani. (2007). Network social capital as an outcome of social movement mobilization. Paper presented at the Annual Meetings of the American Sociological Association, New York.

Diani, M. (1995). *Green Networks: A Structural Analysis of the Italian Environmental Movement*. Edinburgh: Edinburgh University Press.

Diani, M. (1997). Social movements and social capital. *Mobilization*, **2**, 129–147.

Diani, M. and D. McAdam (Eds.) (2003). *Social Movements and Networks: Relational Approaches to Collective Action*. Oxford: Oxford University Press.

Dillman, D. A. (2000). *Mail and Internet Surveys: The Tailored Design Method*, 2nd Edition. Toronto, ON: John Wiley and Sons.

Erickson, B. H. (1988). The relational basis of attitudes. In B. Wellman and S. D. Berkowitz (Eds.), *Social Structures: A Network Approach*. Cambridge: Cambridge University Press, pp. 99–121.

Erickson, B. H. (1996). Culture, class, and connections. *American Journal of Sociology*, **102**(1), 217–252.

Forest Stewardship Council Canada Working Group (2004). *National Boreal Standard*. Toronto, ON: Forest Stewardship Council (FSC) Canada Working Group.

Frame, T. M., T. Gunton and J. C. Day (2004). The role of collaboration in environmental management: an evaluation of land and resource planning in British Columbia. *Journal of Environmental Planning and Management*, **47**(1), 59–82.

Friedkin, N. E. (1998). *A Structural Theory of Social Influence*. Cambridge: Cambridge University Press.

Gartrell, C. D. (1987). Network approaches to social evaluation. *Annual Review of Sociology*, **13**, 49–66.

Halseth, G. and A. Booth (2003). What works well; what needs improvement: lessons in public consultation from British Columbia's resource planning processes. *Local Environment*, **8**(4), 437–455.

Harshaw, H. W. (2008a). Outdoor recreation participation in BC forest-dependent communities. *Forest Chronicle*, **84**(2), 210–220.

Harshaw, H. W. (2008b). *British Columbia Sustainable Forest Management Public Opinion Survey 2006/2007: Synthesis of Results from Nine Communities*. Vancouver, BC: University of British Columbia Collaborative for Advanced Landscape Planning.

Harshaw, H. W., S. R. J. Sheppard and P. Jeakins (2009). Public attitudes toward sustainable forest management: opinions from forest-dependent communities in British Columbia. *BC Journal of Ecosystems and Management*, **10**(2), 81–103.

Harshaw, H. W. and D. B. Tindall (2005). Social structure, identities, and values: a network approach to understanding people's relationships to forests. *Journal of Leisure Research*, **37**(4), 426–449.

Heider, F. (1958). *The Psychology of Interpersonal Relations*. New York, NY: Wiley.

Hemingway, J. L. (1999). Leisure, social capital, and democratic citizenship. *Journal of Leisure Research*, **31**(2), 150–165.

Horne, P., P. C. Boxall and W. L. Adamowicz (2005). Multiple-use management of forest recreation sites: a spatially explicit choice experiment. *Forest Ecology and Management*, **207**(1–2), 189–199.

Hubacek, K., C. Prell, M. Reed *et al.* (2006). Using stakeholder and social network analysis to support participatory processes. *International Journal of Biodiversity Science and Management*, **2**, 249–252.

Inglehart, R. (1977). *The Silent Revolution: Changing Values and Political Styles among Western Publics*. Princeton, NJ: Princeton University Press.

Klenk, N. L., G. M. Hickey, J. I. MacLellan, R. Gonzales and J. Cardille (2009). Social network analysis: a useful tool for visualizing and evaluating forestry research. *International Forestry Review*, **11**(1), 134–140.

Knoke, D. (1990). *Political Networks: The Structural Perspective*. Cambridge: Cambridge University Press.

Lin, N., Y.-C. Fu and R.-M. Hsung (2001). The position generator: measurement techniques for investigations of social capital. In N. Lin, K. Cook and R. R. Burt (Eds.), *Social Capital: Theory and Research*. New York, NY: Aldine de Gruyter, pp. 57–81.

Manning, R. E. (1999). *Studies in Outdoor Recreation: Search and Research for Satisfaction*, 2nd Edition. Corvallis, OR: Oregon State University Press.

Mische, A. (2008). *Partisan Publics: Communication and Contention across Brazilian Youth Activist Networks*. Princeton, NJ: Princeton University Press.

Needham, M. D. and R. Rollins (2009). Social science, conservation, and protected areas theory. In P. Dearden and R. Rollins (Eds.), *Parks and Protected Areas in Canada: Planning and Management*, 3rd Edition. New York, NY: Oxford University Press, pp. 135–167.

Opp, K. (1986). Soft incentives and collective action: participation in the anti-nuclear movement. *British Journal of Political Science*, **16**, 87–112.

Prell, C., K. Hubacek and M. Reed (2009). Stakeholder analysis and social network analysis in natural resource management. *Society and Natural Resources*, **22**, 501–518.

Putnam, R. (1993). *Making Democracy Work: Civic Traditions in Modern Italy*. Princeton, NJ: Princeton University Press.

Putnam, R. D. (1995). Tuning in, tuning out: the strange disappearance of social capital in America. *PS: Political Science and Politics*, **28**, 664–683.

Rogers, E. M. (2003). *Diffusion of Innovations*, 5th Edition. New York, NY: Free Press.

Salant, P. and D. A. Dillman (1994). *How to Conduct Your Own Survey*. New York, NY: John Wiley and Sons.

Sargent-Michaud, J. and K. J. Boyle (2002). Public perceptions of wildlife management in Maine. *Human Dimensions of Wildlife*, **7**, 163–178.

Shaw, K. (2002). Encountering Clayoquot. In W. Magnusson and K. Shaw (Eds.), *A Political Space: Reading the Global through Clayoquot Sound*. Montreal, QC: McGill-Queen's University Press, pp. 25–66.

Sheppard, S. R. J., M. J. Meitner, H. W. Harshaw, N. Wilson and C. Pearce (2006). Extension Note 3 – Public processes in sustainable forest management for the Arrow Forest District. *BC Journal of Ecosystems and Management*, **7**(1), 57–67.

Stokowski, P. A. (1990). Extending the social groups model: social network analysis in recreation research. *Leisure Sciences*, **12**, 251–263.

Stokowski, P. A. and R. G. Lee (1991). The influence of social network ties on recreation and leisure: an exploratory study. *Journal of Leisure Research*, **23**, 95–113.

Suls, J. and R. Miller (1977). *Social Comparison Processes*. Washington, DC: Hemisphere.

Tindall, D. B. (2001). Social science and forestry curricula: some survey results. *Forestry Chronicle*, **77**, 121–126.

Tindall, D. B. (2002). Social networks, identification, and participation in an environmental movement: low-medium cost activism within the British Columbia wilderness preservation movement. *Canadian Review of Sociology and Anthropology*, **39**, 413–452.

Tindall, D. B. (2004). Social movement participation over time: an ego-network approach to micro-mobilization. *Sociological Focus*, **37**, 163–184.

Tindall, D. B. and N. Begoray (1993). Old growth defenders: the battle for the Carmanah Valley. In S. Lerner (Ed.), *Environmental Stewardship: Studies in Active Earthkeeping*. Waterloo, ON: University of Waterloo Geography Series, pp. 269–322.

Tindall, D. B., J. L. Robinson and M. Diani (2010). The concept of social movement revisited: an empirical investigation. Paper presented at the Sunbelt Social Network Conference in Riva del Garda, Italy, July 3.

Valente, T. W. (1995). *Network Models of the Diffusion of Innovations*. Cresskill, NJ: Hampton.

Vining, J. and E. Tyler (1999). Values, emotions and desired outcomes reflected in public responses to forest management plans. *Human Ecology Review*, **6**, 21–34.

Wellman, B. (1979). The community question. *American Journal of Sociology*, **84**, 1201–1231.

Whisman, S. and S. Hollenhorst (1998). A path model of whitewater boating satisfaction on the Cheat River of West Virginia. *Environmental Management*, **22**(1), 109–117.

Williams, P. W., R. W. Penrose and S. Hawkes (1998). Shared decision-making in tourism land use planning. *Annals of Tourism Research*, **25**, 860–889.

Wilson, J. (1998). *Talk and Log: Wilderness Politics in British Columbia, 1965–96*. Vancouver, BC: UBC Press.

KEN A. FRANK

8

Social network models for natural resource use and extraction

8.1 INTRODUCTION: ORIENTATION TO NETWORK ANALYSIS FOR NATURAL RESOURCE USAGE

The analysis of social networks has tremendous capacity to inform social science and policy about how people extract natural resources (e.g. Prell *et al.*, 2009). Attention to social networks frees us from the typical assumptions that individuals act independently or are independent conditional on membership in common organizations (Frank, 1998). Instead attention to social networks embraces the relational (Emirbayer, 1997), and, as it does so, provides a potential bridge between different disciplines and modes of research.

Although social network analysis has great potential to help us understand the causes and consequences of natural resource usage, there are important limitations and pitfalls of which social scientists must be aware (Wellman and Berkowitz, 1997; Degenne and Forse, 1999; Scott, 2002; Breiger, 2004; Freeman, 2004; Carrington *et al.*, 2005; Wasserman and Faust, 2005). In this chapter I will suggest that expressing theory and analysis in formal social network models can help social scientists realize the potential of social network analysis, contributing to scientific dialogue about the effects of, and on, social networks.

8.1.1 Example: the Maine lobster fishery

I anchor my presentation in the case of the Maine lobster fishermen. This is one of the most well-known communities of fishermen, with

Social Networks and Natural Resource Management: Uncovering the Fabric of Environmental Governance, ed. Ö. Bodin and C. Prell. Published by Cambridge University Press. © Cambridge University Press 2011.

special potential for network effects (Acheson, 1988), many of which are quite current (e.g. MSNBC, July 21, 2009). The American lobster fishery has been strikingly robust when compared with other fisheries (Acheson, 1988; Frank et al., 2007). Prior to 1950, lobsters were taken offshore primarily as incidental trawl catches in demersal fisheries (living on or near the bottom of a sea or lake). Reported offshore lobster landings increased dramatically from about 400 metric tons (mt) during the 1950s to an average of more than 2000 mt in the 1960s. In 1969, technological advances permitted the introduction of trap fishing to deeper offshore areas, which helped to increase landings (trap landings: 50 mt in 1969 to 2900 mt in 1972). Total landings were steady from 1977–1986 (~17 600 mt/year). In the 1990s, with improved distribution and market, the landings increased to approximately 32 000 mt per year with a slight decline in 1992–1993. Thus far, the lobster fishermen have not experienced the drop-off in catches indicative of overfishing as in the case of other fisheries (Acheson, 2003; Frank et al., 2007).

The question arises as to why the Maine lobster fisheries, despite what appears to be increased fishing effort, have not experienced declines in their target species as have been typically experienced in other fisheries. Though the answer is complex, involving a range of ecological and social factors, one critical factor resides in the social relations of the local fishermen. Indeed, Acheson (1988, 2003) specifically credits the lobster fishermens' social relations as central to the successful management of the fishery.

The social relations of Maine lobster fishermen are organized within harbor-based gangs (Acheson, 1988). To defy the gang is to risk ostracism, a serious sanction because a fisher's success often depends on social support of others as well as the exchange of local and long-held knowledge regarding fishing. Furthermore, since the gangs are defined by long-standing social and kin-based relationships, ostracism affects an individual's social standing in the community as well as his ability to make a living.

The lobster gangs draw on their social relationships to aggressively protect their territories. If a fisher places traps in a harbor perceived to be the territory of a rival gang, the rival gang members will either first warn the intruder (verbally or by notching the trap) or sabotage the perceived intruder's traps (e.g. cutting the traps, placing debris in them). The social structure of the gang is critical to perpetrating the sabotage and punishing the intruder. It often takes several members to challenge a potential intruder, and all members of the gang are complicit in their support of the saboteur. Although there are

temptations to "second order free-ride" from enforcing sanctions, ultimately the gangs sustain a norm of territorial control (Acheson, 1988,
2003). This territorial control effectively limits the number of traps
local and non-local fishermen can place in the water, with indirect
effects on the sustainability of the resource (Acheson, 1988, 2003;
Frank *et al.*, 2007).

Compare the Maine lobster fishery with the Western Atlantic
spiny lobster (*Panulirus argus*) fishery of the Turks and Caicos Islands
(TCI). Like the Maine lobster, the spiny lobsters live close to shore and
have limited mobility and it is relatively easy for fishermen to observe
and limit each others' trap placements (Frank *et al.*, 2007). Politically,
Haitians, Dominicans, and other "non-belongers" are not allowed to
commercially fish unless a "belonger" (i.e. Island national) is aboard
the vessel with them at all times; akin to having the approval of the TCI
community. On the whole, the social model of the TCI lobster fishery
shares many characteristics with that of the gangs of Maine lobster
fishermen. However, in TCI, unlike in the Maine fishery, there is a
general lack of enforcement of illegal fishing activities. As a result,
foreign poaching vessels and fishermen outside the TCI community
regularly enter the fishery and take lobsters with little or no restraint
so that the TCI spiny lobster fishery has deteriorated while the Maine
lobster fishery has remained sustainable.

It is beyond the scope of this chapter to say for sure whether the
TCI spiny lobster stock could have been better managed had the TCI
fishermen a more extensive and cohesive social network, drawn from
community membership, to enforce fishing practices (see Davis *et al.*'s
(2006) critique of Acheson's conclusions). However, the TCI circumstances provide additional motivation for our use of the Maine lobster
fishery to explore the underlying network models that can affect natural resource usage.

8.1.2   Research questions related to social networks
and natural resource usage

Good social science starts with good research questions. Therefore
I present two fundamental research questions that one might pose
with respect to social networks and the use of natural resources. The
first question concerns how an actor is influenced by members of his or
her network. In the example of the Maine lobster fishery, this might
take the form of how the members of a fisherman's network influence
the technology he uses for fishing, such as a the number and location of

traps he places in the water. The second question concerns how people choose or select with whom to interact. In the example this might concern with whom senior knowledgeable lobster fishermen, known as highliners, share their knowledge of where to place traps. I will use these questions to identify limitations and pitfalls of social network analysis and then relate them to formal models that can inform social science theory and discourse about natural resource extraction.

8.1.3   Limitations and pitfalls of social network analysis

I begin with two limitations of network analysis concerning the nature of social network data, about which the social scientist must make defensible decisions (other limitations can be found in Knoke and Yang, 2008: chapter 3; Wellman and Berkowitz, 1997). The first limitation, tie uncertainty, concerns the uncertainty of the network relation or tie through which actors are influenced. Are natural resource users influenced by all those with whom they come in contact, or are there specific types of relations that are more influential for particular behaviors?

Generally, kinship is a basis of some of the most important ties in subsistence communities (e.g. Levi-Strauss, 1969; Landa, 1994; Bearman, 1997). In the example of lobster fishermen, those with kin in a given community are more likely to be accepted by the community (Acheson, 1988: chapter 2). But even kinship is not an unambiguous basis for a tie, as the definition of kin may vary across cultures or even in the perceptions of members of a given community. Consider the recent dispute in which one Maine lobsterman considered himself a community member by virtue of his marriage while another did not consider him so (New York Times, 2009). Moreover, even if kinship was agreed upon, important relations can emerge through intense socializing experiences that cut across kinship barriers (Acheson, 1988: 58). These other relations could convey knowledge or norms that influence the behavior of natural resource users.

The second limitation, disconnected analysis concerns the definitions of the network boundary (e.g. Zuckerman, 2003; Marsden, 2005). How does one define the relevant boundary from which actors may choose network partners? For Maine lobster fishermen, the answer may seem straightforward because they live and work in communities defined by the geographies of harbors (Acheson, 1988). And yet "many highliners go out of their way to initiate and maintain ties with highline fishermen in nearby communities to exchange information and ideas"

(Acheson, 1988: 58). In other examples the definition of the boundary may be considerably more problematic. Should the network of a natural resource user include anyone who might influence his behavior or with whom he might interact?

The pitfalls of social network analysis emerge more from analytic practices than from fundamental limitations in the data. One pitfall in social network analysis is the inclination to disconnect social network analysis from other forms of analysis. Social network effects should be included alongside other effects (Doreian, 2001; also see Chapter 3). For example, in studying the effect of a lobster fisherman's network on his fishing behaviors, one must also account for the lobsterman's knowledge of the fishery and economic conditions. As one lobsterman put it in the negative, when prices are low "it wouldn't do us any good to catch more lobster because if we do, it'll drive down the prices even more" (USA Today, 2008; see also Acheson, 1988: 156).

A second pitfall, overreliance on image, is the attraction of rendering social networks in pictures such as sociograms without systematically estimating the relationships between networks and individual behaviors. As Zuckerman states in the organization theory blog:

> One of the features of social network analysis that is at once a great strength and a great danger is that network diagrams are highly evocative. In teaching and presenting network material, I have found that if I put up a picture of a network and start spinning a story about it, even untutored audiences follow along easily and they tend to accept the network as an accurate characterization of the actors and the social structure they inhabit. This is great, but the problem is that any such presentation tends to bake in all kinds of assumptions that should always be questioned. (Zuckerman, 2008)

Zuckerman's concern is an example of the need to push social network analysis beyond mere graphics and metaphor (Breiger, 2004).

I recognize that graphical representations of network data can be helpful in developing theory or expressing data in accessible form, especially of systemic phenomena. Indeed, my entry into network analysis came primarily through my technique, KliqueFinder, for embedding subgroup boundaries in sociograms (Frank, 1993, 1995, 1996; Frank and Yasumoto, 1996).

For example, Frank and Yasumoto (1998) identified cohesive subgroups based on friendships among the French financial elite (software available at http://www.msu.edu/~kenfrank/software.htm). After using simulations to establish that the friendships were concentrated within subgroup boundaries at a rate that was unlikely to have occurred by chance alone, they embedded the boundaries in a sociogram (see Figure 8.1). In this sociogram, each number indicates a member of the French financial elite (e.g. chief executive officers of major public or private financial institutions) with the circles representing subgroup boundaries. The lines indicate a friendship between

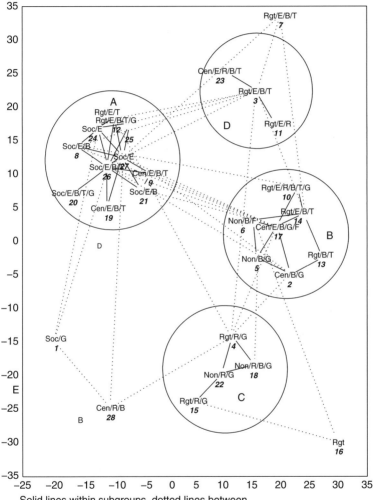

Solid lines within subgroups, dotted lines between
Scale = max weight/(density of exchange), expanded by 6 within subgroups

Figure 8.1 Crystallized sociogram of friendships among the French financial elite (Frank and Yasumoto, 1998). Reprinted with permission from University of Chicago Press.

two people; solid lines within subgroups, dotted between. Distances between actors and subgroups are indicative of patterns of friendship ties, with shorter distances representing denser sets of friendships. Thus the subgroups represent a social space defined exclusively by the pattern of interaction in contrast to kinship or geographic boundaries assumed for the fishermen.

Frank and Yasumoto then showed that resource allocations varied with the subgroup boundaries. First, hostile actions (e.g. a corporate takeover) almost never occurred within subgroups, indicating that trust could be enforced via the dense friendships within subgroups. Second, supportive actions (e.g. large short-term loans in response to informal requests) were more likely to occur amidst the sparse ties between subgroups. Frank and Yasumoto reasoned that members of the French financial elite supported others outside their subgroups because they already had social capital within their subgroups via enforceable trust – the dense social ties within subgroups increased the likelihood that anyone who betrayed the trust of a subgroup member would be sanctioned, socially and otherwise, by the subgroup as a whole. Thus members of the French financial elite sought to engender new obligations and access new information and resources by helping those *outside* their subgroups.

The sociological forces affecting the French financial elite may seem far removed from those forces experienced by those who rely on natural resources for their livelihood. And yet both types of economies are generated by allocation and movement of what are potentially common resources, be they fiscal or natural. In fact, the allegorical tragedy of the commons generated as community members use public grazing land solely for their own good (Hardin, 1968) could as easily apply to members of the French financial elite who directly and indirectly manipulate the financial coffers of France for political or reputational gain.

The methodological contribution of Frank and Yasumoto is that they moved beyond mere graphical representation by formally modeling the effect of friendship on how actors selected others for hostile or supportive action. They then estimated the size of the subgroup effects while controlling for other factors such as attendance at a common post-secondary school or membership in the same political party. Thus Frank and Yasumoto were able to demonstrate an effect of subgroups above and beyond correlates of subgroup membership based on similar career experiences or political affiliations. In the next section I will provide a general example of the models used by Frank and Yasumoto and refer to software for estimating those models.

Generally, the limitations and pitfalls of social network analysis reduce to issues of causal inference (Wellman and Berkowitz, 1997; Doreian, 2001). How confident are we that actors are influenced by the other actors through relations we have measured? How confident are we that actors selected others with whom to interact and were not simply influenced by other common factors? While there are many solutions and approaches the network analyst could take to address these questions, in the next section I show how expressing network effects within formal models can support social scientists' causal inferences by helping them mitigate limitations and avoid pitfalls.

8.2   THE FUNDAMENTAL MODELS FOR SOCIAL NETWORK ANALYSIS: INFLUENCE AND SELECTION

The model of influence expresses how an actor's beliefs, knowledge, or behaviors are affected by the others with whom she or he interacts. This would apply, for example, to how the number of traps a lobster fisherman places in the water is influenced by the norm in his community. The model of selection specifies how actors select with whom to engage in interactions. For example, how do the senior lobster fishermen choose to whom to give advice or support to enter the lobster fishery? These choices affect the distribution of knowledge as well as the potential to create new knowledge through interaction (Schumpeter, 1934). Together models of influence and selection represent processes through and on a social network.

8.2.1   Influences on a fisherman's natural resource usage

I begin by modeling a fisherman's behavior as a function of the behavior of others with whom he interacts (as a norm), his knowledge, the gear he owns, and his own prior behaviors. For example, let sustainable practices$_i$ represent the extent to which fisherman i engages in sustainable practices. For lobster fishermen, sustainable practices might consist of use of traps instead of trawling (National Fisherman, 2007), and the use of a modest number of traps. I model the fisherman's sustainable practices$_i$ as

$$\text{sustainable practices}_i = \beta_0 +$$
$$+ \beta_1 \text{ exposure to previous sustainable practices}$$
$$\text{of others in the network of person } i_i$$
$$+ \beta_2 \text{ knowledge of natural resource}_i \qquad (8.1)$$
$$+ \beta_3 \text{ gear owned}_i$$
$$+ \beta_4 \text{ previous sustainable practices}_i + e_i$$

where the error terms (e_i) are assumed independently distributed, $N(0,\sigma^2)$. In (8.1), "exposure to previous sustainable practices of others in the network of person i" refers to the previous behaviors of those with whom actor i interacts. Thus if fisherman Bob interacts with Al and Joe who engage in sustainable practices at levels of 8 and 10, respectively (for example, these might be the number of days per year they exceeded a trap limit), then Bob is exposed to a norm of 9.[1] Given this definition of the exposure term, β_1 indicates the normative influence of others on fisherman i. This normative influence can be understood as an effect of social capital that complements the fisherman's human capital (knowledge) and physical capital (the gear he owns).

Note that model (8.1) can be estimated as a basic regression model, with a term representing the network effect (Friedkin and Marsden, 1994). As such, and given longitudinal data, the model can be estimated with ordinary statistical software (e.g. SAS, SPSS) once one has constructed the network term (see http://www.msu.edu/~ken-frank/resources.htm [influence models] for SPSS and SAS modules and power point demonstration that calculate a network effect and include it in a regression model). Therefore, within the regression framework one can examine the effects of social networks alongside effects of other theoretically recognized factors, addressing pitfall 1.

Note the use of timing to support the causal inference by identifying the effects in model (8.1). First, controlling for an actor's own prior behavior accounts for the tendency for actors to interact with others similar to themselves (selection based on homophily); the portion of influence that can be attributed to an actor's tendency to interact with others like himself is removed by controlling for the actor's prior attributes including behavior (or beliefs).

---

[1] This definition of exposure extends basic conceptualizations of centrality by accounting for the characteristics of the actors to whom one is exposed. Thus the focus shifts away from the structural towards flows of those attributes or related resources.

Second, the influence effect is specified as a function of a fisherman's peers' *prior* characteristics. This would be natural if one were to model contagion. For example, whether I get a cold from you is a function of my interaction with you over the last 24 hours and whether you had a cold yesterday. I would not argue that contagion occurs if we interacted in the last 24 hours and we both get sick today (see Cohen-Cole and Fletcher's (2008b) critique of Christakis and Fowler's (2007, 2008) models of the contagion of obesity; see also Leenders, 1995).

A key issue in specifying model (8.1) is to identify the relevant network of ties for fisherman i, limitation 1. In the context of the influence model, one should measure the relation through which influence flows will affect a specific behavior. That is, priority is given to the behavior of interest, and the network relation defined relative to that behavior. For example, if one is modeling the extent to which a fisherman engages in sustainable practices then one might use network relations through which fishermen would be exposed to others' practices or knowledge such as through observation or conversation. One would not define the network in terms of with whom a fisherman went to school unless such ties also conveyed resources relevant to current fishing behaviors. Thus limitation 1 is addressed by making a scientific argument relative to the influence process of interest.

Importantly, the influence model does not confine the researcher to estimating influence through a single relation. Friendship defines one possible source of exposures for an actor. Typically, another for subsistence natural resource users would be kinship. Building on the standard network effects model, one could estimate separate effects for the influences of kin versus friends (Doreian, 1989):

sustainable practices$_i$ = β_0+

    + β_1 exposure to previous sustainable practices of friends$_i$

    + β_2 exposure to previous sustainable practices of kin$_i$

    + β_3 knowledge of natural resource$_i$

    + β_4 gear owned$_i$

    + β_5 previous sustainable practices$_i$

    + e_i (8.2)

The terms β_1 and β_2 then represent the separate influences of friends versus kin, and the difference between β_1 and β_2 indicates which set of influences are stronger and can be tested via a standard test of the difference between two regression coefficients (Cohen and Cohen, 1983: 111).[2]

Networks can also be extended beyond direct interactions (limitation 2). For example, one could construct an exposure term based on others whom a fisherman observed, members of a fisherman's cohesive subgroup (where relations are concentrated within cohesive subgroups, but not all members of subgroups have relations with each other – see Figure 8.1), or with whom the fisherman casually interacts. That is, the network can extend beyond direct ties with whom an actor is friends or kin.

Network effects beyond those of direct relations will quickly become difficult to measure and differentiate, especially in small closed communities which allow extensive opportunities for casual interaction and observation of all in the system. One way to model the influence of all in the community is through multi-level models. Multi-level models are a large class of models for estimating effects of nested data such as individuals within organizations (see Raudenbush and Bryk, 2002). As such they have been employed in social network analysis (Frank, 1998; Frank *et al.*, 2008) and have been at the root of some methodological advancements in social network analysis (Lazega and Van Duijn, 1997; Van Duijn et al., 1999; Wellman and Frank, 2001). For example, extend (8.1) to a multi-level framework for fisherman i nested within community j:

At Level 1 (individual level i in community j):

$\text{sustainable practices}_{ij} = \beta_{0j}$
$\quad + \beta_1 \text{ exposure to previous sustainable practices of others}$
$\qquad \text{in the network of person } i_{ij}$
$\quad + \beta_2 \text{ knowledge of natural resource}_i$
$\quad + \beta_3 \text{ gear owned}_i$
$\quad + \beta_4 \text{ previous sustainable practices}_i + \beta_2 \text{ previous}$
$\qquad \text{sustainable practices}_{ij} + e_{ij}$ (8.3)

In model (8.3), β_{0j} represents the level of sustainable practices in community j, controlling for the other terms in the model. Following the

---

[2] Or the difference can be tested by including a main effect of peers (which includes friends and kin) and then an interaction effect of peer by friend: $\text{peer}_{ii'} \times \text{friend}_{ii'}$. The coefficient associated with the second term, $\text{peer}_{ii'} \times \text{friend}_{ii'}$, represents the additional effect of peers who are also friends.

multi-level modeling framework, β_{0j} is modeled at the community level (level 2) as a function of the previous community norm:

Level 2 (community level j):

$$\beta_{0j} = \gamma_{00} + \gamma_{01} \text{ previous sustainable practices}_j + u_{0j} \qquad (8.4)$$

where the error terms (u_{0j}) are assumed independently distributed, $N(0,\tau_{00})$. The parameter γ_{01} then represents the extent to which new sustainable practices are affected by old practices manifesting a community norm. Thus the multi-level model allows one to partially address limitation 2 by extending and testing the boundaries of normative affects. Furthermore, just as in the single level framework, one can adjust (8.4) for community level characteristics such as size of community, or geographical features.

Importantly, the effect of the norm represented by γ_{01} in (8.4) is not a function of direct interactions or relations. Instead it represents the effect of the general community norm that applies equally to all members of the community regardless of the specific networks in which they are embedded. This contrasts with the network effect associated with β_1 in which actors with different networks will be affected differently. Therefore, there is great value in comparing the estimates for β_1 and γ_{01} to evaluate whether effects of the general community (γ_{01}) are stronger than the direct effects (β_1) of the others with whom a fisherman has an observable social relation such as kinship or friend.

8.2.2   The selection of interaction partners

While the influence model represents how actors change behaviors or beliefs in response to others around them, the selection model represents how actors choose with whom to interact. For example, Frank *et al.* (2011) describe how, because of the effects of status and emotional attachment, the provision of help regarding natural resource use is embedded in social networks (Granovetter, 1985). Implied, resources will not flow evenly throughout a social system, but will instead flow differentially depending on the pattern of social relations. For example, the novice lobster fisherman who has marital connections to highliners or who cultivates personal relationships with highliners will be able to access more knowledge than the novice who is new and marginal to a community.

Frank *et al.* (2011) refer to decisions of to whom to allocate help as a "social technology," analogous to the role of production technology.[3] For example, the highliner employs a social technology to determine who to help that yields an expected return in status or conformity to the highliner (Acheson, 1988: 38), just as the highliner employs a fishing technology to extract resources that yields a market return to the highliner. This is clearly borne out in highliners' attempts to deceive specific novices' efforts to discern trap locations, while in other instances a given highliner might share critical fishing knowledge with some novices who are accepted in the community (Acheson, 1988: 103).

Choices such as to whom to allocate resources can be modeled as:

$$\log\left[\frac{p(help_{ii'})}{1 - p(help_{ii'})}\right] = \theta_0 + \theta_1 \ kin_{ii'} \tag{8.5}$$

where $p(help_{ii'})$ represents the probability that actor i' provides help to actor i and θ_1 represents the effect of kinship on the provision of help. Other terms could be included such as friendship, members of one's community, etc.

Importantly, (8.5) can be modified to control for prior tendencies to provide help. This could be done by either modeling only the provision of new help, or by including a term representing whether i' had helped i at a previous time point. This addresses pitfalls 1 and 2 by moving past the general association between characteristics of actors and their relations to a more causal statement about a shared characteristic (e.g. kinship) increasing the likelihood of new ties (e.g. help) emerging.

Marijtje Van Duijn (Van Duijn, 1995; Lazega and Van Duijn, 1997) has shown how θ_0 (the intercept in (8.5)) can be modeled as a function of characteristics of the provider or the recipient of help, enabling one to test many of the effects specified by Acheson (1988, 2003) and others. For example, θ_0 can be modeled as a function of the reputation of the recipient of help (i):

$$\theta_0 = \gamma_{00} + \gamma_{01}^i reputation_i + u_i \tag{8.6}$$

where the u_i are normally distributed with variance τ. A large value of γ_{01}^i would indicate that those with a positive reputation in the

---

[3] I am using the definition of technology as "the application of scientific knowledge for practical purposes" (Oxford English Dictionary, 12th edition). This is different from a common use referring to electronic or mechanical tools.

community are able to access more help from others (Acheson, 1988: chapter 2). Similarly, one can model the likelihood of help provided as a function of the seniority of the potential provider of help:

$$\theta_0 = \gamma_{00} + \gamma_{01}^{i'} \text{seniority}_{i'} + v_{i'} \tag{8.7}$$

where the v_i are normally distributed with variance ω. A positive value of $\gamma_{01}^{i'}$ indicates that those with greater seniority are more likely to be named as providing help, as in a highliner effect. Together (8.5) through (8.7) define a cross-nested random effects model (estimation of these models is described in the Technical Appendix).

8.3   APPLICATION OF THE MODELS
TO CHAPTER 4

The models developed in the previous section express the two basic processes of social networks: influence and selection. While the formal modeling framework may feel constraining, the models are quite flexible. To demonstrate their flexibility I apply them to analyses in Bodin and Crona (Chapter 4, this volume). Bodin and Crona seek to identify the characteristics of those actors who occupy specific social positions in their networks. First, drawing on Guimerà and Amaral (2005a, 2005b), Bodin and Crona identify individuals who are hubs of their subgroups, and those who span between subgroups (see also Gould and Fernandez, 1989). This can be represented with a selection model. Let $CEK_{ii'}$ represent whether actor i' shared ecological knowledge with actor i and let *same subgroup*$_{ii'}$ take a value of 1 if actors i and i' were assigned to the same subgroup by Guimerà and Amaral's (2005a, 2005b) algorithm, 0 otherwise. The selection model at level 1 might then be:

Level 1 (Pair i ,i'):

$$\log\left[\frac{p(CEK_{ii'})}{1 - p(CEK_{ii'})}\right] = \theta_0 + \theta_1 \text{same subgroup}_{ii'} \tag{8.8}$$

The term $\log\left[\frac{p(CEK_{ii'})}{1-p(CEK_{ii'})}\right]$ is known as the log-odds, and transforms the $CEK_{ii'}$ for use in a linear framework. The parameter θ_0 represents the log-odds of knowledge being communicated between members of different subgroups and θ_1 represents the relative increase in the log-odds for members of the same subgroup; θ_1 represents the effect of membership in the same subgroup on the likelihood of knowledge sharing.

Note that model (8.8) is expressed at the level of the pair of actors. The multi-level framework can then be applied to express effects of either the provider (i') or the recipient of knowledge (i). For example, at the provider level:

Level 2a (Provider of knowledge, i'):

$$\theta_0 = \gamma_{00} + \gamma_{01}^{i'}\text{ring net}_{i'} + v_{i'} \tag{8.9}$$

In this model, $\gamma_{01}^{i'}$ represents the extent to which those who use ring nets are more likely to communicate ecological knowledge to others, as hypothesized by Crona and Bodin.

Note that Bodin and Crona's study is more focused on the type of hub a given actor is, not just whether the actor receives many nominations or not. This could be captured by exploiting the multi-level nature of the selection models. In particular, I can model θ_1 from (8.8) as a function of whether or not the fisher uses ring nets:

Level 2b (Receiver of knowledge, i):

$$\theta_1 = \gamma_{10} + \gamma_{11}^{i'}\text{ring net}_{i'} + v_{1i'} \tag{8.10}$$

Assuming $\gamma_{01}^{i'}$ is large and positive, $\gamma_{11}^{i'}$ in (8.10) represents the extent to which a fisherman who uses ring nets is more likely to favor subgroup members versus non-subgroup members in his provision of help. A positive value of $\gamma_{11}^{i'}$ identifies those who use fisher rings as provincial hubs while a negative value would indicate those who use fisher rings as connector hubs.

If one were instead interested in identifying specific individuals who were provincial or connector hubs one could define (8.9) and (8.10) as unconditional models:

$$\theta_0 = \gamma_{00} + v_{i'} \tag{8.11}$$

and

$$\theta_1 = \gamma_{10} + v_{1i'} \tag{8.12}$$

Using models (8.11) and (8.12), provincial hubs would be defined as those actors who had large values of both $v_{i'}$ and $v_{1i'}$ indicating individuals who were nominated frequently and especially likely to be nominated by subgroup members. Connector hubs would then be identified as those individuals who had large values of $v_{i'}$ and small values of $v_{1i'}$, indicating individuals who were nominated frequently but by members of other subgroups.

Bodin and Crona's study also implies an influence model one could estimate. In particular, in their section on individual characteristics and the potential for agency, Bodin and Crona link the structural pattern of relations to behaviors and knowledge concerning sustainability. These could be modeled directly using an influence model. For example:

$$\text{Sustainable practices}_i = \beta_0 +$$
$$\beta_1 \text{ exposure to previous sustainable practices of}$$
$$\text{those from whom one obtained ecological knowledge} +$$
$$\beta_2 \text{previous sustainable practices}_i + e_i \tag{8.13}$$

Here, β_1 indicates the extent to which actors are influenced by those from whom they received ecological knowledge. If Bodin and Crona's hypothesis "It seems highly unlikely that someone engaged in an illegal fishing practice would coordinate or garner support for new or better fishing regulations and enforcement" is correct, then I would expect β_1 to be large and positive, indicating that those who do not engage in sustainable practices induce similar behavior among those with whom they interact.

8.4   DISCUSSION

There are several advantages to the formal models of influence and selection presented here. First, they afford a common framework for communicating theoretical ideas. Any analysis of changes in actors' behaviors as a function of their interactions can be expressed in an influence model. Any analysis focusing on the pattern of nominations can be translated into a selection model and therefore understood by others studying similar phenomena. These models can also include the effects of other attributes representing different theories or different levels of analysis representing contextual effects (avoiding pitfall 1). Social scientists can then use the models to explore the basis of commonalities across contexts, potentially integrating social science dialogue by accommodating effects associated with different disciplines (see Doreian, 2001). Thus a model of how natural resource use is influenced by others can also include effects of social institutions manifest in economic incentives or governmental policies. It can also include biological characteristics of the ecosystem that might constrain or facilitate certain actions.

Second, the models allow specification and testing of specific hypotheses. For example, one can test whether there are normative influences of kin, friends, or community members as well as test whether the effects are different from one another. This avoids vague or idiosyncratic descriptions that can emerge from basic storytelling of social network diagrams (pitfall 2).

The influence and selection models also contribute to discourse about the underlying limitations of network data. In specifying the influence model one must consider through which relation resources or norms flow (concerning limitation 1). This is critical for research on natural resource usage which can be influenced through a number of different types of relations. In specifying the selection model one must consider the pools of potential partners including kin, friends, and community members from which an actor makes a selection (concerning limitation 2). In sum, formally specifying network effects ultimately contributes to scientific discourse that is the basis of policy by helping network analysts avoid pitfalls and mitigate limitations.

8.4.1   New trends in social network analysis

I have attended carefully to the models of influence and selection because they are the bedrock of social network analysis and because there is an emerging consensus regarding their specification and estimation. But there are important extensions to these models which I outline below.

Dynamics of Social Networks (see special issue of *Social Networks*, **32**(1), 2010). I have presented the models of influence and selection in isolation, when in fact both processes likely occur in most social systems. For example, a fisherman may change his trap placement based on interactions with other fishermen, and then change with whom he interacts based on his new practices. This would apply over long periods to the emergence of new highliners. The dynamic interplay between influence and selection is shown in Figure 8.2. At the top of the waves, influence occurs when actors change their behaviors between two time points as a result of interactions occurring between those two time points. At the bottom of the waves selection occurs when actors change their interactions over one interval (e.g. $0 \rightarrow 1$) to the next (e.g. $1 \rightarrow 2$).

The potential for influence and selection processes can pose a challenge to identifying separate effects and for making causal

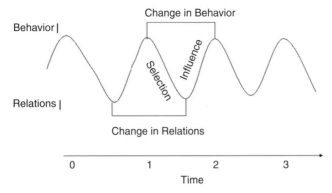

Figure 8.2 The interplay between influence of the network and selection of network partners over time. Adapted from Leenders (1995).

inferences. For example, one might infer that actors have influenced one another when in fact they selected similar others with whom to interact. One way to help identify the separate effects is to use longitudinal data to control for actors' prior attributes. One particular approach to simultaneously estimating models of influence and selection using longitudinal data is Snijders' SIENA models (e.g. Snijders *et al.*, 2010; Steglich *et al.*, in press). In these models, simulations are used to estimate parameters that will generate the state of the network at time 2, given the state at time 1 and a continuous time conceptualization in which network relations are evaluated for change one at a time.

The potential for both processes of influence and selection can be treated as a feature as in dynamic models. The advantage of such dynamic representations is they can be used to track how resources flow through a network and generate changes in the network as they do so. For example, consider Sam who receives certain knowledge from Jack (Jack → Sam), but also from Al who talked with Jack (Jack → Al → Sam). An important question then is the effect of the indirect exposure to knowledge (via Al) on Sam in addition to the effect of direct exposure via interacting with Jack. Frank and Fahrbach (1999) posit that indirect exposures represent normative influences as opposed to informational influences of direct interaction; because Sam receives the knowledge directly from Jack, any influence of Al on Sam is likely not knowledge based but instead evidence of Sam conforming to the norm defined by Al's behavior.

8.4.1.1   Agent-based models via computer simulation

I have grounded the models I presented here in individual behavior and motivations. But it is difficult to extrapolate from them to systemic outcomes, especially those that might be a function of complex feedback. Such systemic implications can be explored using agent-based computer simulations. These simulations are playing an increasingly larger role in the understanding of human–environment interactions (Frank and Fahrbach, 1999; Lim *et al.*, 2002; Parker *et al.*, 2003; Brown *et al.*, 2005). The unique advantage of agent-based modeling comes from being able to simulate the implications of a carefully constructed logic over a series of discrete time steps in order to explore the emergence of macro-level properties from individual-level actions. Critically, the models of influence and selection presented here form a natural basis for the agents' decision-making rules (e.g. Frank *et al.*, 2011). For example, Frank *et al.* compare diffusion when farmers strategically select who to help based on the potential of the recipient to reciprocate, versus when farmers help those in their local network subgroup who come to them in a time of need. One might initially suspect that when there are only strategic allocations, the "rich will get richer" because allocations will be directed to a select few most able to reciprocate, increasing disparities in access to knowledge. However, Frank *et al.* find the resource disparity with respect to knowledge *decreases* dramatically under the scenario where only strategic investments are made. This is partially because more investments are made when people recognize the return on the investment. In turn, more people access the knowledge, reducing knowledge disparities.

Two-Mode Social Networks (see Special Issue of *Social Networks*: http:// www.elsevier.com/framework_products/promis_misc/cfp_socnet_2-mode.pdf). The models I have presented are based on direct social interaction among individuals, but a new trend in social networks is the analysis of two-mode network data, or bipartite graphs. For example, Frank *et al.* (2008) represented high-school transcript data in terms of clusters of students and the courses they took, as in Figure 8.3. They referred to the clusters as local positions, consisting of a set of students with the courses as focal points of the position. They reasoned that local positions defined pools of potential friends because they attracted students with common interests (represented by the courses); provided opportunities to interact with others (during course participation); and defined a venue in which there were third parties who could enforce norms (the other students in the courses). Frank *et al.* (2008) then

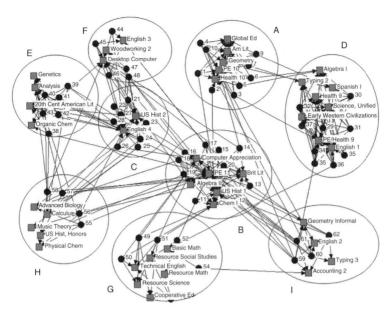

Figure 8.3 Local positions of students focused around courses (Frank *et al.*, 2008). Reprinted with permission from The University of Chicago Press.

theorized that because the local positions anticipated the selection process, adolescents could be influenced by the potential friends who were members of their local positions. This is consistent with recent findings and theoretical arguments that adolescents are influenced as much by the peers with whom *they would like to be friends* as by their current friends who accept them for who they are (Harter and Fischer, 1999; Call and Mortimer, 2001; Haynie, 2001; Giordano, 2003). Frank *et al.* (2008) found that girls' future math course taking was influenced by the existing math levels of other girls in their local positions.

The analysis of two-mode data has important potential in many social contexts, including that of natural resource users. One can imagine defining local positions of natural resource users based on membership in cooperatives, residence in a community, or participation in certain social events. These local positions might then anticipate the formation of close friendships through which knowledge and normative influence can flow.

Doubtless there are myriad advancements in social networks I have not attended to here. I have not addressed in any depth the contribution of those who study communication (Monge and Contractor, 2003), epidemiology (e.g. Valente, 2002), physics (e.g. Barabasi, 2003; Watts, 2003a,

2003b), or economics (Jackson, 2008). My focus here has been more socio-logical to examine how natural resource users make decisions in their social contexts. But interdisciplinary contributions will no doubt be critical in the study of natural resource usage. Here I suggest the models of influence and selection as one way of integrating the contributions from different disciplines.

8.4.2 Implications for managers

The fundamental processes of influence and selection suggest fisheries managers must account for the dynamic social, economic, ecological, and cultural conditions of their fishery because the contagion of behaviors through a network can affect subsequent network ties, and vice versa. Therefore, there will be no silver bullets that work across all contexts (Cochrane *et al.*, 2011). Management approaches that rely largely on markets or property rights may be ineffective, inefficient, or may produce unintended consequences in certain cultures (Ostrom, 1990, 1997, 1998). Similarly, management approaches that draw on underlying networks such as the gangs of lobster fishermen may not work in other contexts with a less intact social system, more fragile natural resource, or unstable political setting, such as the North American cod fishery or the spiny lobster (Frank *et al.*, 2007).

The basic implication then is for managers to adapt general practices to local contexts. Classically, managers have needed to understand the ecology of their natural resources, and how it might differ from other settings. Managers must be similarly aware of how the social networks and norms in their communities differ from those in which practices have been successfully implemented. With greater understanding of the relationship between social networks and natural resources usage, managers might ultimately be able to engage in deliberate action to leverage social networks to change fishing practices. For example, managers can create venues for interaction such as hall meetings or informal committees focused on governance. Managers can also engage social networks by designating individuals for specific roles. For example, managers in a Vietnamese biostation in the Mekong Delta have designated members of villages as "local experts" who work as a liaison between the managers, other villagers, and other communities in efforts to increase small-scale sustainable agricultural practices. Thus the managers are locating knowledge in the social network and strategically modifying specific relations in the network.

8.5 CONCLUSION

There is great potential for existing and new social network methods to inform issues of natural resource use. I believe network analysis will be most helpful when it follows the formal modeling framework presented here. It is through this framework that researchers can engage in high-level and direct discourse about the effects of and on social networks. This discourse is critical to understanding the effects of social context on the decisions humans make about how to use precious natural resources.

8.6 TECHNICAL APPENDIX

8.6.1 Estimation of social network models

One's first inclination to estimate social network models such as in (8.2) might be to use maximum likelihood techniques such as are available to estimate the parameters in standard logit models (e.g. Agresti, 1984). But it is difficult to define the likelihood for the data given the parameters in model (8.2) because the observations are not independent. For example, the relation between i and i' is not independent of the relation between i' and i.

There are currently two new approaches for accounting for dependencies in social network models such as (8.2). First, the p* approach, developed by Frank and Strauss (Frank and Strauss, 1986; Strauss and Ikeda, 1990) and described by Wasserman and Pattison (1996) shows that estimates from the standard logit model as in (8.2) can be described as based on a pseudo-likelihood if one conditions on key relations between other pairs in the network. That is, an explicit set of covariates are entered into the model to control for structural dependencies. For example, whether i' informs i might be a function of the number of informants they have in common, the tendency of i' to inform others, etc. In a key point, Strauss and Ikeda argue that a Markov assumption implies that one need only account for relations that involve either i or i' – the "stars" around the actors involved (although this has been extended to account for less direct ties defining neighborhoods; Pattison and Robbins, 2002).

In another estimation alternative, one can account for the nesting of pairs within nominators (i) and nominatees (i') using an application of multi-level models with cross-nested effects (Lazega and Van Duijn, 1997; Baerveldt et al., forthcoming). These are called p_2 models because they estimate and control for the variances of actors' tendencies to send and receive nominations.[4] One advantage of the p_2 approach over p* is that effects of people can be modeled and tested at a separate level than those of the pair, without attributing most effects to characteristics of the network structure as represented by the p* covariates. Frank (2009) applied this type of p_2 model to estimate the extent to which teachers were more likely to help close colleagues than other members of their schools.

REFERENCES

Acheson, J. (1988). *The Lobster Gangs of Maine*. Hanover, NH: University Press of New England.
Acheson, J. (2003). *Capturing the Commons*. Hanover, NH: University Press of New England.
Agresti, A. (1984). *Analysis of Categorical Data*. New York, NY: John Wiley and Sons.
Baerveldt, C., M. A. J. Van Duijn and D. A. Van Hemert (forthcoming). Ethnic boundaries and personal choice: assessing the influence of individual inclinations to choose intraethnic relationships on pupils networks. *Social Networks*.
Barabasi, A. L. (2003). *Linked: How Everything is Connected to Everything Else and What it Means*. London: Penguin Books.
Bearman, P. (1997). Generalized exchange. *American Journal of Sociology*, **102**(5), 1383–1415.
Brown, D., S. Page, R. Riolo, M. Zellner and W. Rand (2005). Path dependence and the validation of agent-based spatial models of land use. *International Journal of Geographical Information Science*, **19**(2), 153–174.
Breiger, R. L. (2004). The analysis of social networks. In M. Hardy and A. Bryman (Eds.), *Handbook of Data Analysis*. London: Sage, pp. 505–526.
Call, K. T. and J. T. Mortimer (2001). *Arenas of Comfort in Adolescence: A Study of Adjustment in Context*. Mahwah, NJ: Lawrence Erlbaum.
Carrington, P. J., J. Scott and S. Wasserman (2005). *Models and Methods in Social Network Analysis*. Cambridge: Cambridge University Press.
Christakis, N. and J. Fowler (2007). The spread of obesity in a large social network over 32 years. *New England Journal of Medicine*, **357**, 370–379.
Christakis, N. and J. Fowler (2008). The collective dynamics of smoking in a large social network. *New England Journal of Medicine*, **358**, 249–258.
Cochrane, K., W. Emerson and R. Willmann (2011). Sustainable fisheries: the importance of the bigger picture. In W. W. Taylor, A. J. Lynch and M. G. Schechter (Eds.), *Sustainable Fisheries: Multi-Level Approaches to a Global Problem*. Bethesda, MD: American Fisheries Society, pp. 3–19.
Cohen, J. and P. Cohen (1983). *Applied Multiple Regression/Correlation Analysis for the Behavioral Sciences*. Hillsdale, NJ: Lawrence Erlbaum.

[4] p_2 models can be estimated with the Stocnet software at http://stat.gamma.rug.nl/stocnet/.

Cohen-Cole, E and J. M. Fletcher (2008a). Detecting implausible social network effects in acne, height, and headaches: longitudinal analysis. *British Medical Journal*, **337**, a2533.

Cohen-Cole, E. and J. M. Fletcher (2008b). Is obesity contagious? Social networks vs. environmental factors in the obesity epidemic. *Journal of Health Economics*, **27**(5), 1382–1387.

Davis, R., J. Whalen and B. Neis (2006). From orders to borders: toward a sustainable co-managed lobster fishery in Bonavista Bay, Newfoundland. *Human Ecology*, **34**(6), 851–867.

Degenne, A. and M. Forse (1999). *Introducing Social Networks*. London: Sage.

Doreian, P. (1989). Two regimes of network effects autocorrelation. In M. Kochen (Ed.), *The Small World*. Norwood, NJ: Ablex, pp. 280–295.

Doreian, P. (2001). Causality in social network analysis. *Sociological Methods and Research*, **30**(1), 81–114.

Emirbayer, M. (1997). Manifesto for a relational sociology. *American Journal of Sociology*, **103**(2), 281–317.

Frank, K. A. (1993). Identifying cohesive subgroups. Unpublished Doctoral dissertation, University of Chicago.

Frank, K. A. (1995). Identifying cohesive subgroups. *Social Networks*, **17**, 27–56.

Frank, K. (1996). Mapping interactions within and between cohesive subgroups. *Social Networks*, **18**, 93–119.

Frank, K. A. (1998). The social context of schooling: quantitative methods. *Review of Research in Education*, **23**, 171–216.

Frank, K. A. (2009). Quasi-ties: directing resources to members of a collective. *American Behavioral Scientist*, **52**, 1613–1645.

Frank, K. A. and K. Fahrbach (1999). Organizational culture as a complex system: balance and information in models of influence and selection. *Organization Science*, **10**(3), 253–277.

Frank, K. A., S. J. Maroulis, D. Belman and M. Kaplowitz (2011). The social embeddedness of natural resource extraction and use in small fishing communities. In W. Taylor and M. Schechter (Eds.), *Sustainable Fisheries: Multi-level Approaches to a Global Problem*. Bethesda, MD: American Fisheries Society, pp. 309–332.

Frank, K. A., K. Mueller, A. Krause, W. Taylor and N. Leonard (2007). The intersection of global trade, social networks, and fisheries. In W. Taylor, M. G. Schechter and L. Wolfson (Eds.), *Globalization: Effects on Fisheries Resources*. New York, NY: Cambridge University Press, pp. 385–423.

Frank, K. A., C. Mueller, K. Schiller *et al.* (2008). The social dynamics of mathematics coursetaking in high school. *American Journal of Sociology*, **113**(6), 1645–1696.

Frank, K. A. and J. Yasumoto (1996). Embedding subgroups in the sociogram: linking theory and image. *Connections*, **19**(1), 43–57.

Frank, K. A. and J. Yasumoto (1998). Linking action to social structure within a system: social capital within and between subgroups. *American Journal of Sociology*, **104**(3), 642–686.

Frank, O. and D. Strauss (1986). Markov graphs. *Journal of the American Statistical Association*, **81**(395), 832–842.

Freeman, L. (2004). *The Development of Social Network Analysis: A Study in the Sociology of Science*. Vancouver, BC: Empirical Press of Vancouver.

Friedkin, N. E. and P. Marsden (1994). Network studies of social influence. In S. Wasserman and J. Galaskiewicz (Eds.), *Advances in Social Network Analysis*. Thousand Oaks, CA: Sage, pp. 1–25.

Giordano, P. C. (2003). Relationships in adolescence. *Annual Review of Sociology*, **29**, 257–281.

Gould, R. and R. Fernandez (1989). Structures of mediation: a formal approach to brokerage in transaction networks. *Sociological Methodology*, **19**, 89–126.

Granovetter, M. (1985). Economic-action and social-structure – the problem of embeddedness. *American Journal of Sociology*, **91**, 481–510.

Guimerà, R. and L. A. N. Amaral (2005a). Cartography of complex networks: modules and universal roles. *Journal of Statistical Mechanics: Theory and Experiments*, art P02001.

Guimerà, R. and L. s. A. N. Amaral (2005b). Functional cartography of complex metabolic networks. *Nature*, **433**, 895–900.

Hardin, G. (1968). The tragedy of the commons. *Science*, **162**, 1243–1248.

Harter, S. and K. W. Fischer (1999). *The Construction of the Self: A Developmental Perspective*. New York, NY: Guilford Press.

Haynie, D. L. (2001). Delinquent peers revisited: does network structure matter? *American Journal of Sociology*, **106**(4), 1013–1057.

Jackson, M. O. (2008). *Social and Economic Networks*. Princeton, NJ: Princeton University Press.

Knoke, D. and S. Yang (2008). *Social Network Analysis*, 2nd Edition. Los Angeles, CA: Sage.

Landa, J. T. (1994). *Trust, Ethnicity and Identity*. Ann Arbor, MI: University of Michigan Press.

Lazega, E. and M. van Duijn (1997). Position in formal structure, personal characteristics and choices of advisors in a law firm: a logistic regression model for dyadic network data. *Social Networks*, **19**, 375–397.

Leenders, R. (1995). *Structure and Influence: Statistical Models for the Dynamics of Actor Attributes, Network Structure and their Interdependence*. Amsterdam: Thesis Publishers.

Levi-Strauss, C. (1969). *The Elementary Structures of Kinship*. Boston, MA: Beacon Press.

Lim, K., P. J. Deadman, E. Moran, E. Brondizio and S. McCracken (2002). Agent-based simulations of household decision-making and land use change near Altamira, Brazil. In H. R. Gimblett (Ed.), *Integrating Geographic Information Systems and Agent-based Techniques for Simulating Social and Ecological Processes*. New York, NY: Oxford University Press, pp. 277–308.

Marsden, P. (2005). Recent developments in network measurement. In P. J. Carrington, J. Scott and S. Wasserman (Eds.), *Models and Methods in Social Network Analysis*. Cambridge: Cambridge University Press, pp. 8–30.

Monge, P. R. and N. S. Contractor (2003). *Theories of Communication Networks*. Oxford: Oxford University Press.

MSNBC (2009). Police: Maine lobster turf war led to shooting. Available at http://www.msnbc.msn.com/id/32054066/ns/us_news-crime_and_courts.

National Fisherman (2007). Maine lobstermen oppose bill to allow trawled lobsters: supporters cite exodus of draggers to Mass., which permits draggers to land crustaceans. Available at http://www.encyclopedia.com/doc/1G1-162115105.html.

New York Times (2009). http://www.nytimes.com/2009/08/23/us/23lobster.html.

Ostrom, E. (1990). *Governing the Commons: The Evolution of Institutions for Collective Action*. Cambridge: Cambridge University Press.

Ostrom, E. (1997). Self-governance of commonpool resources. W97-2, Workshop in Political Theory and Policy Analysis, Indiana University, Bloomington.

Ostrom, E. (1998). A behavioral approach to the rational choice theory of collective action. *American Political Science Review*, **92**(1), 1–22.

Parker, D. C., S. M. Manson, M. A. Janssen, M. J. Hoffmann and P. Deadman (2003). Multi-agent systems for the simulation of land-use and land-cover change: a review. *Annals of the Association of American Geographers*, **93**, 314–337.

Pattison, P. and G. Robbins (2002). Neighborhood-based models for social networks. *Sociological Methodology*, **32**, 301–337.

Prell, C., K. Hubacek and M. Reed. (2009). Stakeholder analysis and social network analysis in natural resource management. *Society and Natural Resources*, **22**(6), 501–518.

Raudenbush, S. W. and A. S. Bryk (2002). *Hierarchical Linear Models: Applications and Data Analysis Methods*. Thousand Oaks, CA: Sage.

Schumpeter, J. A. (1934). *The Theory of Economic Development*. Cambridge, MA: Harvard University Press.

Scott, J. (2002). *Social Network Analysis*. Newbury Park, CA: Sage.

Snijders, T. A. B., G. G. Van de Bunt and C. E. G. Steglich (2010). Introduction to stochastic actor-based models for network dynamics. *Social Networks*, **32**, 44–60.

Strauss, D. and M. Ikeda (1990). Pseudolikelihood estimation for social networks. *Journal of the American Statistical Association*, **85**(409), 204–212.

Steglich, C. E. G., T. A. B. Snijders and M. Pearson (in press). Dynamic networks and behavior: separating selection from influence. *Sociological Methodology*.

USA Today (2008). Lobster prices fall in Maine, costing no more than sliced turkey. July 30. Available at http://www.usatoday.com/money/industries/food/2008-07-30-lobster-prices_N.htm.

Valente, T. W. (2002). *Evaluating Health Promotion Programs*. Oxford: Oxford University Press.

Van Duijn, M. A. J. (1995). Estimation of a random effects model for directed graphs. In T. A. B. Snijders (Ed.), SSS '95. Symposium Statistische Software, nr. 7. Toeval zit overal: programmatuur voor random-coefficient modellen (Chance is omnipresent: software for random coefficient models). Groningen: iec ProGAMMA, pp. 113–131.

Van Duijn, M., J. van Busschbach and T. Snijders (1999). Multilevel analysis of personal networks as dependent variables. *Social Networks*, **21**(2), 187–209.

Wasserman, S. and K. Faust (2005). *Social Networks Analysis: Methods and Applications*. New York, NY: Cambridge University Press.

Wasserman, S. and P. Pattison (1996). Logit models and logistic regressions for univariate and bivariate social networks: I. An introduction to Markov graphs. *Psychometrika*, **61**(3), 401–426.

Watts, D. J. (2003a). *Six Degrees: The Science of a Connected Age*. New York, NY: Norton.

Watts, D. J. (2003b). *Small Worlds: The Dynamics of Networks between Order and Randomness (Princeton Studies in Complexity)*. Princeton, NJ: Princeton University Press.

Wellman, B. and S. D. Berkowitz (1997). *Social Structures: A Network Approach* (updated edition). Greenwich, CT: JAI Press.

Wellman, B. and K. Frank (2001). Network capital in a multi-level world: getting support from personal communities. In N. Lin, R. Burt and K. Cook (Eds.), *Social Capital: Theory and Research*. Chicago, IL: Aldine De Gruyter, pp. 233–273.

Zuckerman, E. (2003). On networks and markets by Rauch and Casella. *Journal of Economic Literature*, **XLI**, 545–565.

Zuckerman, E. (2008). Blog. http://orgtheory.wordpress.com/2008/11/14/why-social-networks-are-overrated-a-3-when-they-are-at-best-a-2/.

9

Friends or neighbors? Subgroup heterogeneity and the importance of bonding and bridging ties in natural resource governance

9.1 INTRODUCTION

"The more you know, the less you understand" is a well-known proverb that in some ways aptly depicts our relationship with the natural environment around us. This does not mean that science and our understanding of nature has not advanced over time – it has. But with increasing knowledge we have also come to realize that the complexity of natural systems is far greater than imagined and that this complexity causes ecosystems to continuously change in non-linear and sometimes unpredictable ways (Carpenter *et al.*, 2001; Scheffer *et al.*, 2001; Folke *et al.*, 2004). To be able to deal with such uncertainty requires management approaches which can also learn and adapt to changing conditions over time. Adaptive co-management, outlined in more detail in Chapter 3, is one approach which has been championed as a way to deal with uncertainty and surprise in natural resource management. This concept has two key defining characteristics; learning and collaboration. Learning is seen as a key to remaining adaptive. Collaboration, more specifically the involvement of local stakeholders in the governance process, is assumed to provide legitimacy for governance action and management decisions, but it is also a potential source of diversity of perspectives and knowledge which can contribute to increased learning and improved management decisions (e.g. Armitage *et al.*, 2008). However, for adaptive co-management to

Social Networks and Natural Resource Management: Uncovering the Fabric of Environmental Governance, ed. Ö. Bodin and C. Prell. Published by Cambridge University Press.
© Cambridge University Press 2011.

work, (self-) organization of stakeholders and collective action have also been suggested as vitally important (Olsson *et al.*, 2004), and this in turn is influenced by the ability of the involved parties to agree on resource-related problems and resource status (Ostrom, 2005 and references therein). In this chapter we are particularly concerned with how the ability of a community to learn and adapt, and to collectively respond to common resource problems, can be affected by the structure of the social networks within it. Furthermore, we explore to what degree the existence of cohesive subgroups, and their composition in terms of actors' attributes in the form of occupation and tribal ethnicity, can help to explain why a community experiencing significant decline in marine resources over a number of years has not come together to alter unsustainable practices.

Apart from increased legitimacy of management actions, one of the primary arguments for involving local users in management is that they often possess detailed knowledge of their local resource base (Johannes, 1981; Hunn *et al.*, 2003; Ghimire *et al.*, 2004), and that such local ecological knowledge (LEK) can provide a valuable base for resource management (Johannes, 1998; Becker and Ghimire, 2003; Moller *et al.*, 2004). However, it is important to bear in mind that knowledge about a natural resource is unlikely to be evenly distributed across a community. Numerous scholars have shown that communities are rarely one coherent group of stakeholders; rather, they are defined by complicated patterns of subgroups with different perceptions, interests, resources, and amounts of influence (Agrawal and Gibson, 1999; Carlsson and Berkes, 2005; Nygren, 2005). Such perceptions and interests are likely to also be reflected in the type and extent of knowledge about a resource each group has.

Before we embark any further on our discussion of network structure, group cohesion and subgroup composition, it is important to note that subgroups are, of course, made up of individuals. Although social network data can be aggregated to the level of subgroups, as we will show in this chapter, social relations always occur between individuals. Why then should one bother to look at subgroup composition and subgroup connectivity? The simple answer is that humans are social beings. As such we learn and comprehend the world around us as much from interacting with others as from experiencing things first hand. For example, social psychologists and sociologists have long argued that individuals are most influenced by the people with whom they engage in frequent interactions, referred to as primary groups (Cooley, 1909; Festinger *et al.*, 1950; Homans, 1950; Kadushin, 1966).

This implies that individuals are likely to develop an understanding of
the status of a natural resource similar to other members of the same
subgroup, defined for example by the type of resource extraction
technique used. It also suggests that the norms developed within a
primary group are often strong enough to significantly determine
how individuals act, e.g. using illegal gear if your peers also do so, or
fishing in a specific area if your friends usually fish there. This also
suggests that the composition of personal characteristics of the individuals within a subgroup can have a major influence on the norms and
mutual understanding that develops within the group.

If we assume that a reasonable level of mutual understanding of
resource-related issues increases the likelihood that stakeholders will
organize and agree upon common rules for managing the resource (see
e.g. Ostrom, 2005), exchange of information and knowledge among
subgroups emerge as fundamental elements in the successful management of natural resources. The communication between subgroups is
often referred to as bridging ties. This can be contrasted with bonding
ties, which refers to relations within subgroups, which are usually
strong, frequent, and important for trust building (e.g. Gitell and
Vidal, 1998; Newman and Dale, 2005). Bridging ties, on the other
hand, is not only important for intergroup communication, they are
also thought to be important for a community's potential for collective
action (Granovetter, 1973) and conflict resolution (e.g. Schneider *et al.*,
2003; Carlsson and Berkes, 2005). Looked at in this way, the pattern of
relations (structural characteristics such as modularity or connectivity)
of the social network of individuals and subgroups in a community can
influence the potential for successful natural resource management by
its profound effect on the diffusion of information and knowledge, and
therefore, also on the distribution and variability of local knowledge
among users (cf. Weimann, 1982; Gould and Fernandez, 1989;
Abrahamson and Rosenkopf, 1997; Reagans and McEvily, 2003).
Furthermore, cohesion in a social network (sometimes also referred
to as social capital, see Chapter 3) can also have more direct effects on
collective action. Social cohesion creates trust which in turn facilitates
collective decision making, but too much subgroup cohesion (with little
intergroup connectivity) can create feelings of "us and them" (Borgatti and
Foster, 2003) and can also hamper creative thinking (Reagans and McEvily,
2003).

In this chapter we explore how network structure can affect the
ability of a community to learn and adapt, and to collectively respond

to common resource problems. We approach the subject by examining two networks; one used for exchange of resource-related information, and another used for social support. We divide the two networks into coherent subgroups and look at the composition of the subgroups in terms of members' occupations and tribal affiliation. We then describe and quantify the flow of communication within and between subgroups and investigate to what extent network structure can explain the distribution and characteristics of the local ecological knowledge held by the actors. Finally, we explore if the relations among and within, and compositions of, subgroups can help us understand the lack of collective action in the community surrounding a clearly declining fishery. We focus on the overall level of cohesion of the community and thus on the importance of links connecting different subgroups (so-called bridging ties).

9.2 THE CASE STUDY SETTING

The social-ecological system which forms the basis for the analysis in this chapter is a rural fishing village on the south coast of Kenya. It has approximately 200 households and an estimated 1000 inhabitants. The ecological system is characterized by mangroves covering 615 ha with mudflats and seagrass meadows in the shallow part of the lagoon, in turn sheltered from wave impact by shallow reefs at the mouth of the bay (Figure 9.1). Most villagers are in one way or another dependent on the nearby seascape for their livelihood, either directly through the extraction of marine and mangrove forest products, or indirectly since income generated from the fishery is spent in local shops and eateries.

The fishery is characterized as artisanal and based on gear such as seine nets, different types of gillnets, spear guns, and hand lines; methods which have all been found to be spatially separated on a local geographical basis (Obura *et al.*, 2002) (Figure 9.1). This means that although some overlap exists, certain types of gear tend to be associated with certain habitats. For example, set gill nets are often used in the lagoon, while spear guns are used on the reef, and ring nets (purse seines) are primarily used outside the reef crest in deeper waters. The fishery is largely focused on finfish but also includes various crustaceans and molluscs such as juvenile shrimps fished only by women and sold at local markets.

Gradual weakening of traditional governance structures and a lack of capacity to enforce the top–down regulatory measures imposed by national agencies has left the inshore fisheries along the coast as

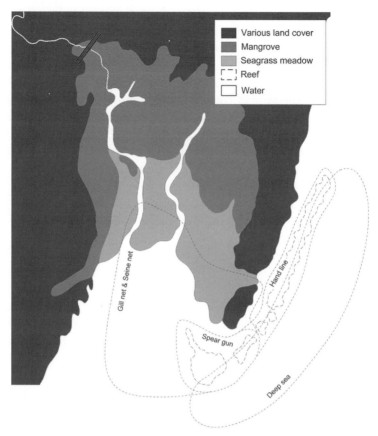

Figure 9.1 Map of the coastal seascape. The respective distribution of
mangroves, mudflats, seagrass beds, and reefs is indicated. The area of
primary fishing effort for each fishing-related occupational category is
marked with dotted lines showing the geographical distribution of
fishing areas at a local scale. The occupational categories associated with
each area are indicated. Adapted from Crona and Bodin (2006).

virtually open-access systems. This has led to overfishing and depletion
of inshore stocks in many areas. In response to the situation, initiatives
towards more inclusive management have been taken. For example, in
2006 the Fisheries Department introduced mandatory local beach management units (BMUs) for all major landing sites along the coast in an
effort to devolve management rights to local communities and increase
effectiveness of monitoring and rule compliance (Cinner *et al.*, 2009).
To date, it is unclear to what degree this initiative has led to any
significant changes in the management of the fishery (Oluoch and

Obura, 2008). However, at the time of initiation one idea was that flexible and sustainable management could be helped by daily information about the state of the fishery from fishers who spend long hours actively observing the resource.

In terms of the human population, approximately 40% of households are recent immigrants, and the majority of these originate from Tanzania, to which they return on a regular basis. Many Tanzanian fishers reside in the village on a semi-permanent basis such that they return to their homeland during seasons of low fishing activity. Migration is linked to economic factors and kinship ties and often plays a significant role in who is recruited as a crew member for the fishing season. Although not the only thing which dictates social relations in the community, tribal affiliation plays an important role for recruitment of crew members and therefore can have an impact on the network of Local Ecological Knowledge (LEK) transfer. Because tribe, but more importantly close family, is also an important aspect of social security in rural Kenya we chose to include tribal affiliation as one of the attributes when we examine cohesion and subgroup formation in the analysis below.

9.3 METHODS

9.3.1 Defining the study population

There are some specific issues of methodological importance in applying a social network research approach to the study of natural resource management, or any other field of inquiry. Here we explain how we dealt with some of these. Readers are referred to Crona (2006) and Bodin and Crona (2008) for more details on these and other issues related to the case presented here.

First, defining the boundaries of the population within which the social interactions of the actors are to be measured and analyzed is in many cases non-trivial (see also Reflection section below). Since everyone in some sense can be considered as connected to everyone else (although via others), one has to carefully define reasonable system boundaries given the research question at hand. Fortunately, in the case discussed here, the population is fairly easy to define as it consists of all households in the fishing village. This equates to 206 households (at the time of data collection) of which we collected network data for 171 households (i.e. 83% of the whole network).

One also has to choose an appropriate unit for inquiry. Often, that is the individual, but it could also be an organization (see Chapter 11), or even a nation (e.g. trade relationship), or a species as in ecological food-web analysis. In this study, we chose households as units of analysis, and our sample consisted of the head of each household. There were several reasons for this. First of all, our primary interest was not in intra-household relationships (such as between and among spouses and siblings) but rather in the exchange of ecological information and social support between households. We acknowledge that in a typical Kenyan household several breadwinners may exist and they may be dependent on different livelihoods and as such each should be interviewed in their own right. However, as in most studies, a trade-off had to be struck between collection of data relevant to the research question and the time and resources available. Our primary concern was to understand how network structure can affect the community's ability to learn, adapt, and collectively respond to a declining fishery. Given resource constraints, households (measured through heads of households) were judged to be the best unit of analysis for this investigation. The reason is that most heads of households are male, and in the predominantly Muslim coastal communities of Kenya, fishing of finfish is reserved only for men.

9.3.2 Defining and measuring appropriate networks

As explained above the rationale behind this chapter is the importance of consensus building and knowledge sharing for collective action around resource management. To be able to address this we first need to define which networks are important. At the onset we stated that local information and knowledge about the status of the environment are key in successfully managing natural resources. Hence, our primary interest is in the social network where such knowledge and information are exchanged. Thus, we posed two questions relating to this to each respondent. These were:

(1)   If you noticed changes in the natural environment, e.g. the number of fish caught, the condition of the mangrove forest or reef, availability of firewood, etc., who would you discuss this with?

(2)   Do you exchange information with anyone which is useful for you to carry out your primary occupation? (Y/N) For example, sharing information about practices, good fishing spots, equipment, timing, and season, etc.?

For the subsequent analysis of network structure we combined the relational data for the two networks elicited by each question into one which we will refer to as the Local Ecological Knowledge (LEK) network.

Different types of networks, however, yield different structures. In this chapter we also look at the network for social support. Social support networks encompass the strongest, most intimate social relations and this is a common way of assessing social cohesion in different cultural settings. It therefore provides a form of baseline measure of cohesion which can be comparable to those of other studies (see e.g. US General Social Survey SDA Archives http://sda.berkeley.edu/archive. htm, or a similar study from China (Ruan *et al.*, 1997)). We therefore include social support here to allow for a discussion of how different types of networks yield different structures and discuss the relevance of this for natural resource management.

To assess social support we asked each respondent the following question:

(3)   With whom can you discuss important matters? Anything you consider important to you.

After defining the population and the networks of interest, the next step is to actually measure the different social networks of interest among the actors. Often, relational data are gathered using interviews and/or questionnaires. Collection of the relational data can be done either using recall methods (i.e. the respondent generates a list of his or her relations) or using recognition methods (i.e. the respondent picks individuals from a precompiled list consisting of all individuals in the studied population). In our case we mainly used the former approach. Using the set of questions outlined above, each head of household in the village was asked about his or her different social relations (see further details in Crona and Bodin, 2006). Social ties mentioned using the recall method tend to be frequent in interaction, intense, and recent, i.e. they are the strongest and most influential ones (Marsden, 1990 and references therein). Thus one can generally say that the recall method primarily elicits data on strong ties whereas the recognition method elicits both stronger and weaker relations.

To get an estimate of how many strong and weak ties existed within the network used for exchange of ecological knowledge we complemented the recall method with a simplified recognition method. Since most of the respondents in the village are illiterate, presenting long lists of individuals to choose between was not feasible (nor was reading out a list of approximately 200 names). Instead, we presented each respondent with a list of ten randomly chosen individuals from the community population. A unique subset of individuals (list of ten individuals) was randomly generated for each respondent. Respondents then pointed out the ones on their list with whom they communicated about LEK. This combined method was only used for eliciting relational data for the exchange of ecological information and knowledge.

9.3.3   Assessing local ecological knowledge

This chapter is concerned with the interaction among groups for transfer of LEK as well as the importance of bonding and bridging ties between groups for natural resource governance. Hence, the network structures that regulate flows of resources, in this case ecological information and social support, can be seen as the independent variables. The dependent variable, on the other hand, is in this study the amount, type, and distribution of LEK. Also, the lack of common management agreements to steer away from resource depletions can be seen as a dependent variable.

Given the objective of this book, we will briefly explain how we measured these dependent variables, and a brief summary of the results are outlined below. For more detailed information we refer to Crona (2006) and Crona and Bodin (2006). We chose to measure LEK at the level of occupational groups or categories. This means that we did not assess LEK at the level of heads of households, but at the level of groups defined by their common occupation, and for fishers, their common use of specific gear, such as gill nets, spear guns, seine nets, etc. For this we used semi-structured interviews and focus group interviews. The decision to study ecological knowledge at the level of groups defined by occupation was based on the fact that in spite of cultural and religious homogeneity, social group identification tends to be strongly connected to occupation. For fishers this has been shown to be related to the use of specific fishing gear types (Glaesel, 2000). Furthermore, in an artisanal fishery setting, gear type largely dictates where principal fishing effort is spatially located in the seascape, thus strongly affecting the type and scale of ecological knowledge accumulated (Figure 9.1).

The level of collective action with regards to resource management was assessed by interviews with key informants within the village, discussion with other researchers on site, and participatory observations under several consecutive years of field studies. In short, no substantial activities among villagers themselves to collectively act on the declining fish stocks were observed, even though focus group discussions revealed that many fishers acknowledged a trend of declining stocks (Crona, 2006). Our assessment of declining resources is also based on other work in the region that shows a general decline of inshore and pelagic fish species throughout this particular coastal region (McClanahan and Mangi, 2001; Ochiewo, 2004; Maina *et al.*, 2008).

9.3.4 Network analysis

Using the relational data collected, social network analysis (SNA) was then used to quantitatively assess structural aspects of the two social networks under investigation (for overview see Wasserman and Faust, 1994; Scott, 2000; Freeman, 2004). Subgroups were derived solely based on relations reported by the respondents, without taking into account individual characteristics such as occupation, i.e. focusing only on the structural pattern of relational groups. The composition of each group, in terms of characteristics such as occupation and tribe, are instead displayed with pie charts representing each subgroup node (Figure 9.2).

There are numerous methods available to formally divide individuals in a network into different subgroups (Wasserman and Faust, 1994; Scott, 2000). All methods have emerged from a desire to distinguish subsets of individuals based on the cohesiveness or reachability of group members, as well as on the relative frequency of relations within the subset as compared to relations with non-members. For this study we chose to use an algorithmic method which maximizes a metric called *Modularity* (Equation 9.1). Modularity as defined here captures to what extent a network can be said to consist of separate subgroups (Guimerà and Amaral, 2005b):

$$M = \sum_{s=1}^{N_M} \left[\frac{l_s}{L} - \left(\frac{d_s}{2L} \right)^2 \right] \tag{9.1}$$

where N_M is the number of subgroups, L is the number of links in the network, l_s is the number of links between nodes in subgroup s, and d_s is the sum of the degrees of the nodes in subgroup s. The stronger the tendency for links to occur within subgroups, the higher the modularity value (M).

a

b

To find the subgroup partition of the networks which maximizes the modularity value, an algorithm based on simulated annealing was used (Guimerà and Amaral, 2005a, 2005b). It is a stochastic optimization technique that is devised to be able to find a global maximum instead of getting trapped in local maxima. Furthermore, in order to assess whether an identified partition actually represent a "true" subgroup structure, the same algorithm was used to find subgroup partitions in a set of 100 randomly generated networks, each with the same degree distribution as the original network (Guimerà et al., 2004). Hence, by comparing the modularities assessed in the random networks with the modularity in the real network, it is possible to define whether the identified subgroup structure in the original network is significant or not.

We also complemented the assessment of subgroups described above by measuring the amount of exchange of ecological information within and between households engaged in different occupations (Crona and Bodin, 2006). The rationale for this was that we were interested in the degree to which occupations define the flows of information. In particular, we were interested in assessing to what extent households communicated within versus across occupations, and if such cross-occupational relations tended to be strong or weak. Technically, this analysis was done by grouping individuals into subgroups according to their occupations (i.e. by dividing the socio-matrix into different blocks, see Table 9.1). To then assess the strength of links between subgroups we compared the number of realized links within each block to the number of links that would be expected within each block if all links were distributed randomly throughout all blocks (further details in Crona and Bodin, 2006). The same procedure was used to estimate the strength of intergroup communications for the subgroup assessment based on the simulated annealing algorithm.

9.4 LOCAL ECOLOGICAL KNOWLEDGE – DIFFERENCES AND SIMILARITIES AMONG GROUPS

Table 9.2 broadly summarizes the main differences between the LEK held by households engaged in the different occupations studied here. The analysis shows that the level of detail of knowledge of marine resources was consistently lower among farmers and businessmen (Crona, 2006). The LEK held by fishers of various occupational categories revealed a wide range, from detailed accounts of feeding of certain target species to acknowledgment of large-scale climatic changes

Table 9.1. *Socio-matrix of relations among subgroups of households engaged in different occupations. All households have been divided into different subgroups based on their primary occupation ("Occupational groups," see also Crona and Bodin, 2006). The numbers refer to the ratio of observed versus expected number of links.*

	Seine net	Businessman	Farmer	Deep sea	Gill net	Middleman
LEK – recall questions (strong links)						
Seine net	**6.13**	0	0	1.02	0	0.29
Businessman		**0.92**	0.21	0.19	0	0
Farmer			**1.64**	0.13	1.15	0.58
Deep sea				**2.79**	1.23	0.72
Gill net					**9.2**	0.46
Middleman						**5.11**
LEK – recognition questions (strong and weak links)						
Seine net	**2.85**	0.89	0.33	1.19	2.14	0.53
Businessman		**0.97**	0.79	0.35	0.16	0.95
Farmer			**1.53**	0.48	1.07	0
Deep sea				**1.47**	1.43	1.33
Gill net					**1.9**	1.28
Middleman						**3.8**
Social support						
Seine net	**4.93**	0	0.66	1.17	0	0
Businessman		**2.16**	1.17	0.35	0.31	0
Farmer			**0**	0	0	0
Deep sea				**2.47**	1.13	1.31
Gill net					**0**	0
Middleman						**1.88**

affecting shrimp stocks and mangrove coverage. On a general level, knowledge common to most groups included, for example, the acknowledgment of the central role played by mangroves for coastal protection, nursery habitat, and water quality. Group-specific knowledge included recognition by seine net fishers that sea urchin aggregations can affect the dynamics of seagrass meadows and associated fauna, while a notion of regional fish stock migrations related to wind patterns and currents were mostly recognized by fish traders, and deep-sea fishers using larger nets and generally fishing further away from the reefs. Deep-sea fishers also have knowledge of currents and linkages between the three subcomponents of the coastal seascape (mangroves, seagrass, and coral reefs) at a scale surpassing that of other

fishing groups. In other words, they have a more holistic perception of
the seascape as compared with all other groups. In addition, their
notion of fish migrations spans a larger geographical scale than seine
netters since they acknowledge that pelagic stocks move up and down
the coast on a regional scale (Table 9.2). A more detailed analysis of the
LEK inventory is presented in Crona (2006).

Table 9.2. *Summary of local ecological knowledge of different occupational
groups in the target community, Kenya. Species refer to marine species of fish and
shellfish targeted by categories of fishers. For each species of fish the functional
groups to which it belongs, based on trophic level, is indicated in parentheses:
pelagic/demersal predator (P), benthic predator (BP), herbivores (H), planktivores
(Pl), omnivores (O). Adapted from Crona and Bodin (2006).*

Occupational category	Species	Ecological links and processes
Deep sea	*Caesio* sp. (Pl)	Notion of regional fish stock
	Carangidae (P)	migrations at a local and regional
	Hyporamphus sp. (O)	scale
	Lethrinus sp. (BP)	Seasonal monsoon-related wind
	Scombridae (P)	patterns and currents affect fish
	Selar sp. (P)	migrations along the regional
	Siganus sp. (H)	coastline
	Squid (P)	Notion that changes in climate (timing of the monsoon rains and El Niño phenomena) have occurred recently resulting in an effect on the artisanal shrimp fishery as well as mangrove coverage
		Recognition of links between the ecosystems mangroves, seagrasses, and reef
Seine net	Carangidae (P)	Notion of regional fish stock
	Caranx sp. (P)	migrations at a local scale
	Lethrinus sp. (BP)	Seasonal monsoon-related wind
	Lutjanus argentimaculatus (BP)	patterns and currents affect fish migrations along the regional
	Mugilidae (H)	coastline
	Pomadasys sp. (BP)	Notion that changes in climate
	Scombridae (P)	(timing of the monsoon rains
	Selar sp. (P)	and El Niño phenomena) have
	Sphyraena sp. (P)	occurred recently resulting in an

Table 9.2. (*cont.*)

Occupational category	Species	Ecological links and processes
	Squid (P)	effect on the artisanal shrimp
	Strongylura sp. (P)	fishery as well as mangrove coverage
		Notion that sea urchin aggregations can affect the dynamics of seagrass meadows and associated fauna
Gill net	*Chanos chanos*(O)	Notion that changes in climate
	Gerres sp. (BP)	(timing of the monsoon rains and El
	Lethrinus harak (BP)	Niño phenomena) have occurred
	Mugilidae (H, P)	recently resulting in an effect
	Siganus sp. (H)	on the artisanal shrimp
	Sphyraena sp. (P)	fishery as well as
	Strongylura sp. (P)	mangrove coverage
		Seasonal monsoon-related wind patterns and currents affect fish migrations along the regional coastline
Fish traders		Notion of regional fish stock migrations
		Seasonal monsoon-related wind patterns and currents affect fish migrations along the regional coastline
		Recognition of interlinkages between seascape components
Farmers		Poor general knowledge of all ecological links and processes in the seascape
Businessmen		Poor general knowledge of all ecological links and processes in the seascape

9.5 NETWORK STRUCTURE AND THE COMPOSITION AND CONNECTIVITY AMONG SUBGROUPS

Looking at the networks used for transmission of LEK and social support, both networks reveal groups which can be determined with statistical significance (e.g. the average levels of Modularity for 2×100 randomly generated networks was more than 9 and 10 standard deviations lower than the Modularity scores for the LEK and the social support networks respectively, i.e. $P < 0.001$).

If we begin by examining the LEK network we see that the network contains one main component with two smaller isolated groups and one large isolated group. This larger group consists of persons who did not report any social relations for this particular type of network, mainly as a consequence of not having been interviewed. The two smaller groups represent two separate dyads. The thickness of the lines between groups indicates the strength of interaction between them (see Method section).

Looking at Figure 9.2 it appears that both occupation and tribe are good predictors of group cohesion. We deduce this because although a few nodes representing groups are more diverse in their composition, most nodes are commonly dominated by one or two types of occupations or tribes. This could indicate that gear-defined occupation does play an important role in defining communication of resource-related knowledge and information in this community. This insight is further reinforced by examining the strength of within-versus between-occupation communications (Table 9.1). Looking at the pattern of within- versus between-occupation interaction in Table 9.1 we see relatively strong within-group interaction (in bold) for all fishing-related occupations, while businessmen and farmers are less confined to their occupational group for resource-related communication (Table 9.1, panel 1). Noteworthy is the fact that the between-group interaction of many of the fishing-related occupational groups is remarkably low, with many zero values in the socio-matrix.

If we also include weaker ties, generated by the recognition method, the pattern changes somewhat. We can then see that interaction between occupations increases while within-occupation interaction decreases for some occupations. For example, the between-group interaction of seine net fishers and gill net fishers increases from 0 to 2.14, while their within-occupation interaction decreases from 6.13 to 2.85. Similar but less pronounced patterns are seen for other fishing-related occupations (Table 9.1, panel 2). At this point we need to make a point of caution. Although it appears that both occupation and tribe are good predictors of group cohesion, and that occupation plays an important role in defining communication of LEK, we have to consider the difficulties in inferring causality in non-longitudinal SNA studies. We must therefore be aware of the fact that

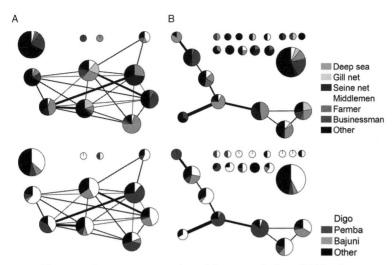

Figure 9.2 Intergroup network used for transmission of (A) local ecological knowledge (LEK), and (B) social support. Each node indicates the percentage representation within each group of occupation (upper half) and tribe (lower half). Note that the thickness of the lines corresponds to the strength of the intergroup communication. Size of the nodes represents relative size based on the number of individuals assigned to each respective group.

another variable (a so-called spurious variable) could be responsible for the observed pattern by linking occupation and communication. We will return to this in our discussion.

The social support network exhibits quite a different structure compared with the LEK network (Figure 9.2). First of all, since networks of social support encompass the strongest, most intimate social relations people have, it is therefore not surprising that fewer relations are reported and that those link to individuals drawn from within the very closest social circle. This is revealed by the lower number of links between subgroups, and the fact that many subgroups are isolated from the main component of the network (i.e. the largest subnet).

Furthermore, we see a remarkably string-like structure. The main reason for this is that the absolute majority of individuals (ego) report only one or at most two relations, but these relations often are not reciprocated. In other words, few of the reported ties in the social support network are reciprocal. We believe this to be an effect of respondents not reporting all of their social support relations rather than the result of non-reciprocal ties (see Marsden, 1990 for a thorough discussion on the issue of respondents which are typically not able to report all of their relations). For this reason there are also a higher number of isolated small groups in this network.

As in the LEK network, both occupation and tribe appear as strong determinants of subgroup composition. Often the alters reported in a social support network are kin. It is therefore not surprising to see the strong dominance of one or two tribal affiliations in the groups reported in Figure 9.2B. In a fishing community, such as the one studied here, it is also reasonable to believe that interconnected households will share occupation. However, the results are striking in that there is also a clear pattern in the social support network where one or two occupations tend to dominate the composition of many of the subgroups.

9.6   SUBGROUPS AND LOCAL ECOLOGICAL KNOWLEDGE DISTRIBUTION

Now let us relate these findings to the knowledge distribution between groups described above. First of all, it was found that the non-fishery-related occupations (such as local businessmen) showed consistently poorer knowledge and understanding of ecological processes. This is hardly surprising given the fact that these persons are not directly dependent on such knowledge, and they are not exposed to this kind of information exchange in their daily routines. Nonetheless, the fact that these persons are only weakly linked to persons engaged in resource-related occupations likely contributes to their poor local ecological knowledge. In Figure 9.2A, most businessmen are confined to only three of the eight subgroups in the main component (of which two are dominated by persons engaged in non-resource-related occupations), thus their "social exposure" to resource-related issues is limited. Table 9.1 (panel 1) also illustrates the weak linkages to fishers of different types.

Some knowledge was found to be shared broadly across the different fishery-related occupations. The causality for the shared knowledge is not possible to assess given our data, and it could be argued that some of the knowledge is surely a result of experiential learning of individual fishers. Nonetheless we believe it is reasonable to assume that the patterns of knowledge distribution are not simply an effect of fishers being exposed to the natural environment on a daily basis. The many linkages between subgroups, and the fact that many subgroups are made up of fishers of different types reveals that there is a fair amount of exchange of ecological information and knowledge among fishers. These interrelations are likely to contribute to the shared knowledge among all fishers.

Another finding was that persons engaged in different types of fisheries exhibited specific knowledge which was not shared with others to any large extent (see further details in Crona, 2006). The reason why persons in different fisheries have different knowledge can of course be attributed to the fact that they fish in different locations using different gear. However, following the arguments above, we believe these differences are also likely to be attributed to the structure of the LEK network. For example, the fact that deep-sea fishers possess a more holistic knowledge, while also resembling much of the gill net and seine net fisher's specific knowledge, is particularly intriguing and something we argue is a result of their central positioning in the network of occupations (Table 9.1, panel 1). This allows them more exposure to communication with all other resource-related occupations. Deep-sea fishers are members of seven of the eight subgroups in the main component (Figure 9.2A), and Table 9.1 (panel 1) reveals that deep-sea fishers, as an occupational group, have relatively strong links to both seine net and gill net fishers. Furthermore, by examining Table 9.1 (panel 1) and Figure 9.2A, it is clear that there is not much exchange of information between seine net and gill net fishers. Incidentally, these two occupational groups also have group-specific knowledge which is not shared (see knowledge regarding sea urchins in Table 9.2). This, we argue, can at least partly explain the differences among these fishers in terms of occupational specific knowledge. In terms of the LEK network, these types of fishers are socially separated, and it is therefore more likely that they will develop their own specific knowledge (Bodin and Crona, 2009). Similar to what we described for non-fishers above, two factors may potentially affect the distribution of knowledge among fisher occupation groups; one is related to the gear used which automatically confines fishers to a specific geographic area within the seascape, the other is the pattern of their intra- and inter-group communication.

In light of these findings, it is interesting to note that when we also account for weak links, the level of interoccupational exchange among gill net and seine net fishers increases significantly, and the tendency to only communicate with similar others decreases (between-occupation interaction increases from 0 to 2.14, while the within-occupation interaction decreases from 6.13 to 2.85, see Table 9.1, panels 1 and 2). Were we to consider only these patterns of relations, the fact that these groups actually have developed group-specific knowledge may seem surprising. However, the kind of local ecological knowledge studied here is far from trivial to acquire since it involves recognizing ecological patterns and processes encompassing different kinds of habitat and species. Hence, to develop common knowledge on these grounds would probably require frequent and intense interactions (cf. discussion on tacit knowledge by Hansen, 1999; Reagans and McEvily, 2003), and following this argument it seems the weak links reported may not be capable of doing this.

9.7   SUBGROUPS AND COLLECTIVE ACTION

As discussed previously, lack of social cohesion can prevent a group of actors to collectively respond to various challenges and opportunities (Putnam, 1993; Pretty and Ward, 2001; Ostrom, 2005). Therefore, ongoing over-harvesting of a common-pool natural resource can be devastating for a group which is not able to act collectively to avoid a situation similar to Hardin's tragedy of the commons (Hardin, 1968). In this study, we were particularly interested in examining if lack of social cohesion in the village could help us to explain the villagers' current inability to respond to declining fish stocks.

9.7.1 Bonding and bridging ties

If we examine the LEK network structure in terms of cohesion we see that the density is relatively high. The strength of interaction between subgroups differs but few subgroups are completely isolated. This between-group interaction is often referred to as bridging social capital, while the within-group interaction is referred to as bonding social capital (Woolcock, 2001), and both types of social capital have been suggested as being important for the ability of communities to engage in collective action. In our case we could say that there appears to be a significant amount of both bonding and bridging social capital in the village, at least as measured through relations used for transmitting knowledge related to the environment. If we instead turn to the social support network, the situation changes a bit. Here, the network is more fragmented with more isolated subgroups and fewer intergroup linkages. However, the majority of the households are still confined within one single large component, and even though the composition of each subgroup is typically skewed in favor of some dominating occupation or tribe, there seems to be a fair amount of exchange of social support among different types of villagers. Hence, lack of social cohesion, both

related to LEK communication and in the more general form as measured through social support, cannot be invoked as a credible explanation. More specifically, lack of bonding and bridging social capital is
also not a reasonable explanation. We therefore needed to examine in
more detail the composition of the subgroups occupying certain key
positions in the networks. The main reason is to examine if any particular group of individuals appears more influential than others in controlling the flows of ecological information and knowledge, and thus in
shaping the development of a common understanding of resource-
related problems. This is of particular interest in the context of natural
resource management as shared understanding of a common problem
is seen as a prerequisite for collective action to emerge (cf. Ostrom,
2005).

9.7.2   Who is occupying key positions?

Looking at the LEK network, two clusters of subgroups are easily
identifiable when only the strongest between-group links were
accounted for (i.e. the thickest lines in Figure 9.2). The first cluster
consists of two subgroups, the first being the one in the middle-top
of the main component, and the other being the one most to the
right. The second cluster consists of the three subgroups that are
linked by the two remaining thick lines in Figure 9.2. Together these
subgroups constitute the majority of the households confined
within the main component, and they are strongly linked with
other subgroups within their respective cluster. Hence, individuals
within either of these two clusters are not only members of fairly
large subgroups, they also possess a comparatively high number of
ties to members of other subgroups within their clusters. Thus, in
comparison with other villagers outside these clusters, they experience a higher level of social cohesion extending beyond their immediate social neighborhood. It is therefore reasonable to assume that
the individuals who are members of these two clusters are, on
average, the most influential when it comes to exchange of ecological information and knowledge in the studied community. We
therefore argue that it is particularly interesting to analyze who
the members of these subgroups are. For example, does any particular occupation dominate a certain subgroup, and how are subgroups linked to each other? For the latter analysis we treat
subgroups as single actors and focus our attention on the pattern
of relations among subgroups.

We start with the cluster consisting of two subgroups. The subgroup to the left is the most heterogeneous one of all subgroups since all seven occupations are represented. However, the single largest type of occupation is represented by deep-sea fishers (approximately 30%). Hence, if any occupation is likely to be more influential than others in this group it is deep-sea fishers. The other subgroup of this cluster is nearly completely dominated by non-resource dependent occupations. This subgroup, as a whole, is likely to be less influential when it comes to influencing the development of LEK than the former subgroup since its members are not directly involved in occupations relating strongly to the marine environment and are probably less motivated to engage in such communications (as well as perceived to be less knowledgeable). As such the potential for deep-sea fishers to exert influence on the framing of the issues surrounding the status of the marine resource in this cluster is high even though they are numerically fewer than the combined total of other occupations.

The other cluster consists of three subgroups, where one subgroup sits in the middle. Returning to the importance of brokers (i.e. actors with high betweenness who can exert influence by controlling the flow of resources between others) (Burt, 2004, 2005), it is reasonable to assume that this middle group, as a whole, has the potential to dominate this cluster. Once again, this key subgroup is dominated by deep-sea fishers (*c.* 45%), with strong potential to influence and shape the development of a mutual understanding of resource-related problems in this cluster as well. Furthermore, it is interesting to note that the two peripheral subgroups of this cluster each contain a large fraction of gill net and seine net fishers respectively, but the structure of the three-node cluster is such that these two fisher groups are largely separated, with seine netters mostly in the top right node and gill netters in the lower node (Figure 9.2). The subgroup in the middle, dominated by the deep-sea fishers, therefore acts as gatekeepers limiting direct communications between large numbers of seine net and gill net fishers.

In sum, this qualitative and quite speculative analysis suggests that although the network is fairly cohesive, it could well be dominated, in terms of agenda setting and framing of issues, by deep-sea fishers. This would be a result of their dominance of the most influential positions. Importantly, this potential dominance cannot only be attributed to their status as the largest group of fishers, but the way they occupy key positions in the network of subgroups further boosts their influence.

This potential dominance is also reflected when looking at the network being divided into subgroups based on respondents' occupations and not based on relational pattern (Table 9.1, panel 1). Deep-sea fishers represent the only occupation that has links to all other occupations, and they are therefore the most central group when the network is divided in subgroups based on respondents' occupations (see Crona and Bodin, 2006 for an extended discussion on this topic).

The potential dominance by deep-sea fishers is not necessarily a problem per se, it can also be seen as an opportunity since they are better positioned than any other group of households engaged in a common occupation to contribute to the development of shared understanding of resource-related problems and thus to initiate collective action. However, as was found in previous studies (Crona, 2006; Crona and Bodin, 2006), deep-sea fishers seem less inclined to perceive the current situation of declining fish stock as a major threat, and accordingly they are probably less inclined to change the current state of affairs. Also, their role as possible gatekeepers between seine net and gill net fishers could block these more peripheral subgroups from acquiring sufficient shared influence in the community to be able to instigate collective action themselves.

9.8   CONCLUDING REMARKS

In this chapter we explored how social network structure can affect the ability of a community to learn and adapt, and to collectively respond to common resource problems, in this case a declining fishery. We approached the subject by examining two networks; one used for exchange of resource-related information, and another used for social support. Our focus was on the overall level of cohesion of the community and we examined to what degree the village social ties were distributed in coherent subgroups. The reason for this was the hypothesized importance of bonding and bridging ties (social capital) for overcoming barriers to collective action.

We found a significant amount of both bonding and bridging ties and therefore conclude that a lack of binding and bridging social capital in the village cannot be seen as a credible explanation for why no collective action has occurred to halt unsustainable fishing practices. Instead we dug deeper into our data and looked at the composition of groups which occupy central positions in the knowledge network – thus potentially shaping the development of a common understanding

Reflections

Network boundary issues

Due to the nature of our research question the village became the natural boundary of our study. This was justified by the fact that the village itself is a distinct cluster of houses and geographically separated from other nearby villages, the closest of which is *c.* 3 km away. Furthermore, our concern with resource management and collective action at the village level made this a natural and easy choice in our case.

Ecological boundaries

The ecological limits were defined as the coastal seascape – including mangroves, seagrasses, and coral reefs fringing the lagoon – where the majority of the village fish and which is the area designated for management by the local Beach Management Unit.

Deciding on the unit of analysis

In this study we chose the head of household as a proxy for the household as a unit of analysis. This was because our primary interest was not in intrahousehold relationships (such as between and among spouses and siblings), but rather in the exchange of ecological information and social support between households. We acknowledge that in a typical Kenyan household several breadwinners may exist and they may be dependent on different livelihoods but due to time and resource constraints we limited our data collection in this manner. Furthermore, as we were interested in the group interactions our unit of analysis was defined as relational and occupational groups. This was because occupation has been shown in the literature to be of strong importance in defining identity in this and similar communities.

Data-gathering issues

Working in communities where a large proportion of respondents are illiterate always presents a problem. Furthermore, in Kenya updated census data at the household level were not available so a complete roster of names was not an option. Also, in many of the Muslim communities along the coast of Kenya individuals are known by several different names (nicknames, father's last name, first name, etc.). This made collection of relational ties difficult and we had to devise a method by which we could ensure the identity of each alter. In our case this required the help of a local informant who could help us decipher and triangulate the identity of all heads of households. As a first step, this included walking around the community and locating each house in the village and establishing the head of the household. Where any doubts remained as to the identity of the person, this was checked with other members of the community.

The string-like structure observed in the social support network is worthy of mention. The main reason for this is that the absolute majority of individuals (ego) report only one, or at most two, alters but these alters often do not name ego. In other words, few of the reported ties in the social support network are reciprocal. We believe this to be an effect of respondents not reporting all of their social support relations rather than the result of non-reciprocal ties but this is an interesting and challenging methodological issue which SNA researchers need to be aware of when interpreting network structures.

Ethical issues

The exact identities of the respondents were not revealed when presenting the results. The name of the village is also kept secret.

Explanatory power of SNA

Causality is notoriously difficult to determine in network studies since it typically requires longitudinal data. Gathering network data is however very labor intense. In addition, the reliability of relational data is sometimes limited. Therefore, comparing relational data collected for the same system at different points in time could potentially reveal differences which are attributed to respondent reliability and not a result of social processes leading to network change. Applying a multiple case study approach, preferably with a combination of longitudinal data and contextually differentiated studies, can begin to address this. In this chapter we presented only one case study. Accordingly, our assertions of casual links between the network structures and what we denote as dependent variables should be seen as grounded speculations and not facts. Nonetheless, the only way in which we can hope to uncover the extent to which social networks among different stakeholders actually matters in the governing of natural resources is by continuing to empirically uncover the structural characteristics of real-world social networks in different resource management situations. Given these constraints we still feel that the SNA approach allows researchers to come up with a set of elaborate and hopefully well-grounded hypotheses which can be taken as inputs to more elaborate studies preferably adopting a multi-case study approach.

Non-network data

We collected detailed data on group-specific local ecological knowledge which was essential to link knowledge distribution to the communication network.

of resource-related problems, something which has been deemed important for collective action to occur (Ostrom, 2005). In analyzing who the members of these central subgroups were we asked: does any particular occupation dominate a certain subgroup, and how are sub-groups linked to each other?

We found that deep-sea fishers tended to dominate the composition of these groups; not because of their absolute numerical abundance but because they dominated the composition in groups of high structural importance, such as nodes in brokering positions. This could allow them to play a strong part in setting agendas and framing topics of discussion related to the fisheries. As noted above, this is not necessarily a problem but previous studies in the same community have shown deep-sea fishers to be less likely to perceive the current situation of declining fish stock as a major threat. This is a result of two things; first, they use gear which is less reliant on the near-shore fish stocks, targeting more pelagic stocks outside the reef crest, and second, a significant portion of the deep-sea fishers are semi-migrant fishers originating from Tanzania, and many harbor less of a sense of place and thus potentially less commitment to the area and the sustainability of its resources. We suggest these as tentative reasons for why this community has not, in spite of apparent and noticeable catch declines, organized to address this issue.

REFERENCES

Abrahamson, E. and L. Rosenkopf (1997). Social network effects on the extent of innovation diffusion: a computer simulation. *Organization Science*, **8**(3), 289–309.

Agrawal, A. and C. Gibson (1999). Community and conservation: beyond enchantment and disenchantment. *World Development*, **27**(4), 629–649.

Armitage, D., R. Plummer, F. Berkes *et al.* (2008). Adaptive co-management for social-ecological complexity. *Frontiers in Ecology and the Environment*, **7**(2), 95–102.

Becker, C. D. and K. Ghimire (2003). Synergy between traditional ecological knowledge and conservation science supports forest preservation in Ecuador. *Conservation Ecology*, **8**(1), 1.

Bodin, Ö. and B. I. Crona (2008). Management of natural resources at the community level: exploring the role of social capital and leadership in a rural fishing community. *World Development*, **36**(12), 2763–2779.

Bodin, Ö. and B. I. Crona (2009). The role of social networks in natural resource governance: what relational patterns make a difference? *Global Environmental Change*, **19**, 366–374.

Borgatti, S. P. and P. C. Foster (2003). The network paradigm in organizational research: a review and typology. *Journal of Management*, **29**(6), 991–1013.

Burt, R. (2004). Structural holes and good ideas. *American Journal of Sociology*, **110**(2), 349–399.

Burt, R. (2005). *Brokerage and Closure: An Introduction to Social Capital*. Oxford: Oxford University Press.

Carlsson, L. and F. Berkes (2005). Co-management: concepts and methodological implications. *Journal of Environmental Management*, **75**, 65–76.

Carpenter, S., B. Walker, J. M. Anderies and N. Abel (2001). From metaphor to measurement: resilience of what to what? *Ecosystems*, **4**(8), 765–781.

Cinner, J. E., A. Wamukota, H. Randriamahazo and A. Rabearisoa (2009). Towards institutions for community-based management of inshore marine resources in the Western Indian Ocean. *Marine Policy*, **33**, 489–496.

Cooley, C. H. (1909). *On Self and Social Organization*. Chicago, IL: University of Chicago Press.

Crona, B. I. (2006). Supporting and enhancing development of heterogeneous ecological knowledge among resource users in a Kenyan seascape. *Ecology and Society*, **11**(1), art 32, http://www.ecologyandsociety.org/vol11/iss1/art32/.

Crona, B. I. and Ö. Bodin (2006). What you know is who you know? Patterns of communication as prerequisites for co-management. *Ecology and Society*, **11**(2), art 7.

Festinger, L., S. Schachter and K. Back (1950). *Social Pressures in Informal Groups. A Study of Human Factors in Housing*. New York, NY: Harper & Brothers.

Folke, C., S. Carpenter, B. Walker *et al.* (2004). Regime shifts, resilience, and biodiversity in ecosystem management. *Annual Review of Ecology, Evolution, and Systematics*, **35**(1), 557–581.

Freeman, L. C. (2004). *The Development of Social Network Analysis – A Study in the Sociology of Science*. Vancouver, BC: Empirical Press.

Ghimire, S. K., D. McKey and Y. Aumeeruddy-Thomas (2004). Heterogeneity in ethnoecological knowledge and management of medicinal plants in the Himalayas of Nepal: implications for conservation. *Ecology and Society*, **9**(3), 6 (online).

Gitell, R. and A. Vidal (1998). *Community Organizing: Building Social Capital as a Development Strategy*. Thousand Oaks, CA: Sage.

Glaesel, H. (2000). State and local resistance to the expansion of two environmentally harmful marine fishing techniques in Kenya. *Society and Natural Resources*, **13**, 321–338.

Gould, R. V. and R. M. Fernandez (1989). Structure of mediation: a formal approach to brokerage in transactions networks. *Sociological Methodology*, **19**, 89–126.

Granovetter, M. (1973). The strength of weak ties. *American Journal of Sociology*, **76**(6), 1360–1380.

Guimerà, R. and L. A. N. Amaral (2005a). Cartography of complex networks: modules and universal roles. *Journal of Statistical Mechanics: Theory and Experiments*, art P02001.

Guimerà, R. and L. A. N. Amaral (2005b). Functional cartography of complex metabolic networks. *Nature*, **433**, 895–900.

Guimerà, R., M. Sales-Pardo and L. A. N. Amaral (2004). Modularity from fluctuations in random graphs and complex networks. *Physical Review E (Statistical, Nonlinear, and Soft Matter Physics)*, **70**, art 025101.

Hansen, M. T. (1999). The search-transfer problem: the role of weak ties in sharing knowledge across organization subunits. *Administrative Science Quarterly*, **44**, 82–111.

Hardin, G. (1968). The tragedy of the commons. *Science*, **162**, 1243–1248.

Homans, G. C. (1950). *The Human Group*. London: Routledge & Kegan Paul.

Hunn, E. S., D. R. Johnson, P. N. Russel and T. F. Thornton (2003). Huna Tinglit traditional environmental knowledge, conservation, and the management of a 'wilderness' park. *Current Anthropology*, **44** (supplement), S79–S103.

Johannes, R. E. (1981). *Word of the Lagoon: Fishing and Marine Lore in the Palau District of Micronesia*. London: University of California Press.

Johannes, R. E. (1998). The case for data-less marine resource management: examples from tropical nearshore fisheries. *Trends in Ecology and Evolution*, **13**, 243–246.

Kadushin, C. (1966). The friends and supporters of psychotherapy: on social circles in urban life. *American Sociological Review*, **31**, 786–802.

Maina, G. W., D. Obura, H. Alidina and B. Munywoki (2008). Increasing catch in an overexploited fishery: Diani-Chale, Kenya, from 1998 to 2006. In *Ten Years after Bleaching – Facing the Consequences of Climate Change in the Indian Ocean*. Mombasa: CORDIO Status Report, Coastal Oceans Research and Development in the Indian Ocean/Sida-SAREC.

Marsden, P. V. (1990). Network data and measurement. *Annual Review of Sociology*, **16**, 435–463.

McClanahan, T. and S. C. Mangi (2001). The effect of a closed area and beach seine exclusion on coral reef fish catches. *Fisheries Management and Ecology*, **8**, 107–121.

Moller, H., F. Berkes, P. O'Brian Lyver and M. Kislalioglu (2004). Combining science and traditional ecological knowledge: monitoring populations for co-management. *Ecology and Society*, **9**(3), 2 (online).

Newman, L. L. and A. Dale (2005). Network structure, diversity, and proactive resilience building: a response to Tompkins and Adger. *Ecology and Society*, **10**(1), art 2.

Nygren, A. (2005). Community-based forest management within the context of institutional decentralization in Honduras. *World Development*, **33**(4), 639–655.

Obura, D. O., I. N. Wanyoni and J. M. Mwaura (2002). Participatory monitoring of an artisanal fishery in Kenya. In *Coral Reef Degradation in the Indian Ocean, Status Report 2002*. Sweden: Cordio, University of Kalmar, pp. 70–82.

Ochiewo, J. (2004). Changing fisheries practices and their social implications in south coast Kenya. *Ocean and Coastal Management*, **47**, 389–408.

Olsson, P., C. Folke and F. Berkes (2004). Adaptive comanagement for building resilience in social-ecological systems. *Environmental Management*, **34**(1), 75–90.

Oluoch, S. J. and D. Obura (2008). Assessment of fisherfolk organizations and beach management units (BMU) in the management of fishery resources in Diani-Chale, Southern Kenya. In *Ten Years after Bleaching – Facing the Consequences of Climate Change in the Indian Ocean*. Mombasa: CORDIO Status Report, Coastal Oceans Research and Development in the Indian Ocean/Sida-SAREC.

Ostrom, E. (2005). *Understanding Institutional Diversity*. Princeton, NJ: Princeton University Press.

Pretty, J. and H. Ward (2001). Social capital and the environment. *World Development*, **29**(2), 209–227.

Putnam, R. D. (1993). *Making Democracy Work. Civic Traditions in Modern Italy*. Princeton, NJ: Princeton University Press.

Reagans, R. and B. McEvily (2003). Network structure and knowledge transfer: the effects of cohesion and range. *Administrative Science Quarterly*, **48**(2), 240–267.

Ruan, D., L. C. Freeman, X. Dai, Y. Pan and W. Zhang (1997). On the changing structure of social networks in urban China. *Social Networks*, **19**(1), 75–89.

Scheffer, M., S. Carpenter, J. A. Foley, C. Folke and B. Walker (2001). Catastrophic shifts in ecosystems. *Nature*, **413**, 591–596.

Schneider, M., J. Scholz, M. Lubell, D. Mindruta and M. Edwardsen (2003). Building consensual institutions: networks and the National Estuary Program. *American Journal of Political Science*, **47**(1), 143–158.

Scott, J. (2000). *Social Network Analysis. A Handbook*. London: Sage.

Wasserman, S. and K. Faust (1994). *Social Network Analysis – Methods and Applications*. Cambridge: Cambridge University Press.

Weimann, G. (1982). On the importance of marginality: one more step into the two-step flow of communication. *American Sociological Review*, **47**(6), 764–773.

Woolcock, M. (2001). The place of social capital in understanding social and economic outcomes. *Canadian Journal of Policy Research*, **2**, 11–17.

10

The role of individual attributes in the practice of information sharing among fishers from Loreto, BCS, Mexico

10.1 INTRODUCTION

A weak regulatory regime, high resource-dependent livelihoods, poor development of social organization, extreme poverty, and signs of over-exploitation of extensive fishery resources characterize the fisheries system in the Loreto area. Fishers have not developed their own institutions to control the access and use of fishery resources, and government fisheries institutions have failed to prevent resource degradation. This would appear to be the familiar tragedy of the open-access situation that many scholars have used to describe the degradation of fishery resources by fishers competing to extract the last fish from the oceans (Ostrom *et al.*, 1994). However, paradoxically, cooperation rather than competition seems to characterize the access to fishery resources in the Loreto area. Indeed, fishers in the Loreto area use trustworthy personal contacts to find out about the abundance of fish resources in adjacent and distant waters to decide where and when to fish (Ramirez-Sanchez, 2007; Ramirez-Sanchez and Pinkerton, 2009).

Information sharing among fishers has been found to be associated with contextual variables such as mobility of the resource; alternative sources of information (e.g. pure observation of other vessels' behavior, equipment to locate fish, two-way marine-band radios); the regulatory structure of a fishery; and long-term relations of kinship and friendship, trust, and solidarity (Forman, 1967; Andersen, 1972; Stiles, 1972; Gatewood, 1984). Furthermore, it has been suggested that fishers

Social Networks and Natural Resource Management: Uncovering the Fabric of Environmental Governance, ed. Ö. Bodin and C. Prell. Published by Cambridge University Press.

may engage in information exchanges to reduce the uncertainties and financial risks involved in the decisions about where and when to fish (Andersen and Wadel, 1972; Acheson, 1981; Gatewood, 1984; Salas and Gaertner, 2004). Despite the manifest function that information sharing can have (Merton, 1957), this form of cooperation is not homogeneous and sometimes this exchange may be intentionally deceptive (Forman, 1967; Andersen, 1972; Stiles, 1972; Gatewood, 1984). What, then, structures or motivates the practice of information sharing among fishers?

There are three theoretical approaches one can draw on to explain what motivates the practice of information sharing. An individualistic approach would propose that individual attributes like interests motivate actors to engage in information exchanges. For instance, in the modern practice of fisheries management, resource users are grouped according to individual attributes such as type of gear or fishery to, for instance, allocate resources and promote collective action (Maurstad, 2000). This practice assumes that such groupings reflect common interests, arguably making them homogeneous groups and thus likely to act similarly (Starr, 1992; Scott, 1998; Maurstad, 2000). Moreover, scholars of "the choice-within-constraints" new institutionalism (Ingram and Clay, 2000) argue that the increasing social diversity (i.e. groups defined by interests) associated with the protection and management of common-pool resources such as fisheries, renders more challenging social cooperation (Dietz *et al.*, 2002). A holistic approach focuses on wholes (e.g. communities) and emergent properties like norms and values that are assumed to be internalized by individuals. For instance, Agrawal and Gibson (1999: 633) indicate that many advocates of community-based conservation and resource management employ the concept of community as small, integrated groups "using locally-evolved norms and rules to manage resources sustainably and equitably." A social relational approach would argue that human action unfolds through, and as part of, relations among actors and not by independent self-contained interacting individuals (Granovetter, 1985; Emirbayer, 1997). Such a conception resembles the more familiar phenomenon of social embedding, which focuses on how human action is channeled (constrained or enabled) and constituted by social relations (Schweizer, 1997). The social relational approach does not dismiss the role of individual attributes (social and demographic factors) in how social life is organized. However, they interpret their role as an issue of social inbreeding or homophily, where actors have a tendency to interact with socially and demographic similar persons (Marsden, 1988; McPherson *et al.*, 2001).

10.1.1   Social inbreeding or homophily

Homophily refers to the idea that if two actors are similar in some way (e.g. having the same age) it is more likely that there will be network ties between them than between those who do not share a particular attribute (McPherson *et al.*, 2001). The conceptual importance of homophily can be appreciated with Blau's (1977) contention that a tendency to homophily is an indicator that an attribute is a meaningful dimension of social structure. Thus, the patterning of social relationships by social and demographic factors has important implications for the stratification of social systems beyond what would be expected on the basis of chance alone (Marsden, 1988; McPherson *et al.*, 2001). The other side of social stratification is social integration. Marsden (1988) argues that "because homophily tendencies reflect the density of relationships among persons sharing an attribute, they are at once indicators of decreased global and increased local integration." Thus, local homophily may enable a set of similar people to coordinate their actions more effectively; however, strong tendencies towards homophily and the lack of ties to outsiders may lead to social fragmentation and compromise collective action (Granovetter, 1973). For instance, Crona and Bodin (2006) have suggested that strong homophily of groups with different knowledge about the ecological condition of fishery resources may account for the lack of collective action in fisheries management and conservation in a rural fishing community in Kenya.

From a network perspective, homophily can be made operational through the network property of density. The most basic network relational property (in graph theoretical terms) is that of node degree or number of ties adjacent to a particular node. In other words, node degree refers to the number of social ties of a particular type in which an individual is involved. Node degree can be generalized to the whole network to assess the density of a network of a particular kind; i.e. the proportion of possible ties in a network as a whole that are actually present in a network. Network density ranges from 0, if there are no ties present, to 1, if all possible ties among network actors are present.

In this chapter, I analyze the role of selected individual attributes in the practice of information sharing among fishers from the

Loreto area (see Chapter 6 for a general description of the Loreto area). The question I address is this: to what extent is information sharing among fishers from the Loreto area structured by individual attributes? The five individual attributes I used are: place of birth, years living in the community, years of fishing experience, seasonal migration, and occupational preference. Moreover, is information sharing more likely to occur among fishers that are kin related or through friendship and acquaintance relations for each of these individual attributes? I discuss the implications of homophily for collective action in the management and conservation of fisheries, and conclude by discussing why the social network relational approach may provide a superior strategy to understand the role of social life in natural resource management and conservation than individualism or holism.

10.2 METHODS

10.2.1 Hypotheses

Multiple socio-demographic (e.g. race, ethnicity, sex, age) and acquired characteristics (e.g. occupation, intrapersonal values) have consistently been found to induce homophily across many different types of relationships (McPherson et al., 2001). Moreover, family ties appear to be homophilous for most characteristics and can induce heterophily in other characteristics (McPherson et al., 2001). This appears to be the case because of family ties' strong affective bonds and slow decay as opposed to more voluntary, easier to dissolve relationships (e.g. friendship relations). In this context, I proposed the following two generic hypotheses:

(1)   Actors who share a socio-demographic or acquired characteristic are more likely to share information on the abundance of fish resources than fishers who do not share the same characteristic; thus, ties within groups defined by a particular characteristic will be greater than ties among groups.

(2)   Ties within groups defined by a particular individual attribute (e.g. place of birth) will conform to the following hierarchical pattern: kinship > friendship > acquaintance relationships.

I test these two general hypotheses using five selected actor attributes. The relevance of each of these attributes to the practice of information sharing is explained below.

10.2.2   Actor attributes

10.2.2.1   Place of birth and years living in the community

Within the broad social category of fisher folk, there is often a strong sense of identity and pride, both of which are part of the fishing practice that is often learned at a young age (Acheson, 1981; Gatti, 1986; McGoodwin, 1990). Moreover, fisher folk often develop a strong sense of place and territory that are largely caused by more face-to-face interactions (Smith and Hanna, 1993; Pinkerton and Weinstein, 1995). A sense of place, however, emerges over time and frequently over generations (Acheson, 1981; Dyer and McGoodwin, 1994; Pinkerton and Weinstein, 1995; McCay, 2000; Aswani, 2002). Indeed, time is of the essence for cooperation to emerge, including information sharing (Stiles, 1972; Singleton, 1998; Biel, 2000; Berkes, 2004). However, fishing communities all over the world are more often than not composed of fisher folk with different socio-demographic backgrounds – fishing communities are not homogeneous (Davis, 1991; Smith and Hanna, 1993; Clay and McGoodwin, 1995; Breton et al., 2006). The lower Baja California Peninsula, where the municipality of Loreto is located, has been characterized by high influxes of people relative to their local population, often facilitated by federal policies aimed at populating these low-density areas (Ramirez-Sanchez, 2007). In particular, the rural coastal communities of the Loreto municipality have been recently populated by migrants from within and outside the state of Baja California Sur, especially during the late 1970s. In the case of the fishers from Loreto considered in my study, the place-of-birth and years-living-in-the-community attributes were determined based on the current residency of fishers. See more on how the place-of-birth attribute was constructed below. To what extent do place-of-birth and years-living-in-the-community reflect the structure of information sharing of the fishers from the Loreto area?

10.2.2.2   Years of fishing experience and seasonal migration

The fishing practice is unique in many respects. It not only develops in a dynamic and uncertain environment that involves high financial risks; fishery resources are often distributed unevenly and the equipment necessary to carry out fishing is very specialized (Acheson, 1981). Perhaps one of the most important acquired characteristics of fishers, and of great interest in recent years in fisheries management, is that of local ecological knowledge (Holm, 2003; Crona and Bodin, 2006). Undoubtedly, such knowledge is culturally transmitted and it is enhanced and possibly refined with experience (Forman, 1967). Knowledge on fish-abundant areas can be very effective when exploiting fishery resources without requiring much help from others. Yet, since fish are mobile, fishers seldom have continuous information on their exact location (Andersen and Wadel, 1972; Acheson, 1981). Thus, decisions in fishing are rarely taken on the basis of detailed, predetermined, or programmed information. The day-to-day information acquired in fishing and accumulated knowledge by fishers form a very valuable resource, although not available to everybody.

An important adaptation to the seasonal variation in fish abundance is human migration. Human migration with the purpose of accessing and using natural resources has been and still is a widespread practice, particularly, although not exclusively, in developing countries (Piddington, 1965; Curran and Agardy, 2002; Curran *et al.*, 2002). In the context of common-pool resources like fisheries, the pressure that migration imposes on extraction rates is far from direct. Seasonal migration operates within economic, political, and cultural systems that mediate its impact on the resources and the environment (Curran and Agardy, 2002). In all, to what extent do the years of fishing experience and seasonal migration structure information sharing among fishers?

10.2.2.3 *Occupational preference*

Small-scale fisheries form a primary sector that supports a large proportion of the world's population in coastal areas (Berkes *et al.*, 2001). Yet, it has been socially in crisis for some time now, in part due to the collapse of multiple fish stocks and because it has been systematically neglected in government programs (González-Méndez, 1986; Berkes *et al.*, 2001). Indeed, small-scale fisheries in many parts of the world are in social, economic, and political distress (McGoodwin, 1990; Durrenberger and King, 2000; Charles, 2001; WRI, 2001). On the one hand, it seems logical that most small-scale fishers would prefer to leave the fishing activity at the first sight of any alternative source of income. On the other hand, the perceptions of the benefits derived from fishing as a way of life may be stronger than the prospects of an alternative, less uncertain, economic activity. Under a hypothetical situation of an alternative occupation providing equal remuneration to the one received in the fisheries sector, 61% of fishers from the

Loreto area would not leave the fishery sector (Ramirez-Sanchez, 2007). Are those fishers who prefer not to leave fishing most likely to share information among themselves than those who would leave fishing?

In sum, it is reasonable to believe that the selected attributes may be factors affecting the fishers' tendency on who they would share information with. The overall question regarding these individual attributes is to what extent does each of these attributes reflect the way fishers from the Loreto area share information on the abundance of fish? Furthermore, do ties within subgroups defined by each of these attributes conform to the following hierarchy pattern of importance regarding the type of social relations: kinship > friendship > acquaintance relationships?

10.2.3   Analysis

To test the extent to which individual attributes affect the tendency of fishers to interact with similar others, I use an analysis of variance (ANOVA) of density under a model of variable homophily. A model of variable homophily tests the likelihood that tie density within each group (defined by an individual attribute, for example, age) differs from all ties that are not within groups (Hanneman and Riddle, 2005). In other words, the hypothesis is that the density within groups (i.e. density of groups predefined by an attribute such as age) differs from what would be expected if an equal number of ties were distributed at random across the network.

The model of variable homophily requires two inputs: relational and individual attribute data (Borgatti et al., 2002). For the relational data, I used the same network data I used in Chapter 6, which includes the trustworthy contacts that fishers rely on to obtain information on the abundance of fish resources. In this chapter, however, I pooled all the ties reported by fishers from all the fishing communities (i.e. Ramadita, San Nicolás, Colonia Zaragoza, Juncalito, Ligüí, Ensenada Blanca, and Agua Verde; see Chapter 6 for details). In addition, I use the information these fishers reported regarding the kind of social relation they have with each of their contacts (i.e. kinship, friendship, and acquaintance relations). The individual attribute data were collected as part of the same survey questionnaire used to collect the relational data. I use the five individual attributes introduced in the previous section. Each attribute was coded into discrete subcategories to create a file containing the actor attributes as required by UCINET (Borgatti et al., 2002). For example, the individual attribute "place of birth" was coded into five subcategories: fishers who were born in the community where they currently reside were coded as 1; fishers born in nearby ranches, but not in the community where they currently reside were coded as 2; and so on.

The ANOVA density model of variable homophily tests were determined using the UCINET suite of social network programs (Borgatti *et al.*, 2002). In this program the statistical significance is established by running a large number of random networks of the same size using the same total density as the original data. The program then applies a predefined partition (according to an individual attribute) to each run and calculates the block densities for the random data. The procedure is repeated for a large number of random trials; thus, providing the proportion of random networks that have block densities higher and lower than the observed data.

In addition, the observed/expected number of ties was calculated according to a Relational Contingency Table Analysis as implemented in the UCINET program. Observed/expected ratios above one indicate more exchanges of information within groups than expected by chance.

The observed number and proportion of ties of a particular type (i.e. kinship, friendship, acquaintance) within subcategories of each attribute (e.g. place of birth) were determined to test the second hypothesis regarding the importance of the type of social relation on how fishers share information.

10.3   RESULTS

Table 10.1 summarizes the results of the ANOVA density model of variable homophily for each of the selected attributes, observed/expected ratios, and proportion of ties for each type of social relation. For expositional convenience, all density values were transformed to percentages from the original values that run between 0, for no ties are present, to 1, when all possible ties between actors are present.

The place-of-birth attribute appears to be a stronger factor in the way fishers share information than the years-living-in-the-community attribute. In particular, the "out of municipality" subcategory is not a significant attribute affecting information sharing, and fishers are significantly more likely to share information within the 21–31 and 31–40 years-living-in-the-community subcategories. Clearly, the subcategories that were found significant by the ANOVA model of variable homophily also have the highest observed/expected ratios. Although within most subcategories of both attributes, kinship ties are proportionally

Table 10.1. *Density of ties and observed/expected ratio by individual attribute (place of birth, seasonal migration, etc.) for all ties, and the number (proportion) of ties for each type of relationship (kinship, friendship, and acquaintance). The * indicates significant densities according to the ANOVA tests with variable homophily model, and the number (proportion) of ties in bold indicate categories that do not fit the hypothesized order of importance among the three type of relationships: i.e. kinship > friendship > acquaintance.*

Category (n)	All ties		Number of ties (Proportion)		
	Density	Obs/Exp	Kinship	Friendship	Acquaintance
Place of birth					
Community (12)	18*	4.12	14 (58)	8 (33)	2 (8)
Ranch (20)	17*	3.82	32 (48)	26 (39)	8 (12)
Town of Loreto (53)	9*	1.99	106 (43)	**132 (54)**	8 (3)
Out Municipality (36)	5	1.22	38 (56)	26 (38)	4 (6)
Years living in the community					
1–10 (14)	7	1.59	4 (33)	**6 (50)**	2 (17)
11–20 (25)	7	1.69	18 (43)	**24 (57)**	0 (0)
21–30 (31)	16*	3.79	96 (65)	46 (31)	6 (4)
31–40 (33)	10*	2.33	56 (54)	46 (44)	2 (2)
41+ (18)	6	1.42	2 (11)	**16 (89)**	0 (0)
Years of fishing experience					
1–20 (43)	7	1.71	70 (52)	56 (42)	8 (6)
21–30 (35)	11*	2.60	54 (42)	**70 (54)**	6 (5)
31–40 (30)	5	1.13	22 (55)	14 (35)	4 (10)
41+ (13)	4	0.94	4 (67)	0 (0)	2 (33)
Seasonal migration					
No (48)	5	1.01	62 (53)	52 (45)	2 (2)
Yes (73)	9*	1.78	238 (50)	222 (46)	20 (4)
Occupational preference					
No (74)	7	1.39	170 (47)	**182 (51)**	6 (2)
Yes (47)	5	1.15	72 (62)	40 (34)	4 (3)

more important than friendship ties, in some cases friendship ties are relatively more important than kinship ties.

In the case of years-of-fishing-experience subcategories, only the 21–30 years subcategory was a significant factor in the sharing of information. It is also within this subcategory that fishers tend to share more information through friendship than kinship ties. Those who reported to migrate to other communities are significantly more likely to share information among themselves than those who do not migrate. In both subcategories of seasonal migration, kinship ties are more important than friendship ties.

Finally, none of the "occupational preference" subcategories significantly structure information exchanges among fishers. Only in the case of the subcategory of fishers who would not leave fishing for another economic activity, are friendship ties more important than kinship ties. Overall, acquaintance ties were consistently less important than friendship and kinship in all five attributes analyzed.

10.4   DISCUSSION

Homophily or the tendency of people to interact with their own kind, whether by preference or induced by opportunity constraints as defined by individual attributes such as race, gender, educational class, and organization unit, etc., has important implications for the capacity of groups to coordinate their actions. On the one hand, interacting exclusively with similar others may be efficient to the extent that similarity facilitates transmission of tacit knowledge, simplifies coordination, and avoids potential conflicts. On the other hand, limiting communication among dissimilar others prevents a group from reaping the benefits of diversity and may promote adversary thinking (Borgatti and Foster, 2003).

My discussion focuses on three aspects. First, I discuss the observed patterns regarding the role of the five selected individual attributes and type of relationship in the practice of information sharing using information from interviews I conducted in 2002 and 2004 with fishers from the Loreto area. Second, I use the distinction between manifest and latent social function to explain why fishers from Loreto have not been able to address fisheries' collective action problems (e.g. over-exploited fisheries). Finally, I reflect on the tri-lemma created by the individualistic, holistic, and relational approach when trying to understand the role of social life in natural resource management. I illustrate this tri-lemma by discussing how each of these three views has a different conception of what a community is and its role in fisheries management and conservation.

10.4.1   Individual attributes and importance of social relations

Except for the occupational-preference attribute, all attributes showed tendencies to homophily in some subgroups. The place-of-birth, and to a lesser extent, years-living-in-the-community attribute showed an important tendency to homophily within their subcategories. During my interviews with some fishers who were not from the area (outside of BCS) or just recently arrived from other communities (within the municipality of Loreto), there was often a perception of less fellowship when it came to sharing information. In 2004, I interviewed a fisher from the Agua Verde community who had recently arrived to the Colonia Zaragoza community after marrying a woman from this community. The way he felt about other members of Colonia Zaragoza sharing information with him was summed up as "here, all are goats," suggesting that the local community members would shy away or ignore you before trying to help you out. With time trust may develop between long-time residents and more recently arrived fishers to a community. Indeed, fishers within the 21–30 and 31–40 years living-in-the-community subcategory have a tendency to share more information within their subcategories than expected by chance; i.e. a stronger tendency to homophily than those who have recently arrived to a community. Interestingly, fishers of 41+ years living in the community do not show a strong tendency to interact among themselves. An explanation for this pattern could be that more senior fishers may not be as engaged in the fishing activity as younger fishers are.

The years-of-fishing-experience attribute is a weak structuring factor in information sharing among fishers from Loreto. In other words, there is a strong tendency to heterophily. This seems to make sense if we assume that relatively inexperienced fishers are likely to seek the advice of more experienced ones, thus promoting heterophily. Moreover, the patchy distribution and mobility of fish resources in the Loreto area may make information sharing less a function of accumulated knowledge than up-to-date information. Migrating fishers, on the other hand, have a strong tendency to homophily. Migration is a widespread social practice in BCS (Young, 1995). Seasonal migration appears to require more cooperative ties in terms of sharing of information in part because of the uncertainty involved, difficult conditions encountered in the migratory destinations, and investment required. During my interviews in 2002 and 2004, many fishers indicated that they were less prone to migrate because of the expenses involved, the difficulty of being away from the family, and harsh living conditions (mostly limited basic services such as food, shelter, and washrooms). An alternative strategy to cope with the uncertainty of the fishing practice is for fishers to diversify their occupation or leave the fishing activity if the opportunity arises. Clearly, neither fishers who prefer to leave the fishing activity if the opportunity arises nor fishers who would not leave the fishing activity form homophilic groups.

Studies of social networks and the commons, including information exchanges, suggest a hierarchy of importance of social relations (kinship > friendship > acquaintance relations) in the extent to which individuals are more likely to cooperate and exchange information (Stiles, 1972; Gatewood, 1984; Taylor and Singleton, 1993; Aswani, 2002). Overall, family ties have been found to be homophilous for multiple characteristics and may induce heterophily in other characteristics (McPherson *et al.*, 2001). This has been attributed to family ties' strong affective bonds and slow decay as opposed to more voluntary, easier to dissolve relationships (e.g. friendship relations). In Mexico, most aspects of social life unfold through family relationships (Smith, 1984; Otero, 1999). In the state of Baja California Sur, family relationships appear to be even more important because of its relatively small and sparse population, particularly in rural communities of the Loreto municipality (Morales-Polo, 1994; INEGI, 2001). In some of the subcategories considered in the practice of information sharing among fishers from Loreto, the proportion of friendship ties was higher than kinship ties. Although it is possible that kinship relations may be operating mostly as a factor towards heterophily, this effect is not consistent across all the selected individual attributes within the practice of information sharing.

In sum, the fact that social life is organized through social categories is not necessarily an unequivocal indicator of homogeneous groups. The role that an individual attribute has in structuring social life is an empirical question with important implications to understand and promote collective action. In the case of the fishers from the Loreto area, even strong homophilic attributes such as community do not limit fishers' interactions to fishers from their own community (Ramirez-Sanchez, 2007). Intra-community ties are very important in the livelihoods of fishers from the Loreto area to access distant fish resources to adapt to the changing abundance of fish stocks (Ramirez-Sanchez and Pinkerton, 2009). If information sharing is widespread, why have fishers not engaged in collective action to tackle key problems of their livelihoods, such as the overexploited state of fish?

10.4.2   Information sharing and collective action

A central hypothesis advanced by social network scientists is that local homophily may enable a set of similar people to coordinate their actions more effectively. However, strong tendencies towards local homophily and the lack of ties to outsiders may lead to social fragmentation and compromise collective action (Granovetter, 1973). While fishers from the Loreto area who share certain attributes have a tendency to homophily, fishers also share information with fishers who display other attributes. Under the structural condition of weak homophily, fishers from the Loreto area should have the potential to engage in collective action. There is evidence that they do.

The account of one of the fishers from the Loreto area involved in the protest against the no-take fishing zones proposed in the first version of the management plan for the Loreto Bay National Marine Park suggests that communicative networks indeed have an important impact on collective action. In 2002, I had an informal interview with a fisher from Juncalito who seemed to have initiated a mass movement by commercial fishers in light of the provisions and restrictions in the first management plan of the Loreto Bay National Marine Park, drafted two years after the park was created in 1994:

> My nephews, who are engineers in fishery sciences, came with the news that the marine park's management plan was going to prohibit most human activity, particularly fishing in the most productive areas used by fishermen, but that the presidential decree required approval by local communities within a time frame of one and a half years. After reading the first version of the management plan it became clear that they were going to exclude most commercial fishing and almost prohibit use of the beaches. We went to visit fishers from Ligüí and Ensenada Blanca to convince them to reject the management plan. Initially there was slow involvement but in not too long there was a large involvement of fishers to protest against the management plan.

The overall effect was such that it took several years for the management plan to be approved by fishers. It is not entirely clear what the role of the communicative social networks was precisely but in the absence of other forms of communication among communities it is possible that they had an important role in disseminating information to support this form of collective action.

Despite the evidence of collective action by fishers from the Loreto area, why have fishers not been able to address collective action problems such as the over-exploited state of fish resources? I suggest that the communication ties used by fishers from the Loreto area have two functions, a manifest and latent one.

10.4.3   Latent and manifest function of social networks

The distinction between latent and manifest function of social systems was first proposed by Merton (1957) and adopted by Mahner and Bunge (2001) to distinguish between manifest or recognized (intended) and latent or unrecognized (unintended) social functions. In the practice of information sharing among fishers from Loreto, social relations and the social networks that emerge serve the manifest function of enabling access to fish stocks. Such manifest function is puzzling given the unpredictability on fish stocks and difficulty of their exclusive use, which, arguably, creates a very competitive context in which the fishing activity unfolds. However, it has been argued that this very condition calls for cooperation rather than competition, at least when it comes to finding out about the abundance of fish. Stiles (1972: 162) eloquently states "the competitors need each other" to contribute to each other's success.

These same social relations and the networks that emerge also fulfill the latent function of social integration – social relations are not purposefully used to bring about social integration. Indeed, the effect of individual attributes in the practice of information sharing does not produce total social stratification and allow for social integration. Thus, the manifest function of social networks narrows its scope to accomplish a particular task (e.g. sharing information for accessing fish) while the latent or non-committed function (e.g. social integration) can potentially support all forms of collective action (e.g. protesting against the provisions of a marine park). To be sure, collective action for fisheries management requires a sophisticated understanding that fishers from Loreto may not have (Ramirez-Sanchez and Pinkerton, 2009).

Indeed, using a network conceptual framework, Crona and Bodin (2006) have recently hypothesized that few communication ties between fairly homogeneous fishing subgroups and lack of a common perception among subgroups of the existence of depleted fish stocks hindered generalized collective action for conservation and management in a fishing community in Kenya.

To summarize, in this chapter I have illustrated the relevance of a social network perspective to study the role of individual attributes in the practice of information sharing and understand how the manifest and latent function of social networks may affect collective action. To conclude, I discuss why a social network perspective represents a superior approach to understand the role of actors' attributes (individualist concern) and the emergent properties of the systems (holist concern) they are part of. I do this by reflecting on the tri-lemma caused by the three contrasting perspectives described in the introduction of this chapter. To do this I reflect on the proposal that we should replace the notion of community predicated on concepts of territory, social structure, and shared values (holistic view) in favor of individuals and their interests structured by institutions – the institutional individualistic view (Agrawal and Gibson, 1999; Allison and Ellis, 2001).

10.4.4   Integrating actors' attributes and emergent properties

It has been argued that advocates of community-based resource management and conservation tend to emphasize homogeneous communities and neglect their political divisions, interests of actors, and the internal and external institutions that shape the decision-making process (Agrawal and Gibson, 1999). Agrawal and Gibson (1999) make an important contribution in analyzing the shortcomings of conceiving communities as territorially fixed, small, and homogeneous (holistic view). Moreover, they point out that "these characteristics supposedly foster the interaction among members that promote desirable collective decisions" in conservation and resource management (Agrawal and Gibson, 1999: 636). These authors suggest that to be more accurate in our efforts to depict communities and their interactions with adjacent natural resources greater attention should be given to "the multiple actors with multiple interests that make up communities, the processes through which these actors interrelate, and, especially, the institutional arrangements [i.e. rules] that structure their interactions" (Agawal and Gibson, 1999: 636).

The analysis of the six individual attributes in this chapter does not support a view of homogeneity among fishers or complete social stratification. I think the critique of Agrawal and Gibson (1999) of communities conceptualized as territorially fixed, small, and homogeneous is well founded and supported by multiple anthropologists and social scientists (Davis, 1991; Smith and Hanna, 1993; Clay and McGoodwin, 1995; Breton et al., 2006). Even though I agree that it is important to consider actors' interests and institutional arrangements, I disagree that such a shift in emphasis can provide a better picture of communities and their role in resource management and conservation. It is the case that traditional depictions of communities often used in conservation and resource management may have failed to articulate a viable definition of human communities or simply assumed it away. This, however, does not invalidate the intuitive idea that social groups are wholes with emergent properties and pro-social behaviors such as relations of trust and reciprocity.

Nowadays, the rational-choice (individualism) and norm-following models (holism) of human behavior appear to be the main contrasting views in the social sciences (Emirbayer, 1997; Checkel, 2001). Seemingly representing opposite views, these models converge in one important aspect: their neglect of the ongoing structures of social relations in human action (Granovetter, 1985). In particular, Granovetter (1985) characterizes the rational-choice model as an "under-socialized" or an atomized-actor conception (i.e. individualism) and the norm-following model as an "over-socialized" one (i.e. holism). On the one hand, in the under-socialized view individuals are detached from their social relations, for example, as a necessary condition for perfectly competitive markets. On the other hand, in the over-socialized view individuals acquire cultural habits, customs, and norms that are followed automatically or mechanically as some sort of "latent variable" (Granovetter, 1985; DiMaggio, 1997). In the final analysis, ironically, both "have in common a conception of action and decision carried out by atomized actors"; either individuals act in pursuit of their self-interest or they enact internalized behavioral patterns (Granovetter, 1985: 485). The fact that both forms converge by focusing on individuals attests to the various shades that ontological and methodological individualism can take despite the seemingly apparent differences (Udehn, 2002; Bunge, 2003). It is also this convergence that directs Emirbayer (1997) to conceive rational-choice and norm-following models of human behavior as essentially the same and separates them from relational forms of thinking in the social sciences.

The social network perspective provides a superior view that, for instance, in the case of human communities, they are conceived as neither organic wholes nor aggregates but social systems characterized by dynamic pro-social behaviors. It is true that the institutional individualism promoted by Agrawal and Gibson (1999) is closer to conceiving human communities as social systems but fails to acknowledge emergence or qualitative novelty, the most important aspect highlighted by holism. Moreover, Agrawal and Gibson's (1999) exaggerated emphasis on individual interests coordinated by institutional arrangements neglects the fact that any social institutional arrangement requires a minimum of pro-social behaviors to be operational (e.g. trust). I submit that a conception of human communities must be predicated on pro-social behaviors and in relational terms. The former emphasizes the human tendency for attachment (Brothers, 1997) that holds together social systems through a sense of fellowship, acts of reciprocity, and, above all, sharing. Indeed, it is only in this sense that speaking of the "commons" has any meaning from a social human perspective. A social relational view avoids totalizing or unifying social groups through cultural, political, or economic social categories and focuses on the intrinsic relational character of pro-social behaviors; i.e. it transcends totalizing categories and treats them as an issue of homophily/heterophily or social stratification/integration. Moreover, it avoids confining communities to a fixed territory by defining communities in relational terms. Focusing on pro-social relations also allows for understanding social integration as a matter of degree, thus making room for internal fractures, divisions, disconnections, or social fragmentation, as I have shown in this chapter through the extent to which fishers who have similar attributes are more likely to share information among themselves than with those with whom they do not share an attribute. Pro-social behaviors are dynamic and not static, thus, human communities are always evolving.

Conceptualizing communities as essentially pro-social in character does not undermine the need to study internal politics, individual interests, and power relations that clearly contribute to their dynamics. Indeed, the concern of institutional individualists with individual agency is important in understanding the dynamics of social systems. However, we can also study the role of individuals in the dynamics of social systems within the social relational framework used by social network analysts, whereby the contribution of individuals to this dynamic is conceptualized as his or her degree of involvement in the web of social relations. In short, a social network approach adopts the best aspects of both individualism and holism: it conceives human action to unfold through, and as part of, relations among actors and not by independent self-contained interacting individuals.

10.5 CONCLUDING REMARKS

In this chapter, I explored the role that actors' attributes (e.g. fishing experience) and the type of social relations (kinship, friendship, and acquaintance relations) have in the practice of information sharing among fishers from the Loreto region, and I hypothesized that the latent and manifest function of the communication networks of fishers from Loreto may help explain the tendency of fishers to engage in collective action. I finally argued that while researchers have at least three perspectives to draw from to study the role of social categories in the practice of information sharing, a social network approach may be superior because it is capable of incorporating the concerns of the other two competing views: actors' attributes (individualism) and emergent properties (holism).

Reflections

Since this study draws from the same data set as in Chapter 6, my reflections presented in that chapter are not duplicated here.

ACKNOWLEDGMENT

Saudiel Ramirez-Sanchez currently works as policy analyst in the Oceans Directorate of the Department of Fisheries and Oceans, Canada. The International Development Research Centre (IDRC) and the Canon National Parks Science Scholar Program supported this research.

REFERENCES

Acheson, J. M. (1981). Anthropology of fishing. *Annual Review of Anthropology*, **10**, 275–316.

Agrawal, A. and C. C. Gibson (1999). Enchantment and disenchantment: the role of community in natural resource conservation. *World Development*, **27**(4), 629–649.

Allison, E. H. and F. Ellis (2001). The livelihoods approach and management of small-scale fisheries. *Marine Policy*, **25**(5), 377–388.

Andersen, R. (1972). Hunt and deceive: information management in Newfoundland deep-sea trawler fishing. In *North Atlantic Fishermen. Anthropological Essays on Modern Fishing*. Newfoundland, Canada: University of Toronto Press, pp. 120–140.

Andersen, R. and C. Wadel (1972). Comparative problems in fishing adaptations. In *North Atlantic Fishermen. Anthropological Essays on Modern Fishing*. Newfoundland, Canada: University of Toronto Press, pp. 141–165.

Aswani, S. (2002). Assessing the effects of changing demographic and consumption patterns on sea tenure regimes in the Roviana Lagoon, Solomon Islands. *Ambio*, **31**(4), 272–284.

Berkes, F. (2004). Rethinking community-based conservation. *Conservation Biology*, **18**(3), 621–630.

Berkes, F., R. Mahon, *et al.* (2001). *Managing Small-scale Fisheries. Alternative Directions and Methods*. Ottawa, Ontario: IDRC.

Biel, A. (2000). Factors promoting cooperation in the laboratory, in common pool resource dilemmas, and in large-scale dilemmas: similarities and differences. In *Cooperation in Modern Society. Promoting the Welfare of Communities, States and Organizations*. New York, NY: Routledge, pp. 15–42.

Blau, P. M. (1977). *Inequality and Heterogeneity*. New York, NY: Free Press.

Borgatti, S. P., M. G. Everett *et al.* (2002). *UCINET for Windows: Software for Social Network Analysis*. Harvard, MA: Analytic Technologies.

Borgatti, S. P. and P. C. Foster (2003). The network paradigm in organizational research: a review and typology. *Journal of Management*, **29**(6), 991–1013.

Breton, Y., D. N. Brown and M. Haughton (2006). Social sciences and the diversity of Caribbean communities. In Y. Breton, D. Brown, B. Davy, M. Haughton and L. Ovares (Eds.), *Coastal Resource Management in the Wider Caribbean: Resilience, Adaptation, and Community Diversity*. Kingston, Jamaica: Ian Randle Publishers, pp. 17–49.

Brothers, L. (1997). *Friday's Footprint. How Society Shapes the Human Mind*. New York, NY: Oxford University Press.

Bunge, M. (2003). *Emergence and Convergence: Qualitative Novelty and the Unity of Knowledge*. Toronto, ON: University of Toronto Press.

Charles, A. (2001). *Sustainable Fishery Systems*. Oxford: Blackwell Science.

Checkel, J. T. (2001). Why comply? Social learning and European identity change. *International Organization*, **55**(3), 553–588.

Clay, P. M. and J. R. McGoodwin (1995). Utilizing social sciences in fisheries management. *Aquatic Living Resources*, **8**(3), 203–207.

Crona, B. and O. Bodin (2006). What you know is who you know? Communication patterns among resource users as a prerequisite for co-management. *Ecology and Society*, **11**(2), 7.

Curran, S. and T. Agardy (2002). Common property systems, migration, and coastal ecosystems. *Ambio*, **31**(4), 303–305.

Curran, S., A. Kumar, W. Lutz and M. Williams (2002). Interactions between coastal and marine ecosystems and human population systems: perspectives on how consumption mediates this interaction. *Ambio*, **31**(4), 264–268.

Davis, A. (1991). Insidious rationalities: the institutionalization of small boat fishing and the rise of the rapacious fisher. *Maritime Anthropological Studies*, **4**(1), 13–31.

Dietz, T., N. Dolšak, E. Ostrom and P. C. Stern (2002). Introduction: the drama of the commons. In E. Ostrom, T. Dietz, N. Dolšak *et al. The Drama of the Commons. Committee on the Human Dimensions of Global Change*. Washington, DC: National Academy Press, pp. 3–36.

DiMaggio, P. (1997). Culture and cognition. *Annual Review of Sociology*, **23**, 263–287.

Durrenberger, P. E. and T. D. King (2000). *State and Community in Fisheries Management. Power, Policy, and Practice*. Westport, CT: Bergin & Garvey.

Dyer, C. L. and J. R. McGoodwin (1994). *Folk Management in the World's Fisheries. Lessons for Modern Fisheries Management*. Niwot, CO: University Press of Colorado.

Emirbayer, M. (1997). Manifesto for a relational sociology. *American Journal of Sociology*, **103**(2), 281–317.

Forman, S. (1967). Cognition and the catch: the location of fishing spots in a Brazilian coastal village. *Ethnology*, **6**(4), 417–426.

Gatewood, J. B. (1984). Cooperation, competition, and synergy: information-sharing groups among Southeast Alaskan salmon seiners. *American Ethnologist*, **11**(2), 350–370.

Gatti, L. M. (1986). *Los pescadores de México: la vida en un lance*. Mexico, DF: Cuadernos de la Chata.

González-Méndez, H. (1986). El fomento a la pesca en el periodo post-revolucionario; problemática y perspectivas. In *Desarrollo pesquero Mexicano*. Mexico, DF: Secretaría de Pesca, pp. 97–120.

Granovetter, M. (1985). Economic action and social structure: the problem of embeddedness. *American Journal of Sociology*, **91**(3), 481–510.

Granovetter, M. S. (1973). Strength of weak ties. *American Journal of Sociology*, **78**(6), 1360–1380.

Hanneman, R. A. and M. Riddle (2005). *Introduction to Social Network Methods*. Riverside, CA: University of California, Riverside (published in digital form at http://faculty.ucr.edu/~hanneman/).

Holm, P. (2003). On the relationship between science and fishermen's knowledge in a resource management context. *Maritime Studies*, **2**(1), 5–33.

INEGI (2001). Tabulados Básicos Nacionales y por Entidad Federativa. Base de Datos y Tabulados de la Muestra Censal. XII Censo General de Población y Vivienda, 2000. Aguascalientes, INEGI.

Ingram, P. and K. Clay (2000). The choice-within-constraints new institutionalism and implications for sociology. *Annual Review of Sociology*, **26**, 525–546.

Mahner, M. and M. Bunge (2001). Function and functionalism: a synthetic perspective. *Philosophy of Science*, **68**(1), 75–94.

Marsden, P. V. (1988). Homogeneity in confiding relations. *Social Networks*, **10**, 57–76.

Maurstad, A. (2000). To fish or not to fish: small-scale fishing and changing regulations of the cod fishery in northern Norway. *Human Organization*, **59**(1), 37–47.

McCay, B. J. (2000). Sea changes in fisheries policy: contributions from anthropology. In *State and Community in Fisheries Management. Power, Policy, and Practice*. Westport, CT: Bergin & Garvey, pp. 201–217.

McGoodwin, J. R. (1990). *Crisis in the World's Fisheries. People, Problems, and Policy*. Stanford, CA: Stanford University Press.

McPherson, M., L. Smith-Lovin and J. M. Cook (2001). Birds of a feather: homophily in social networks. *Annual Review of Sociology*, **27**, 415–444.

Merton, R. K. (1957). *Social Theory and Social Structure*. Glencoe, IL: Free Press.

Morales-Polo, S. (1994). *Loreto. Algunos hechos relevantes acerca de la historia del padre cultural de las Californias*. Loreto, BCS, Mexico.

Ostrom, E., R. Gardner and J. Walker (1994). *Rules, Games, and Common-pool Resources*. Ann Arbor, MI: University of Michigan Press.

Otero, G. (1999). *Farewell to the Peasantry? Political Class Formation in Rural Mexico*. Boulder, CO: Westview Press.

Piddington, R. (1965). *Kinship and Geographical Mobility*. Leiden: E. J. Brill.

Pinkerton, E. W. and M. Weinstein (1995). *Fisheries that Work. Sustainability through Community-based Management*. Vancouver, BC: David Suzuki Foundation.

Ramirez-Sanchez, S. (2007). A social relational approach to the conservation and management of fisheries: the rural communities of the Loreto Bay National Marine Park, BCS, Mexico. PhD thesis. School of Resource and Environmental Management, Simon Fraser University, Burnaby, BC.

Ramirez-Sanchez, S. and E. Pinkerton (2009). The impact of resource scarcity on bonding and bridging social capital: the case of fishers' information-sharing networks in Loreto, BCS, Mexico. *Ecology and Society*, **14**(1), 22.

Salas, S. and D. Gaertner (2004). The behavioural dynamics of fishers: management implications. *Fish and Fisheries*, **5**, 153–167.

Schweizer, T. (1997). Embeddedness of ethnographic cases – a social networks perspective. *Current Anthropology*, **38**(5), 739–760.

Scott, J. C. (1998). *Seeing like a State. How Certain Schemes to Improve the Human Condition have Failed.* New Haven, CT: Yale University Press.

Singleton, S. (1998). *Constructing Cooperation. The Evolution of Institutions of Co-management.* Ann Arbor, MI: University of Michigan Press.

Smith, C. L. and S. Hanna (1993). Occupation and community as determinants of fishing behaviors. *Human Organization,* **52**(3), 299–315.

Smith, T. R. (1984). *Kinship Ideology and Practice in Latin America.* Chapel Hill, NC: University of North Carolina Press.

Starr, P. (1992). Social categories and claims in the liberal state. *Social Research,* **59**(2), 263–295.

Stiles, R. G. (1972). Fishermen, wives and radios: aspects of communication in a Newfoundland fishing community. In *North Atlantic Fishermen. Anthropological Essays on Modern Fishing.* Toronto, ON: University of Toronto Press, pp. 35–60.

Taylor, M. and S. Singleton (1993). The communal resources: transaction costs and the solution of collective action problems. *Political Sociology,* **21**, 195–215.

Udehn, L. (2002). The changing face of methodological individualism. *Annual Review of Sociology,* **28**, 479–507.

WRI (2001). *People and Ecosystems: The Fraying Web of Life. World Resources, 2000–01.* Washington, DC: World Resource Institute.

Young, E. (1995). Elusive edens: linking local needs to nature protection in the coastal lagoons of Baja California Sur, Mexico. PhD thesis. University of Texas at Austin, Austin, TX.

HENRIK ERNSTSON

11

Transformative collective action: a network approach to transformative change in ecosystem-based management

11.1 INTRODUCTION

There is great need for modern societies to find more sustainable ways of securing good living environments and the resources upon which societies depend. In the academic community this has spurred an interest in what has been called *transformative change*, i.e. how "old" regimes of natural resource management deemed as non-sustainable can transform so as to establish "new" regimes of ecosystem-based management (Olsson *et al.*, 2004 and references below).[1] This is often described as a shift from top–down bureaucracies that narrowly focus on a single (and commercially viable) species (e.g. a fish or a crop), to a more integrated approach that acknowledges a wider array of stake-holders, and that monitors and builds knowledge of landscape-level ecological processes (such as water flows and pollination) that under-pin ecological functions (Olsson *et al.*, 2004). Ecosystem-based manage-ment has been argued to better cope with the interconnectedness, uncertainties, and dynamics of ecosystems in a human-dominated world (Holling, 1978; Christensen *et al.*, 1996).

This chapter will strive to add to contributions made by other authors in describing and explaining transformative change. Special

---

[1] There is not a clear usage of terms in this emergent literature. Transformative change is also referred to as transformative (change) processes, transformational change, or simply transitions or transformations, or alternatively, social-ecological transformation.

Social Networks and Natural Resource Management: Uncovering the Fabric of Environmental Governance, ed. Ö. Bodin and C. Prell. Published by Cambridge University Press.
© Cambridge University Press 2011.

attention will be paid to elucidate the collective nature of these trans-formations, hence the title of *transformative collective action*. The analysis will show that in order to bring about radical institutional change of natural resource management, a whole network of individuals and organizations are needed that, through time, can sustain pressure for change. These actors furthermore need to relate to each other through information exchange and repeated collaborations in order to coordi-nate their collective action, to learn as they go along of what works and what does not work, and to negotiate their vision of change to reach some common ground that can unite their collective effort. This type of sustained collective action furthermore needs to operate through, and challenge, already established institutions, modes of thought, and ways of doing things. As such we can talk about collective action as a "collective actor" – the network of actors – that over time builds enough agency to generate institutional change.

With this understanding of transformative collective action, the prime focus of this chapter is to demonstrate how concepts derived from social network analysis, paired with theories from the social movement literature, can be used to analyze transformative change in natural resource management. This in turn will set the chapter on a path to unravel the relational character of transformative change, i.e. to explain and bring understanding of how key social processes emerge from the way social relations are patterned among actors. I will demonstrate the type of analysis I suggest by re-using data from an urban case study in which a diverse set of civil society organizations set out to protect a large green area in Stockholm, Sweden (Ernstson *et al.*, 2008; Ernstson and Sörlin, 2009). The collective action by these organ-izations led to the implementation of a protective law, the recognition of novel values of protecting green space, and the establishment of a landscape scale for collaborative management of the grasslands, for-ests, and lakes that compose this urban park landscape. Before this, however, I will review the subfield of transformative change and selected parts from the field of social movements to more clearly point out how I will contribute to this emergent field.

11.1.1   Transformative change processes as a subfield of social-ecological studies

The subfield of transformative change has been developed in a series of important studies by Olsson and colleagues. In an explorative fashion a row of studies have analyzed how a small set of devoted actors intentionally strive to steer institutions towards ecosystem-based collaborative management, thus often challenging established top–down management arrangements. Based on a social-ecological systems perspective (Gunderson and Holling, 2002), studies have included governance transformations in a peri-urban wetland landscape in southern Sweden (Olsson *et al.*, 2004; Hahn *et al.*, 2006), the Great Barrier Reef in Australia (Olsson *et al.*, 2008), and comparisons between transformations in the Florida Everglades and other hydrological ecosystems in the USA, Thailand, and Australia (Olsson *et al.*, 2006).[2] These authors have described transformative change processes as consisting of three phases: preparing for change, transition to a "new social context," and building "resilience in the new direction" depicted as a greater "capacity to learn from, respond to, and manage environmental feedback from dynamic ecosystems" (Olsson *et al.*, 2006). With theoretical inspiration from organizational sociology and political science, especially Westley (1995; Westley *et al.*, 2002) and to a lesser extent Kingdon (1995), the main analytical categories used for explaining transformation are the following: (i) the building of new (scientific) *knowledge* to demonstrate the interconnectedness of ecosystems and the articulation of a greater spatial scale for management; (ii) the creation of *social networks* that connect different interest groups across societal levels (where the term "social networks" is used more in its metaphorical and descriptive sense; see Chapter 1, this volume); (iii) the emergence of *leaders* (often referred to as key-stewards, or social entrepreneurs) who are seen as guiding change and holding or shaping *visions* that integrate ecological knowledge; and (iv) the seizing of *windows of opportunity* which are changes in the political, ecological, or institutional system allowing transitions to happen. Further, (v) *enabling legislation* is discussed as important but not sufficient institutional and legal conditions that facilitate transformations.

The value of the research on transformative change lies in the descriptions of how processes interlink across societal levels and that structural features are not enough to explain change, but that some form of agency or intentional action is needed. Here I intend to complement this past research by using quantitative analytical tools to improve our understanding of how particular social networks mediate to generate change. This will be done through: (i) identifying social network positions and using these to describe (or hypothesize) *network*

---

[2] A forerunner and inspiration for these studies seems to have been ecologist Lance Gunderson (1999).

level mechanisms that underpin transformative collective action. Network-level mechanisms are here seen as social actions made possible through, and emerging from, the patterns of relations between mobilizing actors, and thus depend on the full structure of the social network, and not just the local surrounding of single actors. Further, I will (ii) describe and distinguish between different types of collective action processes within the same social network. Indeed, one of my main contributions will be to demonstrate that transformative action can be conceptualized as several types of interlinked collective action processes, where the most intense form is made up of strongly interacting individuals and organizations that come to share a similar world view or collective identity, which gives direction and continuity to the change pursued. My effort is consequently also to (iii) emphasize the collective nature of transformative action and that agency can be understood not just at the individual level – as held by key-stewards, entrepreneurs, or leaders – but also as a relational property that is a function of individual skills, the relations among various actors, and on network structures they create. To do this I will argue that the body of work from the broader research field of social movements, contentious action, and voluntary action, especially when merged with social network analysis, can bring to the study of transformative change some useful analytical tools.

11.1.2   Collective action processes: lessons from social movement studies

Social movement research is a field that par excellence has studied transformative change. A main interest has been to explain the emergence of "collective actors," i.e. how a set of individual and autonomous actors (not formally tied through lines of command) across space and time can address similar issues with similar demands, and often using similar methods and practices. During the last three decades, various theoretical approaches have been developed that broadly fall into structuralist, cultural, or rationalist modes of explanations (della Porta and Diani, 2006). I will here follow a social network analytic approach to social movements first developed by Mario Diani (1992) in his seminal work on the Milano environmental movement protecting urban green space (Diani, 1995).

The network approach to social movements extends back to an earlier school of thought called resource mobilization theory (McCarthy and Zald, 1977; Zald and McCarthy, 1980) in which actors are seen as competing – or collaborating – in securing economic, material, and symbolic resources. This school of thought sees the control of more resources coinciding with actors increasing their possibility to become strategic, successful, and influential in expressing their demands and taking action (Zald and McCarthy, 1980). Earlier studies viewed success as originating from within the actor itself, especially in the capacity of building effective organizations, for instance through increasing the capacity to secure economic resources (e.g. by collecting member fees), employing professional "activists" (bureaucratization and professionalization), and dividing the organizations into regional or local chapters (to cover greater geographical areas). With a network perspective, the interactional part between actors is stressed, as well as the structures that emerge from these interactions. The core analytical unit is neither the individual "parts," nor the whole "system", but rather the "relations among parts." This has allowed for the study of how localized interaction between organizations gives rise to larger-scale patterns – or structures – that both enable and/or constrain actors (Diani, 2003a; Borgatti et al., 2009). Technically this is done by quantifying and measuring the "resource flows," or collaborative ties between all pairs of mobilizing actors. The network perspective has demonstrated that social movements are heterogeneous and that smaller organizations – through their interactions with other organizations – can become influential.

Arguing that a social movement framework is useful for studying a broader spectrum of collective action (which makes it useful for us, as we will see), Diani has furthermore come to distinguish between three main types of *collective action processes*: movement processes, coalition processes, and organizational processes (Diani, 2002; Diani and Bison, 2004).[3] This is achieved through separating between three analytical dimensions and then empirically measuring: (i) if networks between a subset of mobilizing actors are *dense* or *sparse* (or between pairs of actors, if relations are strong or weak), and (ii) if actors express a *collective* or *organizational* identity. The former dimension captures the intensity by which actors are tied to each other in mutual exchange of information and collaboration. The latter dimension refers to how recurrent collaboration and the participation in similar events not only can lower the costs for further collaboration, but also can produce

---

[3] Diani and Bison (2004) state that many claiming to have studied "social movements," have in fact studied and built theory for these other types of collective action processes (see also Table 11.1).

a "shared commitment to a cause" (Diani and Bison, 2004: 284), i.e. an aligned world view that encourages individual actors to perceive the world in similar ways and give similar rationales when asked why they are taking action. On the contrary, actors expressing an organizational identity will rather motivate their actions in reference to their individual or organizational aims. A third analytical dimension measures (iii) the presence or absence of *conflictual* or *consensual* attitudes towards identified opponents or other vested interests such as landholders or state agencies. In effect, the full typology consists of six collective action processes as displayed in Table 11.1. Here *social movement processes* are identified as "the building and reproducing of dense informal networks between a multiplicity of actors, sharing a collective identity, and engaged in social and/or political conflict" (Diani, 1992; cf. Diani and Bison, 2004), whereas the other collective action processes are relaxations of this social movement definition. *Coalition processes* are consequently seen as tightly knit alliances to achieve specific goals but that lack clearly agreed upon long-term goals, whereas *organizational processes* are actions taken in reference to specific organizations rather than broader networks.

Table 11.1. *A typology of collective action processes (Diani, 2002; Diani and Bison, 2004).*

Analytical dimension	1. Dense vs sparse informal networks (strong vs weak ties)		2. Collective identity vs organizational identity		3. Conflictual vs consensual attitudes towards opponents/vested interest	
Social movement	Dense		Collective		Conflict	
Consensus movement	Dense		Collective			Consensus
Conflict coalition	Dense			Organiz.	Conflict	
Consensus coalition	Dense			Organiz.		Consensus
Conflict organization		Sparse		Organiz.	Conflict	
Consensus organization		Sparse		Organiz.		Consensus

Some interesting differences can be hypothesized. As Diani and Bison (2004) argue, actors involved in *movement processes* will tend to follow their peers without making instrumental calculations if their organization will gain or lose in participating in a certain collaboration or event. They are engaged in sustained resource exchanges through what Diani and Bison (2004) refer to as "identity ties"; if their peers engage in action, they will also engage and share in solidarity their resources without expecting anything in return.[4] One reason for this lies in that they know they share the same goals and accept the same methods to reach these goals. Interestingly, for actors involved in a consensus movement process there is no reference to a political enemy, but actors could very well collaborate with municipalities, private companies, or other vested interests, or even stress the necessity of doing so, i.e. incorporate a consensus element in their vision of change. In *coalition processes*, actors exchange resources in a more calculated fashion to collaborate on specific projects. After a specific campaign, their "instrumental ties" (Diani and Bison, 2004) – in contrast to "identity ties" – are less important and the formation of a strong collective identity is less likely. In *organizational processes* most resources are harnessed and actions planned internally in one organization.

Given this typology, two things become clear. First, empirical examples of transformative change in natural resource management can be found among the six types. For instance, the previously mentioned studies by Olsson and colleagues would seem to fall under the categories of coalition and organizational processes, with collaborative (rather than conflictual) attitudes between civil servants, researchers, and civil society representatives. This indicates that we indeed can draw upon social movement theory to analyze transformative change in natural resource management. Second, the typology and its underpinning analytical framework allow us to distinguish between different types of collective action processes within the same network. As we will see, this deepens the relational agenda of this chapter: not only can we analyze how actors are related to each other through social networks, but we can also analyze how different collective action *processes* can be interrelated to produce different outcomes.

---

[4] Frank (2009) has developed a similar notion to "identity ties" that he calls "quasi-ties," meaning to direct resources to a collective without specifying to whom. An earlier conceptualization of this was expressed by Molm (2003) as "reciprocal exchange."

Having established this as an analytical departure point, the rest of the chapter is organized as follows. I briefly describe the case study and the methods used to generate network data. This is followed by a two-step social network analysis that in its first step aims to simplify the network so as to reveal its underlying structure, and in its second step identifies different types of collective action processes. These two structural representations are later used in the discussion section to describe three network-level mechanisms, which, supported by interview and participatory data, can be seen as generating transformative capacity and the capacity to protect urban green areas over time.

11.2   THE CASE STUDY, METHODS, DATA, AND RESULTS

The protection of the National Urban Park in Stockholm is used to illustrate a method for analyzing transformative change in ecosystem-based management. In the course of merely five years, 1990 to 1994, these large grassed, wooded, and water areas lying close to Sweden's business and political center went from being perceived as separate entities and under threat, to be elevated into a unified park of national interest protected by one of the first laws in the world for nature reserves in cities. This law also marked the effort of articulating a larger spatial scale for ecosystem management and for establishing a collaborative management arena between municipalities, regional authorities, a royal park organization, and a number of civil society organizations. The diverse collection of 62 organizations that will be analyzed here played a crucial role in this feat, both through the structure of their social network (Ernstson et al., 2008), and through articulating a "protective story" able to explain and legitimize the need for protection of the whole park landscape, previously seen as separate areas (Ernstson and Sörlin, 2009). However, in spite of the success, exploitation plans have continued to be issued and the coalition of organizations has continued to mobilize protection until the present date. The umbrella organization for protecting the park had 22 member organizations in 1992 and this had increased to 50 in 2009, demonstrating a longer-term commitment of many organizations.

In this chapter, I will draw upon and extend analyses from earlier publications, so details on the reliability and validity of data can be found there (Ernstson et al., 2008; Ernstson and Sörlin, 2009). Briefly, however, the interorganizational network was generated through a survey sent to 60 official organizational leaders in April–May 2005.

Using a recognition technique, a list of 92 civil society organizations was composed and added to the survey (cf. Marsden, 1990) through which respondents were prompted to mark four types of collaborative ties to others: regular cooperation, exchange of advice on political and ecological issues, and personal friends. Since all are collaborative ties, the answers could be combined into a single network reflecting shifting strengths of collaboration from 0–5 between pairs of organizations, where cooperation was given double weight (Ernstson *et al.*, 2008). Respondents were also asked to mark organizations they perceived as actively engaging in protecting the park areas; those receiving at least two affirmations were selected as belonging to the network, which included 62 of the 92 listed organizations. The boundary of the network was thus based on mutual recognition by the actors themselves, securing a notion that all actors in the network agree upon that they take action towards a similar broadly defined goal (Diani, 2003a).[5] The survey also generated attribute data. A second list of organizations prompted respondents to report their regular contacts to 36 authorities, which was turned into a number of their "political contacts." By furthermore combining the type and number of days of activity organizations had in the park, their "user intensity" of the park landscape was calculated.[6] Although crude, this index effectively discriminated between for instance an allotment garden reporting six months of organized activity per year in the park, and a cultural conservation organization reporting only three days. Finally, respondents were asked to name their most valuable individual contacts in protecting the park. Selecting among this list of most-cited individuals, five persons were interviewed concerning the emergence, dynamics, and reasons for taking collective action. The qualitative data were paired with participatory observations at four high-profile events.

---

[5] This procedure also allowed me to estimate the validity of my data and send new surveys to organizations included in the network but missed in the first set of 60 respondents. However, those few organizations not completing a survey received few links and few affirmations of being active indicating they would not influence the overall structure of the network. I therefore decided not to send any more surveys.

[6] Different activities were given different weights so that allotment gardening was given more weight than boating or riding as it implies a stronger interaction with local ecosystems. User intensity was then calculated for each organization as the product of an activity's weight and the number of days an organization spent in the park (details in Ernstson and Sörlin, 2009).

11.2.1 Step 1: Using blockmodeling to reveal underlying network structure

In the first analytical step a method called blockmodeling is used that helps to simplify the network by grouping actors into network positions (cf. Burt, 1988; Ansell, 2003; Diani and Bison, 2004). These positions will, in the Discussion section, aid in the identification and description of network-level mechanisms. The idea behind blockmodeling lies in finding those actors in the network that have ties to the same others. If actor A and B have three ties, one each to C, D, and E, then A and B are structurally equivalent and can be grouped into the same "position," or "block." A network of many actors can thus be translated into a simpler network with just a few positions that is easier to make sense of. The Appendix describes in detail how and under what presumptions the real-world data used here were grouped into a network of only three blocks. These were named core, semi-core, and periphery and their average tie densities within and between blocks are given in the simplified network of Figure 11.1. It should be noted that out of the 62 mobilizing actors, only 47 participated in the main component that has been analyzed here. The remaining 15 are organizations with few or no ties to others.

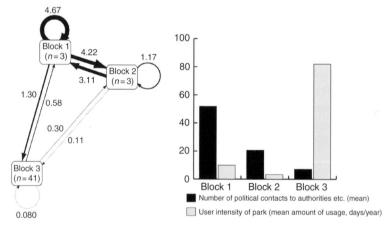

Figure 11.1 The left figure shows how the network of 47 nodes can be transformed to a simplified network with only three blocks. The method used is called blockmodeling based on structural equivalence (see Appendix). The right figure shows how Block 1 and Block 2 have many more contacts to authorities than Block 3, while the latter has organizations that spend many more days using the park landscape (see also Table A11.1). Average network density was 0.237.

Summarizing other results in relation to the simplified network, two significant correlation patterns were found (Table A11.1). Core (N16, N37, N60) and semi-core members (N9, N25, N31) are placed centrally in the network with many more ties to others (higher degree centrality), whereas the 41 periphery members had on average fewer ties resulting in a sparsely connected periphery block. Core and semi-core members were also markedly more active in engaging with authorities and formal actors such as municipalities, regional authorities, and the royal park administration (KDF), giving them significantly higher scores of political contacts. When comparing the blocks across user intensity, the figures were reversed. In the periphery position we find the users of the park landscape, e.g. boating and riding clubs, scouts and orienteering clubs, and allotment gardens (some being completely isolated) that spend significantly more days of organized activity in the park than core and semi-core members. As it happens, core and semi-core groups, being exclusively either nature or culture conservation groups, spend on average less than ten days in the park (with N60 removed; see note in Table A11.1).

11.2.2 Step 2: Identifying types of collective action processes

The second analytical step is based on a method used by Diani and Bison (2004) in their study of different types of collective action processes among civil society organizations in British cities. In their study they asked each organizational leader about preferred alliance partners, participation in the same events, overlapping membership, feelings of solidarity, and about conflictual attitudes. I did not use a list of events, nor asked systematically for shared activists, solidarity, or attitudes. However, there is a degree of comparability with this approach in that I also based my data on organizational leaders and gathered data on different types of collaborative ties. A consequence is nonetheless that a simpler version of their analysis is needed. Instead of blockmodeling and comparing two different types of networks (based on alliance and identity ties), I made use of the strength of ties between pairs of actors and if these ties are reciprocated or not. As a consequence, in following the typology of Table 11.1, I distinguish between actors involved in dense or sparse networks through uncovering subsets of actors engaged with each other in "network of strong ties" or "network of weak ties," respectively. Those sharing ties with strengths of 4–5 are thus approximated to be involved in similar collective processes as those hypothesized earlier by Diani and Bison for "dense" networks, while those participating in ties with strengths of 1–2 are taken as involved in "sparse" networks. "Dense networks" thus means in this analysis that actors engage with each other through multiple relations and that they frequently collaborate and share information with each other. (Note that tie strength 3 is left out so as to create a wider analytical distinction between the two processes and distinguish more robustly between the two. No organization is left out through this operation.)

To find those among "dense networks" that potentially also share a collective identity, and thus are involved in a *movement process*, I use a criteria of complete reciprocity, i.e. instead of using "shared activists" and "shared events" as indicators of collective identity (like Diani and Bison, 2004), I take those organizations tied to each other through reciprocated ties of strength 5 to indicate the presence of the formation of collective identity. The presumption is that those subsets of organizations that have mutually recognized each other on all ties also have a stronger tendency (in relation to others in the network) to negotiate a shared common goal over time and align their way of thinking about themselves and the system they are trying to change. The remaining actors engaged in "dense networks" are taken as involved in a *coalition process*. The set involved in "sparse networks" (strengths 1–2), are seen as exchanging resources based more on their organizational identity than on some overarching collective identity (since they, according to my criteria, have no reciprocated strong ties). The latter are therefore seen as engaged primarily in an *organizational process*. As should be noted I have left out a distinction between consensus and conflictual processes in this analysis due to lack of data.

Although my method is less refined than that of Diani and Bison (2004), Figure 11.2 suggests that there is not just a diversity of actors occupying different structural positions (from step 1), but there is also a set of *collective action processes* at work in the interorganizational network (from step 2). It is noteworthy that the same set of core and semi-core organizations (except N25) come out as distinct, seen in Figure 11.2 as filled circles.[7] These findings suggest that these organizations are engaged in a *movement process*. The subset of actors that the analysis uncovers as being involved in a *coalition process* is considerably

---

[7] Organizations N12 and N39 are also reciprocating their strongest ties (and also stand out in the MDS-plot of Figure A11.1). These are involved in a green area struggle outside the National Urban Park.

larger, being the 35 organizations represented as circles and squares in Figure 11.2. The rest (12 triangles of Figure 11.2) are those not engaged in either movement or coalition processes, but only in *organizational processes*. Furthermore, Figure 11.2 indicates that movement, coalition, and organizational processes are interlinked, since some actors participate in all three processes through their ties to others. These actors thus come to play a crucial role in interlinking the various processes. This can be made clearer by removing core and semi-core actors from the coalition network, which is done in Figure 11.2C and 11.2D. Going from Figure 11.2B to 11.2C, one sees that in removing the core actors there are not many ties left in the coalition network (and even fewer when semi-core actors are removed in Figure 11.2D). This implies that core organizations are crucial in linking the suggested identity-driven movement process to the more loosely held coalition process. This should give core actors a greater ability to build specific and shorter-term coalitions for particular events, and control and guide these coalitions in the direction of those values embedded in their commonly held vision, as I will further discuss in the next section.

11.3   DISCUSSION

It is not obvious how transformative change in ecosystem management can occur given institutional inertia and already established patterns of thought and mental models among managers, politicians, and citizens. Of course, the clearest outcome of transformation in the case study at hand was the acceptance of a new protective law for the particular green areas today known as the National Urban Park, preceded as it was by two parliamentary motions shaped and lobbied in different political parties by core and semi-core organizations in 1994–1995 (notably N31 and N60) (Ernstson and Sörlin, 2009). The argument here is that this shift in legal arrangements, and the creation of a de facto new scale of collaborative management, occurred after years of mobilization to protect the areas from particular development plans spread out in space and time. It was the onset of collective action at various points in time to "fight" particular "threats" that came to structure the social network and gave it its shape, function, and capacity of transformation (Ernstson *et al.*, 2008). It was also through engaging in these particular struggles that a few intensely collaborating organizations developed a more coherent narrative. This emergent narrative framed and explained collective action, and demonstrated to the participants, their external supporters, and their political enemies (which were

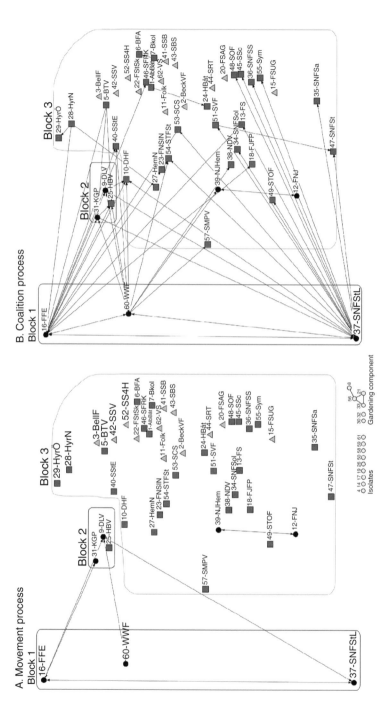

Figure 11.2 The figure shows the results of identifying different types of collective action processes in the network of 47 organizations. Few are involved in a movement process (circles and ties in pane A), many more in a coalition process (circles, squares, and ties in pane B). Those only involved in organizational processes are shown as triangles. Through removing core and semi-core actors (in panes C and D) their key role in interlinking movement and coalition processes is demonstrated. Removing core actors almost completely removes all ties in the coalition network (compare pane B with C). (The 15 organizations at the bottom of pane A are isolated organizations outside the main component of 47 organizations.)

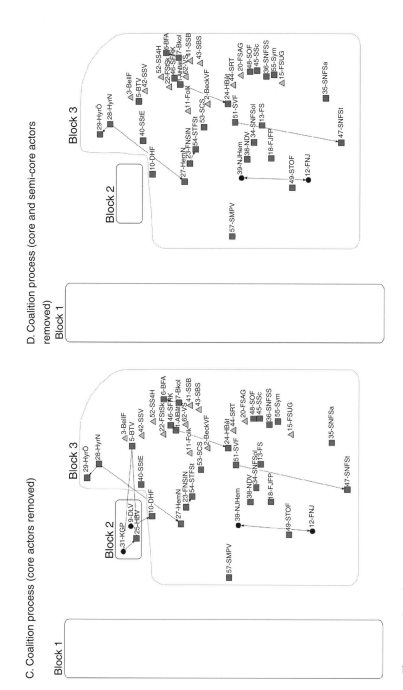

C. Coalition process (core actors removed)

D. Coalition process (core and semi-core actors removed)

Figure 11.2 (cont.)

many, from politicians, building companies, and other citizens) that their action was part of a larger struggle to protect not only these areas, but particular species and biodiversity more generally (e.g. keystone species like the oak tree), and a cultural history unique to Stockholm and Sweden (especially the "royal" park landscapes in the area) (Ernstson and Sörlin, 2009). Bringing together these earlier findings, the discussion that follows situates the significance of the "collective actor," the functions it performs, and how it is reproduced through recurring instances of collective action.

11.3.1   Network-level mechanisms and the interlinking of collective action processes

The capacity of social networks to protect urban park areas from exploitation and degradation can be discussed as the capacity to stop large-scale and small-scale development plans. The former refer to plans that need to be taken through the public participatory planning process. Small-scale plans are minor interventions without needing approval from the local parliament. The interorganizational network in this case study seems capable of dealing with the centralizing tendency of the former, and the distributive practice of the latter. In this section, three network-level mechanisms will be described based on the above analyses.

The first mechanism of "repeated collaboration" is based on that a small subset of actors – the core and semi-core actors – has regularly interacted with one another in trying to solve similar (but slightly different) problems. By turning otherwise single activities into repeated collaborative events, knowledge can be shared and strategies can be developed. As argued by for instance Ostrom (1990), repeated interaction drives down transaction costs as actors get to know each other, which speeds up the process and generates even stronger incentives to continue collaboration, resulting in networks of strong ties (see also network literature: Granovetter, 1973; Schneider *et al.*, 2003; Burt, 2005). Indeed, in our study, more than once have core and semi-core organizations collaborated in organizing supportive galas, debates, and meetings to influence politicians. Throughout the years, a portfolio of strategies to face exploitation plans has evolved (see list in Ernstson *et al.*, 2008), and, through the internal webpage of the umbrella organization (N16), a tool to keep track of the many exploitation threats has been developed where responsibilities to monitor these threats have been divided among the organizations.

In addition, learning is facilitated through a mechanism of repeated collaboration. As argued by social-learning theorists, when persons become embedded in a "community of practice" (Wenger, 1998), cognition and problem-solving happen repeatedly together with the same others, which facilitates the development of shared understanding (Wenger, 1998). Empirical support is found in interviews with core members that displayed detailed and similar knowledge about the decision-making process, how and when it is possible to influence it, including knowledge on the internal organization of different state agencies, and which civil servants could be willing to help. Furthermore, and indicative of strong mutual ties, interviewees also had detailed knowledge about the skills and resources of other core and semi-core organizations and individuals within them, including who can set up meetings with important power-holders. Taken together, the above supports what is suggested in the network analysis, that the strong collaborative ties between core and semi-core actors facilitates the creation of new practices and strategies to stop, postpone, or change development plans.

Further data make it plausible to interpret a second network-level mechanism of "internal and external brokerage" facilitated by the structure of the network. Through repeatedly engaging in protecting the park, core and semi-core organizations have built many more ties to state agencies and political parties than periphery members; on average core members have 2.5 and 7 times more ties than semi-core and periphery members (Table A11.1). They also seem to have collaborated, especially the core, with different periphery organizations at different points in time so as to situate themselves in-between many others in the network. The level of sitting in-between can be measured as "betweenness centrality" (Wasserman and Faust, 1994), and Table A11.1 demonstrates that core members have on average 5 and 30 times higher in-betweenness scores than semi-core and periphery members. Consequently, the dense interaction arena of core and semi-core members is also embedded in the network as an arena of internal and external brokerage, which according to Burt (2005) can be used to control information flows in the network and increase their ability to coordinate collective action. Below I will give telling examples that this seems to be the case. However, at this stage it is important to note how the two described network-level mechanisms so far – repeated interactions and brokerage – seem to work in tandem to interlink the movement process of core and semi-core actors, with the coalition and organizational processes that stretch into the wider network.

Admittedly, a strong hypothesis is emerging that transformative action needs a small subset of actors engaged in a movement process – here identified as the triad of N16, N9, and N37, together with N31 and N60 – that can work as a "navigation bridge" for coordinating and controlling collective action, only drawing on coalition partners in the periphery position when needed (similar results to Diani, 2003b). Their repeated interactions over time serve to generate a common horizon of interpretation, a formation of collective identity that can sustain and steer the political will towards producing a larger-scale transformation.

Moving now to the small-scale development plans, a third network-level mechanism can be identified that draws upon the periphery members, but also on the skewed distribution of political contacts and user intensity (Figure 11.2; Table A11.1). While it is the user groups in the periphery that actually use and need the park landscape for their activities, it is the core and semi-core organizations that take action and have contacts to influence decision making (Figure 11.2). Periphery members consequently need core/semi-core members to wage the struggle. However, the core/semi-core members also need the periphery in at least two explicit ways: for increasing political legitimacy (representing a diverse set of interests), and for being their "eyes and ears" in the park. The latter is especially important for stopping small-scale development plans. As supported both in interviews and observations, it has happened several times that user groups at different locations in the park have informed about activities like the building of smaller car-parks, sheds, or the staging of public events. Reporting such information makes it possible for the politically more skilled core/semi-core actors to take action using their established contacts with authorities. Out of the network structure this third network-level mechanism, which could be called "mutualistic" or "division of labor," seems to have emerged through which periphery members monitor the park, and core/semi-core members meet with authorities.

11.3.2   Explaining single events and bursts of activity

To give further credit to the role of social networks in explaining protective capacity and how repeated actions sustain structure, I will discuss three different episodes of mobilization, which demonstrate that quantitative social network analysis can be useful as a tool for interpreting single events and bursts of activity.

In 2004 the municipality of Stockholm made official the plans for a new town district with 3000–5000 apartments at the *Husarviken* shoreline, arguing for effective re-use of this industrial site just on the border of the National Urban Park.[8] During 2004 the royal management administration of the park (KDF) contacted core and semi-core members in order to mobilize resistance. A task-group was formed with the umbrella organization FFE, along with KGP, HBV, and DLV (N16, N31, N25, and N9). This led to, on the one hand, that KGP and HBV re-used a strategy that they developed in the 1990s. This strategy consisted of developing an alternative plan for the area (called a "citizen's plan"). Through drawings by a landscape architect, sports and cultural activities were stressed, instead of closely built apartment blocks. The argument was that this alternative development would increase ecological connectivity in the areas, and preserve the cultural–historical landscape. To further strengthen these arguments, biological dispersal maps produced by Stockholm University researchers were used (Löfvenhaft and Wikberger, 1996), alongside an eighteenth-century ballad singing of the area's "pastoral landscape" through the "divine window" of the seventeenth-century king's hunting cottage, which lies opposite the site across a small stretch of water. To further articulate these alternative values, KGP and HBV arranged, as in the 1990s, a debate in the prestigious Royal Swedish Academy of Arts to which they invited top politicians and civil servants who were challenged with the alternative plan. At the end of the debate, the FFE chairman threatened the city planners to start a lengthy juridical process if current plans were not revised (which they had successfully managed to do in the past). In parallel, DLV, with a 20-year long record of activities in this particular park area, and thus with good contacts with community groups and residents, co-organized an open information meeting in the local church. DLV produced images of the negative impacts of development, and KGP and HBV were invited to present their alternative plan for the area. Third, the task-group (including KDF) also engaged in a row of lobbying meetings with municipal and county decision-makers. The result of this specific mobilization was that in December 2006, the County Administrative Board decided not to grant the city's detailed building plans, but instead called for plans with increased ecological connectivity and less impact on the cultural–historical landscape.[9]

---

[8] The vignettes are based on interviews with organizational activists, participatory observations, and newspaper articles (details in Ernstson, 2008).

[9] The civil society organizations won a partial victory in 2006. However, plans are still on their way and new legal complaints by core organizations have been

The network analysis in this chapter helps the appreciation that this set of particular events would not have happened if it were not for the fact that they were part of a longer effort of collective action, which in turn had embedded its protagonists in a particular network structure. Knowing this structure, one can deduce plausible explanations of how the core–periphery structure, and the various identified collective action processes, cooperate to facilitate the observed action. First, the management authority KDF chooses to work with the core and semi-core members, not with peripheral network members. The most likely reason behind this lies in that the very active core and semi-core organizations had already established contacts with KDF (which data on their political contacts also show), which makes it easier for KDF to contact them rather than to some other organization in the network. Consequently, and due to their network position, the core and semi-core actors are the ones receiving new and early information. This information gets embedded in a rich field of experience from previous struggles held by core and semi-core organizations, who can re-use developed strategies (alternative plans, meetings, lobbying), take advantage of their enhanced ability to coordinate the network (find local resident's groups, joint lobbying), and influence the decision-making process, both through direct interaction with decision-makers (political contacts, debates), and through mobilizing local residents in the area. In relation to Figure 11.2, we can see how the actors of the movement process come to activate certain ties to generate a specific coalition network to address a particular threat. Of course, in all its details this vignette tell of complex dynamics, but through the previous network analysis we can bring understanding of how the underlying structure of social relations came to structure these dynamics.

Before moving on we also note how this instance of collective action can help to understand the emergence and maintenance of the core–periphery structure. New local organizations are added to the periphery, and through collaborating once again, core and semi-core organizations come to re-use and refine their strategies and further strengthen their ties to authorities. In this way, the core–periphery structure is reproduced.

Another short vignette tells about the exploitation plans at *Tre Vapen* in 2005, where a member of a core organization (N60-WWF) was present during the public consultation meeting being standard procedure in Swedish city planning. Neighbors to the exploitation

issued as late as 2009. The building start of the project has been postponed in steps, from 2006, to 2008, and currently is set to 2010.

site raised concerns and the core member initiated the formation of a residents group. This new group raised a legal complaint and got local press to cover the story so as to put pressure on decision-makers, and exploitation was also delayed. Interpreted from a social network perspective, the core activist can be understood as lending his agency, gained from his network position, to the larger group. Thus, he was able to apply his skills, contacts, arguments, and framing of the park so that a stronger case could be built. This local "NIMBY"-protest (not-in-my-back-yard) was woven into a grander narrative of upholding a park of national interest, and at the same time a new periphery member to the network was added so as to reinforce the core–periphery structure. Again, the social network analysis from above can help interpret these kinds of single events and make visible their relational and collective character, demonstrating that agency does not just originate from single actors and their skills, but also from the pattern of relations that has built up over time among a wider set of actors (Emirbayer and Mische, 1998).

In contrast to the above, in which core and semi-core actors lent their agency and/or came to control instances of collective action towards a certain goal and outcome, a final vignette illustrates how interests and resources of core and semi-core actors are limited and selective. In 2005, an allotment garden (N33) received news that government agencies would move a train station and that the allotment garden would lose several of their gardening plots. Although the allotment gardens openly opposed this threat to their own activity, both through receiving local media press and through publishing petition lists, core and semi-core actors remained passive throughout the struggle, and the allotment garden, together with the gardening umbrella organization (N21) acted in vain to stop exploitation. It seems core and semi-core organizations deliberately chose not to lend their skills and resources, which was also later confirmed by a core member (they thought it was for the better of the park to move the station). As an analyst, to acknowledge such instances of non-action, one can arrive at clues to the nature of the exclusion/inclusion dynamics operating in all collective action.

11.3.3 A social network approach to transformative change

In comparing my explanatory account with other accounts of transformative change towards ecosystem management, there are some differences. In the urban context of the National Urban Park, the struggle has been more openly conflictual and political. Furthermore, although ecological dispersal corridors and ecosystem processes have figured in the struggle, they have rather been mobilized as part of other arguments as to why green areas need protection, especially cultural historical arguments but also as spaces for recreation and education (Ernstson and Sörlin, 2009). Consequently, it has been more difficult to say something about how much or how well the transformation has led to an implementation of ecosystem management. What is clear is that a new scale of collaborative management was institutionalized through the new law, which put rules in place that forced municipalities to collaborate and start working out novel management practices aimed at sustaining ecological processes at a greater landscape scale. To be sure, a very important dimension of transformative change is the social production of a new and "proper" scale of governance (Swyngedouw, 1999), which in this study was a result of the collective action performed by the heterogeneous collective actor under study (cf. Ernstson and Sörlin, 2009).

In further comparing my analysis of transformative change, with those of others, there are also differences pertaining to where in the explanatory accounts the "power to change" is placed. Other authors (Olsson *et al.*, 2004, 2006, 2008) tend to mix structural factors with individual agency (embodied in the skills of key-stewards and institutional entrepreneurs), in which "social networks" figures in a mediating role between the two. Exactly *how* social networks mediate are less clearly described. Although not accounted for in this chapter, there were certainly structural and cultural factors that aided in generating change in the specific case of the National Urban Park, not the least the area's "royal heritage" that made it easier to claim the area's "uniqueness" through aligning it with hegemonic ideas of Sweden's cultural history and elite interest (Ernstson and Sörlin, 2009). A second structural factor was more public in the sense that a wide range of interest and user groups was already active in the park areas when mobilization started in the 1990s. In fact, a steady stream of organizations had found their home in the park areas since 1885, until the present day. On a structural level, this combination of elite and public interest might explain transformative change. However, this misses the point of using social network analysis and social movement theory since there is no identification of the emergent network-level mechanisms that generate change. As such, the value of social network analysis for this chapter lies partly in describing the heterogeneity and structure of the collective actor, but also in identifying the emergent network-level mechanisms that this collective actor generates, i.e. *how* it can transform or translate structured resources (like "cultural heritage" and a pool of existing organizations) into coordinated collective action in the face of change (exploitation threats), and towards a common goal (protecting the park). As was noted, the interlinking of different collective action processes seems key, where repeated collaboration among a few actors sustains a movement process to give thrust, direction, and continuity to the transformative action pursued, while, in times of more acute situations, these actors can draw upon an extended group of coalition partners which have at least partially overlapping interests.

When it comes to placing agency at the individual level (often described as skills held by "leaders" or "entrepreneurs"), a complementary strategy would allow more room for how individuals are relationally embedded in network structures. One way to think this through is to hold that all ties – if they are to be meaningful, i.e. to be able to transfer resources or trust for collaboration – come with a cost, first for establishing them and then for sustaining them (Granovetter, 1973; Degenne and Forsé, 1999). Adding this cost of ties makes it plausible that resources tend to flow along already established patterns of social interaction, and thus why structure matters. Consequently, and despite that very active actors can change parts of the structure (through devoting resources to interact with new others), they cannot change all relations in the network. Thus, their network position – and their possibilities and constraints of taking action – will still be influenced by interactions beyond their reach (Degenne and Forsé, 1999). In highlighting this, one can compare the graph of Figure 11.2 with the three vignettes from above. It is not so that just because there are no links between certain organizations in Figure 11.2 that members of these organizations never meet, or even that they could not collaborate at a certain point in time, which is to read network graphs too literally. Instead, graphs – and structural network analysis – help us to understand dominant patterns of collaboration and resource flows that makes certain collaborations more likely to occur, and more effective if and when they occur. Recurring collaboration – i.e. investments in certain ties – can lower the costs involved in collaborating, which drives further collaboration, but also consume resources to start collaborating with certain others. Actors are always "captured" in their local region of the network, which both constrains and facilitates their action.

11.4   CONCLUSION

The subfield of transformative change in ecosystem management is bound to grow as society faces increasing environmental change (Rockström *et al.*, 2009). This chapter should be seen as a response for how such transformations could be studied by departing from the legacy of using social network analysis to study social movements, a field that has strived to explain and understand both conflictual and consensual transformative changes. A strength from this perspective is that it would allow a greater sensitivity to the conflictual dimensions that all institutional change engenders, and a more relational and structural analysis of these processes. The chapter has demonstrated how such an approach could be used and the type of analysis it would allow, especially how a single social system could hold different types of collective action processes supported by social networks. This chapter has demonstrated that the investment in a social network study can be worthwhile as it brings more analytical dimensions to the "social network" variable, and enhances the possibilities for more detailed understanding of those transformative changes that society is facing, given our predicament of unprecedented environmental change.

Reflections

Social network theory compels us through its structural and relational underpinnings. By necessity it avoids explaining social dynamics by only looking at single individuals or organizations. Instead it helps us – in a systematic fashion – to embed actors in webs of exchange to shift the analytical focus to "the network" from which to build explanatory narratives and understanding. This automatically poses some fundamental choices that one as an analyst needs to make, e.g. what is an actor/node, a tie/link; or the boundary of the network, and the scales of the ecological and social system under study, which I will briefly reflect upon.

   During the course of my study, one member of an organization questioned my focus on organizational ties, saying that "this is all about personal contacts," and not about organizations. In part he was correct since ties between organizations are primarily enacted through personal contacts (at least in this case study). However, organizations gather collective resources that only members can draw upon, and individuals act on the basis of these collective resources. For instance, although one very active individual headed the park project within WWF (N60), his ability to be active rested upon secretarial services, an office with computer, internet access, and phone, not to mention the reputation of an organization that he could draw upon in meetings and engagement with media. Furthermore, several organizations have outlived their activists; while some members have stepped down, others have stepped up, building on the organization's reputation and already-established ties to officials and other civil society organizations. One of my interviewees also told me that it was difficult to take action as an individual citizen. He had called the Department of Environment to arrange for a meeting whereupon the secretary asked: "Who do you represent?" When he said he was just a concerned citizen, a meeting was impossible and his reaction was to join an organization (N25), and he later founded a new organization (N31). This indicates that organizations and organizational ties are plausible units of analysis as they capture something that either constrain or facilitate individual action, thus shaping social dynamics at the level of the "collective actor," this being my focal interest. Nonetheless, there are good ways to survey individuals involved in dynamic social processes. For instance, Sandström and Carlsson (2008) successfully used a method based first upon snowballing to find individuals, and then, in a second step, a complete network survey among identified individuals. Although such a method effectively traces the most active persons to undertake finer-grained analysis, it could, in relation to my study, potentially have missed the less-engaged individuals in the periphery. This in turn would have made it more difficult to identify those relational dynamics and mechanisms that were generated by the periphery position. If nothing else, this importantly demonstrates that our methodological and analytical choices shape our results, and that complementary methods that trace both organizational-level and individual-level networks could be a fruitful option to further understand transformative collective action.

In this study the social system was composed of all those civil society organizations (and their relations) that mobilized to protect the park. The boundary of the network was defined by asking all actors who they consider were participating in the social process in question. Those receiving recognition by other participants in protecting the park were included in the network, while all others were excluded (this follows Diani, see main text). The social system also consisted of actors that influenced and/or had jurisdiction over land use. The scale of the ecological system followed the geographical boundaries of the social struggle. Mobilizing actors came to create a narrative based on cultural history and biological research, which demonstrated that green areas previously seen as disconnected could actually be seen as connected, and treated as a single management unit (Ernstson and Sörlin, 2009). This meant that smaller ecosystems, such as lakes, wetlands, grasslands, and forest patches (that were not necessarily ecologically connected into a larger ecosystem), became part of a new management unit. Although further ecological research might produce arguments that could enlarge (or reduce) the scale of key ecological processes of the park, the current management scale seems to be encompassing enough to allow for ecosystem management, both in order to influence lower-scale processes (like improving pollination networks through collaboration with allotment gardeners, and the holding of cattle to sustain biodiverse pasture grasslands), and larger-scale processes (such as the promotion of oak trees to sustain seed dispersal by birds in the Stockholm metropolitan landscape). In an urban context, where social and ecological dimensions are deeply entwined, letting the social struggle define the ecological scale seems a viable route to unravel how social-ecological management systems could be formed.

Lastly, there are limitations to social network analysis. Without a doubt, collective action towards transformative change involves many dimensions, and while social network analysis can help us understand how the patterning of ties can give rise to network-level mechanisms that facilitate or constrain individual and collective action, it is silent on cultural and meaning-making processes. For instance, you cannot explain with network analysis alone how the mobilizing actors in this case study could construct a narrative to articulate a new scale of governance (Ernstson and Sörlin, 2009). For that reason, and following others (Emirbayer and Goodwin, 1994), there lies a great value in setting quantitative and qualitative analysis in communication so as to better understand the emergence of network structures (Mische, 2003), and to enrich the interpretation of cultural and meaning-making dimensions of collective action (Melucci, 1996).

Blockmodeling using structural equivalence

Blockmodeling aims to simplify the network to search for underlying patterns. This is done through grouping actors that are structurally equivalent, i.e. actors that have the same relations to exactly the same others, in direction, strength, and across all relations (Boorman and White, 1976; Burt, 1988). Although network theorists have argued that such actors are likely to face the same constraints and opportunities in the network, which could generate similar behavior (Boorman and White, 1976; Burt, 1988; Wasserman and Faust, 1994), blockmodeling will not be used here for testing such hypotheses. Instead it is used as a tool to reach a simpler representation of the network. For similar uses, see especially other social movement scholars who have worked with data where nodes represent civil society organizations (Ansell, 2003; Diani, 2003b; Diani and Bison, 2004).

Perfect structural equivalence is rarely found in empirical data so various ways to identify *nearly* structurally equivalent actors have been developed. These are based on calculating an index of similarity (or dissimilarity) between actors' tie patterns, i.e. between their in- and out-going ties. Two commonly used measures (especially for valued and ordinal data as here) are the Pearson correlation (Wasserman and Faust, 1994) and Euclidean distance (Burt, 1988). Modeling has shown they do not give greatly differing results (Burt, 1988), but some differences exist. The former searches tie patterns (disregarding tie strength), while the latter counts tie strength as important structural information (Burt, 1988). If data are based on self-estimated rating scales (e.g. How much do you interact with that person on a scale from 1 to 5?) it could be wise to use the Pearson correlation. In my case, no rating scale was used, but instead the matrix of relations between organizations was constructed from combining four bidirectional relations, which I consider carry vital structural information. There is a great difference between reporting only exchange of information on ecological issues (strength = 1) and reporting that your organization exchanged information on all relations, including collaboration, information exchange, and personal friend (strength = 5). Using Euclidean distance will thus help to discriminate between organizations interacting with the same others but with markedly different intensities. The next step is to hierarchically cluster the distance matrix (or similarity matrix), i.e. to group actors with short distances (or high similarity) into exclusive subsets.[10]

By calculating the Euclidean distances between all organizations in the valued network of the main component ($N = 47$), and then hierarchically clustering these distances, the partition diagram of Figure A11.1 is produced. Perfectly equivalent actors are found on level 0.000 (distance is zero), and less equivalent partitions of actors as we move down. It is necessary to then ask, which of these 43 partitions to choose? Literature tells us quite bluntly, and honestly, to choose "a useful and interpretable partition" where "[t]heory is the best guide" (Wasserman and Faust, 1994: 383; see also Hanneman and Riddle, 2005). An aid for interpretation is also to plot the multi-dimensional scaling (MDS-plot) of Euclidean distances where nodes visually closer are more equivalent, also presented in Figure A11.1.

The clustering diagram demonstrates that there are quite a few closely equivalent actors.[11] Further, actors seem to be added sequentially to one another. My aim is to simplify, but sustain structural features, and at level 11.679 a "valley" appears making organizations N9, N25, and N31 stand out. These are also found closer to each other in the MDS-plot. To the right (and more equivalent), we find a large set of 41 organizations, also grouped in the MDS-plot (but see N39 and N12, which according to Figure 11.2A are also involved in a separate movement process). To the left of these (and less equivalent), we find N37, N16, and N60. These clearly stand out in the MDS-plot and since they have long distances both to each other and others, they should potentially be viewed as three separate positions. However, striving to keep it simple, I could nonetheless gain a meaningful interpretation (see main text) when these were grouped into the same block. This finally gave three blocks: core, semi-core, and periphery (Figure 11.1). Another possibility would have been to define four or five blocks at level 9.397 and 8.784, respectively. Interestingly, using Pearson correlation suggests a block with 11 nodes, composed of blocks identified above using Euclidean distances. This gives credit to the proposition that tie strengths do matter for the

---

[10] Hierarchical clustering means that if two actors have the same distance to all other actors they are collapsed into a class, and then all equivalences (using Euclidean distance here) are re-calculated with these two actors seen as a single "actor." This is repeated until all actors have found a class. There are various algorithms to collapse actors into classes (e.g. average link, single link, and complete link), but they usually differ little (Hanneman and Riddle, 2005: chapter 13). I used single link.

[11] But see at level 4.285 in Figure A11.1, with classes [11, 39]; [25, 24, 15, 35, 38, 44, 26]; [5, 6]; [3, 2, 9, 36]; and [16, 41, 32, 31, 33, 12, 34, 47], while the rest is ungrouped.

HIERARCHICAL CLUSTERING OF STRUCTURAL EQUIVALENCE MATRIX BASED ON EUCLIDEAN DISTANCE

```
Equiv.   Org.id.no (Nxx) --->
Level    3 1 6 2 3 1 3   2 4 1 5 4 5 2 2 2 3 5 1   2 1 4 5 3 3 2 4 4 5 3   1 4 2 5 4 4 4 1 4 6
         7 6 0 9 5 1 2 9 5 3 0 0 7 7 1 7 8 9 8 4 8 1 4 3 9 3 5 4 0 5 8 5 6 6 7 3 2 2 1 3 5 4 2
```

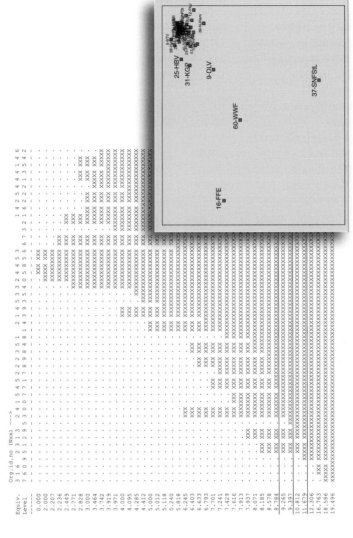

Figure A11.1 Hierarchical clustering of the Euclidean distance matrix as measure of structural equivalence (left). Non-metric MDS of Euclidean distance matrix (right); stress = 0.074.

Table A11.1. *A description of the blocks of actors from the simplified network (Figure 11.1) by using the mean value of their attribute data and network measurements. The second half displays the result from a non-parametric test of the blockmodel (see text in Appendix). The number of missing data, when not zero, is given within parentheses.*

	B1	B2	B3	ANOVA
(a) Block description	Mean	Mean	Mean	F
Degree central. (no. of ties)	117.7	43.3	13.2	131***
Betweenness centrality [1]	0.28	0.056	0.0092	48.2***
Year of foundation	1986	1988	1950 (6)	2.76*
Political contacts	51.7	20.7	7.3 (11)	27.6***
User intensity (raw data) [2]	106.7	3.3	3.3 (9)	4.55**
N60 removed	10 (1)	3.3	82.0	4.55**
(b) Non-parametric test [3]				
Ties within block (standardized coeff.)	0.2431	0.0297	−0.2979	
Significance (P value)	0.0004	0.1114	0.0002	

Note:
[1] Betweenness centrality was measured after the network had been dichotomized (keeping ties with strength > 2) and symmetrized (keeping the maximum value for each link); [2] To clarify the pattern of user intensity, N60 was removed as it is a professional organization with just one employee, in stark contrast to the member sizes of others with high user intensity (e.g. allotment gardens have 20 to hundreds of members); [3] Model fit: adjusted $R^2 = 0.163$ (probability = 0; no. of obs. = 2162); (***$P < 0.001$; **$P < 0.01$; *$P < 0.1$).

structuring of this network since they enhance the separation between structurally equivalent positions.

The next step is to partition the 47-by-47 network matrix according to the blocks – keeping directions and strengths of ties – and calculate the link density between and inside blocks as the mean value of reported ties. This generates Figure 11.1 in the main text. A non-parametric test of tie density within and between blocks demonstrates that the blockmodel of Figure 11.1 is unlikely a random result (Table A11.1); Block 1 actors interact significantly more with each other than with others; B2 actors follow the same pattern (but not significantly); and B3 actors interact significantly less with each other than with others.[12] Leaving the relational analysis, attribute data are then

[12] In UCINET the non-parametric test that was used is called the Variable Homophily test, where "Intercept" can be interpreted as meaning "Ties between any blocks."

used to describe the blocks to facilitate interpretation. In this chapter, the attributes of user intensity and political contacts were most important in interpreting the emergent network-level mechanisms (see main text).

REFERENCES

Ansell, C. K. (2003). Community embeddedness and collaborative governance in the San Francisco Bay Area environmental movement. In M. Diani and D. McAdam (Eds.), *Social Movements and Networks – Relational Approaches to Collective Action*. Oxford: Oxford University Press, pp. 123–144.

Boorman, S. A. and H. C. White (1976). Social structure from multiple networks. II. Role structures. *American Journal of Sociology*, **81**(6), 1384–1446.

Borgatti, S. P., A. Mehra, D. J. Brass and G. Labianca (2009). Network analysis in the social sciences. *Science*, **323**, 892–895.

Burt, R. S. (1988). Some properties of structural equivalence measures derived from sociometric choice data. *Social Networks*, **10**(1), 1–28.

Burt, R. S. (2005). *Brokerage and Closure: An Introduction to Social Capital*. Oxford: Oxford University Press.

Christensen, N. L., A. M. Bartuska, J. H. Brown *et al.* (1996). The report of the Ecological Society of America Committee on the scientific basis for ecosystem management. *Ecological Applications*, **6**, 665–690.

Degenne, A. and M. Forsé (1999). *Introducing Social Networks*. London: Sage.

Diani, M. (1992). The concept of social movement. *Sociological Review*, **40**, 1–25.

Diani, M. (1995). *Green Networks*. Edinburgh: Edinburgh University Press.

Diani, M. (2002). Britain re-creates the social movement: contentious (and not-so-contentious) networks in Glasgow. Conference paper presented at Contentious Politics and the Economic Opportunity Structure, University of Crete, Rhetimno, October 17–18.

Diani, M. (2003a). Introduction: social movements, contentious actions, and social networks: 'from metaphor to substance'? In M. Diani and D. McAdam (Eds.), *Social Movements and Networks: Relational Approaches to Collective Action*. Oxford: Oxford University Press, pp. 1–18.

Diani, M. (2003b). 'Leaders' or brokers? Positions and influence in social movement networks. In M. Diani and D. McAdam (Eds.), *Social Movements and Networks: Relational Approaches to Collective Action*. Oxford: Oxford University Press, pp. 105–122.

Diani, M. and I. Bison (2004). Organizations, coalitions and movements. *Theory and Society*, **33**, 281–309.

Emirbayer, M. and J. Goodwin (1994). Network analysis, culture and the problem of agency. *American Journal of Sociology*, **99**, 1411–1454.

Emirbayer, M. and A. Mische (1998). What is agency? *American Journal of Sociology*, **103**(4), 962–1023.

Ernstson, H. (2008). In Rhizomia: actors, networks and resilience in urban landscapes. PhD thesis. Department of Systems Ecology, Stockholm University, Stockholm.

Ernstson, H. and S. Sörlin (2009). Weaving protective stories: connective practices to articulate holistic values in Stockholm National Urban Park. *Environment and Planning A*, **41**(6), 1460–1479.

Ernstson, H., S. Sörlin and T. Elmqvist (2008). Social movements and ecosystem services – the role of social network structure in protecting and managing urban green areas in Stockholm. *Ecology and Society*, **13**(2), 39.

Folke, C., T. Hahn, P. Olsson and J. Norberg (2005). Adaptive governance of social-ecological systems. *Annual Review of Environment and Resources*, **30**, 441–473.

Frank, K. (2009). Quasi-ties: directing resources to members of a collective. *American Behavioral Scientist*, **52**(12), 1613–1645.

Granovetter, M. (1973). The strength of weak ties. *American Journal of Sociology*, **76**(6), 1360–1380.

Gunderson, L. H. (1999). Resilience, flexibility and adaptive management: antidotes for spurious certitude? *Conservation Ecology*, **3**(1), 7.

Gunderson, L. H. and C. S. Holling (Eds.) (2002). *Panarchy: Understanding Transformations in Human and Natural Systems*. Washington, DC: Island Press.

Hahn, T., P. Olsson, C. Folke and K. Johansson (2006). Trust-building, knowledge generation and organizational innovations: the role of a bridging organization for adaptive comanagement of a wetland landscape around Kristianstad, Sweden. *Human Ecology*, **34**, 573–592.

Hanneman, R. A. and M. Riddle (2005). *Introduction to Social Network Methods*. Riverside, CA: University of California (published in digital form at http://faculty.ucr.edu/~hanneman/).

Holling, C. S. (1978). *Adaptive Environmental Assessment and Management*. Caldwell, NJ: Blackburn Press.

Kingdon, J. W. (1995). *Agenda, Alternatives, and Public Policies*, 2nd Edition. New York, NY: Harper-Collins College Publishers.

Löfvenhaft, K. and C. Wikberger (1996). Biotopkarta och historisk landanvändning (Biotope and historical land-use map). In *Nationalstadsparkens ekologiska infrastruktur (The Ecological Infrastructure of the National Urban Park)*. Stockholm: SBK 1997: 98.

Marsden, P. V. (1990). Network data and measurement. *Annual Review of Sociology*, **16**, 435–463.

McCarthy, J. D. and M. N. Zald (1977). Resource mobilization and social movements: a partial theory. *American Journal of Sociology*, **82**(6), 1212–1241.

Melucci, A. (1996). *Challenging Codes. Collective Action in the Information Age*. Cambridge: Cambridge University Press.

Mische, A. (2003). Cross-talk in movements: reconceiving the culture-network link. In M. Diani and D. McAdam (Eds.), *Social Movements and Networks: Relational Approaches to Collective Action*. Oxford: Oxford University Press, pp. 258–280.

Molm, L. D. (2003). Theoretical comparisons of forms of exchange. *Sociological Theory*, **21**(1), 1–17.

Olsson, P., C. Folke and T. Hahn (2004). Social-ecological transformation for ecosystem management: the development of adaptive co-management of a wetland landscape in southern Sweden. *Ecology and Society*, **9**(4), 2.

Olsson, P., C. Folke and T. P. Hughes (2008). Navigating the transition to ecosystem-based management of the Great Barrier Reef, Australia. *Proceedings of the National Academy of Sciences USA*, **105**(28), 9489–9494.

Olsson, P., L. H. Gunderson, S. R. Carpenter *et al.* (2006). Shooting the rapids: navigating transitions to adaptive governance of social-ecological systems. *Ecology and Society*, **11**(1), 18.

Ostrom, E. (1990). *Governing the Commons: The Evolution of Institutions for Collective Action*. Cambridge: Cambridge University Press.

della Porta, D. and M. Diani (2006). *Social Movements: An Introduction*. Oxford: Blackwell Publishing.

Rockström, J., W. Steffen, K. Noone *et al.* (2009). A safe operating space for humanity. *Nature*, **461**, 472–475.

Sandström, A. and L. Carlsson (2008). The performance of policy networks: the relation between network structure and network performance. *Policy Studies Journal*, **36**(4), 497–524.

Schneider, M., J. Scholz, M. Lubell, D. Mindruta and M. Edwardsen (2003). Building consensual institutions: networks and the National Estuary Program. *American Journal of Political Science*, **47**(1), 143–158.

Swyngedouw, E. (1999). Modernity and hybridity: nature, regeneracionismo, and the production of the Spanish waterscape, 1890–1930. *Annals of the Association of American Geographers*, **89**(3), 443–465.

Wasserman, S. and K. Faust (1994). *Social Network Analysis: Methods and Applications*. Cambridge: Cambridge University Press.

Wenger, E. (1998). *Communities of Practice: Learning, Meaning, and Identity*. New York, NY: Cambridge University Press.

Westley, F. (1995). Governing design: the management of social systems and ecosystem management. In L. H. Gunderson, C. S. Holling and S. S. Light (Eds.), *Barriers and Bridges to the Renewal of Ecosystems and Institutions*. New York, NY: Columbia University Press, pp. 391–427.

Westley, F., S. R. Carpenter, W. A. Brock, C. S. Holling and L. H. Gunderson (2002). Why systems of people and nature are not just social and ecological systems. In L. H. Gunderson and C. S. Holling (Eds.), *Panarchy: Understanding Transformations in Human and Natural Systems*. Washington, DC: Island Press, pp. 103–120.

Zald, M. N. and J. D. McCarthy (1980). Social movement industries: competition and cooperation among movement industries. In L. Kriesberg (Ed.), *Research in Social Movements, Conflict, and Change*, 3, Greenwich, CT: Jai Press, pp. 1–20.

12

Social networks, joint image building, and adaptability: the case of local fishery management

12.1 THE CHALLENGES OF NATURAL RESOURCE GOVERNANCE

It is generally agreed that adaptability – as in the capacity to react and respond to social and ecological change – is a desirable quality of systems governing natural resources (Holling, 1978; Walters, 1986; Folke *et al.*, 2002). Even so, the complex nature of environmental problems makes adaptive governance a far from straightforward task. In addition to the inherent complexity and unpredictability of the natural environment, social processes related to natural resources are often ridden with conflict and feature great uncertainty regarding the substance of the problem, the strategies of other actors, and the overall institutions governing such processes (Koppenjan and Klijn, 2004). In striving for adaptability, governance is faced with various challenges originating from collective action problems, from the existence of divergent and competing interests, values, and problem definitions, and from the fact that ecological knowledge more often than not is contested (Olson, 1965; Hardin, 1968; Hoppe, 1999; Koppenjan and Klijn, 2004). These features significantly aggravate the processes of reaching a joint image regarding the state of the resource and appropriate management rules, which is absolutely essential for adaptive management to evolve. Thus, the social challenges of adaptive governance are many. There is therefore a constant search – among both policy makers and

Social Networks and Natural Resource Management: Uncovering the Fabric of Environmental Governance, ed. Ö. Bodin and C. Prell. Published by Cambridge University Press.
© Cambridge University Press 2011.

researchers – for the type of governance system that can promote the rise and subsistence of social processes dealing with these challenges in an efficient way.

No blueprint for this delicate undertaking exists as the variables that affect the function and performance of these exceedingly complex socio-ecological systems are many, interrelated, and essentially context dependent (Dietz *et al.*, 2003). Still, traditional forms of top-down and state-centered management systems have been criticized for being incapable of dealing with the uncertainties referred to above. As an alternative, recent research has emphasized the particular advantages of collaborative governance structures, or co-management systems (Berkes, 2002, 2008; Rova, 2004; Carlsson and Berkes, 2005; Sabatier *et al.*, 2005). In very broad terms, co-management refers to systems in which authority is divided and in which both public and private actors are involved in management. The underlying assumption is that these types of management systems promote the supply and exchange of resources, mitigate conflicts, and increase the legitimacy of the decisions taken. Thus, the multi-actor and cross-boundary nature is assumed to support a process in which the troublesome social dilemmas of natural resource governance are more easily overcome. However, the concept of co-management covers a rich diversity of different organizational arrangements, both regarding the set of actors involved and the nature of their relationships, towards each other and to the resource being managed (cf. Sen and Nielsen, 1996; Njaya, 2007). The starting point of this chapter is that even though the advantages of co-management systems have been underpinned by solid theoretical arguments and empirical confirmation, the distinguishing characteristics of co-management systems could also serve to render the process of collective action because of the increased diversity in perspectives, interests, and goals they imply. The implementation of co-management should therefore not be regarded as a universal remedy or as the sole answer to the troublesome issues of natural resource governance. Evidently, we need to deepen our knowledge about how different types of co-management systems affect the way they function. The proposition being argued for in this chapter is that a social network approach is a promising way forward to enhancing our knowledge about the features of effective co-management systems.

The aim of this chapter is to show how the adoption of a network approach and the application of social network analysis can enhance our understanding of natural resource management systems, their function, and performance. In order to fulfill this aim, theoretical as well as methodological issues will be dealt with in relation to previously conducted case studies of local fishery management in Sweden (Sandström, 2008; Sandström and Rova, 2010a; Sandström and Rova, 2010b). In this chapter, the results from these studies are comprehensively analyzed, focusing on both the theoretical and methodological aspects of social networks in natural resource research. While the management networks' adaptability was the main performance variable in these studies, this chapter more closely examines the function of joint image building in management. Through a comparative analysis of the structural features of the management networks, their adaptability, and processes of joint image building, the relationship between performance and different types of co-management systems is discussed. Additionally, the methodological choices are reflected on and some critical issues related to the research process are discussed. Even though the empirical cases dealt with in this chapter concern fishery management, the implications are applicable also to similar cases of collective action processes within other policy areas dealing with other kinds of resources. The aim is to illustrate what type of research questions can be elaborated with a network approach and how the methodological considerations associated with the application of social network analysis can be handled. Hopefully, the chapter will also serve to inspire others, researchers, policy makers, and practitioners at various levels of management, to adopt a network approach when engaged in these issues.

The chapter continues with a brief description of the empirical case studies that constitute the focal point of departure for the subsequent theoretical and methodological reasoning. Thereafter, the theoretical perspectives implied by a network approach and the arguments supporting such an approach to study these management systems are presented. The method of data collection is subsequently described and in the empirical section the studied fishery management networks are analyzed in regards to adaptability, joint image building, and network characteristics. Finally, our current findings concerning the network structure of effective co-management is concluded and the methodological experiences, both the advantages and difficulties associated with a social network approach, are summarized pointing towards a research agenda for the future.

12.2   THE EMPIRICAL CASE OF LOCAL FISHERY MANAGEMENT

The discussion in this chapter is based on experiences and results from studies of three local fishery management systems. However, in order to fulfill the aim to examine the relation between network structure and performance, only two of these management systems are included in the comparative analysis. The third study is excluded since it diverges in regards to geography, institutional setting, and socio-economic variables that might jeopardize the comparative validity of the analysis. The other two management systems, though, are both situated within Fishery Conservation Areas (FCAs) in the county of Jämtland. Similar fish species, with similar economic value, are managed and both areas have an, at least with Swedish measures, extensive and expanding fishery tourism. Thus, the two management systems are situated in comparable contexts.

Fishery Conservation Areas constitute a certain type of local co-management regime that is regulated by national law (Swedish Statutes SFS, 1981: 533; Dyhre and Edlund, 1982). The law regulates the constitution for management; the conditions stipulating the formation of new areas, their aim, the composition of actors, and their sphere of authority. The FCAs are intended to function as collaborative arenas for owners of fishing rights within a certain geographic area that want to manage a shared resource system. Thus, they are examples of property-based co-management systems (Piriz, 2005). Decisions regarding access and appropriation rules, regulating resource use, are formally taken during annual meetings and between those meetings an elected board runs the operational work. The rules that are decided on are binding and the FCA has the right to impose sanctions in case of rule-infringements. Appeals towards these decisions are handled by the County Administration Boards (CABs) that are the regional state authorities in Sweden. Accordingly, the FCAs possess far-reaching formal authority to determine how the resource is utilized.

An evaluation of the actions and undertakings of FCAs in Sweden was conducted in the late 1990s (Tengelin, 1997). One conclusion was that there are large variations in management systems operation, a notion that was further verified by the empirical studies upon which this chapter is based. Significant divergences emerge when comparing the set of actors involved in the joint management activities as well as their level of commitment. Further, the FCAs have different goals and apply different measures in order to realize these goals. Thus, even though the management systems are governed by the same formal institutional framework (i.e. the legal regulations briefly described above) they diverge in processes as well as outcomes. They differ, for example, in how ecological knowledge is generated, understood, and integrated into management. The capacity to make rules that are accepted and followed also diverged. While some areas function very well, being able to balance different interests, restrain conflicts, and keep the resource system within ecologically safe limits, others struggle with destructive arguments, a constant lack of resources, or paralyzed decision-making processes. The proposition here is that a network perspective to the study of these management systems will enhance our potential to address and explain these important differences in performances, here framed as adaptability and joint image building.

12.3   SOCIAL NETWORKS AND ADAPTIVE GOVERNANCE

The network approach embraces the fundamental idea that social networks are an important variable in research as the network structures, defined as actors and the patterns of their interactions, provide some explanatory power. The network structure is assumed to affect the social processes, their qualities, and outcome.

12.3.1   The foundation of a network approach

This theoretical stance is justified by drawing on policy network theory, institutional theory, and social capital theory (thoroughly elaborated in Sandström and Carlsson, 2008). Applied to the empirical case study of this chapter, the adopted approach implies that, first, a study of outcomes and explanations thereof must start with the social networks, i.e. the actors involved in the problem-solving processes, that evolve in relation to fishery management (cf. the Action arena) (Hjern, 1987; Hull and Hjern, 1987; Hjern and Porter, 1993; Carlsson, 1996, 2000; Ostrom, 2005). Policies, or management rules, are formed within these networks which imply that they can be perceived as governance networks. Second, it is acknowledged that the task of defining these governing networks, i.e. determining who the involved actors are, what interests they possess, and what external rules they are affected by, must be done empirically. The relevance of formal institutions, organizational boundaries, or hierarchies could not be assumed and the real-world networks of governance might diverge significantly from the boundaries of formal decision-making authority. For example, being on the board of an FCA does not necessary imply involvement in governance. At the same time, a person with no formal connection to an FCA might play an important role in various management activities. Brought together, this is why the social network of individuals involved in the problem-solving processes, and not the elected board or the fishery rights owners, is treated as the main analytical unit of this study. Accordingly, the search for variables affecting joint image building and adaptability must start with these networks.

Moreover, the adopted network approach implies that the very structure of fishery management networks can be ascribed explanatory power. Thus, not merely the characteristics of the involved actors, their aims, interests, resources, etc., but also the patterns of their interactions are assumed to affect adaptability. Networks evolve in situations when individuals share an advantage of collaboration, or when they are dependent upon each other and the achievement of collective action to realize their goals (Coleman, 1990; Lin, 2001). Within these networks, actors meet and exchange various types of resources, such as money, information, knowledge, or legitimacy (Scharpf, 1978; Rhodes and Marsh, 1992; Elmore, 1993; Thatcher, 1998). As a result, webs of social relations are formed and the specific features of these webs matter for the turnout (Friedkin, 1981; Knoke, 1990; Powell, 1990). As formulated by Knoke: "the structure of relations among actors and the location of individual actors in the network have important behavioral, perceptual, and attitudinal consequences both for the individual units and for the system as a whole" (Knoke, 1990: 9). Accordingly, the adaptive processes in the case of fishery management are assumed to be affected by how the network is structured. Both the ability to craft rules within FCAs and the content of the rules, for example whether rules are based on current ecological knowledge or not, are supposedly correlated with certain network characteristics. Then again, the level of social (and ecological) complexity surrounding natural resource management is immense, making the number of variables of interest for research, and their causality, many and difficult to handle. The relationship between context, actors, network structure, and outcome are far from straightforward and a mutual interplay between agency and structure is assumed (Giddens, 1984; Granovetter, 1992; Marsh and Smith, 2000, 2001). However, in this study, reality is significantly simplified by focusing on the variables network structure, adaptability, and joint image building only. Further, the relationship between these variables is discussed in terms of correlations since causality cannot be definitely determined with the adopted research design, investigating the variables at one point in time only.

12.3.2 The importance of closure and bridging

This far, the relevant unit of analysis and arguments for why networks should be treated seriously have been proposed. Still, propositions specifying how network structure presumably affects the processes of problem-solving within the studied fishery management networks are needed. These propositions are derived from social capital theory. Great diversity and range are characteristics that aptly describe the current state of social capital research (Bourdieu, 1986; Putnam, 1992, 2000; Portes, 1998; Portes and Landolt, 2000; Lin, 2001; Lin *et al.*, 2001; Borgatti and Foster, 2003; Ostrom and Ahn, 2003; Rothstein, 2003; Kadushin, 2004; Kwon, 2004). The common denominator, though, is the fundamental idea that some relations or network constellations are more advantageous than others. Mainly two divergent notions, even though differently named in the literature, exist regarding the relation between structure and performance. The reasoning in this chapter comes from Burt's (1997, 2000, 2001) concepts of "social capital as network closure" and "social capital as structural holes," comparable with the terminology of bonding versus bridging ties, respectively (Putnam, 2000; Woolcock and Narayan, 2000; Bodin and Crona, 2009). While closure corresponds to the level of cohesiveness, i.e. the internal structure of the network and the bonding ties, the structural hole argument is essentially based on the importance of bridging, i.e. ties that bridge different network constellations.

The first notion of social capital, as a function of network closure, emphasizes the particular advantage of well-connected structures, i.e. structures in which actors are directly connected by many and strong relations or indirectly through a coordinating unit (Burt, 2000). These types of structures are assumed to facilitate a free communication flow, promoting the creation of common norms and common values, restraining opportunistic behavior among the involved actors (Coleman, 1987; Lin, 2001). The second notion of social capital underlines the importance of non-redundant information channels for the sake of mobilizing new and diversified resources into the management process. This kind of resource flow is secured by ties spanning structural holes (defined by the absence of ties) connecting otherwise sparsely connected or unconnected clusters of actors (Burt, 2000). Granovetter's (1973) weak-tie argument also rests upon the significance of bridging. While network closure describes the internal structures of the fishery management networks, the idea of bridging over structural holes refers to how the networks connect to other networks. Hypotheses that relate these general ideas about structure and performance to the concepts of adaptability and joint image building in fishery management are formulated next.

12.3.3   Hypotheses relating closure and bridging to joint image building and adaptability in fishery management

Adaptive management (Holling, 1978; Walters, 1986; Folke *et al.*, 2002, 2003), or adaptive governance, is defined as a management process in which rules are constantly revised and adjusted to prevailing ecological knowledge in a process of continuous learning. Adaptive management is often described as a circle involving, for example, the steps of knowledge generation, goal formulation, selection of alternatives, action, assessment, and evaluation (Carlsson and Danell, 2006; Plummer, 2009, cf. policy life cycle, Parsons, 1995). Basically, adaptability requires (1) an inflow of ecological knowledge (here scientific knowledge is in the center of attention), (2) an active decision-making process based on prevailing ecological knowledge, and (3) a high level of rule-compliance among users.

As stipulated in the introduction to this chapter, the complex nature of environmental problems and related social and ecological uncertainties pose significant challenges to the realization of all three aspects of the adaptive circle listed above (Koppenjan and Klijn, 2004). One of these critical challenges consists of the development of a joint view regarding the fundamental problem of management and solutions, i.e. appropriate management rules. Action arenas, such as the ones studied here, are likely to be composed of a quite diverse set of actors that represent different interests and strive towards divergent and sometimes opposing goals. Actors are likely to possess different understandings of what the focal problem of management is and how it best should be approached. Then again, organizing processes and collective action are dependent upon people agreeing about a common problem (Carlsson, 2000). Thus, in order to be adaptive, management systems must deal with difficult issues of substantive uncertainties, finding commonly agreed-upon answers to questions regarding what the problem is, what the cause is, and how it could be solved. Or more specifically applied to the context of fishery management; what is the overall problem and goal of the FCA? Whose interest should be obliged? What kind of actions and rules should be adopted? This challenge, and the importance of overcoming it, has been described in natural resource management research. For example, Olsson *et al.* (2004) address the topic when emphasizing the importance of the creation of a common vision and a common goal among concerned stakeholders. Likewise, Carlsson and Sandström (2008) discuss the importance of a common problem definition and prioritizing process in organizing. Disregarding how the function is framed, the process of building a joint image is regarded as critical. Then again, a joint image is not a sufficient condition for adaptive governance. To sustain a process in which rules are constantly adjusted and revised to the ecological environment, the learning processes must be firmly anchored in accepted ecological knowledge. Thus, a common view regarding the status of the ecological system based on agreed and valid knowledge, systematic observation, and science, is a second prerequisite for adaptability.[1]

Four different concepts developed by Koppenjan and Klijn (2004) can, slightly modified,[2] be applied to categorize network processes in regards to differences in the function of joint image building. Successful joint image-building processes, sustaining adaptability, can with the terminology discussed above be described as a process of "negotiated knowledge." In such processes, ecological information is absorbed, processed, and negotiated among stakeholders – generating a common view regarding problems, solutions, and ecological status. If actors fail to agree on a joint view in regards to either the problem or the ecological system, the result will be a network struggling with adaptability. These clearly less desirable scenarios can also be described using the concepts developed by Koppenjan and Klijn

[1] Not only scientific knowledge is emphasized in the adaptive management literature, but also so-called local ecological knowledge (Olsson and Folke, 2001). Sometimes the separation between experiential and experimental knowledge is made (Folke *et al.*, 2003). In this chapter, though, there is a focus on ecological knowledge based on science, and systematic experimentation and observation.

[2] Koppenjan and Klijn (2004) focused on the variables "agreed scientific validity of problem formulation and solutions" and "consensus about problem formulation and solutions." In this chapter, the management processes are studied examining the existence of "a joint view regarding problem and solutions" and "a joint view regarding the ecological system based on agreed and valid science."

(2004). A process in which actors agree upon the fundamental problem of management and appropriate solutions, although no scientifically valid knowledge base motivating these understandings exists, is described as a process of "negotiated nonsense." In this network, actors agree about what to do and why, however, these agreements are not reinforced by ecological knowledge. Then again, if an extensive knowledge base exists, and actors agree about how the status of the ecological system should be described while they disagree on the goals and overall directions for management, a process of "superfluous knowledge" occurs. This type of network essentially lacks the ability to act on the knowledge input. Finally, a network that is struggling with different interpretations regarding the reliability of ecological data, the status of the ecosystem, and the fundamental problem of management is referred to as a process of "ambiguity." This type of network is likely to suffer from a paralyzed decision-making process. The above-mentioned concepts describe different results of joint image building. The proposition of this chapter is that these four scenarios relate to different types of network structures.

Both bridging and closure can be related to these aspects of joint image building in fishery management. Previous research has implied that network closure is positively related with adaptability since collective action and the processes of rule-making and rule-enforcing are enhanced within internally well-connected structures (Sandström and Carlsson, 2008; Sandström and Rova, 2010a, b). In this study, we assume that closure enhances the formulation of a common view regarding the ecosystem and problem of management. However, networks that are merely internally well integrated might obstruct adaptability in the long run since closure fosters convergence in values and perspectives, at least in the long run (Bodin *et al.*, 2006). Network closure might in fact obstruct innovativeness and openness to change, resulting in a process of "negotiated nonsense." Adaptive management requires that rules are made, and constantly revised, based on inflow of new ecological knowledge. The function of resource mobilization, within the supply of ecological knowledge, has previously been related to the presence of bridges and cross-spanning ties (Carlsson and Sandström, 2008). Therefore, bridging ties are considered as a necessity for adaptability. Accordingly, the hypothesis of this chapter is that adaptive management, and processes of negotiated knowledge, are enhanced by networks with high levels of closure and bridging, respectively. Before the relevance of this hypothesis can be empirically explored the network concepts must be translated into a set of social network measures.

12.3.4 Making the concepts measurable

12.3.4.1 Network closure

Network closure refers to structures that are either directly or indirectly well integrated. This feature is here captured by two social network measures, namely density and centralization. Density reflects the level of general activity in a network and is calculated by dividing the number of connections present with the maximum number of possible connections (Scott, 2000). Graph A in Figure 12.1 illustrates a so-called complete graph with the highest density level possible.

Integration and connectivity might also be sustained through the existence of indirect ties, here measured by the concept of network centralization. In a centralized network, the networking activity is mainly coordinated by one central individual. Thus, centralization also reflects differences in connectivity. It is calculated through several steps. First, the centrality of each individual actor is measured. Thereafter, the centrality values are compared and the variations among these are summarized. Finally, this sum is divided with an imaginary value, reflecting the highest variation that is theoretically possible (Wasserman and Faust, 1994; Scott, 2000). Three different notions of centrality exist, from which the concepts of degree centrality and betweenness centrality are applied here (Freeman, 1978/79; Freeman *et al.*, 1979/80; Bonacich, 1987; Friedkin, 1991; Wasserman and Faust, 1994). While the former rests upon the idea that the most central individual is the one with most connections, the latter determine centrality in accordance to how many times an actor is situated "in-between" two other actors. Graph B in Figure 12.1 exemplifies a structure with the highest centralization value possible, disregarding what notion of centrality is applied.

Generally speaking, higher levels of density and centralization indicate the presence of network closure and bonding ties. Still, at least two other network features, namely size and subgroup structure, affect

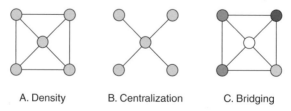

A. Density   B. Centralization   C. Bridging

Figure 12.1 Different network structures.

to what extent density really reflects integration. First, previous studies have shown that when comparing networks of different sizes, similar levels of density reflect different levels of cohesion (Friedkin, 1991; Moody and White, 2003). A small network needs a higher density value than a large one to reflect the same level of cohesion (Friedkin, 1981). Second, a fragmented network composed of several tightly knitted subgroups might have a high density level because of the intense activity going on within each subgroup. At the same time, this kind of structure should not be described as being well integrated. Thus, the comparative validity of the density measure is limited. In this study, both size and the possible existence of subgroups are therefore taken into account when interpreting the level of network closure in the analytic section below.

The interpretation of network centralization might also involve certain problematic concerns. One particular example that is of relevance for this study is when different centralization measures point towards divergent conclusions. In those situations, it is of vital importance to go back to the theoretical framework and to reflect upon the essential ideas behind the theoretical concepts. In this case, this reflexive process generated the standpoint to treat degree centralization as the main indicator of network closure. Previous work on the theoretical power of the centralization measures has shown that the betweenness centralization measure is very responsive to and affected by the presence of long paths of indirect communication (Freeman, 1978/79; Freeman et al., 1979/80). This type of social structure is not compatible with the adopted idea of network closure. Accordingly, in situations when degree centralization is low and betweenness centralization is high the level of closure should be regarded as low.

12.3.4.2 *Heterogeneity as a proxy for bridging*

While network closure describes the internal structure of the fishery management networks, the idea of bridging over structural holes refers to how the networks connect to other networks. In this chapter, the concept of heterogeneity, which refers to networks composed of a rich diversity of different types involved in extensive cross-boundary collaboration, is used as a proxy variable for bridging ties (cf. Reagans and Zuckerman, 2001; Carlsson and Sandström, 2008). This is done since the analytical unit of analysis, i.e. the management networks, consists of stronger connections (otherwise their affect on behavior and outcome cannot be assumed) while bridging ties are essentially weaker connections (Granovetter, 1973; Friedkin, 1980) and, therefore, not captured here. Instead it is assumed that fishery management networks composed of a rich diversity of actors, representing various organizations and sectors of society (i.e. heterogeneous networks) also include many bridging ties, even though these are not explicitly measured. Just like network closure, heterogeneity is a compound measure, with the difference that heterogeneity is captured by one structural measure (cross-boundary exchange) and one attribute measure (actors' diversity). The latter is measured simply by counting how many different organizations are represented in the network. The former, the extent (percentage) of cross-boundary ties (i.e. ties connecting actors with different organizational belongings), is measured by dividing the number of cross-boundary ties with the total number of ties in the social structure. Network C in Figure 12.1 illustrates a graph composed by actors from four different types of organizations (indicated by the different shades of grey) with extensive cross-boundary collaboration. The underlying assumption is that networks of this kind possess bridges to a wide range of different network constellations.

Thus, the guiding hypothesis for the forthcoming analysis can be further specified implying that adaptive networks – in which processes of joint image building and negotiated knowledge occur – are heterogeneous structures with high density and network centralization levels.

12.4   THE COLLECTION OF EMPIRICAL DATA

The adopted network approach has implications for how to empirically define the analytical unit and how to set the network boundaries. This critical undertaking was carried out in several steps. First, an interview study was conducted. A wide range of questions was asked, covering individual attributes of the actors such as age, position in management, organization memberships, but also actors' views concerning ecological knowledge, the state of the ecosystems, the goals and direction of the FCA, and current management rules. The actors were asked questions that altogether describe the work within the FCAs; for example, the processes of knowledge generation, the setting and enforcing of rules, and the customary routines for mitigating and resolving conflicts. These questions provided qualitative information about the management process, adaptability, and joint image building. The respondents were also asked to name other actors involved in the collective activities, thereby nominating new interviewees for the study. The interviews started with the chairmen of the FCAs and with the use of the

snowballing interview technique (Miles and Huberman, 1994) the interviewing continued until no new actor of any central importance was
named. Thus, the very criterion of being an actor stipulates that unconnected individuals are of no interest here, i.e. a whole network data set
was collected. This means that the critique towards snowballing, that
isolated actors or whole subgroups of actors might be excluded from the
analysis (Hanneman and Riddle, 2005) is of no relevance here. The
method is however rather time consuming and also extremely dependent upon the qualities of the interviews. The semi-structured character
of the interviews is open to interpretation and the interviewer might
affect the interviewee in a number of ways, affecting the reliability of the
empirical data negatively. Disregarding these shortcomings, it is the
most appropriate method to ensure that the empirical unit of analysis
reflects the social phenomena that the study aims to capture.

Second, for the purpose of mapping the patterns of interactions
among those involved, a survey was sent out to the individuals who had
been identified through the interview study. The survey asked two
questions aimed at capturing two different types of social relations
communication concerning (i) the rule-forming process and (ii) the
generation of ecological knowledge. In this chapter, though, only the
rule-forming network, reflecting the governing networks of the fishery
areas, are analyzed. The research field shows immense variety in how
sociometric questions are phrased. In this case, the respondents were
given a list of names (generated from the interview study) and asked to
mark the persons that they "*usually* talk to about the *goals*, *rules*, and
routines of the fishery management area." The respondents were also
given the opportunity to add new names to the list. According to the
theoretical framework, the fishery management networks are governance networks, affecting the behavior of individuals, the interplay
among actors, and the outcome in terms of joint image building and
adaptability, which presuppose a certain structural stability. The words
"usually," "goals," "rules," and "routines" were applied based on the
reliance that these terms could capture these rule-forming governance
structures. And based on the same reason – to ensure that the data really
reflect the social phenomena of governance – only the symmetric ties,
reflecting reciprocated and stronger ties, were included in the analysis.

Working with stronger ties only also strengthens the validity of
data. Sociometric data that are referring to the more stable connections
have a higher reliability than data attempting to capture more shallow
or temporal contacts since the accuracy of the information given by the
respondents is higher (Freeman *et al.*, 1987; Marsden, 1990; Wasserman

and Faust, 1994). People might have trouble to recall temporarily
acquaintances or whom they met or talked to last week while they
tend to report more correctly on what they normally do. Previous
research has shown that by asking questions about more stable interactions, covering shorter time frames, and by specifying the questions,
the reliability and validity of social network data can be improved (Bell
et al., 2007). This knowledge supported the approach adopted in this
case study.

The report accuracy is a troublesome question that affects the
validity of the study since analyses made on complete networks
evidently are extremely vulnerable for missing data (Wasserman
and Faust, 1994; Scott, 2000). The studies presented in this chapter
all received response rates of around 90%, which is considered as
satisfactory for the forthcoming analysis. The high response rate
might partly be explained by the fact that many actors, when receiving the questionnaires, already had been introduced to the study as
respondents in the interview study. Finally, the social network analysis was performed using UCINET6 and Netdraw (Borgatti, 2002;
Borgatti et al., 2002).

12.5 ANALYZING SOCIAL NETWORKS, ADAPTABILITY, AND JOINT IMAGE BUILDING IN FISHERY MANAGEMENT

The concept of adaptive governance is easily comprehended on an
abstract level but much more difficult to grasp and measure in real
empirical settings. Basically, adaptability requires an input of scientific
knowledge into the management process, an active decision-making
process based on prevailing ecological knowledge, and finally, a high
level of rule-compliance among users. Based on this notion, the level of
adaptability in the fishery management is determined by examining
four aspects of the management processes. Is there an input of scientific
knowledge? Are rules changed and revised on a regular basis? Are these
rules based on current ecological knowledge? And, finally, are rules
accepted and followed among users? Table 12.1 presents the empirical
findings concerning the adaptive capacities of the studied management
networks, from now on referred to here as Network A and Network B.
It is important to note that these conclusions are based on interpretations of the qualitative data generated through the interviews.

According to Table 12.1, there are both similarities and differences among the management processes. Both networks do have an

Table 12.1. *The management processes and their outcomes.*

Outcomes in terms of adaptability	Network A	Network B
Input of scientific knowledge	Yes	Yes
Rules are continuously changed	Yes	Yes
Rules are based on existing ecological knowledge	Yes	Yes
Level of rule-compliance	Low	High
Adaptive management	**No**	**Yes**

input of scientific knowledge. This comes from the fact that both FCAs have previous experience of working with scientific projects, performing systematic observations and experiments together with researchers in their areas. This ecological knowledge has affected the formulation of new rules and both areas claim that rules are continuously revised as new ecological knowledge is presented. However, the networks diverge in how these rules are received and implemented. Network A complies with the first three conditions of adaptability (see Table 12.1). In this network rules are contested and the area suffers from a comparatively lower rule-compliance. Network B, on the other hand, fulfills all four criteria of an adaptive process, as the concept is defined as measured here. Accordingly, the two management networks diverge in regard to adaptability.

The divergence in adaptability, notable in the aspect of rule-compliance, can be explained and further scrutinized by addressing the process of joint image building within these networks. Natural resource governance was described in the theoretical section of this chapter as the outcome of a process in which different stakeholders meet, discuss, and form a common view regarding the state of the ecological system and appropriate rules. Thus, the establishment of a joint image regarding the status of the ecological system, problems, and solutions (often translated into the goals of the area) is tentatively of particular importance for the outcome of this process, and, as such, a necessary prerequisite for adaptive governance. Accordingly, the deficit in rule-compliance in Network A could possible be related to the absence of a joint image in regard to these important issues. The assumption is that if people do not agree about the state of the ecological system, what problem management should be devoted to and how, the acceptance of rules and willingness to follow them will decrease significantly. The studied

Table 12.2. *The processes of joint image building in management.*

Aspects of joint image building	Network A	Network B
Joint view regarding problem and solutions	No	Yes
Joint view regarding the ecological system based on agreed and valid science	No	Yes
Characterizing the networking process	**Ambiguity**	**Negotiated knowledge**

fishery management networks are compared according to this aspect in Table 12.2.

All management networks have access to scientific knowledge. However, the processes diverge considerably when analyzing how this knowledge is comprehended and processed among the involved actors. To start with, both the quality and usefulness of scientific data are challenged and considerably distrusted among certain groups of actors in Network A. There are competing views regarding the status of the ecological system and fish stocks in this network. This situation is a complicating factor that is likely to affect the chances of finding a common problem and to reach consensus about priorities, rules, and routines. Then again, it might also be the other way around, that divergence in how the focal problem of management is described affect how the ecological data are comprehended. To exemplify, in Network A, the attitudes towards scientific knowledge coincide with how the overall goal for the FCA is formulated. In this network, controversies exist with regard to the aim and future direction of the area. While one group puts emphasis on tourism and sport fishing, and suggests rules to promote these interests, the other group is more focused on the interests of local users. Two groups with opposite interests exist and it is mostly within the group of actors advocating local, non-commercial interests that the skepticism towards science is expressed. The causality between the two factors cannot be determined here, instead a mutual interplay between the variables in Table 12.2 is assumed. It is clear from the analysis that the process in Network A is obstructed by the existence of divergent and competing views.

The lack of belief in the ecological knowledge base that is so clearly manifested in Network A is absent in Network B. Furthermore, the actors in Network B express a united view concerning the overall goal and prevailing management rules. Within this area, there is general support behind the strategy to involve science, make use of science, and also to promote the growing tourism industry. Based on the concepts elaborated in the theoretical section, it can be concluded that while Network A has most resemblance with a process of "ambiguity," a process of "negotiated knowledge" has occurred in Network B. Thus, significant divergence in regards to joint image building are evident.

12.5.1   Social network analysis

The results from the social network analysis are presented in Table 12.3. Based on the logic of comparison, the terms low and high are used to categorize the networks with regard to closure and heterogeneity. Thus, the structural quality of one network is determined in relation to the other network. The FCAs are governed by networks of similar size (enhancing comparability) although with dissimilar structural qualities. Network A is regarded as a structure with relatively low levels of both closure and heterogeneity. Network B, then again, is interpreted as a closed network due to the higher density and centralization levels. Network B is also perceived as highly heterogeneous since it involves actors representing different types of sectors and organizations in extensive cross-boundary exchange. These structural differences are nicely illustrated by the graphs in Figure 12.2.

Figure 12.2 shows two networks involving approximately the same categories of actors in management (see the different shapes of

Table 12.3. *The structural qualities of the management networks.*

Structural features	Network A	Network B
Size (No.)	16	18
Density	0.19	0.20
Degree centralization (%)	31	70
Betweenness centralization (%)	44	55
Actors' diversity (No.)	6	7
Cross-boundary exchange (%)	39	71
Closure	**Low**	**High**
Bridging	**Low**	**High**

Network A   Network B

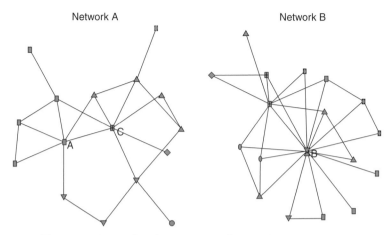

Figure 12.2 Comparing the structures of Network A and Network
B. Square: board of the FCA; downwards triangle: member of the FCA;
circle: neighboring FCA; upwards triangle: public administration; circle
in box: Sport Fishing Association; diamond: university; rounded square:
commercial organization; box: public administration and university;
central node marked B: chairman, board of FCA and commercial
organization.

the nodes). The high centralization in Network B can easily be detected.
The node that is marked with a B represents the chairman of FCA B and
moreover an entrepreneur engaged in commercial activities. This person is in structural terms obviously very important for the turnout of the
common undertakings. This notion is further verified by the qualitative
interviews and it is clear that the chairman works very consciously to
coordinate action, to inform, and to get informed about different opinions, to identify disputes and to solve disagreements, even before these
emerge. This style of coordinating the internal process is reflected in the
network structure and, without anticipating the forthcoming analysis,
constitutes one likely explanation to the features of management. As a
contrast, the chairman of FCA A, represented by the node marked with
an A, has a structurally very different position. In Network A, a representative from the public and academic sector (Actor C) is the most central
actor in the network. This information might denote a situation of
unclear leadership. In this discussion about centralization, the reasons behind and possible implications for management, the interplay
between structure and agency becomes especially evident (cf. Bodin
and Crona, 2008). The conclusion is that the networks diverge

significantly in regard to network closure; they are not equally well connected, foremost reflected through remarkable differences in centralization.

The structural differences concerning the aspect of bridging also become evident in Figure 12.2. The process of extensive cross-boundary exchange in Network B can be contrasted to the process of more intragroup communication in Network A. Figure 12.2 illustrates the fact that while 33% of the ties in Network A span organizational boundaries, the same measure in Network B is significantly higher, more specifically 71%. Thus, the management networks are structural opposites also when regarding the concept of bridges. Next, the connection between these structural properties, adaptability, and joint image building is discussed.

12.6   THEORETICAL FINDINGS AND METHODOLOGICAL CONSIDERATIONS

This far, the structure and performance of the two fishery management networks have been analyzed and compared, making it possible to explore the relation between the two variables. For this purpose, the results from the empirical analysis are brought together in Figure 12.3. Different results of the joint image-building processes (Koppenjan and Klijn, 2004) are combined with different network qualities. The level of network closure is specified on the x-axis and the level of bridging on the y-axis. The performances of networking (in terms of ambiguity,

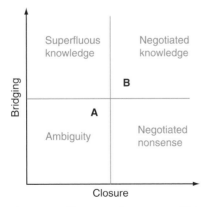

Figure 12.3 The network structure of joint image building.

superfluous knowledge, negotiated knowledge, and negotiated non-sense) are specified in each square. The letters A and B represent the two management networks that are situated in accordance with their structural properties. Network B has a comparatively higher level of closure and heterogeneity than Network A and is therefore situated in the upper right square of the figure.

Figure 12.3 demonstrates an empirical relationship between network structure and joint image building that concurs with the theoretical hypotheses. Both bridging and closure are seemingly required to sustain a process of negotiated knowledge and, accordingly, to increase the prospects of achieving adaptive management. The high level of closure within Network B is one likely explanation of the successful joint image process, in the spirit of negotiated knowledge, and a high rule-compliance within this area. Thus, management networks structured like Network B are most likely to successfully handle the problematic challenges pertinent to substantial uncertainties of natural resource governance. The structure of Network A is more associated with uncertainty and ambiguity, with regards to ecological knowledge comprehension and problem formulation. There are no conditions for adaptability.

According to theory, sparsely and uncoordinated networks, i.e. networks with very low closure situated to the very left side of Figure 12.3 are likely to struggle with ineffective, or even paralyzed, rule-forming processes, lacking any ground for collective action (cf. Sandström and Rova, 2010). Rules are rarely changed within these types of structures. In networks with very low closure, an inflow of ecological knowledge will not contribute to an improved adaptability since the governance process has no common agenda stipulating what to do and why. Instead of generating a process of "negotiated knowledge," the knowledge input might merely end up being "superfluous knowledge" as actors disagree about what to make of it. Or perhaps more likely, the low level of closure will have the effect that scientific information is interpreted differently by different actors, resulting in a situation of overall "ambiguity." The conclusion proposed in this chapter is that network closure is positively correlated with the formulation of a joint view regarding problem and solutions. Bridging ties, for example encompassing contacts with the scientific community, are however considered as essential to counteract the risk of turning "negotiated knowledge" into "negotiated nonsense." Thus, the conclusion is that the desirable state of negotiated knowledge is correlated with both closure and bridging.

A number of objections can be raised towards the analysis presented in this chapter. The most evident problem, commonly noted in social science research in general, concerns the topic of causality. Structure, organizing, and performance are variables likely to affect one another in an ongoing process of governance. Consequently, the main conclusion presented in this chapter is restricted in the sense that it merely states that the variables correlate in a way that concurs with theory. Longitudinal studies that investigate structure and performance over time are needed to disentangle the complicated issue of causality. Another problem with the adopted research design is that the sole focus on one variable, i.e. network structure neglects other, hidden variables that might have the potential to explain success and failure in joint image building. To avoid the possible impact from socio-economic variables in this study two networks embedded in similar contexts were analyzed. However, the issue can be more properly handled by applying a research design that allows for rival hypotheses testing.

Besides the theoretically oriented aim of this chapter, the purpose has also been to highlight some methodological implications of a social network approach in the study of natural resource governance. Every research process involves difficult choices and studies applying social network analysis are of course no exception. Some validity and reliability aspects of network research arise as the methodological considerations and choices made in the fishery management studies are reflected upon. The central message is that quantitative social network analysis is particularly suitable for the task of studying the social structures of these management systems. The particular advantage comes from the fact that structural data and attribute data can be analyzed comprehensively; generating more information about the management processes than if the variables were analyzed separately. The outputs of social network analysis, particularly the visual graphs, are also valuable pedagogical tools, not only for research, but also in communication with concerned stakeholders. However, as exemplified by the research process described in this chapter, an assortment of difficult choices have to be made in relation to the procedures of collecting, analyzing, and interpreting social network data. The particular advantage of a formal network approach – the quantification of social relations – also imposes difficulties since complex and essentially qualitative aspects of human interactions are reduced into quantitative measures. The point proposed here is that these inevitable choices must be made based on a solid theoretical framework stipulating through what lens the empirical world is understood. The first and foremost important issue to work out concerns what kind of social phenomena should be studied. For example, is the study about governance networks, possessing institutionalization characteristics, or networks that should be perceived as mere aggregations of individual actors? In this study, the ambition to capture governance networks has influenced the research design. It affected how the network boundaries were determined, how the questionnaire was designed, and on what level of tie-strength the analyses were performed. Still, even though general guidance is to be found in theory, no manual for how these research design issues should be handled exists.

The lack of general standards, for what social network measures to use and how to interpret these, and the rich diversity in how these issues have been solved by researchers, affect both the validity and comparability of network studies negatively. For example, there are various ways to address and define the concepts of adaptability, closure, and bridging both theoretically and empirically. And while the choice of empirical measures directly affects the results and the validity of conclusions, these choices are far from given. It is important to keep this in mind when scrutinizing the conclusions made in this study, or on any other study struggling with these essentially multifarious concepts.

The formulation of the survey questions constitutes another critical step in the validity of methods. Depending upon how the question is framed, different network structures will emerge. In the stage of designing the study, the researcher also needs to reflect on how to assure a high response rate since there are certain trade-offs between rich data and reliable data that ought to be considered. For example, studies covering multiple relations might have great potential to generate interesting theoretical insights. At the same time questionnaires containing many and complex questions might result in fewer responses and thereby jeopardize the validity of data.

Another troublesome aspect of working with social network measures is that the measures are interrelated, affecting one another, and are therefore likely to have a combined affect on performance. This makes the analysis significantly much more complicated since a multiple set of various network measures must be considered simultaneously when drawing conclusions on the overall network properties. It also becomes increasingly difficult to present any standard, or cut-off values, for how to interpret social network measures. These validity and reliability problems are demonstrated when drawing inferences based on density values. However, many other social network concepts suffer from this "traveling problem" (Denk, 2002) that occurs when the same empirical measure means different things in different settings.

The examples above illustrate the kind of ambiguity that is associated with the use of social network data. They also serve to illustrate the importance of combining the quantitative analysis with a robust qualitative analysis to ensure the construct validity of the research.

12.7   REMARKS ON A FUTURE RESEARCH AGENDA

Despite all the limitations and potential pitfalls of a social network approach, it is clear that research focused on natural resource governance has a lot to gain from social network analysis application. The case studies presented in this chapter have served to illustrate how a network perspective can be applied, what kind of theoretical insights can be generated, and what methodological questions occur throughout the research process. The approach is evidently useful; however, in order to reach its full potential within the area much more empirical work is needed. The research field is not in need of more abstract propositions deduced from theory. Instead the most promising way forward is via more empirical research. Particularly important contributions can be made if research is designed as longitudinal multiple-case studies aimed at investigating the relevance of rival hypotheses.

Given that networks, often referred to as constellations of co-management, receive increasing attention from policy makers, this area of research is believed to have the capacity to generate important policy implications for the future. While the idea of networks as central entities for societal problem-solving has emerged, the question of how to promote the establishment and function of these structures has become absolutely crucial. What types of co-management structures are successful and in what way can the government, the state, and its agencies on various levels of administration, influence the evolvement of these? This question leads us to one particular important topic that has not been discussed in this chapter; the governance of these governing networks. The term "meta-governance"

(Sorensen and Torfing, 2007) has been used to describe how formal government structures exercise control over these networks. At other times the term "network management" is used to describe the same phenomenon (Kickert *et al.*, 1997; Bogason and Toonen, 1998; O'Toole Jr. and Meier, 1999, 2004; Koppenjan and Klijn, 2004; Klijn *et al.*, 2007). The essential difference separating these new forms of public management from traditional public management is the focus on horizontal steering and the ambition to improve inter-organizational decision making and coordination among key actors; for example by managing the content (the initial agenda for management) and the rules of the game (the participating actors and the division of authority). While traditional management attempts to reduce uncertainty, a network approach to public management is more focused on handling uncertainty. Also this area of research would benefit significantly from more empirical studies. There is a need for research addressing the new role of the state, investigating how public actors can set the conditions for successful co-management. For example, what kind of formal institutions enhance collaboration and joint image building within co-management networks?

A final aspect that needs to be addressed concerns the scale of research. In this chapter, a research design adjusted to the study of small local management systems has been presented. However, what kind of methodological challenges would be manifested in attempts to understand network structure and performance within larger and more widely spanning multi-level policy networks? With regard to fishery policy or policy concerning a cross-scale issue like biological diversity, for example, could the basic ideas of the social network approach suggested in this chapter be applied in the study of these types of policy structures, and if so, in what way? No answers to these questions have been elaborated within the framework of this chapter; still it is important to put the questions on the future research agenda since these types of policy processes would be interesting subjects to study applying the theories and tools of social network analysis.

Finally, the social network approach adds new and interesting perspectives to the study of natural resource governance in particular and to policy making in general. Hopefully, the discussion held in this chapter will serve to inspire managers and policy makers to think in network terms and researchers to consider a future research agenda working with these issues.

Reflections

Deciding the unit of analysis

The aim of the study was to address how the structure of governance networks affects their function and performance. This means that the governance network constitutes the main analytical unit. The research question was formulated based on the current state of knowledge in policy network research. While networks are ascribed greater importance in public policy making, systematic knowledge about these structures is still lacking. This, coupled with the great possibilities provided by social network analysis, justified the choice to explore the relation between networks and performance.

The individuals, representing various types of organizations, are embedded units in the main analytical unit. Even though the structural characteristics of some individual actors are discussed and the organization memberships of individual actors are regarded, this information is predominantly used to make inferences regarding the network as a whole. The choice to consider the network as the relevant unit of analysis was briefly motivated by the theoretical section in this chapter. The general proposition is that not only the actors and their attributes influence performance but also their patterns of interactions – i.e. the network structure. The bottom line is that networks – as the ones studied here – constitute something more then simply aggregations of individuals and therefore ought to be treated seriously. Thus, the network structure affects actors' behavior, their interactions and, accordingly, the ability to craft rules and the content of rules.

Looking back, it would have been very useful if I had collected data on other variables as well, for example the historical and cultural contexts of the FCAs and more attribute data. This would have made it possible to test rival hypotheses and to determine the explanatory power of network structures in relation to other explanatory variables.

Defining network boundaries

In accordance with a methodological bottom–up approach (that disregards formal organizational boundaries and formal authority when structures of policy making are defined), the network boundaries were empirically determined in a process of several stages. First, the actors were identified through a snowballing interview technique. Second, the relations among these actors were determined through questionnaires. This approach is not unproblematic, not the least since it leaves the issue of determining who is involved and who is not to the judgment of the respondents. The question asked in order to capture relations might be interpreted differently and some people might be more prone to nominate other actors, or even leave out certain actors. Still, given the theoretical notion about the studied fishery management networks, and the adopted bottom–up approach, it is difficult to think of a method more suited for the assignment.

The fishery management networks are considered structures of governance forming the rules of the game. Since a certain extent of stability and regularity is required for processes of institutionalization to occur, only actors with stronger (empirically captured by regularity and reciprocity) connections to other actors involved in the rule-forming process were included. Weaker, or shallower, contacts cannot be assumed to have an effect on governance. I would like to emphasize the standpoint that not all networks can be treated as governance networks.

Data-gathering issues

It was very difficult to decide on how to formulate the questionnaire so that it would capture the rule-forming processes, i.e. the stronger and repetitive communication ties in regards to management. I long considered how to quantify the question. For example, should a tie reflect communication on a weekly or monthly basis? Finally, I chose to leave this interpretation to the respondents and asked for their *usual* communication patterns. If I would repeat the study I would perhaps reformulate the question to more directly relate to resource exchange. For example, by asking the respondents to name the individuals with whom they share important resources, knowledge, finances, etc. in relation to fishery management.

Two different network relations were mapped in the studies presented in this chapter, i.e. the rule-forming network and the knowledge network (only the first one was analyzed here). It would indeed have been interesting to collect data on other relations as well. To further refine the social network analysis, by describing the structures of different functions in governance; for example the processes of problem definition, resource mobilization, and prioritization. However, the advantages of gaining access to this type of information must be carefully considered knowing that complicated questionnaires severely decrease response rates. This risk should not be neglected since social network analysis is very sensitive to missing data.

Ethical issues

Social network analysis has ethical implications. These are, however, less delicate when analyzing data on the network level. When working with complete network analysis, the behavior and performance of individual actors are not particularly important for the analysis and it is usually possible to conceal their identity. My experience is that by thoroughly explaining how the data will be presented and perhaps showing some examples of network graphs, the respondents will feel comfortable in participating in the study.

In the case studies presented here, names were listed in the questionnaires. I have reflected upon the ethical aspects of this practice. So far, no respondent has raised any objections in regards to this matter. This potential problem is probably more pressing in studies of networks within negative contexts or in the study of politically sensitive processes.

Explanatory power of social network analysis

The SNA approach encompasses a network perspective and the analytical tools for mapping and analyzing network structures. In order to search for explanations though, this approach must be combined with theory specifying why and in what respects network structure assumingly affects performance. In this chapter, the relevance of network structure is motivated by drawing upon ideas from policy network theory, institutional theory, and social capital theory. According to the findings presented here, network structure correlates with performance in a way that concurs with theory. Still, social processes are complex and it is unclear how network structure relates to other variables and how these many variables interact over time. Put differently, the issue about causality and hidden variables are complicating facts that should not be ignored. One way of disentangling these important issues in the future is to study management networks over a longer period of time, using different theories and formulating and testing rival hypotheses.

Other data than social network analysis

In order to build explanations, it is absolutely necessary to collect qualitative data describing the organizing processes that take place within the fishery management networks. My opinion is that it is the combination of quantitative and qualitative data that actually makes the approach so useful.

Is social network analysis static?

One limitation of the empirical analysis is that it merely provides a snapshot of the networks. I therefore agree with the critique that social network studies more often than not fail to generate more than static illustrations. Once again, the collection of longitudinal data should be encouraged since software to handle network dynamics exists.

ACKNOWLEDGMENTS

This chapter has been written in connection to the research programs *Adaptive management of fish and wildlife*, financed by the Swedish Environment Protection Agency, and *BaltGene*, founded by the Baltic Organizations Network for funding Science EEIG, BONUS, and the Swedish Research Council for Environment, Agricultural Sciences and Spatial Planning, FORMAS. I am most thankful to the founding organizations and to colleagues in the above-mentioned programs. A special thanks to Carl Rova, Luleå University of Technology, for collaboration in the empirical case studies presented herein.

REFERENCES

Bell, D. C., B. Belli-McQueen and A. Haider (2007). Partner naming and forgetting: recall of network members. *Social Networks*, **29**, 279–299.

Berkes, F. (2002). Cross-scale institutional linkages: perspective from the bottom up. In E. Ostrom, T. Dietz and N. Dolšak (Eds.), *The Drama of the Commons*. Washington, DC: National Academy Press, pp. 293–321.

Berkes, F. (2008). Commons in a multi-level world. *International Journal of the Commons*, **2**(1), 1–6 (online).

Bodin, Ö. and B. Crona (2008). Community-based management of natural resources: exploring the role of social capital and leadership in a rural fishing community. *World Development*, **36**, 2763–2779.

Bodin, Ö. and B. Crona (2009). The role of social networks in natural resource governance: what relational patterns make a difference? *Global Environmental Change*, **19**(3), 366–374.

Bodin, Ö., B. Crona and H. Ernstson (2006). Social networks in natural resource management: what is there to learn from a structural perspective? *Ecology and Society*, **11**(2), r2 (online).

Bogason, P. and T. A. J. Toonen (1998). Introduction: networks in public administration. *Public Administration*, **76**, 205–227.

Bonacich, P. (1987). Power and centrality: a family of measures. *American Journal of Sociology*, **92**(5), 1170–1182.

Borgatti, S. P. (2002). *Netdraw*. Included in *UCINET 6 for Windows: Software for Social Network Analysis*. Harvard, MA: Analytic Technologies.

Borgatti, S. P., M. G. Everett and L. C. Freeman (2002). *UCINET 6 for Windows: Software for Social Network Analysis*. Harvard, MA: Analytic Technologies.

Borgatti, S. P. and P. C. Foster (2003). The network paradigm in organizational research: a review and typology. *Journal of Management*, **29**(6), 991–1013.

Bourdieu, P. (1986). The forms of social capital. In J. G. Richardson (Ed.), *Handbook of Theory and Research for the Sociology of Education*. Westport, CT: Greenwood Press, pp. 241–258.

Burt, R. S. (1997). The contingent value of social capital. *Administrative Science Quarterly*, **42**, 339–365.

Burt, R. S. (2000). The network structure of social capital. In B. M. Straw and R. I. Sutton (Eds.), *Research in Organizational Behaviour*, 22. Greenwich, CT: JAI Press, pp. 345–423.

Burt, R. S. (2001). Structural holes versus network closure as social capital. In N. Lin, K. Cook and R. S. Burt (Eds.), *Social Capital. Theory and Research*. New York, NY: Walter de Gruyter, pp. 31–56.

Carlsson, L. (1996). Nonhierarchical implementation analysis. An alternative to the methodological mismatch in policy analysis. *Journal of Theoretical Politics*, **8**(4), 527–546.

Carlsson, L. (2000). Policy networks as collective action. *Policy Studies Journal*, **28**(3), 502–520.

Carlsson, L. and F. Berkes (2005). Co-management: concepts and methodological implications. *Journal of Environmental Management*, **75**, 65–76.

Carlsson, L. and K. Danell (2006). Förvaltning i standing förändring. Vilt och Fisk. Aktuell forskning om vilt, fisk och förvaltning. Nr. 1/2006.

Carlsson, L. and A. Sandström (2008). Network governance of the commons. *International Journal of the Commons*, **2**(1), 33–54 (online).

Coleman, J. S. (1987). Norms as social capital. In G. Radnitsky and P. Bernholz (Eds.), *Economic Imperialism: The Economic Approach Applied Outside the Field of Economics*. New York, NY: Paragon House Publishers, pp. 133–155.

Coleman, J. S. (1990). *Foundations of Social Theory*. Cambridge, MA: Harvard University Press.

Denk, T. (2002). *Komparativ metod: förståelse genom jämförelse* (The comparative approach: understanding through comparison). Lund: Studentlitteratur.

Dietz, T., E. Ostrom and P. C. Stern (2003). The struggle to govern the commons. *Science*, **302**, 1907–1912.

Dyhre, G. and L. Edlund (1982). *Fiskevårdsområden: Bildande och Förvaltning.* (Fish management areas: formation and administration). Stockholm: Norstedt.

Elmore, R. E. (1993). Organisational models of social program implementation. In M. Hill (Ed.), *The Policy Process. A Reader.* London: Harvester Wheatsheaf, pp. 313–348.

Folke, C., S. Carpenter, T. Elmqvist *et al.* (2002). Resilience and sustainable development: building adaptive capacity in a world of transformations. *AMBIO: A Journal of the Human Environment*, **31**(5), 437–440.

Folke, C., J. Colding and F. Berkes (2003). Synthesis: building resilience and adaptive capacity in social-ecological systems. In F. Berkes, C. Folke and J. Colding (Eds.), *Navigating Social-Ecological Systems: Building Resilience for Complexity and Change.* Cambridge: Cambridge University Press, pp. 352–387.

Freeman, L. C. (1978/79). Centrality in social networks. Conceptual clarification. *Social Networks*, **1**, 215–239.

Freeman, L. C., D. Roeder and R. R. Mulholland (1979/80). Centrality in social networks: II. Experimental results. *Social Networks*, **2**, 119–141.

Freeman, L. C., A. K. Romney and S. C. Freeman (1987). Cognitive structure and informant accuracy. *American Anthropologist*, **89**(2), 310–325.

Friedkin, N. E. (1980). A test of structural features of Granovetter's strengths of weak ties theory. *Social Networks*, **2**, 411–422.

Friedkin, N. E. (1981). The development of structure in random networks: an analysis of the effects of increasing network density on five measures of structure. *Social Networks*, **3**, 41–52.

Friedkin, N. E. (1991). Theoretical foundations for centrality measures. *American Journal of Sociology*, **96**(6), 1478–1504.

Giddens, A. (1984). *The Constitution of Society.* Cambridge, MA: Polity Press.

Granovetter, M. S. (1973). The strength of weak ties. *American Journal of Sociology*, **78**, 1360–1380.

Granovetter, M. S. (1992). Economic institutions as social constructions: a framework of analysis. *Acta Sociologica*, **35**, 3–11.

Hanneman, R. A. and M. Riddle (2005). *Introduction to Social Network Methods.* Riverside, CA: University of California.

Hardin, G. (1968). The tragedy of the commons. *Science*, **162**, 1243–1248.

Hjern, B. (1987). Policy analysis: an implementation approach. Paper presented at the Annual Meeting of the American Policy Science Association, September 3–6, Chicago.

Hjern, B. and D. O. Porter (1993). Implementation structures. A new unit of administrative analysis. In M. Hill (Ed.), *The Policy Process. A Reader.* London: Harvester Wheatsheaf, pp. 248–265.

Holling, C. S. (Ed.) (1978). *Adaptive Environmental Assessment and Management.* London: John Wiley & Sons.

Hoppe, R. (1999). Policy analysis, science and politics: from 'speaking truth to power' to 'making sense together'. *Science and Public Policy*, **26**(3), 201–210.

Hull, C. J. and B. Hjern (1987). *Helping Small Firms Grow. An Implementation Approach.* Worcester: Billing & Sons.

Kadushin, C. (2004). Review: too much investment in social capital? *Social Networks*, **26**, 75–90.

Kickert, W. J. M., E.-H. Klijn and J. F. M. Koppenjan (Eds.) (1997). *Managing Complex Networks: Strategies for the Public Sector.* London: Sage.

Klijn, E.-H., J. Koppenjan and K. Termeer (2007). Managing networks in the public sector: a theoretical study of management strategies in policy networks. *Public Administration*, **73**(3), 437–454.

Knoke, D. (1990). *Political Networks. The Structural Perspective.* Cambridge: Cambridge University Press.

Koppenjan, J. F. M. and E.-H. Klijn (2004). *Managing Uncertainties in Networks.* London: Routledge.

Kwon, H. (2004). Associations, civic norms and democracy: revisiting the Italian case. *Theory and Society,* **33**(2), 135–166.

Lin, N. (2001). *Social Capital. A Theory of Social Structure and Action.* Cambridge: Cambridge University Press.

Lin, N., K. Cook and R. S. Burt (Eds.) (2001). *Social Capital. Theory and Research.* New York, NY: Aldine.

Marsden, P. V. (1990). Network data and measurement. *Annual Review of Sociology,* **16**, 435–463.

Marsh, D. and M. Smith (2000). Understanding policy networks: towards a dialectical approach. *Political Studies,* **48**, 4–21.

Marsh, D. and M. Smith (2001). Debates: there is more than one way to do political science: on different ways to study policy networks. *Political Studies,* **49**, 528–541.

Miles, M. B. and A. M. Huberman (1994). *Qualitative Data Analysis – An Expanded Sourcebook,* 2nd Edition. Thousands Oaks, CA: Sage.

Moody, J. and D. R. White (2003). Structural cohesion and embeddedness: a hierarchical concept of social groups. *American Sociological Review,* **68**, 103–127.

Njaya, F. (2007). Governance challenges for the implementation of fisheries co-management: experiences from Malawi. *International Journal of the Commons,* **1**(1), 137–153 (online).

O'Toole Jr., L. and K. J. Meier (1999). Modelling the impact of public management: implications of structural context. *Journal of Public Administration Research and Theory,* **9**(4), 505–526.

O'Toole Jr., L. J. and K. J. Meier (2004). Public management in intergovernmental networks: matching structural networks and managerial networking. *Journal of Public Administration Research and Theory,* **14**(4), 469–494.

Olson, M. (1965). *The Logic of Collective Action: Public Goods and the Theory of Groups.* Cambridge, MA: Harvard University Press.

Olsson, P. and C. Folke (2001). Local ecological knowledge and institutional dynamics for ecosystem management: a study of Lake Racken Watershed, Sweden. *Ecosystems,* **4**(2), 85–104.

Olsson, P. C. Folke and T. Hahn (2004). Social-ecological transformation for ecosystem management: the development of adaptive co-management of a wetland landscape in southern Sweden. *Ecology and Society,* **9**(4), 2 (online).

Ostrom, E. (2005). *Understanding Institutional Diversity.* Princeton, NJ: Princeton University Press.

Ostrom, E. and T. K. Ahn (2003). *Foundations of Social Capital. Critical Studies in Economic Institutions.* Cheltenham: Edward Elgar.

Parsons, W. (1995). *Public Policy. An Introduction to the Theory and Practice of Policy Analysis.* Cheltenham: Edward Elgar.

Piriz, L. (2005). *Praktiskt samtal om samförvaltning av fiske (Conversations on fishery co-mangement).* Göteborg: Fiskeriverket (Swedish Board of Fisheries).

Plummer, R. (2009). The adaptive co-management process: and initial synthesis of representative models and influential variables. *Ecology and Society,* **14**(2) (online).

Portes, A. (1998). Social capital: its origins and applications in modern sociology. *Annual Review of Sociology,* **24**, 1–24.

Portes, A. and P. Landolt (2000). Social capital: promise and pitfalls of its role in development. *Journal of Latin American Studies*, **32**, 529–547.

Powell, W. W. (1990). Neither market nor hierarchy: network forms of organization. *Research in Organizational Behaviour*, **12**, 295–336.

Putnam, R. (1992). *Making Democracy Work: Civic Traditions in Modern Italy*. Princeton, NJ: Princeton University Press.

Putnam, R. (2000). *Bowling Alone: The Collapse and Revival of American Community*. New York, NY: Simon & Schuster.

Reagans, R. and E. W. Zuckerman (2001). Networks, diversity, and productivity: the social capital of corporate R&D teams. *Organization Science*, **12**(4), 502–517.

Rhodes, R. A. W. and D. Marsh (1992). New directions in the study of policy networks. *European Journal of Political Research*, **21**, 181–205.

Rothstein, B. (2003). *Sociala fällor och tillitens problem* (Social dilemmas and the problem of trust). Stockholm: SNS Förlag.

Rova, C. (2004). Flipping the pyramid. Lessons from converting top-down management of bleak-roe Fishing. PhD thesis. Department of Business Administration and Social Sciences, Luleå University of Technology.

Sabatier, P. A., W. Focht, M. Lubell *et al.* (Eds.) (2005). *Swimming Upstream. Collaborative Approaches to Watershed Management*. Cambridge, MA: MIT Press.

Sandström, A. (2008). Policy networks. The relation between structure and performance. PhD thesis. Department of Business Administration and Social Sciences, Luleå University of Technology.

Sandström, A. and L. Carlsson (2008). The performance of policy networks: the relation between network structure and network performance. *Policy Studies Journal*, **36**(4), 497–525.

Sandström, A. and C. Rova (2010a). The network structure of adaptive governance – a single case study of a fish management area. *International Journal of the Commons* (online).

Sandström, A. and C. Rova (2010b). Adaptive co-management networks: a comparative analysis of two Fishery Conservation Areas in Sweden. *Ecology and Society*, **15**(3), 14.

Scharpf, F. W. (1978). Interorganizational policy studies: issues, concepts and perspectives. In K. Hanf and F. W. Scharpf (Eds.), *Interorganizational Policy Making: Limits to Coordination and Central Control*. London: Sage, pp. 345–370.

Scott, J. (2000). *Social Network Analysis. A Handbook*, 2nd Edition. London: Sage.

Sen, S. and J. R. Nielsen (1996). Fisheries co-management: a comparative analysis. *Marine Policy*, **20**(5), 405–418.

Sorensen, E. and J. Torfing (Eds.) (2007). *Theories of Democratic Network Governance*. New York, NY: Palgrave Macmillan.

Swedish Statutes (1981). Lag (1981:533) om Fiskevårdsområden. (Fishery Conservation Areas Act (SFS 1981:533)). Stockholm: Jordbruksverket (Ministry of Agriculture).

Tengelin, B. (1997). Fiskevårdsområdenas betydelse för fritidsfiskemöjligheterna, fiskevattenägarna och fiskevården – en utvärdering. Slutrapport. (Fishery Conservation Areas and their impact on leisure fishing, fishing right owners and conservation – an evaluation. Final report). Sveriges Fiskevattenägareförbund (The Swedish Federation of Fishing Right Owners). Hushållningssällskapet Östergötland.

Thatcher, M. (1998). The development of policy network analyses. From modest origins to overarching framework. *Journal of Theoretical Politics*, **10**(4), 389–416.

Walters, C. (1986). *Adaptive Management of Renewable Resources*. New York, NY: Macmillan.

Wasserman, S. and K. Faust (1994). *Social Network Analysis. Methods and Applications.* Cambridge: Cambridge University Press.

Woolcock, M. and D. Narayan (2000). Social capital: implications for development theory, research and policy. *The World Bank Research Observer*, **15**, 225–249.

13

Agrarian communication networks: consequences for agroforestry

13.1 INTRODUCTION: AGRARIAN NETWORKS

Current challenges associated with soil degradation and land scarcity will have significant impacts on agricultural productivity, with far-reaching consequences for agroecosystem services and food security (Altieri, 2002; Sanchez, 2002; Lal, 2004; Vitousek *et al.*, 2009). Research has shown that by increasing agrodiversity, ecological benefits operating at various spatial and temporal scales mitigate environmental risks (Sanchez, 2002; Garcia-Barrios and Ong, 2004; Nair, 2007). Accordingly, the implementation of diverse agricultural systems has become of increasing interest (Pattanayak *et al.*, 2003). Of particular importance is the distribution of information on agrodiversity, and agroforestry, management (Montambault and Alavalapati, 2005; Isaac *et al.*, 2007a, 2009).

As continuously changing biophysical interactions operate in diverse agricultural systems, producers require access to specialized information in order to appropriately manage productive and persistent systems. However, institutionally derived agrarian information and technologies may in fact not reach the desired recipients, confounded by irregular diffusion of agrarian information (Boahene *et al.*, 1999; Warner, 2007). Presumably, the development of informal information on relevant management may counteract such barriers to information flow between producers and from regional institutions. Bodin *et al.* (2006) and Janssen *et al.* (2006) recognized the importance of informal social networks to resource management, however there are

Social Networks and Natural Resource Management: Uncovering the Fabric of Environmental Governance, ed. Ö. Bodin and C. Prell. Published by Cambridge University Press.

currently few empirical studies that investigate the effects of such informal networks on agricultural information transfer as well as consequences for agrarian management.

Based on data from cocoa producers in Ghana, this chapter presents informal communication networks, with particular emphasis on the potential flow of agrarian management information through these networks. Increasingly, regional response to agrarian-derived environmental degradation in Ghana is made through practices that enhance agrodiversity, such as agroforestry, particularly in the economically important cocoa sector (Amanor, 1994; Boni et al., 2004). There is an urgency to uncover information barriers on such practices and subsequent environmental decision making. Therefore, we apply a social network approach to identify such critical aspects of agro-environmental management.

13.2 ANALYTICAL FRAMEWORK: SOCIAL NETWORKS AND INFORMATION FLOW

The adoption of new techniques within an agricultural context is shown to partially depend on ties within social systems (Valente, 1995; Rogers, 2003). A focus on these relationships and the resultant structure of such relations is considered a social network. Network theory in part describes the transfer of information via network ties, while the concurrent use of network analysis allows for the measure and examination of ties and network characteristics (Wasserman and Faust, 1994). The flow of information embedded in these networks may be more evident in the context of relationships and interactions between actors (Granovetter, 1973; Burt, 1992; Burt, 2000; Lin, 2002; Davidson-Hunt, 2006).

For the agrarian context discussed in this chapter, minimal sources of formal information on pertinent agricultural techniques exist, particularly official and verifiable information derived from regional institutions or organizations. Communication networks are important for the transfer of such formally sourced information on agriculture management (Foster and Rosenzweig, 1995; Lyon, 2000; Conley and Udry, 2001; Romani, 2003; Davidson-Hunt, 2006; Kiptot et al., 2006). However, it can be assumed that to balance a deficit of formal information, particularly in remote farming areas, other types of informal information are produced and endure within farming communities (Mortimore and Adams, 2001; Campbell, 2004), creating two pools of knowledge. Farmers who

cannot access information from external sources, such as government or academic institutions, presumably draw on knowledge
within their social networks and access agricultural information
via social interactions (Boahene *et al.*, 1999; Conley and Udry,
2001). The diffusion of information and the process of adopting
farm-management techniques may rely heavily on social relationships in the larger farming community and subsequent informal
networks (Foster and Rosenzweig, 1995; Valente, 1995; Lyon, 2000;
Romani, 2003; Davidson-Hunt, 2006; Kiptot *et al.*, 2006). It is the
structure of these networks that can play a key role in the success
of social processes to advance or weaken sustainable agrarian
management.

Organizationally, local network structures may in fact be subgroups of larger regional-scale networks. Dependent on geographic
locations, regional institutions, rural actors, and/or agencies may
include extension and government agencies, formal research institutions, local support providers, non-governmental organizations
(NGOs), local expert sources, informal opinion leaders, or even buyers
(Allen, 1977; Pretty and Smith, 2004; Matuschke *et al.*, 2007; Bodin and
Crona, 2009). Hoang *et al.* (2006) illustrated that agricultural extension
and research-development institutions, as well as community-based
sources of informal information, were very active; the latter was used
effectively to supplement extension agents' work in the diffusion of
agrarian practices. However, regardless of the network scope, the identification of emerging network structures and the position of key
actors in the transfer of agroecological techniques will help define
pools of information and highlight diffusion of information on agrarian management.

Communication patterns may evolve into multiple forms of
social networks with structural characteristics that may either
impede or promote information diffusion. Two basic measures of a
network are size, composed of the number of actors, and ties, the
number and direction of connections in a network. Networks can be
at the individual scale (ego-network) or larger scale, such as at a
community level (whole-network). Regardless of scale, structural
features such as density have implications for transfer of information within a network. For instance, density, the percentage of
actual ties out of all possible ties in a network, is an important
structural attribute for information flow (Scott, 1991; Knoke and
Yang, 2008). A greater understanding of barriers to information
flow may require an examination of network density at either the

ego-network or whole-network level. A highly dense network can have an elevated frequency of communication amongst actors but may not receive new information (Valente, 1995), whereas a low-density network may have new information but low information flow. The density level may not be equal throughout the network but may vary within subsections of a network. For example, a core–periphery structure may arise in the form of a high-density group (core) surrounded by a low-density group (periphery) (Wasserman and Faust, 1994). The core position in this type of structure generally exhibits a high density of ties, whereas the periphery position is minimally connected to each other (Borgatti and Everett, 1999). Such a high density between actors in the core can be positive for information exchange when members of that core are connected to actors in a low-density, weakly tied periphery. Therefore, unlike a hierarchical structure for example, a web-like core–periphery structure can facilitate information flow through low-density elements (Muller-Prothmann, 2005), as in this case for information flow on agrarian management techniques.

Although limited, recent studies have investigated informal communication networks in agroecology and agroforestry management (Hoang et al., 2006; Kiptot et al., 2006; Isaac et al., 2007a, 2009; Warner, 2007). It has been shown that agroforestry producers play an active role in the development and transfer of management knowledge, particularly for rural and remote producers. We respond to the current discourse on social networks and resource management by examining emerging communication patterns, and consequences of such patterns to the use of agroforestry practices and resource management in general. To investigate these phenomena, we examine whole-network communication structures, particularly advice seeking, at the community level in order to characterize network positions and to determine the consequences of such structures on management information and agroforestry practices. Subsequently, a structural examination of personal producer-to-producer and producer-to-rural institution networks is undertaken to investigate the larger regional features of agrarian management. Individual network metrics are correlated to management, using species richness as an estimate of agroforestry management intensity, in order to establish some measures between network structural characteristics and sustainable agrarian management.

13.3   BACKGROUND

13.3.1   Agroforestry management

Agroforestry, a diverse system incorporating and/or maintaining trees in the agricultural landscape for both production and function purposes, is emerging as a win-win production system, mitigating risk in regions facing ecological and economic challenges (Nair, 1998; Sanchez, 2002; Garrity, 2004). While agroforestry principles have shaped and guided international policy and on-farm management over the years (Nair, 2007), new insights and advances in system management are still required to overcome barriers to diverse crop production and sustainable rural livelihoods.

The general principle of minimizing competition and maximizing facilitation between species in agroforestry systems remains a primary focus of research for successful agroforestry management practices. By managing agroforestry systems in accordance with ecological processes, many different benefits can be achieved (Beer *et al.*, 1998; Garcia-Barrios and Ong, 2004). Montagnini *et al.* (2000) demonstrated effective nutrient uptake, nutrient interception, recycling of nutrients, and synchronization of nutrient release with crop uptake under agroforestry management. Appropriate light-level regulation for target shade-tolerant species grown in agroforestry systems has been documented, while interactions between light and nutrient resources in perennial- and annual-based systems remain critical (Garcia-Barrios and Ong, 2004; Isaac *et al.*, 2007b).

13.3.2   Cocoa agroforestry in Ghana

Cocoa, a tree crop of high economic importance throughout the tropics, is particularly prevalent in Ghana. Small-scale farm production of cocoa in Ghana has developed from a minimal proportion of world production in the early nineteenth century to currently Ghana being the second largest global producer, maintaining 1 200 000 ha of land in cocoa production (Amoah, 1995; ICCO, 2004). Currently, the expansion rate of agricultural land in Ghana is 2.5% annually for tree and food crops, exhibiting like neighboring Cote D'Ivoire, Cameroon, and Nigeria, widespread deforestation through forest conversion to cocoa production (MOFA, 1991). However, current production is low due to multiple factors, including aging farms, high production costs, and climate change challenges. Long-term on-site consequences of nutrient depletion and unpredictable rainfall patterns have resulted in declining crop yields. Moreover, additional costs originating from environmental impacts such as accumulation of fertilizer residues and soil degradation accompany this decline (Nyanteng, 1993; Amanor, 1994). A large portion of the cocoa-farming population in Ghana is dependent on successful production of cocoa (*Theobroma cacao* L.) while simultaneously producing subsistence food crops and commodity tree crops (Asare, 2006). Amid low soil fertility and constraints to fertilizer access, farmers have developed techniques to promote soil and crop nutrition as well as maintain shade for healthy plants (Amanor, 1994; Boni *et al.*, 2004).

In response to the economic and ecological needs of smallholder farmers in Ghana, agroforestry practices are an option in cocoa ecosystems. Intricate small-scale production systems, incorporating trees and understory crops integrated with the cocoa stratum, have advanced farm health and production in Ghana (Isaac *et al.*, 2005; Asare, 2006, 2007b; Dawoe *et al.*, 2010). These techniques of farmer-based system management are often put into action through means such as planting schemes and species selection (Isaac *et al.*, 2009). Farmers have been active in managing forest timber species on their cocoa farms for shade and other functions. These upper canopy trees are retained or planted during farm establishment for light regulation and enhancement of biomass inputs for improved soil fertility and plant nutrition, which consequently increases farm diversity (Beer *et al.*, 1998; Hartemink, 2005).

Although some conflicting results exist on the success of cocoa-shade systems, a number of trends can be noted. In general, most cocoa research demonstrates high levels of nutrient transfer, providing evidence for nutrient-use efficiency and nutrient cycling (Hartemink, 2005). While shade trees have been shown to compete for soil resources, ameliorative effects have also been demonstrated, particularly through changes in microclimatic conditions, reduction in soil erosion, and as mentioned above, nutrient use efficiency (Beer *et al.*, 1998; Hartemink, 2005; Isaac *et al.*, 2007b). Generally, these cocoa-shade systems are emerging as a sustainable form of diverse cash crop production.

13.4 METHODS

13.4.1 Study regions

Gathering of empirical data for network analysis took place in two regions of Ghana: in the Western region (Region 1: 06°12′ N and

02°29′ W) and in the Ashanti region (Region 2: 06°75′ N and 01°40′ W). Communities in these regions were selected as representational of the respective regions. Both regions are characterized by a natural vegetation of semi-deciduous forests with predominantly smallholder farms, typically for cocoa perennial systems. Region 1 is characterized by highly weathered ochrosol-oxisol intergrades (Rhodic Ferralsol). Region 2 is characterized by deep, moderately well-drained silty-loam soils of the classification Ferric Lixisol (Soils Survey Division, 1969). Both regions have bi-modal rainfall, ranging from 1300 mm per year to 1850 mm per year. Similarly, the dominant naturally regenerated non-cocoa species in the region, on cocoa farms and in taungya systems, are *Terminalia superba* Engl. & Diels, *Triplochiton scleroxylon* K. Schum., *Alstonia boonei* de Wild, and *Ceiba pentandra* (L.) Gaertn. Fruit trees may also be planted; e.g. orange (*Citrus sinensis* (L.) Osbeck), avocado (*Persea americana*), and mango (*Mangifera indica* L.) (Isaac and Dawoe, 2009).

Regions 1 and 2 vary in accessibility to formal information accessed through institutions or rural agencies/actors. Region 2 is approximately 30 km from Kumasi, the second largest city in Ghana and has a much greater access to markets, extension agents, research for development organizations, and educational institutions, whereas Region 1 is approximately 120 km from Kumasi, located in a more remote area of Ghana near the Ivory Coast border. In Region 1, extension agencies have a much less frequent visitation pattern to farms than Region 2. Furthermore, in Region 1, the presence of NGOs that prioritize agriculture research for development is inconsistent as compared to Region 2. If a local development project is active in the region, there is a high level of contact but when no projects are active, there is little to no formal contact with NGOs.

13.4.2   Approach

Both whole-network (community) and ego-network (individual) scales were used to study the flow of agrarian management information, particularly the structure of communication networks and network features in relation to agroforestry adoption. Specifically, whole-network data (an exhaustive list of ties within a geographically bounded community) from Region 1 was derived from on-site producer interviews. All participants were asked questions on socio-demographics and specific management practices, as well as advice seeking and communication patterns. We specifically asked: "Whom do you go to for advice on agroforestry techniques and management?"

Such network data were collected through the name-generator technique (Marsden, 2004). Region 1 interviews were conducted in four separate agrarian communities, creating four whole-networks. These communities were similar in population, location (distance from markets and towns), and access to land, but had no apparent crossover in social relations. The adult farming population of the village was interviewed (~22 people per community), where a producer is one who currently owns or rents land and has established a cocoa farm. Data for individual networks (bounded to one step from ego) were extracted from the whole-network data set for Region 1. For Region 2, data for individual networks was gathered through a comparable interview process to Region 1, with alters and alter ties identified by ego as well as determined from pooled ego-network data. Twelve individual networks, representing half of a community network, from Region 1 and 11 individual networks from Region 2 were analyzed. As described above, based on geographical distance of the two regions, participants in Region 2 also included non-producers, in particular rural institutional actors (extension agency officers, research for development agencies employees, and local development actors) in the network data-gathering process on information seeking, whereas Region 1 participants did not. Once a producer in Region 2 identified a non-producer as a source of information in their ego-network, semi-structured interviews were conducted with individuals from each institution, which again focused on information seeking in agroforestry practices. Participant responses were coded as binary variables, i.e. the presence (1) or absence (0) of a tie, and entered into an actor-by-actor adjacency matrix (Hanneman, 2001).

Data for the advice networks in the four communities in Region 1 were analyzed with a core–periphery model to test for a group of actors with high density and groups with low density. The density of ties within each group was determined based on a predefined algorithm by Borgatti and Everett (1999) for categorical core–periphery structures. Again, core members were those that had a significantly higher density of ties amongst themselves as compared with others in the network. Participant attributes were then tested to see whether they correlated with core membership. Here, we present one attribute: "producer origin" which is divided into local (producer is from the community) and settler (producer migrated to the community). This attribute was selected to investigate the strength of pre-existing ties and social proximity as drivers of core–periphery formation. Ego-network data were analyzed for size (number of actors), ties (number of connections), and density (a measure of existing ties as a percentage of all possible ties).

Some farm physical attributes were also recorded. Producers were asked to report on the quantity and diversity of species established on their farms. Specifically, we employed the number of tree species on a farm plot basis (species richness) as a measure of agrodiversity and used this as a correlate of the intensity of agroforestry adoption. We tested correlations between relational attributes of actors (individual density score) to a non-relational variable (species richness).

All network analysis was conducted with UCINET (Borgatti *et al.*, 2002) and visualization in Netdraw (Borgatti, 2002). Although the data are not presented, note that for whole-networks, we used four independent replications of whole-networks to test for core–periphery structures. Density data derived from the core–periphery analysis was then subjected to analysis of variance to test for differences between networks in this region. Again, although the raw data are not presented, we relate an attribute (origin of producer) to a measure of the actor's position in a network (core or periphery) with t-tests (see Isaac *et al.*, 2007a for data). Density data from ego-networks had 12 replications for Region 1 and 11 replications for Region 2. All statistical tests were performed using SAS version 8.0.

13.5   EMPIRICAL FINDINGS: ADVICE NETWORKS AND INDIVIDUAL NETWORK STRUCTURE

In all four communities, information on agrarian management was noticeably sought from within a smaller, densely connected group (core) compared with a loosely connected periphery. Low tie density was observed between these two structural positions and within the periphery group (example network in Figure 13.1; see Isaac *et al.*, 2007a for core–periphery data). Follow-up interviews showed that of these highly sought core producers, 84% explored some level of formal information, predominately from government institutions (Table 13.1). Although producers in the peripheral positions sought a similar type of externally sourced information, peripherally positioned actors sought such information much less frequently than core-positioned actors (Table 13.1). Information on general farm techniques, such as species selection, organic matter management, and tree and crop densities, tended to be sought from producer-to-producer ties within communities (Table 13.1). Although core membership was not significantly

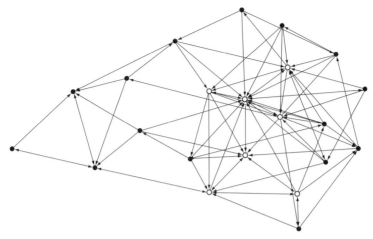

Figure 13.1 An example of one of the four community networks on agrarian management advice seeking from Region 1. Nodes represent individual producers and directed arrows represent advice ties. Filled nodes are periphery members and empty nodes are core members.

dependent on origin of producer, a slight over-representation of settler producers was found in the core. Community members at large were approximately evenly divided between local and settler producers, however, self-identified settlers comprised 73% ± 20% of the core.

To further uncover factors affecting agrarian information for individual producers in the larger organizational landscape, we undertook a comparative analysis of individual network structural measures, using informal producer-to-producer communication ties for Regions 1 and 2 but also institutional ties for Region 2. This allowed for an assessment of emergent network structures with varying sources on agrarian management. Individual networks composed exclusively of producers had significantly greater number of ties ($P = 0.029$) in Region 1 compared with Region 2. When institutions were included, ego-network density scores were significantly lower ($P = 0.005$) in Region 2 (Table 13.2; Figure 13.2). In this region, 69% of all producers had immediate ties with non-producer actors, such as individuals from institutions. However, even when exclusively comparing producer networks by removing institutional ties from the analysis, ego-networks were overall much more dense with lower access to institutions (Table 13.2).

Although we tested ego-network density scores from Regions 1 and 2 individually, to determine correlations between density and tree species richness (number of species reported on-farm), the data

Table 13.1. *Percentage of producers averaged over the four community networks (N = 4 ± SD) in Region 1 seeking information from various sources: informal information and on-farm experimentation for producers positioned in the core and formal information categorized into core and periphery positions. The most highly mentioned types of information are also provided.*

Source of information	Farmers seeking information (%)	Type of information
	Core members	
Informal	100	• Species selection • Farm establishment • Planting patterns • Shade management • Organic matter management
Experimentation	92.5 ± 9.57	• Species selection • Planting densities • Organic matter management
Formal	84 ± 17.05	• Pest control • Disease control • Planting densities
Periphery members		
Formal	32.3 ± 9.43	• Pest control • Disease control • Planting densities

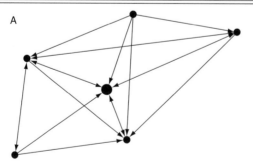

Figure 13.2 Example individual networks on advice seeking for agrarian management information in (A) Region 1 and (B) Region 2. The larger nodes represent the target individual (ego), the other nodes represent individual alters. Directed arrows represent advice ties. Filled circular nodes are producers and empty circular nodes are actors from regional institutions. Note that alter ties were not recorded between institutions.

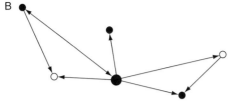

Figure 13.2 (cont.)

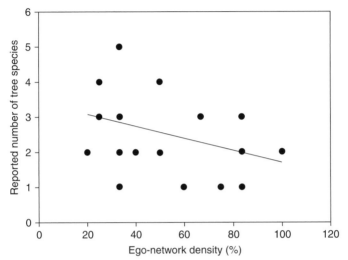

Figure 13.3 Correlation between individual network density (%) and species richness (number of tree species reported on-farm) pooled for Region 1 and 2 ($r = 0.35$; $P < 0.100$).

presented here are pooled from the two regions. In doing so, we found a negative relationship between individual network density (excluding institutions) and the number of shade tree species ($r = 0.35$) (Figure 13.3). This suggests that increasing ties between community members did not forecast adoption of agroforestry practices as approximated by agrodiversity. Regardless of weak or strong institutional support, higher reporting of agrodiversity occurred from individuals with relatively low-density ego-networks. However, some caution should be noted. Although variation in data-collection procedures in the two regions was minimized (see Methods section) and density scores were not significantly different between the two regions, correlations using pooled data may be influenced by other confounding methodological factors.

Table 13.2. *Mean (± SD) individual network measures (number of actors (size),
number of connections (ties) and percentage of ties (density)) for producer
networks in Region 1 and Region 2 and producer + institution network for Region
2 (Region 1: N = 12; Region 2: N = 11).*

Location	Mean ego-network measure		
	Size*	Ties**	Density (%)
Region 1 [Producer]	3.4 ± 1.00a	5.8 ± 3.52a	64.6 ± 20.59a
Region 2 [Producer]	3.3 ± 1.01a	2.9 ± 1.04b	48.0 ± 27.56ab
Region 2 [Producer + institutions]***	4.1 ± 1.30a	3.7 ± 2.10ab	30.3 ± 8.39b

* Including ego
** Directed ties
*** Institutional alters have been added.
Means within a column followed by the same letter are not significantly
different accordingly to Tukeys test, $P < 0.05$.

13.6   DISCUSSION

13.6.1   Advice networks: informal ties and agroforestry management

Due to increasing commodity prices of cocoa, and the availability
of land in the western region of Ghana, many people from outside
this region are buying or renting land for cocoa production; thus
farmers from other areas of Ghana as well as neighboring countries are often attracted to this region. Furthermore, as a result of
long-term fluctuating cocoa prices, local community members have
both started and abandoned cocoa farming (Boni *et al.*, 2004).
Consequently, both "local" farmers with a family history from
the dominant lineage in the community and newer "settler" farmers (migrant farmers from an external group) reside together
within these communities. A slight over-representation of settler
farmers was found in the core position (see Isaac *et al.*, 2007a for
data), which is presumably a result of multiple factors. For
instance, settler individuals may more easily adopt innovations
because of less pressure for social conformity. The introduction
of new producers who have lost previous associations may have a
greater willingness to implement new techniques and an enhanced
opportunity to activate new ties, thus resulting in a core advice-
seeking position. Although kin ties can encourage information

flow, the similarity of actor characteristics or actor homophily can impede transfer (Warriner and Moul, 1992). The low level of homophily (in this case, similar origin) found amongst core-positioned producers might in fact lead to a higher likelihood of information transfer. This suggests that advice ties were indeed motivated by farming practices, and social proximity was not a driving factor in forming network structure.

Interestingly, agrarian practices leading to meaningful advice may be derived from settler producers who have adapted their management to a new environment and/or condition; or settler producers may have pertinent adaptive management strategies from previous experience in other regions. It should be noted that these migrating settler producers are primarily from northern regions of Ghana. Climate change impacts in the north of the country may in fact be acting as a push factor leading to southern migration into cocoa-growing regions. There are as of yet undetermined consequences of drought-related farmer migration on localized agroforestry management (Van der Geest and de Jeu, 2008; Gyampoh et al., 2009), forces of which are presumably strongest in countries with a large ecological transition zone such as Ghana. The resultant impacts of farmer migration on agricultural innovation and land-use management may be of particular interest as locally developed technologies under climate change scenarios may be easily transferred to new recipient groups currently coping with unpredictable climate. This is particularly important in southern Ghana which is currently experiencing unpredictable rainfall.

Core- and periphery-positioned producers within each community used informal ties as a means to access agroforestry information. Generally, producers relied on pre-existing local information and on-farm experimentation. These experiments investigated, amongst other management practices, growth comparisons under different shade trees, testing previously unused species on small plots of land. Information derived from these experiments indicates a new pool of knowledge and a source of original information on farming practices under local conditions. Further studies on decision making and management in these cocoa-growing communities showed that the most prominent variable in farm management was managing the tree stratum (Isaac et al., 2009). This was not unexpected as management of the tree canopy is frequently the focus of farming practices, either for ecological advantages, such as shade and nutrient additions or financial benefits from on-farm products, such as fruits or fuelwood (Beer et al., 1998; McNeely, 2004).

Core and periphery producers gathered technical information on farm pests and diseases; they sourced answers to current farm problems predominately from outside the community. However, core members of the whole advice networks had a much higher level of contact with institutions from outside the immediate community, thus functioning as bridging links. The presence of these bridging ties formed between the community and outside institutions suggests a path of information diffusion. These connections to external sources may increase the flow of information into the community and/or counteract the frequently observed low level of information flow to all community members (Boahene *et al.*, 1999).

13.6.2   Individual networks: institutional ties and consequences for agroforestry adoption

Previous work has shown that adoption of agricultural technologies is typically linked to access to information and resources, such as credit (Valente, 1995; Rogers, 2003; Matuschke *et al.*, 2007). Remembering that Region 2 is characterized by higher access to formal information and institutions such as extension agents, government ministries, NGOs, and local development support, we recorded a decrease in the number of ties of informal networks. This may be a result of increased resources, thus a decrease in dependence on community members. As ties become more formalized, producer-to-producer reliance declines, and perhaps results in a simultaneous decline in localized knowledge. This also shows that individual networks are not restricted to producers. And some level of reciprocity exists insofar as actors from institutions may seek information from producers.

New approaches to information distribution, particularly through development agencies such as farmer field school, may complement information provided by traditional extension services (Hoang *et al.*, 2006). For instance, Prell *et al.* (2009) demonstrated that agricultural extension services might utilize well-selected community members as demonstrators of new practices. This may promote the formation of stronger informal networks for information flow, particularly under scenarios with strong institutional contact. With weak support from rural agencies and a corresponding large producer-dominated individual network, bridging ties could be activated to source formal information on management, as was the case with core actors in our community-level advice networks.

It is also possible that with increasing ties, information becomes redundant or even conflicting. We showed that higher individual network density does not necessarily lead to adoption of agroforestry practices as approximated by on-farm species richness. Although with time this abundance of information may in fact be successful at providing a full spectrum of support for rural producers, more ties do not necessarily mean better information. Information excess may lead to information homogenization and thus declining sustainable resource use. This saturation may also lead to an abandonment of innovative ideas and suggests a need for greater focus on optimal information flow, rather than the amount of information – quality over quantity. Although it has been suggested that a greater number of ties, and hence network density, would positively impact resource governance (Bodin and Crona, 2009) and improve information exchange (Pretty and Ward, 2001), other studies showed that agrarian innovativeness had no relationship to network density (Valente, 1995). Conversely, Bodin and Norberg (2005) demonstrated a positive consequence of low to moderate number of ties on the potential of diverse management practices. Low numbers of ego-network ties and/or densities are derived from either small network size or nominal levels of alter ties. As our data set captured no ego-networks with very low densities, it is difficult to say whether even at lower densities we would find a corresponding positive impact on adoption of agroforestry practices. This may be a function of our methods insofar as complete lists of ego-identified alters may be quite difficult to recall, leading to smaller ego-networks and perhaps artificially capturing high density.

13.6.3   Scaling up agroforestry practices with social networks

Under agrarian scenarios, a networks approach exhibits sources of innovation and information on sustainable management (Warner, 2007). And with appropriate institutional networks, higher rates of sustainable management adoption can be encouraged with proper organizational structures. Sustainable agrarian systems can be additionally promoted by scaling up environmentally appropriate practices. This may be achieved through networks of varying scales; specifically in this case, plot-to-community-to-regional levels. This work empirically studied informal communication networks at individual actor as well as more regional levels. By investigating common management issues such as the flow of information on agroforestry practices at various scales, obstacles to diffusion may become evident. However, comprehensive policy is needed due to the large geographical, as well as social, distance that may play a significant role in the movement of information (Schneider *et al.*, 2003). Less formally, local management networks can be encouraged to compensate for barriers to specialized information. Crossing such scales for improved resource management may be achieved through subgroup connections (Berkes, 2008; Bodin and Crona, 2009). This bottom–up focus is essential to the improvement of rural livelihoods, because large-scale policy that is dependent on global markets yet enforced at the local scale could be ineffectual. Over time, the passive yet persistent adoption of sustainable agroforestry management practices through previously established communication networks may be of use. This would ensure on-ground permanence of agroforestry practices and subsequent landscape-scale benefits of such practices.

13.7 CONCLUSIONS

Under weak institutional support and in the face of large ecological challenges, further investigation into the barriers and benefits of social networks to agrarian management information is critical. Although specific predictions may be unfeasible, data are emerging on network characteristics and natural resource management, particularly in this case for agrarian management. Network heterogeneity and bridging ties between networks have been regularly positively linked to sustainable management practices (Crona and Bodin, 2006; Isaac *et al.*, 2007a; Newman and Dale, 2007; Prell *et al.*, 2009). Our work showed a lack of homophily between highly sought producers, which in turn could lead to a higher likelihood of information transfer.

The structure of informal communication networks in relation to small-scale agricultural production varied with the degree of access to formal information; individual producer networks had fewer ties with increasing dependency on formal institutions. Regardless of where a producer sourced information (producer-derived or formally sourced), higher agrodiversity was correlated to individual networks with low density. This may be a product of greater institutional ties or in fact, a higher adoption frequency with fewer informal ties, particularly among alters. Despite this, characterization of emerging network structure and density as well as the identification of highly sought producers may play a critical role in the introduction, transfer, and implementation of new agroforestry techniques.

Reflections

Network boundary, ecological boundaries, and unit of analysis

In the advice network, our unit of analysis is the whole-network. To determine the boundaries of each network, we relied on the name-generator technique. Participants provided names of community members from whom they seek advice on farm management until no new names were provided, creating a complete list. We found the name-generator approach in this situation appropriate for two reasons: (1) we were working in a similar socio-economic group, reducing dissimilar interpretation of questions and (2) we assessed unidirectional ties, which presumably increased the stability of the network measures.

The individual (ego) networks were bounded by a one-step "neighborhood" from the central individual. Both individual producers and other actors in the rural landscape, such as extension agents, non-governmental agencies, and rural development support, were included in this neighborhood. Unlike common-pooled resources, we deemed ecological boundaries as simple to define. We used the farm plot as an ecological unit of analysis, which was defined by the producer. For instance, when we gathered data on species richness, the unit of analysis was the farm plot. Therefore, our network boundary (ego-network) and our ecological boundaries (farm plot managed by that individual) corresponded.

Data-gathering issues

To resolve obstacles associated with social network universality for agrarian resource management, we undertook a variety of steps to overcome barriers to data rigor and richness. First, a multi-community approach was carried out; similar whole-network analysis was conducted in geographically separate but socio-economically comparable communities. With regard to such community networks, we were interested in the variability and consistency among the distinct advice networks of four communities. Specifically, we asked: "Do informal advice networks within these farming communities have comparable structures, and can some general statements be made about farming advice networks?" By focusing on one type of relationship in multiple communities, we sought to increase the rigor and accuracy of the analysis and to test whether the emerging communication patterns were community specific or whether structural characteristics were generalized. The replication among communities allowed whole-network characteristics to be compared statistically, revealing general attributes of network structure for advice and information transfer. The applicability of a multi-communities approach enhanced our ability to state with some certainty the existence of a particular network structure as well as testing of network similarity.

Explanatory power of social network analysis

The explanatory power of our social network analysis lies in the qualitative data and additional quantitative data that were collected. The advice-seeking tie structure in and of itself is informative but is practical only when placed in context of position attributes, e.g. who seeks who and for what type of information? We used (and highly recommend) a multi-methods approach. Further work on cocoa agroforestry management was undertaken using cognitive mapping and decision making models as a unit of analysis to assess the process of local knowledge use (Isaac *et al.*, 2009). This allowed for comparison between individual producers to determine the degree of similarity among on-farm decision-makers and to expand information on the quality of information being transferred through social networks.

   When examining biophysical attributes of a resource, quantitative data were essential as a dependent variable. As we were interested in using network structure as a correlate to agrarian management techniques, it became invaluable to select a quantifiable variable, for instance biodiversity indices, yields, or growth rates. By collecting data on farm species richness, we operationalized farm management into a measurable variable. We then linked this variable, as an estimate of management, to an aspect of network structure, specifically density, in order to establish some measures between network structural characteristics and agrarian management.

In the current discourse on localized information in natural resource management, importance should be placed on the dynamic nature of information production and flow. This work conducted on cocoa agroforestry in Ghana explored the process-oriented nature of information seeking, decision making, and management of on-farm practices by employing social network analysis. Access to both informal and formal information sources as well as the structural characteristics of local social networks among producers influenced decision making to adopt more sustainable practices. Collectively, informal networks remain instrumental for the successful transfer of this information throughout the farming community and provide a foundation for sustainable agrarian management.

ACKNOWLEDGMENTS

We would like to acknowledge helpful comments from colleagues at the University of Toronto. We are grateful to field support provided by J. Hagan (Sefwi Wiawso) and A. Owusu (Kumasi), Ghana. This work was financially supported by Natural Science and Engineering Research Council of Canada.

REFERENCES

Allen, T. J. (1977). *Managing the Flow of Technology, Technology Transfer and the Dissemination of Technological Information within the R&D Organization*. Cambridge, MA: MIT Press.

Altieri, M. (2002). Agroecology: the science of natural resource management for poor farmers in marginal environments. *Agriculture Ecosystems and Environment*, **93**, 1–24.

Amanor, K. S. (1994). *The New Frontier; Farmers' Response to Land Degradation: A West African Study*. London: UNRISD.

Amoah, J. E. K. (1995). *Cocoa Outline Series: Development of Consumption, Commercial Production and Marketing*. Takoradi, Ghana: Jemre Enterprises Limited.

Asare, R. (2006). *A Review on Cocoa Agroforestry as a Means for Biodiversity Conservation*. Brussels: World Cocoa Foundation Partnership Conference.

Beer, J., R. Muschler, D. Kass and E. Somarriba (1998). Shade management in coffee and cacao plantations. *Agroforestry Systems*, **38**, 139–164.

Berkes, F. (2008). Commons in a multi-level world. *International Journal of the Commons*, **2**, 1–6.

Boahene, K., T. Snijders and H. Folmer (1999). An integrated socioeconomic analysis of innovation adoption: the case of hybrid cocoa in Ghana. *Journal of Policy Modeling*, **21**, 167–184.

Bodin, O. and B. Crona (2009). The role of social networks in natural resource governance: what relational patterns make a difference? *Global Environmental Change*, **19**, 366–374.

Bodin, O., B. Crona and H. Ernstson (2006). Social networks in natural resource management – what's there to learn from a structural perspective? *Ecology and Society*, **11**(2), r2 (online).

Bodin, O. and J. Norberg (2005). Information network topologies for enhanced local adaptive management. *Environmental Management*, **35**, 175–193.

Boni, S., R. I. Nuhu, F. Reuter and G. Da Re (2004). *Anthropological, Environmental and Soils Assessment of the Sefwi Wiawso District, Ghana*. Italy: Ricerca e Cooperazione.

Borgatti, S. P. (2002). *Netdraw Network Visualization*. Harvard, MA: Analytic Technologies.

Borgatti, S. P. and M. G. Everett (1999). Models of core/periphery structures. *Social Networks*, **21**, 375–395.

Borgatti, S. P., M. G. Everett and L. C. Freeman (2002). *UCINET for Windows: Software for Social Network Analysis*. Harvard, MA: Analytic Technologies.

Burt, R. (1992). *Structural Holes: The Social Structure of Competition*. Cambridge, MA: Harvard University Press.

Burt, R. (2000). The network structure of social capital. In R. I. Sutton and B. M. Staw (Eds.), *Research in Organizational Behaviour*. Greenwich, CT: JAI Press, pp. 213–243.

Campbell, M. O. (2004). The role of socio-environmental networking in the sustainability of rain-fed agriculture in the coastal savanna of Ghana. *Geojournal*, **61**, 79–88.

Conley, T. and C. Udry (2001). Social learning through networks: the adoption of new agricultural technologies in Ghana. *American Journal of Agricultural Economics*, **83**, 668–673.

Crona, B. and O. Bodin (2006). What you know is who you know? Communication patterns among resource users as a prerequisite for co-management. *Ecology and Society*, **11**(2), 7 (online).

Dawoe, E., M. E. Isaac and S. J. Quashie-Sam (2010). Litterfall dynamics in cocoa-agroforestry systems of lowland Ghana. *Plant and Soil*, **330**, 55–64.

Davidson-Hunt, I. J. (2006). Adaptive learning networks: developing resource management knowledge through social learning forums. *Human Ecology*, **34**, 593–614.

Foster, A. and M. Rosenzweig (1995). Learning by doing and learning from others: human capital and technical change in agriculture. *Journal of Political Economy*, **103**, 1176–1209.

Garcia-Barrios, L. and C. K. Ong (2004). Ecological interactions, management lessons and design tools in tropical agroforestry systems. *Agroforestry Systems*, **61**, 221–236.

Garrity, D. (2004). Agroforestry and the achievement of the Millennium Development Goals. *Agroforestry Systems*, **61**, 5–17.

Granovetter, M. (1973). The strength of weak ties. *American Journal of Sociology*, **78**, 1360–1380.

Gyampoh, B. A., S. Amisah, M. Idinoba and J. Nkem (2009). Using traditional knowledge to cope with climate change in rural Ghana. *Unasylva*, **60**, 70–74.

Hanneman, R. A. (2001). *Introduction to Social Network Methods*. Riverside, CA: University of California, Riverside.

Hartemink, A. E. (2005). Nutrient stocks, nutrient cycling, and soil changes in cocoa ecosystems: a review. *Advances in Agronomy*, **86**, 227–253.

Hoang, L. A., J. C. Castella and P. Novosad (2006). Social networks and information access: implications for agricultural extension in a rice farming community in northern Vietnam. *Agriculture and Human Values*, **23**, 513–527.

ICCO (International Cocoa Organization) (2004). *International Cocoa Organization's Quarterly Bulletin of Cocoa Statistics.*

Isaac, M. E. and E. Dawoe (2009). Promoting long-term farm diversity: integrative management of cocoa agroforestry systems in Ghana. *Journal of Science and Technology, Ghana*, **26**, 26–33.

Isaac, M. E., E. Dawoe and K. Sieciechowicz (2009). Assessing localized knowledge use in agroforestry management with cognitive maps. *Environmental Management*, **43**, 1321–1329.

Isaac, M. E., B. Erickson, J. Quashie-Sam and V. R. Timmer (2007a). Transfer of knowledge on agroforestry management practices: structure of informal advice networks. *Ecology and Society*, **12**(2), 32 (online).

Isaac, M. E., A. M. Gordon, N. Thevathasan, S. K. Oppong and S. J. Quashie-Sam (2005). Temporal changes in soil carbon and nitrogen dynamics in tropical multistrata agroforestry systems: a chronosequence of pools and fluxes. *Agroforestry Systems*, **65**, 23–31.

Isaac, M. E., V. R. Timmer and S. J. Quashie-Sam (2007b). Shade tree effects in an 8-year-old cocoa agroforestry system: biomass and nutrient diagnosis of *Theobroma cacao* by vector analysis. *Nutrient Cycling in Agroecosystems*, **78**, 155–165.

Janssen, M. A., O. Bodin, J. M. Anderies *et al.* (2006). A network perspective on the resilience of social-ecological systems. *Ecology and Society*, **11**(1), 15 (online).

Kiptot, E., S. Franzel, P. Hebinck and P. Richards (2006). Sharing seed and knowledge: farmer to farmer dissemination of agroforestry technologies in western Kenya. *Agroforestry Systems*, **68**, 167–179.

Knoke, D. and S. Yang (2008). *Social Network Analysis*, 2nd Edition. Thousand Oaks, CA: Sage.

Lal, R. (2004). Soil carbon sequestration impacts on global climate change and food security. *Science*, **304**, 1623–1627.

Lin, N. (2002). *Social Capital.* New York, NY: Cambridge University Press.

Lyon, F. (2000). Trust, networks and norms: the creation of social capital in agricultural economies in Ghana. *World Development*, **28**, 663–682.

Marsden, P. (2004). Recent developments in network measurement. In P. Carrington, J. Scott and S. Wasserman (Eds.), *Models and Methods in Social Network Analysis*. New York, NY: Cambridge University Press, pp. 8–30.

Matuschke, I., R. Mishra and M. Qaim (2007). Adoption and impact of hybrid wheat in India. *World Development*, **35**, 1422–1435.

McNeely, J. A. (2004). Nature vs. nurture: managing relationships between forests, agroforestry and wild biodiversity. *Agroforestry System*, **61**, 155–165.

MOFA (Ministry of Agriculture) (1991). *Agriculture in Ghana: Facts and Figures.* Accra, Ghana: Policy Planning, Monitoring and Evaluation Department, Ministry of Agriculture.

Montagnini, F., C. F. Jordan and R. M. Machado (2000). Nutrient cycling and nutrient use efficiency in agroforestry systems. In M. S. Ashton and F. Montagnini (Eds.), *Silvicultural Basis for Agroforestry Sysytems*. Boca Raton, FL: CRC Press, pp. 131–160.

Montambault, J. and J. R. R. Alavalapati (2005). Socioeconomic research in agroforestry: a decade in review. *Agroforestry Systems*, **65**, 151–161.

Mortimore, M. J. and W. M. Adams (2001). Farmer adaptation, change and 'crisis' in the Sahel. *Global Environmental Change*, **11**, 49–57.

Muller-Prothmann, T. (2005). *Leveraging Knowledge Communication for Innovation: Framework, Methods and Application of Social Network Analysis in Research and Development.* Frankfurt: Peter Lang.

Nair, P. K. R. (1998). Directions in tropical agroforestry research: past, present and future. *Agroforestry Systems*, **38**, 223–245.

Nair, P. K. R. (2007). The coming of age of agroforestry. *Journal of the Science of Food and Agriculture*, **87**, 1613–1619.

Newman, L. and A. Dale (2007). Homophily and agency: creating effective sustainable development networks. *Environment, Development and Sustainability*, **9**, 79–90.

Nyanteng, V. K. (1993). The prospect of the Ghanaian cocoa industry in the 21st century. Paper presented at the International Conference on Cocoa Economy. Bali, Indonesia, October 19–22.

Pattanayak, S., D. E. Mercer, E. Sills and J. Yang (2003). Taking stock of agroforestry adoption studies. *Agroforestry Systems*, **57**, 173–186.

Prell, C., K. Hubacek and M. Reed (2009). Stakeholder analysis and social network analysis in natural resource management. *Society and Natural Resources*, **22**, 501–518.

Pretty, J. and H. Ward (2001). Social capital and the environment. *World Development*, **29**, 209–227.

Pretty, J. and D. Smith (2004). Social capital in biodiversity conservation and management. *Conservation Biology*, **18**, 631–638.

Rogers, E. M. (2003). *Diffusion of Innovations*, 5th Edition. New York, NY: Free Press.

Romani, M. (2003). Love thy neighbor? Evidence from ethnic discrimination in information sharing within villages in Côte d'Ivoire. *Journal of African Economies*, **12**, 533–563.

Sanchez, P. (2002). Soil fertility and hunger in Africa. *Science*, **295**, 2019–2020.

Schneider, M., J. Scholy, M. Lubell, D. Mindruta and M. Edwardsen (2003). Building consensual institutions: networks and the National Estuary Program. *American Journal of Political Science*, **47**, 143–158.

Scott, J. (1991). *Social Network Analysis*. London: Sage.

Soils Survey Division (1969). *Great Soil Groups*. Accra: Survey of Ghana.

Valente, T. W. (1995). *Network Models of the Diffusion of Innovations*. Cresskill, NJ: Hampton Press.

Van der Geest, K. and R. de Jeu (2008). Climate change and displacement: Ghana. *Forced Migration Review*, **16**, 31.

Vitousek, P. M., R. Naylor, T. Crews *et al.* (2009). Nutrient imbalances in agricultural development. *Science*, **324**, 1519–1520.

Warner, K. D. (2007). *Agroecology in Action: Extending Alternative Agriculture through Social Networks*. Cambridge, MA: MIT Press.

Warriner, G. K. and T. M. Moul (1992). Kinship and personal communication network diffusion in the adoption of agriculture conservation technology. *Journal of Rural Studies*, **8**, 279–291.

Wasserman, S. and K. Faust (1994). *Social Network Analysis – Methods and Applications*. Cambridge, MA: Cambridge University Press.

Part III   Summary and outlook

ÖRJAN BODIN AND CHRISTINA PRELL

14

Social network analysis in natural resource governance – summary and outlook

14.1 THE RELATIONAL APPROACH IN NATURAL RESOURCE GOVERNANCE

Our intention with this book has been to introduce the social relational approach to scholars and practitioners who, in one way or another, are interested and/or engaged in natural resource governance. At this point, we hope that all the studies presented in this book have conveyed the message that a social relational approach, coupled with formal analytical methods (captured under the term Social Network Analysis (SNA)), can help one acquire new and exciting insights on a number of natural resource governance issues – conceptually, analytically, and practically.

Making use of SNA in the context of natural resource governance is an emerging field of research, and as such, much work is needed in exploring, in depth, the ways a relational approach to natural resource governance can lead to new and/or better theories, insights, tools, and techniques. This book is thus only a starting point. In this final chapter, we highlight some present and future issues in applying the relational approach to natural resource governance, and we take a look forward into what might be some of the future trends of this emerging field. We do not try to summarize all the insights from the contributing studies in this book since the studies themselves cover much more ground and provide for a much richer contextualization than a short summary would be able to grasp (see

Social Networks and Natural Resource Management: Uncovering the Fabric of Environmental Governance, ed. Ö. Bodin and C. Prell. Published by Cambridge University Press.
© Cambridge University Press 2011.

however Bodin and Crona (2009) for an attempt to bring together and synthesize some of the early findings in this research field). Instead, the bulk of this chapter is focused on discussing broader theoretical and methodological issues of concern that emerge from the different studies in this book.

14.1.1   Using social network analysis to explain versus intervene in natural resource governance

Before we proceed, we think it is appropriate to discuss two different purposes when using SNA in studying natural resource governance. In the chapters by Prell *et al.* (Chapter 5) and Ramirez-Sanchez (Chapter 6), SNA was either directly applied, or proposed as a suitable tool, to be used by managers when selecting and engaging stakeholders in participatory processes. The other chapters in this book, on the other hand, use SNA as a means to help understand and explain how structures of social relations affect natural resource governance. Although these different approaches do not present a strict methodological or theoretical dichotomy, they are however very different in terms of the intent of the research. In one instance, SNA is being used in a practical way to help managers make informed decisions on how to identify, select, and include different kinds of stakeholders for social learning or other purposes. The other approach is less direct in practical application, yet still informative to managers in shedding light on how networks are important for a number of different management issues. Taken together, the two styles of usage are actually very complementary – through understanding the role of social networks, one can then harness and make use of social networks for informed governance of natural resources (Prell *et al.*, 2010). With this in mind, one area of future research could be the use of social network analysis for evaluative purposes. That is, examining how social networks in a given resource governance context have changed over time as the result of certain learning or other initiatives on the part of practitioners or scholars. If social network analysis is used for selecting stakeholders for deliberative or other co-management purposes, then the same tool can be used to ascertain the extent to which, after a period of time, social relations amongst certain stakeholders have altered or changed as a result of these deliberative processes.

14.2   NETWORK CHARACTERISTICS AND WHAT ELSE?

Social networks and their structural features have been the focus of this book. Yet social networks have not been studied in isolation; all the case studies in this book have positioned social networks as a key variable alongside other variables of interest. These other variables have reflected aspects of the resource governance processes – either particular behaviors or characteristics of actors involved in these processes; contextual features such as institutions, culture, or environment; and also characteristics and/or changes in the resources themselves. In linking social networks to these other variables, the authors have traced relationships such as how social networks and their structure affect aspects of resource governance, or how, in turn, these aspects have affected social networks. More precisely, social networks have been studied in relation to other resource governance variables to (i) explore resource governance *outcomes*; (ii) explain *why* certain network features exist; (iii) uncover *which* stakeholders might be important for management processes. Each of these is summarized below.

In exploring resource governance outcomes, many of the contributing studies in this book are in fact measuring governance outcomes indirectly. For example, several case studies make use of the concept of homophily as an indirect measure of resource governance. Homophily refers to the situation where two actors who are similar to one another on a number of characteristics or behaviors are also socially tied (see also Chapter 3). The level of homophily can have several implications in terms of governance outcomes. For example, the level of heterogeneity of actors in the network has implications on knowledge generation and diffusion (e.g. Bodin and Crona, 2009; also see Chapter 9), and on actors' collective ability to mobilize resources of various kinds (Chapter 12). In measuring homophily, attribute data of actors are used in conjunction with social network data to determine the extent to which the presence of ties (the network variable) coincides with similarity in actors' characteristics (the resource governance variable). Thus, the case studies in this book have measured the extent to which homophily exists, in an attempt to then draw inferences about how such homophily might affect ongoing and future governance processes (Chapters 7, 9, and 10).

Another resource governance outcome is exemplified in Sandström's chapter (Chapter 12). Here, the author assesses a set of variables to capture the level of adaptability of the governing process.

Using these assessments, she finds a significant correlation between the level of adaptability and the structural characteristics of closure and actor heterogeneity. Isaac and Dawoe (Chapter 13) measured a set of biophysical variables. Using these data, they related on-farm biodiversity with the ego-network density of cocoa producers. In doing so, they actually manage to link some social features of the social network with measurable governance outcomes of the natural environment. Ernstson also linked some network features to governance outcomes (Chapter 11). In his study of an urban park, he found that the socially peripheral actors spent a lot of time in the park, while the more socially well-connected actors were more active in engaging with formal authorities. However, he goes on to suggest that these different roles, in combination, made the whole group of actors more effective in monitoring and protecting the park from further housing developments.

In exploring how or why certain network features arise, other authors in this book have looked to the contextual features of resource governance processes. For example, Chapter 11 looks at how core–periphery structures are maintained over time through the inclusion of new network members: as new, local organizations are added to the network's periphery, core and semi-core organizations reinforce their ties to one another and to local authorities. In doing so, these actors maintain their positions as core actors in the network structure.

For identifying which actors in the network are most important for resource governance processes, several of the authors in this book have made use of attribute data in conjunction with social network data to ascertain the role of individual actors in a given network. For example, Prell *et al.* (Chapter 5) used stakeholder category data, alongside data of actors' network positions, to develop a picture of the different roles actors played in the network, which in turn informed their stakeholder selection. Ernstson's chapter used social network data to identify network positions that, by using data on the different categories of organizations, could be used to disentangle the roles that different civil society organizations were playing vis-à-vis government organizations (Chapter 11). Finally, Bodin and Crona as well as Ramirez-Sanchez (Chapters 4 and 6) used a series of centrality measures to identify sets of potentially influential individuals. These individuals were then analyzed in terms of their personal characteristics, such as how long they have been fishing, which fishing gear they are using, and their tribal affiliation.

In conclusion, all the studies in this book investigate the "network variable" in conjunction with other variables pertaining to resource governance, and thus, the structural characteristic of the network is not of primary interest in itself. Furthermore, the variety of kinds of data outside social network has been noteworthy: biophysical data; ethnographic and other qualitative data; and multiple kinds of actor attribute data are some examples of the variety and scope of data found in these case studies. Furthermore, all the case studies gathered these data with certain social theories in mind, e.g. social learning, adaptive co-management, social capital, social influence, and social movement theory. Taken together, social networks have emerged in this book as a key concept and variable, and when studied in conjunction with well-known theories in resource governance and variables reflective of resource governance processes, studies on social networks can result in new kinds of insights into the role social relations play in the resource governance process (Chapters 1 and 3).

14.3 COMMON CHALLENGES IN USING SOCIAL NETWORK ANALYSIS IN NATURAL RESOURCE GOVERNANCE

In this subsection, we focus on two broad areas of concern in this line of research which all contributing studies in this book have addressed in one way or another. We are not trying to cover all possible methodological and theoretical challenges in applying a relational perspective when studying natural resource governance. Instead, we here focus on the two perceived as most salient to this line of research.

14.3.1 Define relevant systems boundaries

Typically, one of the first questions that faces a researcher doing empirical work in natural resource governance is to define and box-in the system under study. In other words, how to define appropriate boundaries of your study system? This question stems from both theoretical and methodological concerns. From a theoretical standpoint, a relevant system definition is to some extent defined by the research question and the applied theoretical framework. From a methodological and also practical standpoint, how your study system is defined will very much set the stage for how to design your research, and which techniques and approaches would be appropriate to deploy in collecting and analyzing data. This we will elaborate further by drawing on how the authors in this book have addressed this issue. However, before we proceed into that discussion, we present a simple topology of social and ecological systems based on how "open" or "closed" they are. We will then use this topology when we discuss different ways to define relevant boundaries of a study system.

14.3.1.1   *Open and closed social and ecological systems*

For simplicity, one could think of any system as being either open or closed. An open system does not exhibit any clear and obvious boundaries, but rather it is closely intertwined with other systems and contexts. An example of such a system is the atmosphere, which does not exhibit any clear boundaries within the scale of the planet. A closed system, on the other hand, is a system where "natural" boundaries do exist. A social network of all children in a classroom could serve as an example of a fairly closed system. Obviously, most if not all systems are neither completely open or completely closed. The atmosphere does not extend out in the rest of the universe, and the social networks of young children are normally not restricted to only include their classmates. However, the concept of openness versus closedness is useful when discussing system boundaries. In systems that are, by their nature, very open, defining and boxing-in the system under study generally becomes more complicated than in cases where the system exhibits clear (and manageable) boundaries. Furthermore, a governance *arena* inevitably comprises both a social and an ecological (sub) system (social-ecological system, see e.g. Berkes and Folke, 1998). From a boundary-setting perspective, we could therefore envisage each of these subsystems (the ecological and social system) as falling into two different categories; those that are effectively open and those that are effectively closed. Below we briefly discuss openness versus closedness for ecological and social systems respectively.

ECOLOGICAL SYSTEMS

All ecosystems are obviously "open" and have interactions with other ecosystems. But if the bulk of the biological resources being governed, in a particular setting, are fairly stationary and not inherently dependent on other biological resources that are more "free-floating," one might be able to come up with a fairly good approximation of a bounded ecological system. In other cases this might not be feasible. This largely follows the approach taken by Agrawal (2001) and Ostrom (2007) who define natural resources as stationary (e.g. forests) and non-stationary (e.g. pelagic fish stocks).

SOCIAL SYSTEMS

Social systems are similar to an ecological system in that they are rarely completely closed; rather they are situated somewhere in-between being completely open and completely closed. Furthermore, a social system can be approached from various different perspectives. However, since the focus of this book is on social networks, we will limit our discussion on open/closed social systems to the questions "Who are the relevant actors to consider given the social processes and structures in focus for the study?" and "Which of their social relations are important to consider in this context?" Here one could say that the larger the number of *potentially relevant* actors (and the more connected they are) the harder it will be to delimit an appropriate social system/network.

Putting these ecological and social considerations in defining system boundaries together, we can devise a simple classification scheme that could be used when defining boundary characteristics of the social-ecological system under study (Table 14.1). Global carbon and nutrient cycles typically operate on very large temporal and geographic scales (upper left corner in Table 14.1). These biophysical processes are affected by human activities, which also operate on large scales across several contexts. Hence, there are no obvious and manageable boundaries a researcher can rely on when investigating these issues. Similarly, pelagic fish stocks often do not adhere to any clear and manageable boundaries since they can migrate over large distances. However, if a rural coastal village is dependent upon these stocks for their livelihood, one could characterize this as a governance arena with an open ecological and a closed social system (upper right corner in Table 14.1 and Chapter 4). Inversely, the governance of an urban park serves as an example of a governance arena characterized by a fairly closed ecological system (the park has clear geographical borders), while the large

Table 14.1. *Simple classification scheme of types of system boundaries.*[*]

		Social	
Ecological		Open	Closed
	Open	Global carbon and nutrient cycles	Small-scale pelagic marine fisheries
	Closed	Green parks in large cities	Agroforestry in rural villages

[*] This classification scheme emerged from discussions where Beatrice Crona contributed substantially.

variety of people having a stake in the use of the park makes it harder to distinguish any clear boundaries of the social system (lower left corner in Table 14.1 and Chapter 11). Finally, agroforestry in a rural village serves as a good example of a governance arena consisting of fairly well-defined social and ecological system boundaries (lower right corner in Table 14.1 and Chapter 13).

Even though the classification as such does not necessarily help a researcher to tackle all the challenges in defining the appropriate system boundaries outlined here, as the stock of acquired knowledge and experience in this research field builds over time, the classification scheme could evolve into a set of guidelines as well as provide a starting point for detailed comparative analyses. It also helps organize one's thinking about defining appropriate system boundaries, and we do not think it is too far-stretched to say that different theories and concepts will be more or less applicable than others depending on where in the classification scheme the studied system is situated.

14.3.1.2   Different strategies to define boundaries

Here we make use of the classification scheme (Table 14.1) when discussing how the authors of this book set the boundaries around their study systems. Again, we will limit the discussion on defining a social system to the question of defining relevant actors and ties. Answering that question is however closely intertwined with considering, for example, what natural resources are being studied, where those resources are situated, and how (from an ecosystem perspective) these resources depend on other ecological resources. Consequently, most authors in this book needed to pay special attention to the geographic setting in which they were operating, the nature of the resource under question, the uses of those resources, and who made use of them.

CLOSED ECOLOGICAL AND CLOSED SOCIAL SYSTEM

This clearly presents the most straightforward way in defining the study system, but it is only relevant in cases where natural boundaries do exist and are manageable from a research perspective. To exemplify, a small rural village using a mostly locally bounded natural resource could be approximated as a fairly closed and autonomous governance arena/system although it is still socially and economically tied to the outside world. The definition of the study system in the chapter by Isaac and Dawoe (Chapter 13) relied on the geographic boundaries of a village. Here, the authors defined a priori the social system as consisting of producers who currently own or rent land and have established a cocoa farm in the studied villages. Everything and everyone else outside the village was then considered external to the system under study.

In cases where the social system is defined as closed the researcher (presumably) has knowledge about who are the relevant actors beforehand and thus only has to gather data on the ties among these actors (here we do not consider the need for non-network data). Hence, he or she then has the choice to gather social network data using recognition methods where the relevant actors (the respondents) are given a list of the other relevant actors of the system under study. From that list, the respondents only have to tick those he or she recognizes as being socially connected with. This approach not only generates *complete* network data, it also typically yields more ties than the recall method, which is relying on respondents being able to recall their contacts (e.g. Marsden, 1990).

Finally, precaution is needed since most systems are not completely closed; rather defining them as closed is by necessity an approximation that should be justified.

CLOSED ECOLOGICAL AND OPEN SOCIAL SYSTEM

Even if the natural resources being studied are fairly well boxed-in, it is still not always clear who has a stake in extracting and making use of them. For example, all relevant actors in an agricultural village do not necessarily have to be limited to the farmers themselves; there could be other types of actors that have a stake in the governance processes. Researchers may in such cases have a hard time to define, by themselves, the social system a priori. Instead, defining who the relevant actors are becomes a research question in itself. Broadly, the approaches used to tackle this issue in this book are two: either use informed experts to identify all relevant actors, and/or resort to some form of snowball sampling. Using snowball sampling, researchers typically start by asking respondents perceived as core actors of the governance arena to nominate other relevant actors and then proceed to asking the nominated peers until all those actors that are actively engaged in the governance processes are identified. Sandström's study of the designated Fishery Conservation Areas (FCA) serves as a good example of the use of snowball sampling to define relevant actors (Chapter 12). The FCAs are intended to function as collaborative governance arenas within a certain geographic area (therefore being classified as closed ecological systems for this purpose). However, defining a priori who all the relevant actors are, among a multitude of possibly relevant actors being more or less actively engaged in resource use and extraction in these areas, poses a potential challenge. In her study, Sandström started by recognizing that the scope of her research was limited to only include those actors who were actively engaged in the governance processes maintained by these FCAs, therefore other actors being active *outside* the realm of these FCA were, by definition, excluded. By using the formally designated chairmen of these FCAs as seeds for the snowball sampling, she made sure all relevant actors, *given the preposition that only governance processes maintained by the FCAs should be considered*, were used to define the social system.

Ernstson made use of both informed experts and snowball sampling in defining his study system (Chapter 11). His research revolved around governance issues of an urban park. The park itself could be seen as closed since it had, at the onset of his research, clearly defined borders within the urban landscape. However, given the multitude of users and managers linked to the park in various ways, defining a set of relevant actors was more difficult. Ernstson decided to focus his study on voluntary organizations, and he consulted informed experts to devise a list of potentially relevant organizations. He then asked each and every one on the list who they perceived as being active in the governance of the urban park. Only the organizations who received at least two nominations were then considered as being part of the study system. Hence, he started out with a large list, and then used this kind of inverse snowballing technique to reduce the social system to only include those organizations being nominated by others as active.

OPEN ECOLOGICAL AND CLOSED SOCIAL SYSTEM

Similar to the approach taken by Isaac and Dawoe (Chapter 13), Bodin and Crona (Chapters 4 and 9) defined the relevant actors in their studies as the villagers being residents of a chosen village. From a strict social systems perspective, defining the social system was therefore fairly easy (all households in the village). However, in their case the governed resources (fish stocks) cannot be defined as closed (at least not the pelagic fish stocks). The fact that the ecological system was open did not, in this case, affect how the social system was defined. It was however taken into consideration when interpreting the results from the study. Among other things, Bodin and Crona suggest that the fact that some of the fishermen were more geographically mobile than others (and thus have the possibility to geographically extend their fishing operation, making them less reliant on the status of the local fishing grounds) might have made them less inclined to impose fishing restrictions. Hence, the openness of the ecological system might have negatively affected the fishermen's collective ability to deal with the ongoing fish-stock degradation.

OPEN ECOLOGICAL AND OPEN SOCIAL SYSTEM

This is the most complicated (and probably most common) type of system in terms of defining relevant boundaries. We note that authors of this book tended to use a two-pronged strategy for defining such system boundaries that involved tacking back and forth between both social and ecological systems, guided by particular research questions or concerns, and aided by the use of approaches such as using informed experts and snowball sampling. The study by Prell *et al.* illustrates this (Chapter 5). They used a mixture of approaches in defining their study system. They first used informed experts to come up with a large list including all potentially relevant actors given a quite broad definition of the governance arena. Then, they narrowed this list down by reducing the scope of the types of ecological resources (or ecosystem services) that were being studied. In other words, they limited the list of potential actors by imposing boundaries on the ecological system. Last, they asked this remaining and small(er) sample of actors about who they engaged with given the governance issues being studied, thus they in effect finalized the definition of the studied social system using snowball sampling.

The study system of Ramirez-Sanchez also adheres to this category of open social and ecological systems (Chapters 6 and 10). From an ecological systems point of view, his study system (a coastal region) encompassed many kinds of marine resources which made boxing-in unfeasible (similar to Chapter 4 and 9). Furthermore, his study region also included several fishing villages, which made the issue of defining relevant social boundaries more difficult. However, Ramirez-Sanchez made the issue of social boundaries an integral part of his research question. In other words, he differentiated actors on the basis of their residency in the different villages situated along the coastline of the study area, and he differentiated the ties that connected fishermen of the same village versus ties crossing village boundaries. In the analysis he then investigated how the centrality of the fishermen, taking either type of social ties in consideration, was affected. Hence, he investigated to what extent fishermen's centrality was dependent on the applied boundaries of the social system.

Finally, the study system by Tindall *et al.* could also be characterized as open (both socially and ecologically) (Chapter 7). However, since their research questions were focused on how individuals might be influenced by specific *types* of network contacts, they did not have to consider all possible types of network contacts that might be relevant in the governance arena. Instead, they could limit themselves to a subsample of the network contacts belonging to the predefined types.

The challenges and strategies listed above, moreover, often did not take a simple, linear path (see e.g. Chapter 5). In other words, multiple issues were often considered simultaneously in defining the system boundaries, and this multiplicity reflects the complex nature of studying natural resource governance contexts and processes. More good examples on how to go about addressing these difficult issues are needed and to this end we hope this book makes a contribution. Also needed is more theory about natural resource governance in general. As already outlined, the decision on how to define the studied system partly derives from theory. But well-grounded theories on what processes, which actors, what setting, etc. that make a difference in natural resource governance are poorly developed and would make a significant contribution in informing the process of defining relevant system boundaries.

14.3.2   At what level of scale should one look for what kinds of governance explanations?

A key challenge facing anyone investigating different aspects of natural resource governance is how to choose appropriate scales of analysis. With level of scale we refer to both physically defined scales such as time and space, but we assign equal importance to human-made social, organizational, and economical scales. In a natural resource governance setting, the issues of choosing appropriate biophysical and social levels of scales are intertwined because choosing a certain spatial scale of analysis for the ecological system under study (i.e. a lake used for fishing) has implications for the social level of scale appropriate to analyze (e.g. individual fishermen, groups of fishermen, or fishermen in conjunction with various governing agencies).

The issue of scales is obviously linked to the problem of defining your system boundary (as discussed earlier, and exemplified in Chapter 5). However, in defining system boundaries, much of the attention is focused on how to best define and map out the system under study, whereas choosing an appropriate scale of analysis is more linked to the issue of deciding at what level explanations for certain governance outcomes are most likely to be found. To exemplify, if the research is concerned with questions related to the implementation of greenhouse gas emission reductions, the most appropriate social and ecological levels of scale for the study would likely be larger than if the issue of investigation is inshore overfishing in rural coastal communities. Having said that, we wish to clearly emphasize that many issues of importance in natural resource governance have relevance at a range of scales, from the very local to the global. Furthermore, a problem at one scale is often a result of processes operating at different levels of scale (see e.g. Frank *et al.*, 2007 on the interplay between global drivers and local structures in fisheries).

Although the issue of scale in ecological systems is obviously important and interesting in itself (Holling, 1992), in addition to being inevitably linked to the issue of scale in social systems (Folke *et al.*, 2007), the rest of this section will focus on the discussion of scale in social systems. The social network perspective itself is, as we will argue, very suitable when addressing and operationalizing different levels of scale. Furthermore, we also argue that the social network perspective is especially suitable when discussing cross-scale interactions (i.e. when processes at one level of scale interact with processes at another level of scale, see e.g. Bodin and Crona, 2009; Ernstson *et al.*, in press).

Simplified, one can think of a social network as encompassing three different levels of scale. For the remaining discussion, we will use the term *level* instead of *scale* because that term is more commonly used among SNA scholars. The lowest level comprises the individuals (i.e. the nodes) and their ties, the middle level can be constructed by aggregating nodes into distinguishable subgroups along with ties linking these subgroups together, and the highest level comprises the network as a whole where focus is on high-level structural characteristics such as density, centralization, etc. (see e.g. Chapter 2). Thus, when gathering complete network data (that is, all possible ties between the actors/nodes are measured), the researcher essentially has the possibility to investigate the social systems from any or all of these three different levels. If an egocentric network approach has been applied in gathering the network data (see e.g. Chapters 7 and 13), however, the researcher is typically limited in analysis to the level of individual actors.

These different levels of scale in networks are, in practice, not as clearly distinguishable as the discussion above might suggest. This

becomes apparent when studying the methods typically used in analyzing the network data. For example, in order to identify single actors
that are potentially more influential than others, different forms of
centrality measures are often utilized (e.g. Chapter 2). These centrality
measures are defined either locally (like degree centrality only taking
adjacent ties into account) or globally (like betweenness centrality
taking all ties in the whole network into account). Hence, the outcome
of a centrality analysis often depends on structural characteristics of
the network spanning multiple levels of scale (e.g. Chapter 4). This is
not a weakness. On the contrary, these kinds of analyses enable studies
where levels are "mixed." For example, Frank shows how it is possible,
using explicit multi-level statistical models, to simultaneously study
issues at multiple levels of scale (Chapter 8). Finally, it should be
pointed out that it is indeed very common that more than one level
of scale is addressed in any given study. This is exemplified in this book
as basically none of the contributing studies concerned with whole
network data are completely confined within one level of scale.
However, the focus of any given study is typically centered on one
certain level, and below we will use the contributed studies to illustrate
how structural network characteristics at different levels can be analyzed in order to increase understanding and seek explanations for
different issues of concern in natural resource governance.

14.3.2.1   *Lowest level – the individual actors*

As stated, analyses at the level of individuals are often targeted at
identifying actors who, as a consequence of their position in the social
network, are potentially more influential than others. This is interesting in studying natural resource governance for a number of reasons.
Ramirez-Sanchez (Chapter 6) and Prell *et al.* (Chapter 5) use different
centrality measures in identifying highly central individual actors that
could be efficient to include in a participatory process due to their
potential capacity to influence many others, to spread information
and knowledge among large groups of stakeholders, and also their
ability to represent many similar others. Assuming that central actors
are better situated to exert influence on others, and assuming that this
capacity is instrumental in, for example, initiating and maintaining
institutions regulating natural resource extraction, it becomes interesting to study those actors in particular. This is what Bodin and Crona
do in their study (Chapter 4). Their study system is characterized by
governance inertia in spite of ongoing resource degradations, and they

are seeking potential explanations for this governance failure in the forms of (lack of) problem perceptions and/or (lack of) incentives to engage among the potentially most influential individuals in the community of resource users.

Tindall *et al.* uses an egocentric network approach in investigating to what extent the composition of an individual's personal social network influences his or her attitudes towards current forest management on the local as well as on the regional geographic scale (Chapter 7). Similarly, Isaac and Dawoe use an egocentric approach in investigating to what extent size, density, and composition of cocoa producers' personal social networks influence their management practices (Chapter 13). However, these egocentric network studies did not analyze how the studied individuals were structurally situated in a larger social network context, thus the influence they might have on others beyond their immediate social neighborhood (and vice versa) was not considered.

14.3.2.2   *Intermediate level – the subgroup*

Subgroups are agglomerations of individual actors (nodes), and these aggregates can be constructed in numerous different ways. Among the contributing studies in this book, two different approaches have been applied. Ernstson and Prell *et al.* both use positional analyses to group actors into subgroups (Chapters 11 and 5). Using this approach, actors are grouped based on their similarity in terms of their pattern of ties to others. Ernstson used this approach to identify different actors with different types of structural positions; a categorization that he then used to define different functions that were essential in the transformation and structuring of a new governance arrangement of the studied urban park (Chapter 11). One particular function was, for example, provided by a core set of structurally similar actors (in his case an actor is an voluntary organization), and that function was to interact with policy makers and the media making sure no exploitations of the park would be carried out unnoticed. Prell *et al.* (Chapter 5) use positional analysis to identify different network positions that could, when combined with centrality measures and stakeholder categories, identify which stakeholders could be suitable in representing different parts of the network according to three different criteria (position, centrality, and stakeholder category).

Another conceptually different way to define subgroups is based on cohesion, i.e. that members of a subgroup are somehow more tightly linked to each other than they are linked to others (see Chapter 2). In their study, Crona and Bodin identified and deconstructed a social network of rural villagers into a set of cohesive subgroups (Chapter 9). Using this method, they found that fishermen's choice of fishing gear largely coincided with the gear their fellow subgroup members were using. They expanded this analysis by suggesting different hypotheses on how and why the internal compositions of the subgroups, and the pattern of inter-subgroup ties, might have contributed to the observed inability of the community at large to respond to the ongoing resource degradation.

14.3.2.3 *Highest level – the complete network*

At this level of scale, the structural characteristics of the social network as a whole are of primary interest. One such characteristic is what Sandström refers to as network closure (Chapter 12). In her study, she defines network closure as a kind of composite measure of density and centralization, both of which are complete network characteristics. Drawing on data from three different case studies, she argues that network closure is one key factor that is positively correlated to actors' collective ability for adaptability in the governing processes. Furthermore, both Ernstson and Isaac and Dawoe found evidence of an overall core–periphery structure of their studied networks (Chapters 11 and 13). Among other things, Isaac and Dawoe suggest that this network characteristic contributes to increased flows of knowledge exchange in the villages, and that it enhances the abilities of formalized knowledge providers (such as extension agents) to spread information, particularly in remote villages (Chapter 13).

14.4 WHERE TO GO FROM HERE – CHALLENGES AND OPPORTUNITIES

Throughout this book we have argued for the benefits of using a relational approach when studying natural resource governance. That is, we have tried to explain and exemplify how a researcher, by measuring and analyzing social networks using well-defined systematic and quantitative approaches, can gain new insights about key issues of importance in natural resource governance. In particular, in applying a social relational approach it is possible to reveal how different structural characteristics of social networks of resource users, stakeholders, agencies, etc. significantly influence governance processes and outcomes.

At this point, we can only hope that this message has been convincingly conveyed, and that you as a reader have found this emerging research field exciting and relevant.

Although the relational approach in natural resource governance is a fairly new field of research on its own, it comprises and transcends well-established scientific disciplines and research fields (as outlined in Chapter 3). Hence, there are firmly established theoretical and methodological platforms to build upon (or put another way, there are shoulders of giants on which to stand). This means that we can draw extensively from decades or even centuries of theoretical and methodological developments and experiences, and there is no need to invent the wheel all over again. However, there are still many challenges and opportunities ahead that we argue are specific for this emerging field, and which have not yet received much attention. The challenges are both methodological and theoretical, and in the following subsection we highlight some of these future challenges and opportunities.

14.4.1   Causal inference

As explained earlier, the various structural characteristics of the studied social networks are often treated as independent variables whereas the dependent variable is something different (e.g. governance outcome). This outcome could be broadly defined, for example, as whether the studied group of actors has been able to achieve collective action or not; or more narrowly defined as their ability to adjust their extractions of the governed natural resources in accordance with temporal and spatial variations of abundance. However, using the "standard" single case study or cross-sectional approach, where one system is studied at one point in time, causal inference is never fully possible (at least empirically, although one might make theoretical arguments regarding the causal relationship of variables). Thus, in most instances, the researchers have resorted to making correlational or associative claims regarding the relationships among variables of interest (although see, for example, Chapter 7 which makes causal claims based on theoretical assertions).

Although the insights these kinds of studies can generate should not be underestimated, they typically cannot be used to identify causality. Hence, it will not be possible to differentiate whether a particular outcome is the result of the structure of the network, or if the structure is the result of the same processes that gave rise to the measured outcome. In order to be able to investigate causes and consequences of various structural characteristics of networks with more precision and empirical backing, longitudinal network data are needed (as many of the authors of this book emphasized in their reflection boxes). This is currently a critical shortcoming of this emerging research field, and we argue that the next logical step would be to initiate research programs where longitudinal data gathering will be an integral part of the research design. Fortunately, there are methods and tools readily available for longitudinal analyses. Tom Snijders's work on models and tools making use of longitudinal network data is instrumental in this regard (e.g. Snijders *et al.*, 2010). In this book, Frank also provides a modeling framework that uses longitudinal network data to infer causal inference (Chapter 8).

However, there are at least two approaches that can be used to gather longitudinal data. Either data are gathered at several points in time (the standard way), or a set of similar, but independent study systems that are undergoing similar processes are identified, but the systems differ in age or developmental stage. In effect, time is substituted by space/place in the form of gathering data at various sites differing in their successional or development stage. This is a commonly used approach in the field of ecology. Sampling from such systems according to differences in age could yield insights similar to those gained from longitudinal data on a single system.

14.4.2   Attention to process and emergence

Here we discuss how to get a better understanding of processes and emergence in natural resource governance. However, before we start we need to clarify the distinction between causal inference and what we mean by process and emergence. Causal inference, in this case, is when you test whether a particular network characteristic gives rise to a particular outcome. In other words, continual feedback mechanisms are not considered in the analyses, especially the kind of feedbacks that could be characterized as non-linear. Investigating processes and emergence, on the other hand, is when the focus of the research is more oriented towards understanding how, for example, actors, intentionally or not, change and adapt themselves and their relationships as a result of dynamic changes in the social and ecological contexts. In other words, more focus is put on how the "rules of the game" might change dynamically, often as a response to the entire social-ecological system undergoing changes. This notion of continual feedback

mechanisms and emergence is in fact one of the defining characteristics of *complexity* (see e.g. Kaufmann, 1995). We argue that such a
dynamic perspective is particularly relevant in studying natural
resource governance. One important reason for this is that it is becoming more and more apparent that contemporary natural resource governance practices are unsustainable, and therefore we need to develop
better understanding of how various self-reinforcing feedbacks can be
unlocked in order to make transformative change of unsustainable
governance regimes possible (e.g. Olsson *et al.*, 2006; Walker *et al.*,
2009; Chapter 11). Hence, there are compelling reasons to start investigating systems undergoing changes in order to begin disentangling
the feedback processes that facilitate (or inhibit) change. Such an
endeavor calls for research approaches designed to continuously
track processes, feedback, and subsequent changes.

In measuring a cross-sectional social network, one gets a snapshot of the social structure at one point in time. That is, what is
revealed is the *result* of various processes that have given rise to a social
relational structure, but data on these processes may or may not have
been gathered. This structure can then feed back on the same social
processes in a cyclic and iterative way as described above (see also
discussion in Degenne and Forsé, 1999). Most studies applying social
network analysis are, as stated earlier, mostly concerned with the latter
part of this iterative loop, i.e. from social structure to various outcomes
(here, the outcome of the governance processes). All case studies presented in this book have broadly followed such an approach. Thus, a
range of network structural characteristics has typically been identified, and various social outcomes of relevance in natural resource
governance have (indirectly or directly) been discussed in relation to
these structures. However, none of the case studies have explicitly
investigated the processes that give rise to the structures of the networks (although Ernstson comments on how core–periphery structures can be maintained and reinforced over time in a cyclical
process in Chapter 11). Instead, the structures have largely been
taken "as is," and then used for further analysis. Investigation of the
emergence and evolution of network structures would, however, be
very relevant to undertake in studying natural resource governance (as
stated earlier). In addition to previous arguments, natural resource
governance settings are characterized by a multitude of actors that
are all (potential) stakeholders competing for a limited and often
highly dynamic resource. In such a setting, gathering support from
others is one important strategy in pursuing different objectives

(e.g. Hahn *et al.*, 2006; Olsson *et al.*, 2006; Chapter 11). Hence, one would expect lots of deliberate networking activities among actors, which would result in both continual and abrupt changes of the social network structures themselves. In this context, the statistical models presented by Frank (Chapter 8), where both the influence and the deliberate selection of peers in social network can be analyzed simultaneously, provide a solid modeling framework in studying these issues.

There is, indeed, a fairly large stream of scholars who are researching processes and structural changes in social networks, although currently not with a specific focus on natural resource governance. One kind of statistical model typically used for cross-sectional network data is the Exponential Random Graph Model (ERGM), of which the p* model is most well known (see e.g. Robins *et al.*, 2007). This suite of models investigates the statistical distribution of a set of archetypical micro-structures (or network configurations), such as reciprocal ties and closed triangles, in relation to a whole network. Here, the question becomes, what sort of global network structure emerges from local (or micro) structures? Thus, through using these models, it would be possible to start unpacking micro-level processes (such as the tendency to form closed triangles) that generate larger-level social network structures (such as small-world structures or star structures).

One essential factor in researching dynamic systems is, again, to gather longitudinal data. In doing so, one can make use of a similar sort of statistical model as p*, the actor-oriented models of Snijders *et al.* (2010). Here, *longitudinal* network data, alongside actor attribute data, are gathered and analyzed via stochastic models to capture distinctions between social networks as independent variable (the networks causing changes in actors' behavior, for example), and social networks as dependent variable (where actors' attributes or behavior are resulting in changes in the network structure). Furthermore, the models presented by Frank (Chapter 8) would also make it possible to investigate evolving networks using longitudinal network data alongside attribute data. Finally, besides the benefit of being able to infer causality and track network evolution, gathering data on the network at different points in time can act as a means of evaluating whether certain intentionally designed interventions, such as those proponents of social learning initiatives suggest (e.g. Pahl-Wostl *et al.*, 2007), have worked in strengthening ties amongst previously disconnected actors in the network, and also evaluating whether deliberative discussions and changes in social relations result in changes in thinking and behavior in relation to the environment.

Besides gathering longitudinal data and using these data to infer and discuss process and emergence, there are other approaches. Computer simulations are one such important approach. Here, a virtual world is created as a computer software program. The program simulates dynamics of the real world (although heavily simplified), and thus generates "virtual" longitudinal data. Both p* and actor-oriented models make use of simulations to generate distributions of possible network states, against which real-world data can be compared to test the extent to which certain network effects or tendencies (e.g. the tendency to reciprocate ties) are present in an observed social network. In other cases, simulation models are used without explicit consideration to real-world data. Here, the focus is often on using simulations as "thought experiments" to explore patterns, processes, and outcomes, and the results from such exercises can help to provide insights about various real-world phenomena, their underlying causes and potential long-term effects. Often, such models are based on the assumption of systems as consisting of interacting agents, i.e. agent-based simulation models. In social network analysis, there is a stream of research that uses agent-based simulation models to uncover: (i) what local processes and/or decisions of agents give rise to certain global network structures (e.g. Bala and Goyal, 2000; Robins *et al.*, 2005; Buskens and van de Rijt, 2008), or alternatively (ii) how global network structures affect the actions of individual agents (e.g. Centola and Macy, 2007). This body of research could be mined by scholars interested in exploring the processes of resource governance processes in relation to those of network formation. In research on natural resource governance, agent-based models have been used to study actor collaboration/competition in governing common-pool resources (e.g. Janssen, 2003), effects of network structures on farmers' abilities to change and adapt (Bodin and Norberg, 2005), and on fisheries (e.g. Little *et al.*, 2004). As argued by Frank (Chapter 8), agent-based models provide a very interesting modeling approach in investigating complex feedbacks in social-ecological systems.

14.4.3   Extending social theories

Although we acknowledge that the prime concern in resource governance research is to develop theories for this specific, yet very broad, context, we anticipate that findings from this field could also reflect back on broader and less context-dependent theories. In other words, there will eventually be a need to revisit those original social theories in order to maybe tweak them to better account for specific characteristics of governance in a natural resource context.

This book, when linking social networks to other social theory, has done so by applying theories already in existence in the resource governance community (see also Chapter 3). This is a strength and we argue that social network analysis helps one gain more precise understanding of the ways social learning, social capital, and other theoretical perspectives unfold in actual governance contexts. However, a forthcoming step could be to start building more grounded theories from specific case studies making use of social network analysis, and then begin to generalize across these case studies. This would involve a larger range of case studies across contexts, times, resources, and cultures, to start stitching together possible theoretical frameworks. Such a goal is linked to the potential to integrate social network data with data on natural systems to formulate models of coupled social-ecological networks (see concluding remarks below).

As stated above, there are reasons to believe that alongside the further development of this field, there will be a need to return back to those theories and, if needed, adjust them to be more relevant when studying resource governance in particular. However, this rather bold statement leads to the inevitable question, what is so special with natural resource governance to make us suggest such a thing? We propose several reasons. The natural environment is, as repeatedly stated, characterized by immense complexity and boundlessness, resulting in the inevitable need to involve many different actors in the governing processes. These actors often have opposing interests and they often need to be engaged on a more or less voluntary basis. In short, governance of natural resources is characterized by:

(1)   The necessary involvement of many actors/stakeholders of different types, with different objectives and interests, and with differing incentives and willingness to cooperate versus engage in conflicts (e.g. Ostrom *et al.*, 1994; Carlsson and Berkes, 2005).

(2)   Unclear jurisdictions/ownership rights/usage rights (i.e. common-pool and/or open-access resources, see e.g. Ostrom, 1990).

(3)   Surprises. By this we refer to the inherent unpredictability of natural systems, implying that ways to deal with unforeseen events are to be seen as a norm rather than the exception to a greater extent than that typical in many other management and

governance settings (cf. Holling and Meffe, 1996; van der Leeuw, 2000; Kinzig *et al.*, 2003).

What we are arguing here is that these key contextual features characterizing natural resource governance are often much more pronounced in comparison with the typical empirical base that underlies the very foundation of many of the social theories used to study natural resource governance. For example, Burt's very influential work on social capital and networks is largely drawn from research within corporations (Burt, 2005). If insights drawn from such studies are applied "off the shelf," and applied in researching natural resource governance settings, this might lead to incomplete conclusions since the very nature of the governance arena in a resource governance context is typically very different from what characterizes a corporation.

In all, this suggests that although we do not propose these social theories to be invalid in the context of natural resource governance, we do propose they may need adjustments to take into account the many peculiarities of natural resource governance. Accordingly, when the empirical base of natural resource governance builds up, not only will we be positioned to start to develop a theoretical framework that would be tailor-made for the specifics of natural resource governance, we also suggest that this development will involve re-evaluations of many social theories and how they should be applied when investigating natural resource governance. Although we are definitely not in a position today to seriously start questioning these social theories' applicability in a natural resource governance setting, we here provide a speculative discussion on the topic as an illustration. As implicitly outlined above in points 1–3, we think that governance of natural resources is in many aspects very different from management of, for example, private firms or governmental agencies. This applies in particular to studies of issues of leadership. In private corporations, for example, leaders often have the ability and the authority to command others, the objectives are often much clearer (e.g. make profit or enforce regulations) with less need for conciliating opposing interests, and the contextual environment is not fully as complex as when managing complex, non-linear, scale-dependent, self-organizing, and constantly evolving ecosystems (although we acknowledge, for example, global markets as being highly unpredictable). Hence, what defines successful leadership strategies in a natural resource governance setting might be different from other settings. In fact, recent research has shown that there are a number of issues that, although being of general relevance elsewhere, seem to be of particular importance for successful leadership in natural resource management. Examples of these issues are leaders' ability for sense making, collaboration, and linking different types of actors and context (Hahn *et al.*, 2006; Olsson *et al.*, 2007).

In concluding this discussion on how studying natural resource governance might bring new insights into social theories in general, we also want to make the point that using social network analysis in itself can contribute to such developments in a much broader and general way. Indeed, many scholars would argue that the relational approach is very under-utilized in many research fields where it actually has great potential to provide new insights. For example, the theory of social learning, which has seen a lot of use within environmental and resource management (Chapter 3), has rarely been measured using SNA. In this book, social learning has been extended by being combined with social influence and homophily, two intertwined research agendas within the social analytic field, and as a result, more precise predictions on the way social relations and their structuring can affect how actors learn from, or influence, one another has been achieved (see Chapters 5, 7, and 9). In a similar way, the literature on adaptive management and co-management often discusses social interaction (see Chapter 3). Yet, in this book, the roles of social relations and structure have been dealt with in greater detail, as certain structures have been hypothesized for meeting certain management outcomes (Chapter 12), and thus, more precision on the role of social relations within the overall framework of adaptive management and co-management has been gained. Indeed, Crona *et al.* (Chapter 3) attempt to lay out the ways in which SNA can be used to measure and explore common perspectives and theories in natural resource governance, and the case studies found in this book exemplify the different ways this can be done. The point we wish to make here is simply that in integrating an SNA perspective into these already well-established theories within natural resource governance, these theories have gained more precision and predictive capacity from the perspective of the role of social relations.

14.5   CONCLUDING REMARKS – TRANSCENDING THE BOUNDARIES OF SCIENTIFIC DISCIPLINES

Throughout this book, compelling arguments have been given concerning the intricate and inevitable linkages that exist between human societies and the biophysical environment, showing that these systems should not be seen as independent and autonomous subsystems. Instead they should each be seen as an integrated whole – a tightly coupled social-ecological system (Berkes and Folke, 1998). Therefore, even when studying social-ecological systems using a social science perspective, the characteristics, behaviors, and dynamics of the underlying biophysical environment cannot be left out of the analysis. For example, our earlier discussions on the system boundary issues illustrate this inevitable linkage, as does the discussion in the introduction of the book.

Throughout this book, the social and ecological systems have been analyzed separately from a methodological perspective (although the inevitable linkages between the subsystems have shaped the research design, objectives, system definitions, and the interpretation of the results). This is largely a consequence of the lack of common methods shared between the natural and social sciences. However, researchers have recently suggested network analysis as a way to enable integrative analyses of social-ecological systems where the methodological distinction between analyzing social and ecological systems' characteristics is reduced (Janssen *et al.*, 2006; Webb and Bodin, 2008; Cumming *et al.*, 2010; Johnson and Griffith, 2010). Since network approaches have been successfully applied in various fields both within the natural and the social sciences, suggesting that integrated social-ecological network models could enable novel cross-disciplinary analyses of social-ecological systems seems reasonable. Specifically, the reason network approaches might be suitable for this task is the generality of the network modeling approach, i.e. the model specifies the system to be composed of entities (nodes) and relations among these (links). These entities could be anything, and here in this book they have been individual persons, households, or even organizations. But such entities could also be species or habitat patches (e.g. Bodin, 2009). When the network model has been constructed, no matter what entities and relations have been used in giving substance to the model, network analysis is subsequently applied to characterize and quantify various structural aspects of the modeled social-ecological system. However, although promising, the challenges in developing such a cross-disciplinary framework should not be underestimated. Many challenges remain to be solved before such research will be able to deliver substantial contributions to this field of research (Janssen *et al.*, 2006; Cumming *et al.*, 2010).

ACKNOWLEDGMENT

Bodin acknowledges support from the Foundation for Strategic Environmental Research (MISTRA) for his work on this book.

REFERENCES

Agrawal, A. (2001). Common property institutions and sustainable governance of resources. *World Development*, **29**(10), 1649–1672.

Bala, V. and S. Goyal (2000). A non-cooperative model of network formation. *Econometrica*, **68**, 1181–1229.

Berkes, F. and C. Folke (1998). *Linking Social and Ecological Systems*. Cambridge: Cambridge University Press.

Bodin, Ö. (2009). Ecological topology and networks. In *Encyclopedia of Complexity and Systems Science*. New York, NY: Springer, pp. 2728–2744.

Bodin, Ö. and B. I. Crona (2009). The role of social networks in natural resource governance: what relational patterns make a difference? *Global Environmental Change*, **19**, 366–374.

Bodin, Ö. and J. Norberg (2005). Information network topologies for enhanced local adaptive management. *Environmental Management*, **35**(2), 175–193.

Burt, R. (2005). *Brokerage and Closure: An Introduction to Social Capital*. New York, NY: Oxford University Press.

Buskens, V. and A. van de Rijt (2008). Dynamics of networks if everyone strives for structural holes. *American Journal of Sociology*, **114**, 371–407.

Carlsson, L. and F. Berkes (2005). Co-management: concepts and methodological implications. *Journal of Environmental Management*, **75**, 65–76.

Centola, D. and M. Macy (2007). Complex contagions and the weakness of long ties. *American Journal of Sociology*, **114**, 702–734.

Cumming, G. S., Ö. Bodin, H. Ernston and T. Elmqvist (2010). Network analysis in conservation biogeography: challenges and opportunities. *Diversity and Distributions*, **16**(3), 414–425.

Degenne, A. and M. Forsé (1999). *Introducing Social Networks*. London: Sage.

Ernston, H., S. Barthel, E. Andersson and S. T. Borgström (in press). Scale-crossing brokers and network governance of urban ecosystem services: the case of Stockholm, Sweden. *Ecology and Society*.

Folke, C., L. Pritchard, F. Berkes, J. Colding and U. Svedin (2007). The problem of fit between ecosystems and institutions: ten years later. *Ecology and Society*, **12**(1), 30.

Frank, K. A., K. Mueller, A. Krause, W. Taylor and N. Leonard (2007). The intersection of global trade, social networks, and fisheries. In W. Taylor, M. G. Schecter and L. Wolfson (Eds.), *Globalization: Effects on Fisheries Resources*. New York, NY: Cambridge University Press, pp. 385–423.

Hahn, T., P. Olsson, C. Folke and K. Johansson (2006). Trust-building, knowledge generation and organizational innovations: the role of a bridging organization for adaptive comanagement of a wetland landscape around Kristianstad, Sweden. *Human Ecology*, **34**(4), 573–592.

Holling, C. S. (1992). Cross-scale morphology, geometry, and dynamics of ecosystems. *Ecological Monographs*, **62**(4), 447–502.

Holling, C. S. and G. K. Meffe (1996). Command and control and the pathology of natural resource management. *Conservation Biology*, **10**(2), 328–337.

Janssen, M. A. (2003). *Complexity and Ecosystem Management: The Theory and Practice of Multi-Agent Systems*. Cheltenham: Edward Elgar.

Janssen, M. A., Ö. Bodin, J. M. Anderies *et al.* (2006). A network perspective on the resilience of social-ecological systems. *Ecology and Society*, **11**(1), 15.

Johnson, J. C. and D. C. Griffith (2010). Linking human and natural systems: social networks, environment, and ecology. In I. Vaccaro, E. Alden Smith and S. Aswani (Eds.), *Environmental Social Sciences: Methods and Research Design*. Cambridge: Cambridge University Press, pp. 212–237.

Kaufmann, S. (1995). *At Home in the Universe: The Search for Laws of Complexity*. London: Viking.

Kinzig, A. P., D. Starrett, K. Arrow *et al.* (2003). Coping with uncertainty: a call for a new science-policy forum. *AMBIO: A Journal of the Human Environment*, **32**(5), 330–335.

Little, L. R., S. Kuikka, A. E. Punt *et al.* (2004). Information flow among fishing vessels modelled using a Bayesian network. *Environmental Modelling and Software*, **19**(1), 27–34.

Marsden, P. V. (1990). Network data and measurement. *Annual Review of Sociology*, **16**, 435–463.

Olsson, P., C. Folke, V. Galaz, T. Hahn and L. Schultz (2007). Enhancing the fit through adaptive co-management: creating and maintaining bridging functions for matching scales in the Kristianstads Vattenrike Biosphere Reserve, Sweden. *Ecology and Society*, **12**(1), 28.

Olsson, P., L. H. Gunderson, S. R. Carpenter *et al.* (2006). Shooting the rapids: navigating transitions to adaptive governance of social-ecological systems. *Ecology and Society*, **11**(1), 18.

Ostrom, E. (1990). *Governing the Commons: The Evolution of Institutions for Collective Action*. Cambridge: Cambridge University Press.

Ostrom, E. (2007). A diagnostic approach for going beyond panaceas. *Proceedings of the National Academy of Sciences USA*, **104**(39), 15181–15187.

Ostrom, E., R. Gardner and J. M. Walker (1994). *Rules, Games, and Common-pool Resources*. Ann Arbor, MI: University of Michigan Press.

Pahl-Wostl, C., M. Craps, A. Dewulf *et al.* (2007). Social learning and water resources management. *Ecology and Society*, **12**(2), 5.

Prell, C., K. Hubacek, M. Reed and L. Riacin (2010). Competing structures, competing views: the role of formal and informal structures in shaping stakeholder perceptions. *Ecology and Society*, **15**(4), 34. http://www.ecolo gyandsociety.org/vol15/ISS/4/art34.

Robins, G., P. Pattison, Y. Kalish and D. Lusher (2007). An introduction to exponential random graph (p*) models for social networks. *Social Networks*, **29**(2), 173–191.

Robins, G., P. Pattison and J. Woolcock (2005). Small and other worlds: global network structures from local processes. *American Journal of Sociology*, **110**, 894–936.

Snijders, T. A. B., G. G. van de Bunt and C. E. G. Steglich (2010). Introduction to stochastic actor-based models for network dynamics. *Social Networks*, **32**(1), 44–60.

van der Leeuw, S. E. and The Archaeomedes Research Team (2000). Land degradation as a socionatural process. In R. J. McIntosh, J. A. Tainter and S. K. McIntosh (Eds.), *The Way the Wind Blows: Climate, History, and Human Action*. New York, NY: Columbia University Press, pp. 357–383.

Walker, B., S. Barrett, S. Polasky *et al.* (2009). Looming global-scale failures and missing institutions. *Science*, **325**(5946), 1345–1346.

Webb, C. and Ö. Bodin (2008). A network perspective on modularity and control of flow in robust systems. In J. Norberg and G. Cumming (Eds.), *Complexity Theory for a Sustainable Future*. New York, NY: Columbia University Press, pp. 85–118.

Index